MW00761408

ZAGAT®

Connecticut
Restaurants
2011/12

Plus Nearby
New York State
and the Berkshires

LOCAL EDITORS
Elizabeth Keyser, John Bruno Turiano, Julia Sexton and
Lynn Hazlewood
STAFF EDITOR
Yoji Yamaguchi

Published and distributed by
Zagat Survey, LLC
4 Columbus Circle
New York, NY 10019
T: 212.977.6000
E: conn@zagat.com
www.zagat.com

ACKNOWLEDGMENTS

We thank Kathleen Cei, Frank Cohen, Janet Crawshaw, Jan Greenberg, Carrie Haddad, Susan Kessler, Lora Pelton, Dale Salm, James Sexton, Alex Silberman, Jenn Smith and Michael Zivyak, as well as the following members of our staff: Josh Rogers (senior associate editor), Anna Hyclak (editorial assistant), Brian Albert, Sean Beachell, Maryanne Bertollo, Reni Chin, Larry Cohn, Bill Corsello, Nicole Diaz, Alison Flick, Jeff Freier, Michelle Golden, Matthew Hamm, Marc Henson, Cynthia Kilian, Natalie Lebert, Mike Liao, Polina Paley, Art Yaghci, Sharon Yates, Anna Zappia and Kyle Zolner.

The reviews in this guide are based on public opinion surveys. The ratings reflect the average scores given by the survey participants who voted on each establishment. The text is based on quotes from, or paraphrasings of, the surveyors' comments. Phone numbers, addresses and other factual data were correct to the best of our knowledge when published in this guide.

Our guides are printed using environmentally preferable inks containing 20%, by weight, renewable resources on papers sourced from well-managed forests. Deluxe editions are covered with Skivertex Recover® Double containing a minimum of 30% post-consumer waste fiber.

SUSTAINABLE FORESTRY INITIATIVE	Certified Sourcing www.sfiprogram.org SFI-00993

ENVIROINK

The inks used to print the body of this publication contain a minimum of 20%, by weight, renewable resources.

Contents

Ratings & Symbols

Zagat Top Spot	Name	Symbols	Cuisine	Zagat Ratings			
				FOOD	DECOR	SERVICE	COST

Area, Address & Contact

Ⓩ Tim & Nina's ◑ *American* — ▽ 23 | 9 | 13 | $15

Litchfield | Litchfield Green (West St.) | 860-555-1234 | www.zagat.com

Review, surveyor comments in quotes

A "former 18th-century stagecoach stop" on the Litchfield Green, this American draws in both CT Yankees and "staid out-of-staters" with a menu that marries New England classics with Nuevo Latino accents, like their "spicy" Beantown pot roast con plantains; though the "fusty Colonial furnishings" fall flat and service is "slow as mid-winter molasses", "prices won't sting" at this "Waspy bastion."

Ratings

Food, Decor & **Service** are rated a 30-point scale.

0	–	9	poor to fair
10	–	15	fair to good
16	–	19	good to very good
20	–	25	very good to excellent
26	–	30	extraordinary to perfection
	▽		low response | less reliable

Cost

The estimated price of a dinner with one drink and tip. Lunch is usually 25% less. For unrated **newcomers** or **write-ins,** the price range is shown as follows:

| **I** | $25 and below | **E** | $41 to $65 |
| **M** | $26 to $40 | **VE** | $66 or above |

Symbols

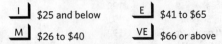

Ⓩ   highest ratings, popularity and importance

◑   serves after 11 PM

Ⓢ Ⓜ   closed on Sunday or Monday

⊄   no credit cards accepted

About This Survey

 Here are the results of our **2011/12 Connecticut Restaurants Survey,** covering 902 eateries in Connecticut (plus nearby New York State and the Berkshires). Like all our guides, this one is based on input from avid local consumers – 4,146 all told. Our editors have synopsized this feedback, highlighting representative comments (in quotation marks within each review). To read full surveyor comments – and share your own opinions – visit **ZAGAT.com,** where you'll also find the latest restaurant news plus special events, deals, reservations, menus, photos and lots more, all for free.

ABOUT ZAGAT: In 1979, we started asking friends to rate and review restaurants purely for fun. The term "user-generated content" had not yet been coined. That hobby grew into Zagat Survey; 32 years later, we have over 375,000 surveyors and cover everything from airlines to shopping in over 100 countries. Along the way, we evolved from being a print publisher to a digital content provider, e.g. **ZAGAT.com** and Zagat mobile apps (for iPad, iPhone, Android, BlackBerry, Windows Phone 7 and Palm webOS). We also produce customized gifts and marketing tools for a wide range of corporate clients. And you can find us on Twitter (twitter.com/zagat), Facebook and just about any other social media network.

THREE SIMPLE PREMISES underlie our ratings and reviews. First, we believe that the collective opinions of large numbers of consumers are more accurate than those of any single person. (Consider that our surveyors bring some 590,000 annual meals' worth of experience to this survey. They also visit restaurants year-round, anonymously – and on their own dime.) Second, food quality is only part of the equation when choosing a restaurant, thus we ask surveyors to separately rate food, decor and service and report on cost. Third, since people need reliable information in a fast, easy-to-digest format, we strive to be concise and we offer our content on every platform – print, online and mobile.

THANKS: We're grateful to our local editors, Elizabeth Keyser, food journalist and restaurant critic; John Bruno Turiano, managing editor of *Westchester Magazine*; Julia Sexton, restaurant critic, food writer and award-winning blogger; and Lynn Hazlewood, freelance journalist and former editor-in-chief of *Hudson Valley* magazine. Thank you, guys. We also sincerely thank the thousands of surveyors who participated – this guide is really "theirs."

JOIN IN: To improve our guides, we solicit your comments; it's vital that we hear your opinions. Just contact us at **nina-tim@zagat.com.** We also invite you to join our surveys at **ZAGAT.com.** Do so and you'll receive a choice of rewards in exchange.

New York, NY
Jume 8, 2011

Nina and Tim

Nina and Tim Zagat

What's New

Like many diners elsewhere, Nutmeggers reacted to the recession by cutting back on restaurant meals. Our surveyors report eating out 2.7 times a week, down just slightly from our last Survey (2.8) but still well below the pre-recession rate (3.1). On the upside, the average meal cost has remained virtually flat ($37.73, vs. $37.71 last time). And restaurateurs are finding new opportunities as the economy rebounds.

THE BOOT IS BOOMING: Italian was named the most popular cuisine by far, easily outpacing the runner-up, American (33% vs. 15%). Connecticut's *abbondanza* of Italian restaurants is being boosted by newcomers that are making the Old Country new again. In Stamford, **Tappo**'s young Italian owners and chef prepare simple, ingredient-driven dishes. A few blocks away, the **Napa & Co.** team is behind **Bar Rosso,** where they'll be focusing on artisan house-cured meats and small plates.

PLANTING THE SEEDS: Sixty-one percent of surveyors find sustainable or locally sourced cooking at least somewhat important (although they're divided over whether they'd pay more for it). Accordingly, chefs at some highly rated newcomers, such as John Holzwarth (**Boathouse at Saugatuck** in Westport), Joel Viehland (Washington's **Community Table**) and Ryan Jones (**Mill at 2T** in Tariffville), are making the state's tables greener. Meanwhile, Jonathan Rapp, chef-owner of Chester's **River Tavern,** holds special dinners on local farms, while **Le Farm**'s Bill Taibe offers 'Souterrain' pop-up dinners in surprise locations that sell out in minutes online.

IS HAUTE OUT? The question "is formal fine dining dead?" received a firm "no" from a majority (57%) of surveyors, but there are signs that money doesn't always talk. The winner of the state's Top Food honors, Roy Ip's **Le Petite Café** in Branford, with its $48.50 four-course prix fixe menu, replaced the long-standing champ, luxe **Thomas Henkelmann.** The recent overhaul of the formal dining room at Ivoryton's Copper Beech Inn into the less formal **Brasserie Pip** is consistent with a trend away from pomp. Still, even at lower price points, chef Tyler Anderson's creative French-based cuisine indicates that fine food never goes out of fashion.

&C., &C.: Service remains the top dining-out irritant, cited by 63%, but that's down from 66% last time . . . CT surveyors eat out far more for leisure (86% of the time) than business . . . Only 26% favor chefs becoming celebrities.

Fairfield, CT
June 8, 2011

Elizabeth Keyser

Vote at ZAGAT.com

Key Newcomers

Our editors' favorites among this year's top arrivals. See a full list on page 197.

Bar Bouchée | *French* | Madison bistro spin-off of the Union League Cafe

Boathse./Saugatuck | *American* | locavore New American in Westport

Brasserie | *French* | brasserie replacing former Saint Tropez in Fairfield

Café d'Azur | *Mediterranean* | midpriced Darien Med

Cask Republic | *American* | beer-centric New Haven New American pub

Fez | *Med./Moroccan* | Stamford Med and Moroccan tapas

Gabriele's | *Italian/Steak* | Italian steakhouse in Greenwich

Goose | *American* | Darien American in the former Black Goose Grille

Millstone Café | *American* | locally sourced New American in Kent

Oaxaca Kitchen | *Mexican* | New Haven Mexican by the owner of Thali

Pine Social | *American* | New Canaan American in former Rocco's space

Red Lulu | *Mexican* | sexy Mex SoNo sibling of Greenwich's Lolita

Sails | *American* | Norwalk nautical-themed New American

Suburban | *American/Med.* | American-Med gastropub in Branford

Tappo | *Italian* | locally sourced Stamford Italian

The most eagerly anticipated arrival is the new branch of Mario Batali and Joe Bastianich's Italian **Tarry Lodge,** set to open in the summer of 2011 in Westport's Saugatuck neighborhood, on the site previously occupied by **Bonda,** which moved to Fairfield. It will be the partners' first venture in the Nutmeg State. Other upcoming entries include New Canaan's **Tuscan,** a 100-seat restaurant with an attached butcher shop and cafe, and **Zaza,** a Stamford Italian gastropub. Both are set to open in spring 2011. Meanwhile, a renovated firehouse in New Haven is slated to be the new home of **Box 63,** a New American bar and grill, which will open later this year.

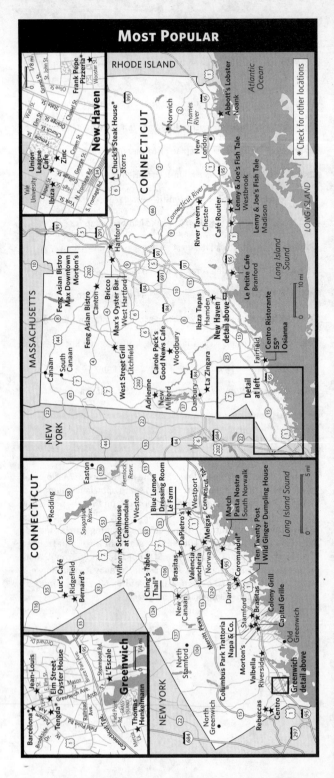

RHODE ISLAND

Atlantic Ocean

* Check for other locations

New Haven

Frank Pepe Pizzeria*
Union League Cafe
Ibiza
Zinc
Chuck's Steak House*

Yale University

CONNECTICUT

Abbott's Lobster
Noank
Norwich
Thames River
New London
Storrs

Lenny & Joe's Fish Tale
Westbrook
River Tavern
Chester
Café Routier
Lenny & Joe's Fish Tale
Madison

Hartford
Connecticut River

Feng Asian Bistro
Max Downtown
Morton's

Bricco
Max's Oyster Bar
West Hartford
Canton

Feng Asian Bistro

Le Petite Cafe
Branford

Ibiza Tapas
Hamden

MASSACHUSETTS

West Street Grill
Litchfield
South Canaan
Canaan

Carole Peck's
Good News Cafe
Woodbury

New Haven
detail above

Centro Ristorante
55°
Osianna
Fairfield

Adrienne
New Milford

La Zingara
Danbury

Long Island Sound

Detail at left

NEW YORK

LONG ISLAND

10 mi

CONNECTICUT

Easton
Redding

Schoolhouse
at Cannondale
Weston

Blue Lemon
Dressing Room
Le Farm
Westport

Match
Pasta Nostra
South Norwalk

Wild Ginger Dumpling House
Ten Twenty Post

Luc's Café
Ridgefield
Bernard's

Wilton

Ching's Table
Thali*
New Canaan

Brasitas
DaPietro's

Valencia
Luncheria
Norwalk

Coromandel*

Darien

Brasitas
Colony Grill
Capital Grille
Stamford

Morton's
Columbus Park Trattoria
Napa & Co.

Valbella
Riverside

Rebeccas
Centro

Old Greenwich

Greenwich
detail above

Long Island Sound

5 mi

Greenwich

Barcelona
Jean-Louis
L'Escale
Elm Street
Oyster House

Tengda
Thomas Henkelmann

North Stamford
North Greenwich

NEW YORK

Most Popular

1. Frank Pepe | *Pizza*
2. Barcelona | *Spanish*
3. Union League | *French*
4. Coromandel | *Indian*
5. Thomas Henkelmann | *French*
6. Carole Peck's | *American*
7. Capital Grille | *Steak*
8. Bernard's | *French*
9. Jean-Louis | *French*
10. Napa & Co. | *American*
11. Ibiza | *Spanish*
12. Elm St. Oyster | *Seafood*
13. Thali | *Indian*
14. Brasitas | *Pan-Latin*
15. Max Downtown* | *Amer./Steak*
16. Bricco | *Italian*
17. Ten Twenty Post | *French*
18. Tengda | *Asian*
19. Valbella* | *Italian*
20. Dressing Room | *American*
21. Le Farm | *American*
22. Max's Oyster* | *Seafood*
23. Ching's/Wild Ginger | *Asian*
24. Match | *American*
25. Schoolhouse | *American*
26. DaPietro's | *French/Italian*
27. Le Petit Café | *French*
28. Valencia* | *Venezuelan*
29. L'Escale | *French*
30. Luc's Café | *French*
31. Colony Grill | *Pizza*
32. Abbott's Lobster | *Seafood*
33. Rebeccas | *American*
34. Chuck's Steak | *Steak*
35. Columbus Park | *Italian*
36. 55° | *Italian*
37. Morton's | *Steak*
38. West St. Grill* | *American*
39. La Zingara | *Italian*
40. Osianna | *Mediterranean*
41. Lenny & Joe's | *Seafood*
42. Feng Asian Bistro | *Asian*
43. River Tavern | *American*
44. Meigas* | *Spanish*
45. Pasta Nostra | *Italian*
46. Café Routier | *French*
47. Centro | *Italian/Mediterranean*
48. Blue Lemon | *American*
49. Zinc* | *American*
50. Adrienne | *American*

Many of the above restaurants are among Connecticut's most expensive, but if popularity were calibrated to price, a number of other restaurants would surely join their ranks. To illustrate this, we have added two pages of Best Buys starting on page 16.

* Indicates a tie with restaurant above

Top Food

29 Le Petit Café | *French*

28 PolytechnicON20 | *American*
Thomas Henkelmann | *French*
Mill at 2T | *American*
Jean-Louis | *French*
Basso Café | *Mediterranean*

27 Isabelle et Vincent | *Bakery*
Harvest Supper | *American*
Max Downtown | *Amer./Steak*
Café Routier | *French*
Bernard's | *French*
Valencia | *Venezuelan*
Tawa | *Indian*
Schoolhouse | *American*
Woodward House* | *American*
Union League | *French*
Bricco | *Italian*
Ibiza | *Spanish*
Bonda | *American*
Le Farm | *American*

DaPietro's | *French/Italian*

26 Paci | *Italian*
Cavey's | *French/Italian*
Peppercorn's Grill | *Italian*
Bar Americain | *American*
Water St. Café | *American*
Harry's Pizza | *Pizza*
Luca Ristorante | *Italian*
La Zingara | *Italian*
Rebeccas | *American*
Match | *American*
Ondine | *French*
Max's Oyster | *Seafood*
SoNo Baking Co. | *Bakery*
Bistro Basque | *French/Spanish*
Cafe Silvium | *Italian*
Bin 100 | *Eclectic*
David Burke Prime | *Steak*
Carole Peck's | *American*
Bravo Bravo | *Italian*

BY CUISINE

AMERICAN (NEW)

28 PolytechnicON20
Mill at 2T
27 Harvest Supper
Max Downtown
Schoolhouse

AMERICAN (TRAD.)

25 Max Burger
24 Noah's
22 Woodland
American Pie Co.
21 Shady Glen

ASIAN

24 Ching's/Wild Ginger
23 Baang Cafe
Wasabi Chi
22 Feng Asian Bistro
Tengda

BARBECUE

25 Jeff's Cuisine
22 Cookhouse
21 Wood's Pit BBQ
Bobby Q's
20 Wilson's BBQ

BURGERS

25 Max Burger
22 Burgers/Shakes
Burger Bar
Plan B Burger Bar
Louis' Lunch

CHINESE

25 Royal Palace (New Haven)
Forbidden City
23 China Pavilion
22 Taste of China
20 Great Taste

FRENCH

28 Thomas Henkelmann
Jean-Louis
27 Bernard's
DaPietro's
26 Cavey's

FRENCH BISTRO

29 Le Petit Cafe
27 Café Routier
Union League
25 Bistro Bonne Nuit
24 Luc's Café

Excludes places with low votes

Vote at ZAGAT.com

INDIAN

27	Tawa
25	Coromandel
24	Thali
23	Bangalore
22	Bombay

ITALIAN

27	Bricco
	DaPietro's
26	Paci
	Cavey's
	Peppercorn's Grill

JAPANESE

25	Miya's Sushi
	Wasabi*
	Kazu
24	Nuage
	Toro

MEDITERRANEAN

28	Basso Café
25	Osianna
24	Oliva Cafe
23	John's Café
	Tapas/Ann

MEXICAN

22	Lolita Cocina
	Besito
21	Wood's Pit BBQ
20	Agave Grill
19	Coyote Flaco

PIZZA

26	Harry's Pizza
25	Sally's Apizza
	Modern Apizza
	Bru Room at BAR
24	Colony Grill

SEAFOOD

26	Max's Oyster
25	Liv's Oyster Bar
24	Elm St. Oyster
	Pacifico
23	Osetra

SPANISH

27	Ibiza
26	Bistro Basque
25	Costa del Sol
	La Paella
24	Olive Market

STEAKHOUSES

27	Max Downtown
26	David Burke Prime
25	Capital Grille
	Ruth's Chris
	J. Gilbert's

THAI

24	King & I
23	Little Thai/Buddha/Spice
21	Kit's Thai
20	Hot Basil
	Papaya Thai*

VEGETARIAN

27	Tawa
24	Thali
23	Bloodroot
	Lime
21	Claire's Corner

BY SPECIAL FEATURE

BREAKFAST

27	Valencia
26	SoNo Baking Co.
25	Meli-Melo
24	Pantry
	Versailles

BRUNCH

27	Bernard's
26	La Zingara
24	Roger Sherman Inn
23	Rest./Water's Edge
22	Splash

BUSINESS DINING

28	Thomas Henkelmann
	Jean-Louis
27	Max Downtown
	Union League
26	Cavey's

HOTEL/INN DINING

28	Thomas Henkelmann
26	Bar Americain
	David Burke Prime
	Bravo Bravo
24	Mayflower Inn

LUNCH

28 PolytechnicON20
    Thomas Henkelmann
    Jean-Louis
    Basso Café
27 Harvest Supper

NEWCOMERS (RATED)

25 Boathse./Saugatuck
24 Brasserie
18 Bank St. Tavern

PEOPLE-WATCHING

28 Jean-Louis
27 Max Downtown
    Union League
    Bricco
    Ibiza

RAW BARS

27 Max Downtown
    Union League
26 Bar Americain
    Water St. Cafe
    Max's Oyster

SINGLES SCENES

25 Bru Room at BAR
    J. Gilbert's
    Max Burger
24 Barcelona
21 Molto

WATERSIDE

28 PolytechnicON20
26 Ondine
25 Boathse./Saugatuck
23 Apricots
    Rest./Water's Edge*
    L'Escale

WINNING WINE LISTS

29 Le Petit Cafe
28 PolytechnicON20
    Thomas Henkelmann
    Mill at 2T
    Jean-Louis

BY LOCATION

BRIDGEPORT

24 Joseph's
    King & I
23 Ralph 'n' Rich's
    Bloodroot
20 Two Boots Pizza

DANBURY

26 Ondine
23 Koo
22 Café on the Green
21 Sesame Seed
18 Chuck's Steak

DARIEN

25 Coromandel
24 Ching's/Wild Ginger
    Aux Délices/Ponzek
23 Little Thai
22 Tengda

FAIRFIELD

27 Isabelle et Vincent
    Bonda
25 Osianna
24 Frank Pepe
    Brasserie

GLASTONBURY

25 J. Gilbert's
23 Max Amore
    Max Fish
22 Plan B Burger Bar
21 Luna Pizza

GREENWICH

28 Thomas Henkelmann
    Jean-Louis
26 Rebeccas
25 Meli-Melo
24 Elm St. Oyster

HARTFORD

28 PolytechnicON20
27 Max Downtown
26 Peppercorn's Grill
25 Costa del Sol
24 Firebox

LITCHFIELD COUNTY

27 Woodward House
26 Carole Peck's
25 Adrienne
24 Mayflower Inn
    Oliva Cafe

MYSTIC

- 26 Bravo Bravo
- 22 Go Fish
- 21 Capt. Daniel Packer
- 18 Steak Loft
- 16 Zhang's

NEW CANAAN

- 27 Harvest Supper
- 25 Bistro Bonne Nuit
- Chef Luis
- 24 Ching's
- Thali

NEW HAVEN

- 27 Union League
- Ibiza
- 25 Sally's Apizza
- Miya's Sushi
- Caseus

NORWALK

- 28 Basso Café
- 27 Valencia
- 25 Brasitas
- La Paella
- Blackstones

OLD SAYBROOK

- 25 Liv's Oyster Bar
- 23 Atlantic Seafood
- 22 Alforno
- 21 Johnny Ad's
- 20 Aspen

RIDGEFIELD

- 27 Bernard's
- 24 Luc's Café
- Thali
- 23 Sagi
- Little Pub

SOUTH NORWALK

- 26 Match
- SoNo Baking Co.
- Strada 18
- 25 Coromandel
- Jeff's Cuisine
- Pasta Nostra*

STAMFORD

- 27 Tawa
- 26 Cafe Silvium
- 25 Capital Grille
- Coromandel
- Columbus Park

WEST HARTFORD

- 27 Bricco
- 26 Harry's Pizza
- Max's Oyster
- 25 Grant's
- Max Burger

WESTPORT

- 27 Le Farm
- DaPietro's
- 25 Boathse./Saugatuck
- Tarantino's
- 24 Dressing Room

Top Decor

28	PolytechnicON20		Griswold Inn
	Thomas Henkelmann	24	David Burke Prime
	Mayflower Inn		Capt. Daniel Packer
	Mill at 2T*		Bespoke
27	Union League		Dressing Room
	Woodward House		Il Palio
26	Bernard's		Luca Ristorante
	Rest./Water's Edge		Boathse./Saugatuck
25	Toro		Le Petit Cafe
	L'Escale		Max's Oyster
	Boulders Inn		Firebox
	Max Downtown		Capital Grille
	Bar Americain		Rainforest Cafe
	Roger Sherman Inn		Jean-Louis
	116 Crown	23	Valbella
	Craftsteak		Ondine
	Besito		Feng Asian Bistro
	Paci		Aspen
	Kudeta		Schoolhouse
	Morello Bistro		Heirloom

OUTDOORS

Abbott's Lobster	La Zingara
Apricots	L'Escale
Bill's Seafood	Mill on the River
Bloodroot	Schoolhouse
G.W. Tavern	Splash

ROMANCE

Bernard's	Chestnut Grille
Bespoke	Jean-Louis
Brasserie Pip	Mayflower Inn
Cavey's	Ondine

ROOMS

L'Escale	Rest. L&E/French 75
Luc's Café	Still River Café
Mayflower Inn	Thomas Henkelmann
Morello Bistro	Union League
Red Lulu	Winvian

VIEWS

Boathse./Saugatuck	L'Escale
Boulders Inn	Mill on the River
Flood Tide	PolytechnicON20
Grist Mill	Positano's
Harbor Lights	Rest./Rowayton Seafood

Top Service

29	PolytechnicON20

28	Le Petit Cafe
	Thomas Henkelmann

27	Bernard's
	Max Downtown

26	Bistro Basque
	Mill at 2T
	Woodward House
	Ondine
	Union League*
	Luca Ristorante

25	Café Routier
	Capital Grille
	Bar Americain
	David Burke Prime*
	Jean-Louis
	DaPietro's
	La Bretagne
	Bonda
	Rest./Water's Edge

Harvest Supper
Valbella
Joseph's
Cavey's

24	Bricco
	Gabrielle's
	Schoolhouse
	Mayflower Inn
	Carbone's
	Ruth's Chris
	La Zingara
	Craftsteak
	Il Palio
	Blue Lemon
	Toro
	Cafe Allegre
	Métro Bis
	Café on the Green
	Consiglio's
	Morton's

Best Buys

Everyone loves a bargain, and Connecticut offers plenty of them. All-you-can-eat options are mostly for lunch and/or brunch. For prix fixe menus, call ahead for availability.

ALL YOU CAN EAT

25	Coromandel
23	Bangalore
22	Splash
21	Flanders Fish
	Bombay
19	Abis
	Brewhouse
18	Griswold Inn
17	Saltwater Grille
16	Squire's

BYO

28	Basso Café
27	Valencia
25	Meli-Melo
	Chef Luis
23	Lenny & Joe's (Madison)
	Little Thai/Buddha
22	Burgers/Shakes (Greenwich)
	Penang Grill
19	Olé Molé (Stamford)
18	Atticus

EARLY-BIRD

25	Osianna
22	Saybrook Fish
	Scribner's
20	Vazzy's
19	Putnam House
18	Chuck's Steak
16	Bull's Bridge Inn

FAMILY-STYLE

25	Coromandel
22	Splash
	Cookhouse
21	Vito's (Hartford)
	Eclisse
20	Two Boots Pizza
	Vazzy's
19	Pellicci's

PRIX FIXE LUNCH

28	Jean-Louis ($29)
27	Tawa ($11)
	DaPietro's ($12)
25	Osianna ($13)
24	Brasserie ($13)
	La Bretagne ($23)
	Polpo ($22)
	Chez Jean-Pierre ($15)
	Pacifico ($17)
23	John's Café ($13)

PRIX FIXE DINNER

27	Woodward House ($28)
	DaPietro's ($33)
26	Cavey's ($35)
24	Bespoke ($40)
	Meigas ($20)
	Chez Jean-Pierre ($25)
23	John's Café ($29)
22	Rest./Rowayton Seafood ($28)
20	Village ($18)
	Mill on the River ($23)

PUB GRUB

25	Bru Room at BAR
23	Little Pub
19	Penny Lane Pub
	White Horse
	Brewhouse
18	Archie Moore's
17	Wood-n-Tap
	John Harvard's
16	Mackenzie's
	Southport Brewing

SEAFOOD SHACKS

23	Lenny & Joe's
	Abbott's Lobster
21	Johnny Ad's

BEST BUYS: BANG FOR THE BUCK

In order of Bang for the Buck rating.

1. Shady Glen
2. Super Duper Weenie
3. Isabelle et Vincent
4. Sycamore Drive-In
5. Louis' Lunch
6. Burgers/Shakes
7. SoNo Baking Co.
8. Firehouse Deli
9. Lucky's
10. Layla's Falafel
11. American Pie Co.
12. Claire's Corner
13. Modern Apizza
14. Atticus
15. Luna Pizza
16. Johnny Rockets
17. Harry's Pizza
18. Jeff's Cuisine
19. Così
20. Harry's Bishops Corner
21. Bru Room at BAR
22. Two Boots Pizza
23. Valencia
24. Frank Pepe
25. Plan B Burger Bar
26. China Pavilion
27. It's Only Natural
28. Meli-Melo
29. Colony Grill
30. Little Pub
31. Pantry
32. Tapas/Ann
33. Orem's Diner
34. Max Burger
35. Rein's NY Deli
36. Sesame Seed
37. Flipside Burgers
38. Mystic Pizza
39. Aux Délices/Ponzek
40. Post Corner Pizza

BEST BUYS: OTHER GOOD VALUES

Alforno
Angelina's Trattoria
Ay! Salsa
B.J. Ryans
Bobby Valentine's
Café Azur
Café Giulia
Cask Republic
Cast Iron Soul
Char Koon
Coromandel
Donovan's
Fat Cat Pie
Fez, The
Fin/Fin II
Goose
Ibiza
King & I
La Bretagne
La Paella
Miya's Sushi
Molto Wine
Noah's
Omanel
Osianna
Pellicci's
Pizzeria Lauretano
Quattro Pazzi
Rizutto's
Sal e Pepe
Sarah's Wine Bar
Scoozi
Sono Bana
Soul de Cuba
Union League
West St. Grill
When Pigs Fly
Wood-n-Tap

NEARBY NEW YORK'S TOP FOOD

29 Sushi Nanase | *Japanese*
27 La Crémaillère | *French*
    La Panetière | *French*
    Arch | *Eclectic*
    Serevan | *Mediterranean*
    No. 9 | *American*
26 Big W's Roadside | *BBQ*
    Rraci | *Italian*
    Rest. North | *American*
    Spadaro | *Italian*

25 Hajime | *Japanese*
    McKinney & Doyle | *American*
    Coromandel | *Indian*
    Tratt. Vivolo | *Italian*
    Emilio Ristorante | *Italian*
    Le Château | *French*
    Bedford Post/Farm | *American*
    Plates | *American*
24 Mulino's | *Italian*
    Lusardi's | *Italian*

BY LOCATION

HUDSON VALLEY

27 Arch
    Serevan
    No. 9
26 Big W's Roadside
    Rraci

PORT CHESTER

24 Sonora
    Il Sogno
    Tarry Lodge
    Piero's
    Willett House

RYE

27 La Panetière
24 Frankie & Johnnie's
23 Ruby's Oyster
    Koo
    Watermoon

WHITE PLAINS

29 Sushi Nanase
24 Mulino's
    Morton's
    Benjamin Steak
23 Seasons Japanese

CONNECTICUT AND NEARBY NEW YORK TOWNS RESTAURANT DIRECTORY

	FOOD	DECOR	SERVICE	COST

Abatino's *Italian*
| 20 | 14 | 18 | $27 |

North White Plains | Super Stop & Shop Ctr. | 670 N. Broadway (bet. Central Westchester Pkwy. & Cloverdale Ave.), NY | 914-686-0380 | www.abatinosrestaurant.com

Every neighborhood needs a "local haunt" and this "likable" Italian in North White Plains fits the bill with "better-than-average" fare, "solid" pizzas and a "friendly" vibe; the decor is on the "spartan" side, but the pricing's "economical" and it's a "low-stress" stop for takeout.

Abbott's Lobster *Seafood*
| 23 | 13 | 14 | $29 |

Noank | 117 Pearl St. (Smith Ct.) | 860-536-7719 | www.abbotts-lobster.com

"Wear your flip-flops and a T-shirt" at this "rustic" "Connecticut classic" where "succulent" lobster rolls and other "outstanding seafood" are ordered from the counter and brought to picnic tables with a "pleasing view of the Noank shoreline" and the Mystic River; "reasonable prices" are appreciated, but "beware" the "aggressive seagulls" that try to "steal" your meal; P.S. open May–October.

Aberdeen *Chinese*
| 23 | 12 | 19 | $31 |

White Plains | Marriott Residence Inn | 3 Barker Ave. (Cottage Pl.), NY | 914-288-0188

"When you can't make it to Flushing", try this "authentic" Chinese in the White Plains Marriott Residence Inn, a "classic" famed for its "wonderful" dim sum and "excellent" Cantonese seafood straight "from the tanks"; although the "run-down" looks are "not up to the quality of the food", tabs are modest and service is "personal" so there's a reason it's a "mob scene" on weekends.

Abis *Japanese*
| 19 | 16 | 19 | $36 |

Greenwich | 381 Greenwich Ave. (Grigg St.) | 203-862-9100 | www.abis4u.com

"Kids love" this "popular" Greenwich Japanese, a "solid standby" for "tween birthdays" thanks to its "entertaining" hibachi show (it's "a hoot") and "reliable" sushi dinners; "good-value" pricing and "welcoming" service overcome the "hectic" vibe and "dated", "no-frills" decor that's certainly "not the place for a romantic dinner."

Abruzzi Trattoria *Italian*
| ▽ 21 | 20 | 20 | $35 |

Patterson | 3191 Rte. 22 (Danby Ln.), NY | 845-878-6800 | www.abruzzitrattoria.com

"Solid" red-sauce Italian deemed "very good for the price" plus "cheerful" hospitality make this "friendly" Patterson spot a local "favorite", whether "to grab a bite" at lunch or linger on "date night"; the "comfortable" room is "often crowded" and loud, but an "energetic" staff willing to "go that extra mile" makes up for it.

Acqua *Mediterranean*
| 22 | 21 | 20 | $45 |

Westport | Parker Harding Plaza | 43 Main St. (bet. Elm St. & Post Rd.) | 203-222-8899 | www.acquaofwestport.com

"Everything's great, from the pizza right out of the wood-burning oven to the excellent seafood dishes" at this somewhat "pricey"

Westport Med with a "modern" bi-level setting boasting river views "if you get a window seat" and a staff that's mostly "cordial", though occasionally "rude"; insiders recommend you go during the day (when there's an "amazing lunch deal") or on weeknights, because on weekends, the noise can be "ear-splitting."

Adriana's *Italian* | 22 | 19 | 21 | $40 |

New Haven | 771 Grand Ave. (bet. I-91 & Jefferson St.) | 203-865-6474 | www.adrianasrestaurant.net

"Spiffed up" relatively recently, this "reasonably priced" New Haven Italian doles out "huge portions" of "quality" dishes, among which "the veal is legendary"; the "accommodating" staff and owner "make everyone feel valued", and while the neighborhood is a bit "dicey", don't let that "dissuade you" from going – "your car will be safe" in the restaurant's "own lighted parking lot."

Adrienne Ⓜ *American* | 25 | 21 | 23 | $53 |

New Milford | 218 Kent Rd. (Rocky River Rd.) | 860-354-6001 | www.adriennerestaurant.com

Ordering from the "seasonal American menu" is a "delightful task" at Adrienne Sussman's "cozy" New Milford eatery, where the "talented" toque "caters to each customer with special care" while creating "ingenious, fresh" fare at "reasonable prices", and the rest of the staff is "friendly" as well; the circa-1774 Colonial is "quaint, but not luxurious", with a fireplace and an outdoor patio that's a "true joy" in the warmer months; P.S. the "cooking classes are also fun."

Agave Grill *Mexican* | 20 | 19 | 19 | $30 |

Hartford | 100 Allyn St. (bet. Ann Uccello & High Sts.) | 860-882-1557 | www.agavehartford.com

"Celebrate Cinco de Mayo" whatever the day at this Downtown Hartford Mexican where the "guacamole made at your table is a treat" and the "lively bar" "pays homage to the agave plant" with "plenty of tequila" options; that you "never have to wait" for service is a bonus, as are the "cool surroundings" and wholly "fun" atmosphere.

AJ's Burgers ⊖ *American* | 20 | 13 | 18 | $17 |

New Rochelle | 542 North Ave. (Hamilton Ave.), NY | 914-235-3009 | www.ajsburgers.com

They "make a mean burger", "killer milkshakes" and a range of "hearty" American eats "served in a skillet" at this "reliable" New Rochelle eatery; the "diner atmosphere" doesn't faze the "Iona college crowd" or "locals with small children" who think the "obliging" staff and "incredible value" are "way cool."

Akasaka *Japanese* | ▽ 21 | 16 | 22 | $35 |

New Haven | 1450 Whalley Ave. (Glenview Terrace) | 203-387-4898

"Fine sushi", "great specialty rolls" and cooked dishes are brought by "gracious, attentive servers" at this "small", "unpretentious" Japanese "standby" in the Westville section of New Haven; ok, so there's "not much that's exciting here", but it's "reliable", and best of all, the prices equal a "good bang for the buck."

Aladdin ● *Mideastern*   - | - | - | I

Hartford | 121 Allyn St. (bet. Ann Uccello & High Sts.) | 860-278-0202 | www.aladdinhalal.com

"Decent Middle Eastern food" and specialty pizzas are what's on the menu at this inexpensive counter-serve Downtown Hartford establishment, which has some dine-in seating but a definite "take-out pizza-joint ambiance"; it's open late on weekends, but don't expect a rowdy scene – alcohol is not permitted, as it's a halal establishment.

Alba's ⑤ *Italian*   23 | 20 | 21 | $54

Port Chester | 400 N. Main St. (Wilkins Ave.), NY | 914-937-2236 | www.albasrestaurant.com

"Old-fashioned Italian done well" sums up this Port Chester "standard" offering "first-rate" Northern-style cuisine and "wonderful wines" in an "attractive" recently expanded space equipped with a working fireplace; its "attentive", "service-oriented" staff appeals to the "older crowd" that doesn't flinch at the "pricey" tabs.

Alforno *Italian*   22 | 18 | 19 | $31

Old Saybrook | Bennie's Shopping Ctr. | 1654 Boston Post Rd. (Rte. 166) | 860-399-4166 | www.alforno.net

"Everything is prepared with care" at this "unprepossessing" Old Saybrook strip-mall trattoria whose "wonderful Italian specialties" include "delicious" brick-oven pizza; moderate prices and "good wine" make it "an easy dining choice", as does the "professional service."

Altnaveigh Inn ⑤Ⓜ *Continental*   ▽ 23 | 24 | 24 | $52

Storrs | Altnaveigh Inn | 957 Storrs Rd. (bet. E & Spring Hill Rds.) | 860-429-4490 | www.altnaveighinn.com

"Quite tasty" Continental cuisine comes with "personal attention" from the staff at this "atmospheric" Storrs inn eatery in a 1734 farmhouse "close to UConn", offering three "beautiful" dining rooms; true, it's a "pricey" "throwback" of sorts, but for an "intimate, romantic dining experience" or "a special occasion", it "never disappoints."

NEW Alvin &   ▽ 26 | 26 | 26 | $45
Friends Ⓜ *Caribbean/Southern*

New Rochelle | 49 Lawton St. (bet. Huguenot & Main Sts.), NY | 914-654-6549 | www.alvinandfriendsrestaurant.com

Early reports on this "exciting" newcomer to Downtown New Rochelle laud the "interesting flavors" of its "spectacular" modern Caribbean-Southern cooking (think jerk duck), the "gracious" service and "beautiful setting" spiced up with "welcoming host" Alvin Clayton's "evocative paintings"; a few find they still "have to work out a few kinks", but the majority maintains they'll "definitely be back."

American Pie Company *American*   22 | 16 | 21 | $21

Sherman | 29 Rte. 37 (Old Greenwoods Rd.) | 860-350-0662 | www.americanpiecompany.com

The bakery counter selling "amazing pies" and "divine" cookies makes you "want to eat dessert first" at this "affordable" Sherman Traditional American, the "epitome of a cute country restaurant",

	FOOD	DECOR	SERVICE	COST

which offers "hearty country-style breakfasts, lunches and dinners" in a "cozy" setting; the staff is "welcoming", but it's so popular the "wait can be unbearable."

Angelina's Trattoria *Italian*
17 | 9 | 17 | $22

Westport | Post Plaza | 1092 Post Rd. E. (bet. Church St. & Morningside Dr.) | 203-227-0865

Despite its "middle-of-the-road" Italian entrees, "average pizza", merely "ok" service and "untempting" digs, this "been-there-forever" Westport strip-maller is "well regarded by locals"; maybe "reasonable prices" explain why "it's so popular", especially among "large families" that also "depend" on it for delivery.

Anna Maria's Ⓜ *Italian*
21 | 18 | 22 | $43

Larchmont | 18 Chatsworth Ave. (bet. Addison St. & Boston Post Rd.), NY | 914-833-0555 | www.annamariasrestaurant.com

"Eat like Giuliani without the stress of New York politics" at this "comfortable", "old-world" Larchmont Italian helmed by former Gracie Mansion chef Anna Maria Santorelli who turns out "family-style" fare "that doesn't stray far from tradition"; though the atmosphere's "warm", prices relatively moderate and service "aims to please", a few find the "pedestrian" fare's "not up to what you'd expect."

🆕 Anthony's Coal-Oven Fired Pizza *Pizza*
22 | 16 | 19 | $22

White Plains | 264 Main St. (bet. B'way & E.J. Conroy Dr.), NY | 914-358-9702 | www.anthonyscoalfiredpizza.com

"Sports-bar" ambiance teams up with "crispy, paper-thin" pizza "with just enough chew" and chicken wings that "will knock your socks off" at this new, large and loungey White Plains outpost of a Florida chain; "friendly" service, a "nice full bar" and "lots of flat-screen TVs" also make it a good place to "go with a group" and "catch a game."

Apricots *American*
23 | 21 | 21 | $46

Farmington | 1593 Farmington Ave. (Highwood Rd.) | 860-673-5405 | www.apricotsrestaurant.com

"As sweet as its name", this New American delivers "fabulous", "inventive" cuisine in a "pricey", "elegant, upscale" upstairs dining room, "less expensive" fare in a "casual, cozy" downstairs pub and "lovely views of the Farmington River" throughout, especially from the patio; "friendly", "accommodating" staffers and an "excellent", "reasonable wine list" complete the "charming" picture.

🅉 Arch, The Ⓜ *Eclectic*
27 | 25 | 27 | $71

Brewster | 1292 Rte. 22 (end of I-684), NY | 845-279-5011 | www.archrestaurant.com

"A golden oldie that never loses its luster", this "delightful" Brewster Eclectic "changes just enough to keep up with the times", offering "exceptional", "refined" "classics" and "amazing soufflés" in a "pretty" stone house where "fireplaces, well-spaced tables" and "charming", "never-stuffy" service make "romantic evenings a natural"; of course, it's "not cheap" (although "Sunday brunch is a rel-

FOOD | DECOR | SERVICE | COST

ative bargain"), but "worth every penny" for something "special";
P.S. jackets suggested at dinner.

Archie Moore's *Pub Food*
| 18 | 13 | 17 | $23 |

Derby | 17 Elizabeth St. (bet. Main & 3rd Sts.) | 203-732-3255
Fairfield | 48 Sanford St. (Post Rd.) | 203-256-9295 ◑
Milford | 15 Factory Ln. (S. Broad St.) | 203-876-5088 ◑
New Haven | 188½ Willow St. (bet. Foster & Orange Sts.) |
203-773-9870 ◑
Wallingford | 39 N. Main St. (Center St.) | 203-265-7100 ◑
www.archiemoores.com

Disciples pronounce this CT chainlet "the Wing King" for its "killer
chicken", and they call the rest of the "standard pub grub" "not bad"
either, especially since it's slung in "humongous portions" and sold
at "budget" prices; the "boisterous happy-hour" atmospheres are
"fine for families as well", even though service is only "fair" (still, it's
"better than usual for these types of places").

NEW Arrosto Ⓜ *Italian*
| ▽ 23 | 24 | 22 | $45 |

Port Chester | 25 S. Regent St. (William St.), NY | 914-939-2727 |
www.arrostorestaurant.com

The wood-burning oven takes center stage at this "pretty" new Port
Chester Italian from Godfrey Polistina (founder of NYC's Carmine's),
where you can choose among a "vast" array of "outstanding" family-
style meat and fish roasts, pizzas and "amazing" housemade pastas
elevated by almost two dozen wines by the glass; there's a "lively
bar scene" to go with the "NY-esque" vibe, and it's all "priced fairly."

Arugula Ⓜ *Mediterranean*
| 23 | 19 | 20 | $38 |

West Hartford | 953 Farmington Ave. (S. Main St.) | 860-561-4888 |
www.arugula-bistro.com

"Simple, tasteful decorations" craft a "relaxed atmosphere" at this
West Hartford bistro where the Mediterranean menu is "always different, never boring" and "priced reasonably for the area"; there
"aren't many tables" in the "intimate" setting, so be sure to book – and
prepare for service that swings between "good-natured" and "curt."

Ash Creek Saloon *American*
| 17 | 16 | 17 | $28 |

Bridgeport | 2895 Fairfield Ave. (bet. Brewster & Jetland Sts.) |
203-333-2733
Norwalk | 2 Wilton Ave. (Cross St.) | 203-847-7500
www.ashcreeksaloon.com

You'll feel like "you're a thousand miles away in the ol' West" at
these "funky", "laid-back" saloons hashin' out "basic", "dependable" BBQ and Traditional American eats; ok, so it's "not spectacular" in any way, but it "fills a real need" for "casual", "family-friendly"
dining at "reasonable prices."

Asiana Cafe *Asian*
| 21 | 18 | 20 | $34 |

Greenwich | 130 E. Putnam Ave. (Milbank Ave.) | 203-622-6833 |
www.asianacafe.com

"Kid-friendly" and "quick", this Greenwich Pan-Asian is a "reliable"
standby "when you don't want to cook", offering a "Chinese-

American mash-up with a sushi bar" at "reasonable prices"; dissenters say the "trendy"-looking decor "could use some spiffing up", though, and some purists pan the fare as being "designed for the Waspy palate."

Asian Temptation *Asian*   20 | 21 | 19 | $36

White Plains | City Ctr. | 23 Mamaroneck Ave. (bet. Main St. & Martine Ave.), NY | 914-328-5151 |
www.asiantemptationrestaurant.com

There's a "hip" "techno feel" to this "sleek" White Plains canteen turning out "fresh" sushi, "unique" rolls and a "wide array" of "tasty" Asian fusion items with martinis and bubble tea in a "modern" setting with a koi pond; just be prepared for a "loud", "lively" "girls'-night-out crowd" and prices that are "not cheap" ("broccoli should not cost so much green").

Aspen ⓜ *American*   20 | 23 | 20 | $44

Old Saybrook | 2 Main St. (Boston Post Rd.) | 860-395-5888 |
www.aspenct.com

"Après-ski" style comes to the shoreline via this "cozy" New American in Old Saybrook, whose "contemporary" environment is bedecked with branches from the namesake tree and whose "reasonably sophisticated" seasonal menu is rife with "local flavors"; a downstairs lounge offers its own "lighter" selection of victuals, as well as specialty cocktails concocted by "skilled and pleasant bartenders."

Assaggio *Italian*   24 | 20 | 22 | $39

Branford | 168 Montowese St. (bet. Main St. & Wilford Ave.) |
203-483-5426 | www.assaggiobranford.com

"A fine dine" say aficionados of this "quaint" Branford Northern Italian presenting "consistently delicious", "attractively presented" dishes alongside "interesting wine selections"; while the quarters are "cramped", "passionate" staffers who treat patrons "like family", "pretty" decor and moderate prices go a long way toward making it "comfortable."

Atlantic Seafood *Seafood*   23 | 17 | 21 | $36

Old Saybrook | 1400 Boston Post Rd. (School House Rd.) | 860-388-4527 |
www.atlanticseafoodmarket.com

Gourmet take-out meals comprising "impeccably fresh fish" are prepared by "thoughtful" owners at this seatless seafood shop in Old Saybrook; even folks from out of the area say the "quality" and affordable tabs make it "well worth the extra travel."

@ the Corner *American*   ▽ 20 | 20 | 20 | $38

Litchfield | 3 West St. (Rte. 61) | 860-567-8882

There's "something for everyone" on the menu at this Litchfield New American where aficionados are "delighted" by the "fun twists on old faves" and "friendly, attentive" service in the "cozy" setting with a "lively bar scene"; critics, though, find the fare "just ok" and evincing surprisingly "little imagination" for the "upper-moderate prices."

	FOOD	DECOR	SERVICE	COST

Atticus *American* | 18 | 15 | 15 | $18 |

New Haven | 1082 Chapel St. (bet. High & York Sts.) | 203-776-4040 | www.atticusbookstorecafe.com

"Basically a deli in a bookstore", this all-day New Haven "mainstay" provides a place for "bibliophiles" to tear into a tome and people-watchers to check out "Yalies young and old", all while noshing on "nicely prepared" American sandwiches and other "coffeehouse" fare at the "few tables"; furthermore, everything's "reasonably priced", appropriate considering the "benign" (yet "pleasant" enough) surroundings.

Aurora *Italian* | 21 | 21 | 21 | $44 |

Rye | 60 Purchase St. (bet. Elm Pl. & W. Purdy Ave.), NY | 914-921-2333 | www.auroraofrye.com

For a "reasonably priced" bite in "upscale Rye", try this "reliable", "modern" Italian turning out brick-oven pizzas and mains "with a Northern spin"; it's especially "lovely for lunch" in warm weather when the French doors are flung open, just beware of "loud acoustics" in the dining room during prime time.

Aux Délices Foods | 24 | 14 | 16 | $24 |
by Debra Ponzek *American/French*

Darien | Goodwives Shopping Ctr. | 25 Old Kings Hwy. N. (Sedgewick Ave.) | 203-662-1136
Greenwich | 3 W. Elm St. (Greenwich Ave.) | 203-622-6644
Riverside | 1075 E. Putnam Ave. (Wampus Ln.) | 203-698-1066
www.auxdelicesfoods.com

This trio of "upscale" "delis for foodies" in Darien, Greenwich and Riverside offers "healthy, tasty and imaginative" French–New American dishes and "wonderful pastries" that'll earn "high-end praise from your guests"; "limited seating", "no atmosphere" and the "attitudes" of the mostly "young, thin clients" make many opt for takeout, however – and "unless you are a hedge fund millionaire", it's "outrageously expensive."

Avellino's *Italian* | 20 | 17 | 21 | $41 |

Fairfield | 1813 Post Rd. (Mill Plain Rd.) | 203-254-2339 | www.avellinosfairfield.com

"Well-prepared" Italian fare is served by "warm, friendly" staffers at this "casual" "staple" in a Fairfield strip mall; "it's not an inexpensive place", but most surveyors consider it a "good value" nonetheless, not least of all because it's a "a safe bet" for "the entire family" (no wonder it's sometimes "noisy").

Aversano's *Italian* | 21 | 21 | 21 | $28 |

Brewster | 1620 Rte. 22 (Rte. 312), NY | 845-279-2233 | www.aversanosrestaurant.com

When brothers John and Paul Aversano expanded their Brewster pizzeria into a "sit-down" eatery a couple of years ago, it "quickly became a go-to" for "dependable", "classic Italian" fare, "and plenty of it"; a staff that "aims to please" adds a "warm atmosphere" to the simple space, while "pizzeria prices" "won't dent the wallet."

FOOD | DECOR | SERVICE | COST

Ay! Salsa 🗷⇗ *Pan-Latin*
— | — | — | I

New Haven | 25 High St. (Messina Dr.) | 203-752-0517 | www.aysalsa.net
Even if you're "not hungry", "the fragrance" of the Pan-Latin fare – especially the "delicious" arepas – makes it "so difficult to walk by" this "hole-in-the-wall" storefront in New Haven; cheap tabs are another draw, but there's "no seating", so plan on eating somewhere else; P.S. there's also a lunchtime food truck on Cedar Street.

Azu Restaurant & Bar *American*
▽ 23 | 20 | 21 | $38

Mystic | 32 W. Main St. (Water St.) | 860-536-6336 | www.ckrestaurantgroup.com
"Rather urbane" for Mystic, this "sexy, sassy" New American offers "appealing", "creative small dishes" and entrees along with "great people-watching when the windows are open" and relatively "modest" pricing; "lively" (read: "noisy") crowds make for "fun" times – indeed, it might be "called Azu because it's always a zoo."

Baang Cafe & Bar *Asian*
23 | 21 | 19 | $48

Riverside | 1191 E. Putnam Ave. (Neil Ln.) | 203-637-2114 | www.decarorestaurantgroup.com
A "favorite for 15 years", this "pricey" Riverside Pan-Asian still pulls "chic singles" into the colorful, "club"-like space with its "clever", "inventive" menu, "satisfying, sexy" cocktails and "still-hoppin'" bar scene; it's "aptly named" say those who wince at the "deafening" decibel levels, and cynics disparage it as a "faded star" that's getting "long in the tooth."

Bacchus 🗷Ⓜ *Italian/Steak*
— | — | — | E

South Norwalk | 120 Washington St. (bet. N. Main & Water Sts.) | 203-956-6220 | www.bacchussono.com
After a hiatus, this SoNo Italian steakhouse has reopened its doors and is serving traditional dishes such as slow-cooked osso buco as well as modern offerings such as tuna tartare on a crispy wonton, along with a big global wine list; the warm, brick-walled space features a glass-enclosed kitchen and a large granite bar.

Back Porch *New England*
▽ 18 | 17 | 17 | $28

Old Saybrook | Between the Bridges Marina | 142 Ferry Ln. (off I-95) | 860-510-0282 | www.backporcholdsaybrook.com
"An appealing vista" of the marina and the Connecticut River elevates the "ho-hum" setting of this seasonal Old Saybrook New Englander doling out "large quantities of simple but nicely prepared food" for affordable tabs; live music Wednesdays–Sundays draws a "dancing and drinking crowd", especially on weekends when it becomes quite "busy."

Bailey's Backyard Ⓜ *American*
21 | 17 | 21 | $38

Ridgefield | 23 Bailey Ave. (Main St.) | 203-431-0796 | www.baileysbackyard.com
"Savory" New American fare is "served professionally" by an "amiable staff" at this "cozy" bistro on a quaint street in Downtown Ridgefield, where the owners "seem like they care"; the "casual" in-

terior, which resembles a backyard "under a fun starry sky", is appealing, but it's so "small" that insiders caution "your wait will be outside" if you come at peak hours.

Ballou's Wine Bar *Eclectic*

∇ 18 | 18 | 23 | $24

Guilford | 51 Whitfield St. (bet. Boston & Broad Sts.) | 203-453-0319 | www.ballouswinebar.com

"Off-the-beaten-path in more ways than one", this "casual", "lovely wine bar" next to Guilford Green pairs its "great" selection of *vini* with chocolates, coffee and Eclectic nibbles; it may be "not so good if you're really hungry, because the light bites are really light", but for a snack and a tipple (accompanied by live music on weekends), "it's just the thing"; P.S. the "outdoor area is fun during warm weather."

Bamboo Grill Ⓜ *Vietnamese*

- | - | - | M

Canton | 50 Albany Tpke. (Colonial Rd.) | 860-693-4144 | www.bamboogrillcuisine.com

Non-locals say it's worth a trip to "the far reaches of the 'burbs" (namely, Canton) for this "attractive" Vietnamese BYO whose "cooked-to-order" specialties offer "fine quality for the price"; the "earnest family that runs the place" "tries hard to please", which helps set the "friendly" tone.

Bambou Asian Tapas & Bar *Asian*

21 | 22 | 21 | $36

Greenwich | The Mill | 328 Pemberwick Rd. (Glenville Rd.) | 203-531-3322 | www.bambourestaurant.com

"Creative" Pan-Asian dishes (including some of the "best sushi in town") and "friendly", "unobtrusive" service draw families and others to this restored mill by the river in Greenwich's Glenville neighborhood, a "lovely modern hideaway" with a "large" outdoor patio; critics grouse that the "desserts leave something to be desired" and the "con-fusion" cooking can be "hit-or-miss", but "great lunch specials" make it a "good value" for many.

Bangalore *Indian*

23 | 17 | 22 | $30

Fairfield | 1342 Kings Hwy. (Commerce Dr.) | 203-319-0100

There's "no shortage of spice" at this Fairfield subcontinental where the fare is "not your run-of-the-mill Indian" and the "delightful staff" "can guide you" around the more "imaginative" options; what's more, supporters say the "decor is pleasant" and the prices are "reasonable", especially those who come for the "reliable, generous" weekday lunch prix fixes and weekend brunch buffet.

Bangkok Gardens *Thai*

19 | 15 | 19 | $26

New Haven | 172 York St. (Chapel St.) | 203-789-8684

Yalies mingle with patrons of nearby "theaters and museums" at this "solid", "consistent Thai" located in Downtown New Haven, where the mostly "friendly" staffers provide "speedy" service, "even when busy" (which is pretty much always); the setting with a sun-filled atrium seems "slightly upscale", while "cheap" tabs make it "the kind of place students can treat their parents to thank them for the tuition."

	FOOD	DECOR	SERVICE	COST

Bangkok Thai *Thai*

20 | 9 | 17 | $26

Mamaroneck | 1208 W. Boston Post Rd. (Richbell Rd.), NY | 914-833-1200
"It's not much to look at", but this Mamaroneck Thai has regulars "returning again and again" for "authentic" dishes that are "consistently good"; service is "friendly" and prices low, but given the "drab" digs, it may be "better suited for takeout."

NEW Bank Street Tavern *Eclectic*

18 | 18 | 19 | $35

New Milford | 31 Bank St. (bet. Main & Railroad Sts.) | 860-799-7991
Early boosters "bank on" this New Milford tavern serving "innovative" Eclectic fare and "great microbrews" at "reasonable" prices in arguably the "best atmosphere in town"; but critics say it still "suffers from growing pains" and "needs to decide what it wants to be."

Bao's Chinese Cuisine *Chinese*

20 | 15 | 19 | $26

White Plains | White Plains Mall | 200 Hamilton Ave. (Cottage Pl.), NY | 914-682-8858
"Not your ordinary Chinese restaurant", this "affordable" grotto in the basement of the White Plains Mall slings "tasty", "authentic" cuisine that celebrates "seasonal, fresh veggies" with "no heavy sauces"; a staff that's "helpful" with ordering makes up for decor that's "a throwback to the '70s" and its somewhat "dismal" subterranean locale.

Bar Americain *American*

26 | 25 | 25 | $62

Uncasville | Mohegan Sun Casino | 1 Mohegan Sun Blvd. (bet. Rtes. 2 & 32) | 860-862-8000 | www.baramericain.com
Fans feel like they "hit the jackpot" at this "upscale Flay-vorite" at the Mohegan Sun casino, a "beautiful behemoth" of a New American brasserie serving Bobby Flay's "incredible" cuisine "blending bold colors and flavors" in a "cavernous but tasteful" setting with "well-spaced tables", where it's "quiet enough to talk", "away from the smoke and casino crowds"; "top-quality" service seals the deal.

NEW Bar Bouchée *French*

▽ 28 | 26 | 25 | $46

Madison | 8 Scotland Ave. (Rte. 1) | 203-318-8004
A "remarkable version of a classic small Paris bistro" can be found in Madison, courtesy of the folks behind New Haven's Union League Cafe, where "spectacular" Gallic dishes are served by an "attentive", "welcoming" staff in a "charming", "Frenchy-chic" room; "good luck" securing a reservation say those suffering from "table envy."

Barça *Spanish*

▽ 20 | 20 | 18 | $44

Hartford | Design Ctr. | 10 Bartholomew Ave. (Park St.) | 860-724-4444 | www.barcatapasct.com
"Authentic", "bangin'" tapas served in a "hip", modern room make this Hartford Spanish worth "looking for" according to amigos; critics, though, say the staff needs "better training" and quip that the noise level makes it a "great place for bad conversationalists."

Z Barcelona
Restaurant & Wine Bar *Spanish*

24 | 21 | 21 | $42

Fairfield | Hi Ho Motel | 4180 Black Rock Tpke. (Rte. 15) | 203-255-0800
(continued)

(continued)

Barcelona Restaurant & Wine Bar

Greenwich | 18 W. Putnam Ave. (Greenwich Ave.) | 203-983-6400
New Haven | Omni Hotel | 155 Temple St. (Chapel St.) | 203-848-3000
South Norwalk | 63 N. Main St. (bet. Ann & Marshall Sts.) |
203-899-0088
Stamford | 222 Summer St. (Broad St.) | 203-348-4800
West Hartford | 971 Farmington Ave. (Main St.) | 860-218-2100
www.barcelonawinebar.com

"*Viva Espana!*" exclaim amigos over the "intense flavors" of the Spanish tapas that "take hold of your taste buds" at this "jumping" sextet where the "young at heart in heat" share small plates, sangria and Iberian *vini* served by an "attentive" staff amid "eclectic, urbane" surroundings; frugal types grouse about "pricey" bites and "high markups", but give an "*olè*" to half-price wines on Sundays.

NEW Bar Rosso *Italian*

 — | — | — | E

Stamford | 24 Spring St. (Bedford St.) | 203-388-8640 |
www.barrossoct.com

Mary Schaffer and Charles Morgan (Napa & Co.) have transformed the former Bennett's in Stamford into an upscale contemporary Italian that's set to open at press time; expect rustic small plates, wood-fired pizza, pastas and house-cured charcuterie from executive chef Dan Kardos (ex Harvest Supper) plus a carefully chosen list of 250 Italian wines (including 25 by the glass) served by a staff schooled in food and wine pairings in a space featuring a 50-ft. bar and an outdoor patio.

NEW Bartaco ◑ *Mexican*

 — | — | — | M

Port Chester | 1 Willett Ave. (Abendroth Ave.), NY | 914-937-8226 |
www.bartaco.com

From the folks behind the ultrapopular Barcelona group comes this beach-chic taqueria in Port Chester vending gussied-up Mexican street fare in an airy space with an exhibition kitchen; it's full service and features a lengthy bar with fresh-fruit cocktails poured until 3:30 AM; P.S. branches in Stamford and Westport are coming soon.

☑ Basso Café Ⓜ *Mediterranean*

28 | 18 | 23 | $46

Norwalk | 124 New Canaan Ave. (Bartlett Ave.) | 203-354-6566 |
www.bassobistrocafe.com

"Shh" say fans of this "charming" cafe in an "unlikely" strip-mall location in Norwalk's Broad River, for it's still a "great secret" among those in the know with "discerning palates" who appreciate its "imaginative", "high-quality" Mediterranean fare with "interesting" South American accents; what's more, the "understated" space is "surprisingly comfortable" and "BYO keeps the price reasonable."

Basta *Italian*

25 | 20 | 23 | $42

New Haven | 1006 Chapel St. (College St.) | 203-772-1715 |
www.bastatrattoria.com

A "favorite of locals and Yalies" in the heart of New Haven, this "homey" trattoria offers "excellent" Italian "comfort food" featuring organic and sustainable ingredients and "first-rate" service from owners and a staff that "couldn't be more welcoming"; the "little space" is

	FOOD	DECOR	SERVICE	COST

"warm" and "cozy" – "unless you suffer from claustrophobia" – and it can get "noisy" when it's "crowded."

Beach House Ⓜ *Seafood* — 22 | 22 | 21 | $46

Milford | 141 Merwin Ave. (Abigail St.) | 203-877-9300 | www.beachhousemilford.com

There's a "vacation feel" to this "off-the-beaten-path" New American seafooder on the Milford waterfront, where management is "passionate" about the "dependable" food and wine; a dramatic, hand-carved 19th-century bar imported from New Orleans is the "focal point" of the "interesting" space, which offers a "mix of different interior designs", and while most praise the "attentive" service, a few say it "can be spotty" when the room gets "crowded."

Beach House Café *American* — 18 | 20 | 18 | $34

Old Greenwich | 220 Sound Beach Ave. (Arcadia Rd.) | 203-637-0367 | www.beachhousecafe.com

"You feel like you're at the beach" at this Old Greenwich American that attracts a mostly local clientele (including a "stroller-crowd" contingent) with a "comfortable" "shore-town" setting, "solid", seafood-centric "pub fare" and a "laid-back staff that makes you feel welcome", while evening bar action, "special nights" and live music on weekends add to the "fun"; a few critics say the "menu gets old fast", however, and complain about the "cacophonous" scene.

Bedford Post, The Barn *American* — 23 | 24 | 21 | $48

Bedford | Bedford Post | 954 Old Post Rd./Rte. 121 (bet. Indian Hill Rd. & Rte. 137), NY | 914-234-7800 | www.bedfordpostinn.com

The "swankiest barn you've ever set foot in", this "trendy" Bedford New American cafe and bakery from Richard Gere attracts a "sophisticated crowd" of "local celebrities" for "delicious homemade pastries" and an "amazing" "farm-to-table" breakfast and lunch; many "wish the portions were bigger" and the service less "disorganized", but "pricey" though it be, the majority insists it's "worth the indulgence"; P.S. dinner is served on Mondays and Tuesdays.

Bedford Post, The Farmhouse Ⓜ *American* — 25 | 26 | 23 | $78

Bedford | Bedford Post | 954 Old Post Rd./Rte. 121 (bet. Indian Hill Rd. & Rte. 137), NY | 914-234-7800 | www.bedfordpostinn.com

"Elegance and class" define the more formal of Richard Gere's Bedford Post eateries, a "charming" "getaway" that "romances its guests" with a "relaxed pace", "lovely ambiance" and "unfailingly excellent" New American cuisine focused on "local meat and produce"; a relatively new chef is in the kitchen, and there's still some murmuring about "small portions", occasionally "mediocre" service and tabs "not for the faint of wallet", but overall it's a "treat."

Beehive *American/Eclectic* — 21 | 16 | 21 | $33

Armonk | 30 Old Rte. 22 (Kaysal Ct.), NY | 914-765-0688 | www.beehive-restaurant.com

"New and improved" after a "major renovation", this Armonk "mainstay" is back with "large portions" of Eclectic-New American "upscale diner" fare that shows its "Greek roots" as well as covering the "comfort-food" "standards"; the "friendly" proprietors now preside over a "more spacious, airy" establishment that promises to be a "great place to meet."

Bellizzi *Italian*   15 | 12 | 15 | $23

Larchmont | 1272 Boston Post Rd. (Weaver St.), NY | 914-833-5800 | www.bellizzi.us

There's a "super-fun" playroom and "video-game mayhem" along with "standard" "thin-crust" pizza and pastas at this child-centric Larchmont Italian hosting birthday parties galore; adults who can't "tolerate noise, confusion and a hectic atmosphere" are in for an "instant headache", "liquor license" notwithstanding.

NEW Bellota at 42 ⑤ *Spanish*   - | - | - | M

White Plains | Ritz-Carlton Westchester | 1 Renaissance Sq., 42nd fl. (Main St.), NY | 914-861-3226

This casual enclave in the bar of Restaurant 42 atop White Plains' glitzy Ritz-Carlton features chef Anthony Goncalves' idiosyncratic take on Spanish tapas; expect moderately priced Iberian snacks prepared with playful twists in an evocative setting framed by ashen birch trunks springing from pools of acorns ('bellota' simultaneously refers to acorns and the elite porkers that eat them).

NEW Benjamin Steak House Ⓜ *Steak*   24 | 23 | 24 | $76

White Plains | 610 Hartsdale Ave. (Dobbs Ferry Rd./Rte. 100B), NY | 914-428-6868 | www.benjaminsteakhouse.com

"Running smoothly" from the get-go, this "outstanding" newcomer gives Hartsdale a "true NYC steakhouse" (almost a "clone" of its Manhattan sibling), complete with "wonderful" beef, "delicious sides" and "excellent" service; the "clubby environment" can get "loud" and the tab is "not cheap", but most find it an "enjoyable" experience nonetheless.

Bentara *Malaysian*   24 | 22 | 21 | $39

New Haven | 76 Orange St. (Center St.) | 203-562-2511 | www.bentara.com

This "longtime favorite" helped "put New Haven on the culinary map" with its "diverse" menu of "outstanding", "authentic" Malaysian dishes that includes ample "vegetarian options" and a "range of spiciness", plus an "amazing" wine list and "excellent" draft beer selection; the "vibrant" setting is "noisy and comfortable", and though some complain that service "can be quite slow" and the fare has "lost its luster", most still consider it a "good value" and "worth a trip."

☑ Bernard's Ⓜ *French*   27 | 26 | 27 | $68

Ridgefield | 20 West Ln. (High Ridge Ave.) | 203-438-8282 | www.bernardsridgefield.com

Chef-owner Bernard Bouissou turns out "superbly crafted" "classic" French fare "with a twist" at this Ridgefield "favorite" situated in an "upscale", "comfortable county-inn" setting; a "warm", "knowledgeable" staff, "outstanding wine list" and live piano on weekends help make it "the place to go for a special occasion" and "worth every penny"; P.S. the "more casual" Sarah's Wine Bar is upstairs.

Bertucci's *Italian*   16 | 14 | 16 | $25

Avon | 380 W. Main St. (Avon Rd.) | 860-676-1177
Danbury | 98 Newtown Rd. (I-84, exit 8) | 203-739-0500
Darien | 54 Boston Post Rd. (I-95, exit 13) | 203-655-4299
Glastonbury | 2882 Main St. (Griswold St.) | 860-633-2225
Newington | 2929 Berlin Tpke. (Main St.) | 860-666-1949
Orange | 550 Boston Post Rd. (Peck Ln.) | 203-799-6828
Shelton | 768 Bridgeport Ave. (bet. Old Stratford Rd. & Parrott Dr.) | 203-926-6058
Southington | 20 Spring St. (Queen St.) | 860-621-8626
Waterbury | Brass Mill Mall | 495 Union St. (Franklin St.) | 203-755-6224
Westport | 833 Post Rd. E. (I-95, exit 18) | 203-454-1559
www.bertuccis.com

This "decent" Italian chain is a "surefire thing" for families with kids who get to "play with dough" at the table; insiders advise just "stick with" the brick-oven pizzas, "hot rolls" and "nice salads" (some dishes can seem "processed"), and you'll get a "solid", "predictable" meal for a "fair price."

Besito *Mexican*   22 | 25 | 22 | $40

West Hartford | Blue Back Sq. | 46 S. Main St. (Memorial Rd.) | 860-233-2500 | www.besitomex.com

Admirers throw *mucho besitos* (kisses) to this "swanky" Nuevo Mexican in West Hartford's Blue Back Square where a "wall of candles" and "very high ceilings" give the "amazing" "mission-style" interior a "sense of drama"; "inventive", "upscale" dishes are served by a "friendly" staff to a "beautiful crowd" in a "lively atmosphere", but be prepared to pay *mucho dinero.*

Bespoke *American*   24 | 24 | 21 | $51

New Haven | 266 College St. (Chapel St.) | 203-562-4644 | www.bespokenewhaven.com

An "excellent Downtown choice" in New Haven, this "hip" New American spot offers "creative", "amazing" fare featuring "local and sustainably grown" ingredients and an eco-friendly wine list in a "stylish" space that includes a "candlelit" dining room, "beautiful" bar and a "hidden treasure" of a rooftop patio; a few critics pan the service as "spotty" and feel it's "lost its mojo" since changing hands in 2009, but most laud it as an "incredible" experience.

Big W's Roadside Bar-B-Que Ⓜ *BBQ*   26 | 7 | 21 | $19

Wingdale | 1475 Rte. 22 (Rock Hill Dr.), NY | 845-832-6200 | www.bigwsbbq.com

"Ace pitmaster" and "gregarious" host Warren Norstein (aka Big W) gets "kudos" for his Wingdale "winner" of a BBQ joint that's "worth a drive" for "melt-in-your-mouth, marvelous" pulled pork and brisket, "tender, meaty ribs" and chicken "smoked to perfection", all at "low prices"; those who find the "sterile, fluorescent-lit" setting a turnoff get the grub "boxed to take home", or picnic roadside under the willow when it's warm.

	FOOD	DECOR	SERVICE	COST

Bill's Seafood ⌀ *Seafood* | 19 | 16 | 17 | $29 |

Westbrook | 548 Boston Post Rd. (Hammock Rd.) | 860-399-7224 |
www.billsseafood.com

Old salts advise "no summer is complete without a dinner" at this
"typical New England shoreline joint" in Westbrook, where you can sit
on the "lively" outdoor deck overlooking the Patchogue River and tuck
into "straight-up good lobster" and "fresh, fried and fabulous" fin fare
to the strains of "awesome" live music; some report "hit-or-miss" service, though, and cognoscenti caution "don't expect anything fancy."

Bin 100 *Eclectic* | 26 | 23 | 23 | $43 |

Milford | 100 Lansdale Ave. (Bridgeport Ave.) | 203-882-1400 |
www.bin100.com

A "delightful surprise" in a Milford strip mall, this "wonderful"
Eclectic leaves diners "impressed" with "extraordinary", 'imaginative" cuisine, an "extensive" wine list and "attentive", "engaging"
servers who don't "interrupt conversation or interfere with a
guest's dining experience"; the ambiance is "welcoming" in the
"chic", modern setting, and while some find it "a bit pricey", others
consider it a "bargain."

Bin 228 Panini & Wine Bar ⧄ *Italian* | 22 | 21 | 20 | $32 |

Hartford | 228 Pearl St. (bet. Ann St. & Service Ct.) | 860-244-9463 |
www.bin228winebar.com

A "phenomenal wine list" lets you find the "perfect complement to
anything you order" from the "well-presented" menu of "delicious"
small plates at this Italian "hot spot" "right across the street from
TheaterWorks" in Hartford; the "tiny" digs are "pleasant", the
owner and staff are "knowledgeable" and "friendly", and the location makes it "perfect for before and after the theater."

⧉ Bistro Basque *French/Spanish* | 26 | 22 | 26 | $42 |

Milford | 13 River St. (bet. Daniel St. & New Haven Ave.) | 203-878-2092 |
www.bistrobasqueusa.com

Boosters basque in the "warm, inviting" ambiance of this French-
Spanish bistro in the center of Milford's historic district, where the
"charming, witty" chef creates "outstanding" tapas and entrees,
which are backed by a "good variety" of "moderately priced" wines,
and the "agreeable" servers "want to please, and they do"; the
outdoor patio is "lovely in the summer months", and while a few
quibble about the "noise level", most regard it as a "good value"
that's only "getting better."

Bistro Bonne Nuit *French* | 25 | 22 | 23 | $57 |

New Canaan | 12 Forest St. (bet. East & Locust Aves.) | 203-966-5303
Delicieux" French fare and one of the "best wine selections in town"
make for an "excellent bistro experience" at this Gallic spot on New
Canaan's Restaurant Row, where the "newly added" sidewalk seating is a welcome addition to the space where some find the tables
"too close for comfort", especially if you find yourself next to "three
tipsy Lovey Howells"; some howl that it's "unbelievably overpriced",
but *amis* insist it's "worth every" centime.

	FOOD	DECOR	SERVICE	COST

Bistro Twenty-Two ⊠ *American/French* | 24 | 23 | 24 | $64 |

Bedford | 391 Old Post Rd./Rte. 22 (bet. Lake Ave. & The Farms Rd.), NY | 914-234-7333 | www.bistro22.com

Like a "Rolls-Royce", this "quiet, elegant" Bedford "standout" purrs along, providing its "regulars" with "exceptional" French–New American repasts enhanced by an "outstanding wine list"; a "gracious host" and "professional" service attract an "older crowd" as well as those who enjoy a "civilized experience" and can afford the "pricey" tariff.

B.J. Ryan's ● *American* | 20 | 17 | 19 | $28 |

Norwalk | 57 Main St. (Hoyt St.) | 203-866-7926 | www.bjryans.com

Though it "may seem like a typical pub at first glance", this Wall Street watering hole in Norwalk dishes out "no-nonsense" New American grub that's "so much better than you'd expect", including "damn fine hamburgers" and "first-rate specials"; sure, it's "loud" – it's a "sports bar", after all – but the staff is "amiable", the atmosphere is "welcoming" and many regard it as an "oasis of comfort and consistency."

Black-Eyed Sally's BBQ & Blues ⊠ *BBQ* | 20 | 17 | 18 | $29 |

Hartford | 350 Asylum St. (bet. Ann & High Sts.) | 860-278-7427 | www.blackeyedsallys.com

As "funky as it gets", this "friendly" "Dixie roadhouse" in the center of Hartford is the "go-to" spot of fans in need of a "BBQ fix", dishing out "outstanding" 'cue and Cajun eats in a "hyper-hip" "blues cave" with a "Mardi-Gras-party" vibe; some say that it's "all about the music" and the "experience", rather than fare that critics dismiss as "so-so."

Blackstones Steakhouse *Steak* | 25 | 20 | 22 | $56 |

Norwalk | 181 Main St. (Plymouth Ave.) | 203-840-9020

Local carnivores "save the train fare to NYC" and head to this "first-class steakhouse" housed in an "unassuming storefront" in Norwalk, where "exquisite" dry-aged steaks and "excellent" seafood are served by a "friendly, quick" staff in a "masculine"-looking space sporting "red tones and beautiful dark wood"; some beef about the "high prices", but others insist "you get what you pay – a lot – for."

Blazer Pub ⊅ *Pub Food* | 22 | 11 | 19 | $22 |

Purdys | 440 Rte. 22 (Rte. 116), NY | 914-277-4424 | www.theblazerpub.com

Boosters "blaze a path" to this "quintessential local pub" in Purdys for "wear-a-bib juicy" burgers and "bar-food" "classics" in a "convivial" atmosphere that can get "a bit noisy"; "friendly, prompt" service helps ease "the wait" for a table, but "remember, it's cash only."

Bloodroot Ⓜ *Vegan/Vegetarian* | 23 | 15 | 15 | $25 |

Bridgeport | 85 Ferris St. (Harbor Ave.) | 203-576-9168 | www.bloodroot.com

"Charming, bohemian" and "feminist-to-the-core", this stalwart in Bridgeport's Black Rock neighborhood offers "inventive", "eclectic"

| | FOOD | DECOR | SERVICE | COST |

vegan-vegetarian dishes that are "healthy and comforting" and may make you "forget you eat meat", while the "service is excellent – as you serve yourself"; the outdoor seating overlooking Long Island Sound is a "must in warm weather", and there's a bookstore and gift shop indoors.

BLT Steak *Steak*   23 | 23 | 22 | $70

White Plains | Ritz-Carlton Westchester | 221 Main St. (bet. Church St. & Renaissance Sq.), NY | 914-467-5500 | www.bltsteak.com

This "lavish, modern" chophouse import from NYC hosts a well-heeled crowd for "amazing" steaks and sides plus "incredible" Gruyère popovers that are "worth the price of admission"; though service is "generally attentive" and the Ritz-Carlton setting "sophisticated", some find the tabs "overpriced, even for an expense-account dinner."

Blue Ⓢ *American*   20 | 21 | 20 | $50

White Plains | 99 Church St. (Hamilton Ave.), NY | 914-220-0000 | www.bluerestaurantwhiteplains.com

It's "quite a scene" at this "sleek" White Plains boîte purveying "creative" Asian-inspired New American bites and "to-die-for martinis" in "dark", azure-hued environs; "uneven" service and "head-achingly noisy" acoustics are among the downsides, and some don't like paying "Manhattan prices for food that misses the mark."

Blue Dolphin Ristorante Ⓢ *Italian*   23 | 14 | 21 | $34

Katonah | 175 Katonah Ave. (Jay St.), NY | 914-232-4791 | www.thebluedolphinny.com

Definitely "not fancy", but "deservedly popular", this "tiny" Katonah Southern Italian in a converted diner is "bursting with mounds" of "authentic, flavorful" Caprese cuisine served up by a "cheerful" crew; "moderate prices" combined with a "no-reservations" policy mean it's "usually packed", but "worth the wait."

Blue Lemon *American*   24 | 20 | 24 | $48

Westport | Sconset Sq. | 15 Myrtle Ave. (Post Rd.) | 203-226-2647 | www.bluelemonrestaurant.com

Fans declare this "intimate" New American in a "quiet corner" of Westport a "winner" thanks to "master" chef-owner Bryan Malcarney's "creative" cuisine, featuring "fresh ingredients and what's in season", as well as Mediterranean, Latin and Asian touches; "well-informed, gracious" servers attend to diners in a "cozy", "quiet" setting, and while some say it's so "cramped" that you "always feel you're eavesdropping", for most, that doesn't detract from a "memorable dining experience."

Boathouse *American*   17 | 20 | 19 | $41

Lakeville | 349 Main St. (Walton St.) | 860-435-2111 | www.boathouseatlakeville.com

Rowing skulls round out the boathouse motif at this Lakeville spot whose "varied menu" of "reliable" American fare also includes "stupendous" sushi, all served by a "friendly" staff in a "cozy" space with a "lovely patio"; "so-so food at high prices" is how antagonists assess it, however, and others warn that "when the country club set hits" in summer, the "wait can be tedious."

NEW Boathouse at Saugatuck Ⓜ *American*   25 | 24 | 23 | $49

Westport | Saugatuck Rowing Club | 521 Riverside Ave. (Bridge St.) | 203-227-3399 | www.saugatuckrowing.com

"Hiding in the Saugatuck Rowing Club", this Westport New American is the showcase for John Holzwarth's "fabulous, fresh" "locavore" cuisine that comes in "beautiful presentations", served in a "tasteful", "nautical" setting with a "picturesque balcony" that commands a "gorgeous view" of the Saugatuck River; the staff is generally "friendly" and "attentive", and while the prices may be on the "high side" for some, fans insist the "quality is way up there" too.

Boathouse at Smokey Joe's *BBQ/Seafood*   19 | 16 | 18 | $26

Stamford | 1308 E. Main St. (Weed Ave.) | 203-406-0605 | www.smokeyjoesribs.com

"Perched above a stream", this Stamford gastropub offers "superb" seafood and "first-class" BBQ in a space that "gleams like the inside of a boat" and "makes you feel like [you're on] a summer vacation", where "adults eat and drink while the teenagers play billiards downstairs"; critics quip the "pace of the service is similarly relaxed", but others observe that "takeout is very fast."

Bobby Q's Barbeque & Grill *BBQ*   21 | 16 | 18 | $28

Westport | 42 Main St. (Post Rd.) | 203-454-7800 | www.bobbyqsrestaurant.com

Bringing the West to Westport, this "smoking" BBQ joint serves up "authentic", "reasonably priced" 'cue and "fantastic sides" in a "kid-friendly" "barn setting" that gets "noisy and crowded"; some cynics sniff the fare is "ok" but "not the best", and the service, "oh well", but others insist "you'll leave stuffed and satisfied"; P.S. live music on the rooftop is a "blast on a nice night."

Bobby Valentine's Sports Gallery Café ◑ *American*   15 | 16 | 16 | $24

Stamford | 225 Main St. (Washington Blvd.) | 203-348-0010 | www.bobbyv.com

"Basic" pub grub fills the bill at this "reasonably priced" "all-American sports bar"/restaurant in Downtown Stamford that's "perfect to catch a game", thanks to "tons of large HD TVs"; though critics gripe about "faded" decor, "so-so" service and an "overly testosterone-ated" atmosphere, baseball fans cheer the "fabulous" memorabilia from the collection of the namesake former Mets manager, who's "often there."

Bogey's Grille & Tap Room *American*   17 | 15 | 18 | $28

Westport | 323 Main St. (Canal St.) | 203-227-4653

"You shouldn't need a mulligan" as long as you "stick to the basics" at this "easygoing" golf-themed Westport "institution", where con-

FOOD · DECOR · SERVICE · COST

sistent", "well-prepared" Traditional American eats and ample "spirits and suds" are par for the course; a few find the "limited" wine selection a hazard, while the duffers' motif (e.g. 'sandwedges' and Augusta National ribs on the menu) is a "turnoff" to others, but many just "play right through" this "no-frills experience that never fails to please."

Bombay *Indian*

| 22 | 14 | 18 | $30 |

Westport | 616 Post Rd. E. (bet. Crescent & Rayfield Rds.) | 203-226-0211 | www.fineindiandining.com
See review in The Berkshires Directory.

Bombay Olive *American/Indian*

| ∇ 19 | 14 | 19 | $25 |

West Hartford | 450 S. Main St. (New Britain Ave.) | 860-561-3000 | www.bombayolive.com
Fans praise the "terrific lunch buffet" at this West Hartford Indian that puts out a "varied" spread of "flavorful" dishes, including American, Persian and Nepalese selections, as well as à la carte offerings, at "reasonable" prices; the staff is "accommodating" and the digs are "clean", but some cynics find the fare too "mild" and leave it for "beginners."

Bonda 🅱Ⓜ *American/Eclectic*

| 27 | 22 | 25 | $55 |

Fairfield | 75 Hillside Rd. (bet. Cedar & Hill Farm Rds.) | 203-292-9555 | www.bondarestaurant.com
Jamie Cooper's globally influenced American-Eclectic cuisine remains "creative and consistently outstanding" and the "wonderful" staff "still makes you feel at home" at his establishment, which moved from Westport to Fairfield's tony Greenfield Hill section in 2010; many say the "inviting" space is "much improved" from the previous site and "really showcases his talents" – just "don't plan on a quiet intimate evening" some caution, for "it gets a bit noisy in the front."

Bond Grill *Asian*

| ∇ 21 | 20 | 20 | $30 |

Norwalk | 250 Westport Ave. (bet. Lovatt St. & Vollmer Ave.) | 203-840-0610 | www.asianbistrogroup.com
Admirers are stirred, not shaken, by this Norwalk establishment's "wide variety" of "exceptional" Pan-Asian cuisine, including "great-quality" sushi, teppanyaki grill fare and "standard (but quite good)" take-out selections; "friendly" service and an "inviting" modern space add to its allure, but some critics lament that while the "menu looks interesting on paper", the fare "loses something in translation."

Booktrader Café *Coffeehouse*

| ∇ 18 | 13 | 14 | $13 |

New Haven | 1140 Chapel St. (bet. Park & York Sts.) | 203-787-6147 | www.booktradercafe.com
This New Haven bookstore cafe "feels like a part of the Yale campus" where "hipsters in Urban Outfitter clothes", students and self-proclaimed "dorks" gather to indulge in "fresh coffee, tasty sandwiches" and "great baked goods" while browsing used books or studying in the "sunroom"; "friendly" service is a plus,

| | FOOD | DECOR | SERVICE | COST |

but a few grouse that while the hardcovers may be "cheap", the edibles are "overpriced."

Boom Restaurant *American* | 22 | 20 | 20 | $41 |

Old Lyme | 90 Halls Rd. (Rte. 95) | 860-434-0075 🖂
Westbrook | Brewer's Pilots Point Marina | 63 Pilot's Point Dr. (Rte. 1) | 860-399-2322
www.boomrestaurant.net

In summer it's "dreamy" to sit on the deck of this waterfront Westbrook spot and "watch boats come and go" under "fabulous sunsets" on the Sound, and boomers boast the New American "food is as good as the view"; when it's closed mid-March through November, many head to the year-round Old Lyme location, where some have to "close their eyes to the strip-mall setting", a task made somewhat easier by "pleasant" service.

Boulders Inn Ⓜ *American* | 21 | 25 | 21 | $58 |

New Preston | The Boulders Inn | 387 E. Shore Rd. (bet. Rte. 202 & Tanner Hill Rd.) | 860-868-0541 | www.bouldersinn.com

Housed in a "romantic, rustic" antique inn on 42 acres on Lake Waramaug, where the "view at sunset is sublime", this "charming" New Preston Contemporary American should be "saved to share with someone really special"; while critics claim the "ambiance carries the erratic food" and "unprofessional", if "well-intended", service, defenders insist the experience is so "memorable" "you may not even notice the price"; P.S. open Fridays, Saturdays and Sundays only in the winter.

Boxcar Cantina *Southwestern* | 21 | 18 | 19 | $32 |

Greenwich | 44 Old Field Point Rd. (Prospect St.) | 203-661-4774 | www.boxcarcantina.com

Organic and local ingredients shine in the "healthy", "high-end" Southwestern fare at this longtime Greenwich favorite that's "as close to authentic Santa Fe without taking your private jet to your New Mexico ranch", and the "hard-to-resist" fresh-lime margaritas may require a "designated driver"; a "friendly" staff works the "noisy" room (aka "kid city"), though adults can escape the din in the bar ("soft music, crackling fire") or by coming after 8; a caveat from cognoscenti – "you'll pay for the quality."

⧫ Brasitas *Pan-Latin* | 25 | 18 | 21 | $37 |

Norwalk | 430 Main Ave. (bet. Creeping Hemlock Dr. & Valley View Rd.) | 203-354-7329
Stamford | 954 E. Main St. (Lincoln Ave.) | 203-323-3176
www.brasitas.com

The "innovative" Pan-Latin cuisine at these "upscale" "foodie finds" in Norwalk and Stamford is a "refreshing" "feast for your eyes" and "happy mouth", and "killer" drinks add to the "buzz"; the staff is "friendly" but some report that "service suffers" when it "gets very busy" on weekends ("parking is always a challenge" too), and while the "lush" "tropical decor" may not obscure the "lack of curb appeal", most agree the "sophisticated" fare does.

	FOOD	DECOR	SERVICE	COST

NEW Brasserie, The *French*

24 | 20 | 23 | $40

Fairfield | 52 Sanford St. (Post Rd.) | 203-254-8094 |
www.thebrasseriect.com

The former Saint Tropez has "absolutely pulled off" the "change from bistro to brasserie" with an "expanded", "lower cost" menu of "succulent" French classics and tapas ("little bites of heaven") that "hits the spot for your stomach and your wallet", plus an "affordable wine list" that's a "real winner" as well; "attentive", "friendly" service and a "cozy, inviting" ambiance add to its allure.

Brasserie Pip *American*

- | - | - | E

Ivoryton | Copper Beech Inn | 46 Main St. (Johnny Cake Ln.) |
860-767-0330 | www.copperbeechinn.com

The owners of the "gorgeous" Copper Beech Inn in Ivoryton have combined the erstwhile Copper Beech restaurant and Brasserie Pip under one *parapluie*, and the result is "a little more brasserie" than the former and "a bit more upscale" than the latter; toque Tyler Anderson – "certainly one of Connecticut's top 10 chefs" – is still in the kitchen, creating a "less expensive" French–New American menu, which is served in the chic bistro and formal dining room.

Bravo Bravo Ⓜ *Italian*

26 | 18 | 21 | $44

Mystic | Whaler's Inn | 20 E. Main St. (Holmes St.) | 860-536-3228 |
www.bravobravoct.com

An "encore worth repeating", this "trendy" Italian in Mystic's Whaler's Inn "never disappoints" with its "absolutely amazing" cuisine with a "modern flair", and it "doesn't forget it's a Shoreline eatery", which is evident in its "excellent" seafood; cognoscenti recommend you "sit by the window and watch the passing scene", which may help distract you from what some describe as "deafening" noise ("you might as well be mute") or service that critics carp is "not up to the quality of the chef."

Brazen Fox ☻ *Pub Food*

17 | 17 | 17 | $26

White Plains | 175 Mamaroneck Ave. (bet. E. Post Rd. & Maple Ave.), NY | 914-358-5911 | www.thebrazenfox.com

This beyond-"bustling" White Plains pub tucked in among the many watering holes on Mamaroneck Avenue "packs in" a post-collegiate crowd with "lots of beers on tap", "solid bar fare" ("decent burgers and wings") and high-def TVs "everywhere you look"; yes, the fare's "predictable" and "there's not much personality" to the decor, but tabs are cheap and there's live music on weekends, so it's a fine place to "hang out."

Brewhouse *American*

19 | 19 | 18 | $29

South Norwalk | 13 Marshall St. (N. Main St.) | 203-853-9110 |
www.sonobrewhouse.com

Offering an "eclectic collection" of "down-home" Traditional American cooking and "international fare", plus a Sunday brunch buffet "with unlimited champagne", carving stations and raw bar, this "family-friendly" pub near South Norwalk's Maritime Center can "please the pickiest of eaters"; the "accommodating" servers

	FOOD	DECOR	SERVICE	COST

"really know their beers", but despite the antique copper brewing kettles in the "charming" space, some hopsters grumble that "they don't actually brew anything" here.

☑ Bricco *Italian*   27 | 23 | 24 | $40

West Hartford | 78 Lasalle Rd. (Farmington Ave.) | 860-233-0220 | www.billygrant.com

Billy Grant's "clubby" "mainstay" in West Hartford is "always busy – for good reason": namely, "spectacular", "creative" Italian cuisine and a "wonderful wine list" that are both "reasonably priced"; a "caring, well-informed staff" oversees the "lively dining room filled with happy people" as well as the "busy bar scene", while the "outdoor space is especially inviting in warm weather", so the only caveat is that "waits can be long", since it takes "no reservations for parties of five or less."

Brix ⑤Ⓜ *French/Italian*   ▽ 21 | 15 | 20 | $41

Cheshire | 1721 Highland Ave. (Fieldstone Ct.) | 203-272-3584 | www.brixct.com

A "surprise" in the "hinterland", this Cheshire "standby" serves up French and Italian cuisine in a "smartly casual" setting; a few sniff that the "menu needs updating", but boosters insist it "hits the ball out of the park" with its "fresh, tasty" fare and declare it a "winner."

Brooklyn's Famous Subs & Pasta *Diner*   17 | 16 | 21 | $18

White Plains | 51 Court St. (bet. Main St. & Martine Ave.), NY | 914-422-0115 | www.brooklynsfamous.com

"If you're young enough to be able to digest it", supporters suggest this "piece of 1950s nostalgia" in White Plains putting out "simple" sandwiches and diner-style grub in predictably "retro" digs; "quick service", low prices and a "fun" vibe make it a fallback for "parents with their kids", even if many maintain the eating's "inconsistent" at best.

Bru Room at BAR *Pizza*   25 | 17 | 16 | $23

New Haven | 254 Crown St. (bet. High & York Sts.) | 203-495-1111 | www.barnightclub.com

"Dependably superb" pizzas, including the "total must-try" mashed potato version, and "excellent" beers are what this New Haven brewpub "does well, nothing more, nothing less" (though the "fresh, crisp salads" are also recommended when you need a "dose of virtue"); the scene is "boisterous" in the "cool" space that once housed an auto showroom, and while critics chide the servers for being "too cool for school", most agree the "amazing" pies are "worth the attitude and the wait."

Bull's Bridge Inn *American*   16 | 15 | 19 | $36

Kent | 333 Kent Rd. (Bull's Bridge Rd.) | 860-927-1000 | www.bullsbridge.com

"Friendly" service and "consistent" "Traditional" American fare (plus a "super salad bar") are offered in a "warm, cozy" circa-1762 building near a historic covered bridge at this Kent establishment, where the "old-fashioned bar scene" is "always filled with interesting locals" (a few hipsters jeer it's "been a decade since anyone was carded here"); fans find it a "great value" and a "perfect" option "after a day of antiquing or pumpkin-picking."

Buon Amici *Italian*

22 | 16 | 24 | $41

White Plains | 238 Central Ave. (Tarrytown Rd.), NY | 914-997-1399 | www.buonamicirestaurant.com

They "make you feel like a million bucks" at this White Plains Italian where the servers "take pride in reeling off a long list of the nightly specials" and the "delicious" "red-sauce" dishes are "delivered with a smile"; the "comfortable" beige digs may be nothing to write home about, but prices are "affordable for what you get", so you really "can't go wrong."

Buon Appetito Ⓜ *Italian*

▽ 26 | 12 | 20 | $35

Canton | 50 Albany Tpke. (Secret Lake Rd.) | 860-693-2211

"You'll never spot a vampire" at this Canton Italian whose chef-owner "loves the stinking rose" and it shows in his "superb", "down-home" cooking, which comes in "huge portions"; though most describe the decor as "nonexistent" in the room that can feel "a bit crowded even when it's not", many consider it a "great little find" "for the money" – and BYO "makes it more affordable."

Burger Bar & Bistro *Burgers*

22 | 15 | 15 | $23

South Norwalk | 58 N. Main St. (bet. Ann & Marshall Sts.) | 203-853-2037 | www.burgerbarsono.com

The "eclectic" selection of "creative carnivorous concoctions" – aka hamburgers – inspires "lofty epicurean aspirations" at this SoNo favorite that also pleases with its "amazing" mac 'n' cheese and truffle fries "to die for"; the "laid-back", bovine-themed space was recently enlarged, and while a few fret that the "small kitchen just can't keep up" with the expansion, exacerbating what they describe as "indifferent" service, the "delicious" eats and proximity to the local cinema make it a popular option for an "affordable night on the town."

Burgers, Shakes & Fries *Burgers*

22 | 8 | 17 | $14

Darien | 800 Post Rd. (Sedgewick Ave.) | 203-202-9401
Greenwich | 302 Delavan Ave. (New Lebanon Ave.) | 203-531-7433 Ⓢ⊄
www.burgersshakesnfries.com

At this Greenwich "hole-in-the-wall" (and its new, larger sit-down sibling), the "succulent" build-your-own burgers of "bodacious beef" "nicely served" on toasted bread "will leave you with a big, fat, greasy smile"; "seating is limited" in the original location's "closet-size" space, but "what it lacks in ambiance" it makes up for with "friendly" service and "16-napkin", "finger-lickin' deliciousness" (those in the know "order ahead" and get it to go, anyway); P.S. Darien also serves beer and wine.

Butterfly Chinese *Chinese*

19 | 15 | 18 | $27

West Hartford | 831 Farmington Ave. (Lancaster Rd.) | 860-236-2816 | www.butterflyrestaurantct.com

A "solid choice" for "well-prepared" Chinese, this "nice sit-down" spot in West Hartford is a "go-to" option for a "mostly local" crowd, offering "reliable" eats and "prompt" service in a setting straight out of central casting, complete with "fish tanks"; cynics find its popularity "perplexing", however, and describe the eats as a "bland" simulacrum of Sino cooking you might've seen in "Kansas City in 1952"; P.S. the piano player in the Koi Lounge is an "institution" – "be sure to ask him if he knows *Freebird*."

Cafe Allegre ⓜ *Italian* | 23 | 22 | 24 | $40 |

Madison | Inn at Lafayette | 725 Boston Post Rd. (Wall St.) | 203-245-7773 | www.allegrecafe.com

"Professional, friendly" service from a staff that "tries hard" is the hallmark of this "classy", "well-run" Italian in Downtown Madison, whose "solid menu" of "consistently good" ("unimaginative" to some) traditional Italian cuisine offers "good value"; the atmosphere is "formal" and "quiet" in the "timeless-classic" dining room, while things are "jumpin'" at the "more casual" bar.

𝗡𝗘𝗪 Café d'Azur *Mediterranean* | - | - | - | M |

Darien | 980 Post Rd. (bet. Center St. & Corbin Dr.) | 203-202-9520 | www.cafedazur.com

The successor to the owners' late Myrna's Mediterranean Bistro in Stamford, this moderately priced bistro and crêperie in the heart of Darien offers French, Italian, Greek and Lebanese fare, plus wines and beers from each region, in a contemporary setting that's casual and family-friendly by day, white-tablecloth romantic by night, with outdoor seating too; takeout and delivery service is also available.

Cafe Giulia *Italian* | ▽ 22 | 20 | 20 | $44 |

Lakeville | 2 Ethan Allen St. (Rte. 41) | 860-435-9765 | www.cafegiuliact.com

"A terrific additional to Lakeville", this Italian is becoming a "favorite of locals" for "informal suppers or a super-duper special meal" thanks to a "limited, but changing menu" of "fresh" fare "deftly cooked and presented", with an emphasis on "local ingredients" in the summer; the "open, airy space" is "warm and comfortable", the staff is "knowledgable" and the owner "could not be more welcoming."

Cafe Goodfellas *Italian* | 20 | 17 | 20 | $40 |

New Haven | 758 State St. (Bradley St.) | 203-785-8722 | www.cafegoodfellas.com

At this "old-school mobster"-themed Southern Italian in New Haven, waiters "provide service fit for a don" and the "top-shelf" "traditional" fare reminds some diners of their "childhood"; surveyors either "love or hate" the "gangster movies" that play on big-screen TVs in the "small" room, which is filled with the strains of Sinatra and Dean Martin crooning, and though some critics find the "wiseguy" motif "degrading", for many the experience is "an offer they can't refuse."

Cafe Livorno ⓩ *Italian* | 19 | 17 | 18 | $50 |

Rye | 92 Purchase St. (Purdy Ave.), NY | 914-967-1909

This "family-owned" Northern Italian "in the heart of Rye" earns its "steady" "neighborhood" following with "satisfying" fare served up

	FOOD	DECOR	SERVICE	COST

in a "quiet" setting that "feels like home"; it's a "bit pricey for what it is", but even if you "wouldn't go out of your way for it", supporters say it's "pleasant" enough.

Cafe Lola *French*

| 24 | 21 | 22 | $47 |

Fairfield | 57 Unquowa Rd. (bet. Post & School Rds.) | 203-292-8014 | www.cafelolarestaurant.com

The owners of this "pricey" Fairfield French "have put a great deal of love into their venture, and it shows" in the "impressive" "bistro fare" (including a "brunch full of sinful delights"), "friendly" hospitality and "romantic, cozy" surroundings; snug seating compels some to caution "make sure you keep your secrets to yourself", while others report that service can be "haphazard", but most regard it as a "great addition to Downtown."

Café Manolo 🗷 Ⓜ *Mediterranean*

| 23 | 19 | 21 | $48 |

Westport | 8 Church Ln. (State St.) | 203-227-0703 | www.cafemanolo.com

"Hidden in plain sight" in Downtown Westport, this "high-end" Mediterranean offers "complex, imaginative" fare featuring "fresh ingredients" from local purveyors, including small plates that are "not all that small", which can be paired with "nice wines by the glass"; the "knowledgeable" staff "always seems happy to see you", and the vibe is "relaxed" in the former bank vault space (although some say it gets "noisy when full") – in sum, it's a "welcome addition" to the town's "bleak dining scene."

Cafe Mirage *Eclectic*

| 22 | 12 | 20 | $36 |

Port Chester | 531 N. Main St. (Terrace Ave.), NY | 914-937-3497 | www.cafemirageny.com

A "funky setting in a converted gas station" forms the backdrop for this "happening" Port Chester Eclectic showcasing an "inventive" menu that foodies find "invariably delicious"; yes, it's "a little cramped", but a "staff that aims to please" makes up for it, and it's "open late" for the area too.

Cafe Mozart *Coffeehouse*

| 17 | 13 | 16 | $26 |

Mamaroneck | 308 Mamaroneck Ave. (Palmer Ave.), NY | 914-698-4166

A "lovely place to meet" "for coffee or brunch", this "cozy", "European"-style cafe in Mamaroneck is a "neighborhood" standby for "simple" salads, sandwiches and "caloric desserts"; perhaps the fare's "nothing to write home about", but the atmosphere's "relaxed", live music on weekends is a "nice touch" and many find it especially "enjoyable" in summer when the sidewalk scene is in full swing.

Café on the Green *Italian*

| 22 | 21 | 24 | $48 |

Danbury | Richter Park Golf Course | 100 Aunt Hack Rd. (Mill Plain Rd.) | 203-791-0369 | www.cafeonthegreenrestaurant.com

You may "need a GPS" to locate this "hidden culinary gem overlooking the rolling landscape" of the Richter Park Golf Course, but aficionados insist "it's worth the trek" for summer "drinks on the balcony" or "sophisticated" Northern Italian cuisine served by an "attentive", "professional" staff in a "relaxed" but "classy" setting; "beautiful views" of the 10th fairway and 18th green round out what most describe as a "superior dining experience."

☑ Café Routier *French*

27 | 22 | 25 | $48

Westbrook | 1353 Boston Post Rd. (bet. Burdick & Goodspeed Drs.) | 860-399-8700 | www.caferoutier.com

A "Shoreline star", this French bistro is an "oasis of quality" in Westbrook, serving "creative" seasonal menus featuring locally sourced ingredients, "eclectic" regional menus full of "surprises" from around the globe, "inventive" specials and its "regular winners", all complemented by a "superb" wine list and "impeccable" service; the dining room is "quiet" and "cozy", but some say the lounge (which offers a separate menu) can get "really noisy", and even though it's "tough to get into during the summer", many conclude it's "worth the wait."

Cafe Silvium ☒ *Italian*

26 | 17 | 22 | $39

Stamford | 371 Shippan Ave. (Park St.) | 203-324-1651 | www.cafesilvium.com

The "lines are legendary" at this *molto bene* Italian in Stamford's Shippan neighborhood, so "get there early" or "have a drink while you wait"; the "well-prepared, enormously comforting" fare is "as authentic as you can get" and comes in "generous" portions at "reasonable" prices, and the service is "friendly and seriously efficient", so even if some think the "casual" space is "not much to look at", seriously, "who cares?"

California Pizza Kitchen *Pizza*

17 | 13 | 16 | $24

Farmington | Westfarms Mall | 3 Westfarms Mall (New Britain Ave.) | 860-561-1027
Ledyard | Foxwoods Resort Casino | 39 Norwich Westerly Rd. (bet. Grand Pequot Ave. & Watson Rd.) | 860-859-2912
Stamford | Stamford Town Ctr. | 230 Tresser Blvd. (bet. Atlantic St. & Greyrock Pl.) | 203-406-0530
www.cpk.com

"Clever", "unusual" pizzas (such as "BBQ chicken and Thai") and "creative" salads are the "stars" at this "gourmet" pie chain that's a haven for the stroller set; it's "inexpensive", "prompt" and "consistent", though some complain the "wannabe eclectic offerings" have grown "tired" and the "overlit" surroundings just "don't have any charm."

☑ Capital Grille *Steak*

25 | 24 | 25 | $63

Stamford | Stamford Town Ctr. | 230 Tresser Blvd. (bet. Atlantic St. & Greyrock Pl.) | 203-967-0000 | www.capitalgrille.com

"Superb" cuts of beef are "served with style" to "lots of suits" at this "top-notch" Stamford chain link that seems to be "hiding undercover as a locals' steakhouse and doing a good job of it"; boasting a "fantastic" wine list, "superior" service and a "manly club atmosphere", it's "wonderful" "for a date" or "impressing a client", so "if you're on an expense account, go for it."

	FOOD	DECOR	SERVICE	COST

Captain Daniel Packer Inne *Eclectic*

21 | 24 | 21 | $43

Mystic | 32 Water St. (Noank Rd.) | 860-536-3555 |
www.danielpacker.com

The "authentic English pub" at this "historic inn" housed in a
250-year-old Colonial on the banks of the Mystic River is the
"place to be on a cold winter night", with a "fireplace blazing", "excellent" pub grub and a "hopping bar scene" that includes "live,
loud music", while upstairs, the "more refined" dining room is the
showcase for "well-prepared", "reasonably priced" Eclectic dishes
in a "quaint", "old-fashioned" atmosphere; some critics find the
cooking "inconsistent" and the service "spotty", but others are
"never disappointed" here.

Carbone's Ristorante Ⓩ *Italian*

24 | 20 | 24 | $47

Hartford | 588 Franklin Ave. (bet. Goodrich & Hanmer Sts.) |
860-296-9646 | www.carboneshartford.com

"After three generations", this Northern Italian "institution" in
Hartford still "outperforms" many with "spot-on" service and
"dependable", "classic" cuisine, including "old-school" tableside
preparations that "make it dinner and a show", delivered in a "white-
tablecloth" setting; some critics contend it's "past its prime" and
"needs an update", but many others believe it delivers "everything
you expect in fine dining."

Carmen Anthony Fishhouse *Seafood*

22 | 20 | 22 | $48

Avon | The Shops at River Pk. | 51 E. Main St. (Mountain View Ave.) |
860-677-7788
Wethersfield | 1770 Berlin Tpke. (Pawtuckett Ave.) |
860-529-7557
Woodbury | 757 Main St. S. (Middle Quarter Rd.) |
203-266-0011
www.carmenanthony.com

At this family-friendly local chainlet, the "fresh seafood selection"
shows "some splashes of creativity", such as crab cakes "crusted in
thin potato slices", and comes in "ample" portions, while the cocktails are "large and powerful"; the setting is "comfortable, not
stuffy", but opinions are split on the service – it's either "first-class"
or in need of "more training" – and some critics find the fare
"overpriced" and "dated."

Carmen Anthony Steakhouse *Steak*

22 | 21 | 23 | $52

New Haven | 1 Audubon Bldg. | 660 State St. (Audubon St.) |
203-773-1444
Waterbury | 496 Chase Ave. (Nottingham Terrace) | 203-757-3040
www.carmenanthony.com

The "wonderful smell" of "perfectly cooked" steaks makes carnivores' "mouths water" at this pair of "traditional" steakhouses in
New Haven and Waterbury, where "knowledgeable servers" "full of
spunk and personality" work the "large", "classy" rooms, which can
get "loud", some report; critics find it "overpriced" and "inconsistent", and suggest that while it's "good for a business meeting", it's
"not for foodies."

	FOOD	DECOR	SERVICE	COST

⚡ Carole Peck's Good News Cafe *American*

| 26 | 21 | 23 | $49 |

Woodbury | Sherman Village Plaza | 694 Main St. S. (Rte. 64) | 203-266-4663 | www.good-news-cafe.com

A "locavore trailblazer" "before it was the 'big thing'", Carole Peck's "foodie delight" in Woodbury is "still fresh and inventive" with its "truly original" seasonal New American menu featuring "old favorites and intriguing specials", served by an "eager-to-please staff" in a "quirky" room graced with "rotating artwork" by area artists; a few critics think the interior "could use a face-lift" while others say it all works best when the "gracious" chef-owner is in the kitchen, but for most it's "always a pleasing dining experience."

Carrabba's Italian Grill *Italian*

| 18 | 16 | 19 | $32 |

Manchester | 31 Red Stone Rd. (Buckland St.) | 860-643-4100 | www.carrabbas.com

"Outback goes to Rome" at this "energetic" sister-chain that "satisfies a craving for Italian", providing "solid", "generous" dishes in a "busy", sometimes "raucous" setting (watch out for "long waits") tended by an "accommodating" staff; while detractors maintain it's "run-of-the-mill" and "hardly authentic", if you "keep your expectations reasonable", it's a "good-value" option.

Caseus ⧄ *Eclectic*

| 25 | 18 | 21 | $35 |

New Haven | 93 Whitney Ave. (entrance on Trumbull St.) | 203-624-3373 | www.caseusnewhaven.com

A "cheese-lover's haven" in New Haven, this bistro grew out of the attached gourmet fromagerie and offers "innovative", "spot-on" Gallic-accented Eclectic fare boasting "intense flavors with an earth-friendly flair" and "friendly service" in a "colorful basement-and-sidewalk" setting with a bar area that has "a lot of energy"; for those who squirm at the "cramped seating", there's always takeout; no dinner service Mondays or Tuesdays.

🆕 Cask Republic *American*

| - | - | - | M |

New Haven | 179 Crown St. (bet. Church & Temple Sts.) | North Haven | 475-238-8335 | www.thecaskrepublic.com

Hopsters are in heaven at this tavern in Downtown New Haven, which features more than 50 artisan beers on tap and bottles from around the world, plus a moderately priced menu of New American fare with global influences; the dimly lit, clubby space boasts a long mahogany bar, plush sofas and a glassed-in cooler that holds beer aging in casks; a private room is also available.

Cava Wine Bar & Restaurant *Italian*

| 22 | 21 | 21 | $46 |

New Canaan | 2 Forest St. (East Ave.) | 203-966-6946 | www.cavawinebar.com

A "mainstay" on New Canaan's Restaurant Row, this Northern Italian draws "couples, small groups and ladies'-night-out gatherings" with "a wonderful wine selection" and a "good mix of casual and more formal fare", served by an "amiable staff" in a "cozy, cavernous setting" that gets "loud" (though some "like the acoustic privacy the high noise level provides"); a few critics decry it as "inconsistent" and "overpriced", but others regard it as a "real gem", and the summer sidewalk seating "makes it that much better."

Cavey's Restaurants 🗷Ⓜ *French/Italian*   26 | 23 | 25 | $60

Manchester | 45 E. Center St. (Main St.) | 860-643-2751 |
www.caveysrestaurant.com

What some say is Manchester's "most elegant venue" is "still great after all these years", offering "consistently excellent" French cuisine in a formal, "old-world" setting downstairs and "wonderful", less-expensive Italian in a Med-inspired room upstairs, plus a "superb" wine list full of "old, rare vintages", all served by an "extremely knowledgeable" staff; though a few feel the "prices are too high" and liken the atmosphere to a "funeral parlor", for most, this "old faithful" is "still the place east of the river to impress" or "celebrate something special."

Cedars *Steak*   ▽ 28 | 23 | 24 | $53

Ledyard | Foxwoods Resort Casino | 39 Norwich Westerly Rd.
(bet. Grand Pequot Ave. & Watson Rd.) | 860-312-4252 |
www.foxwoods.com

Aces advise "treat yourself with your slot winnings" to some "first-rate steak and seafood" at this Ledyard meatery in the "heart of fun central" (aka Foxwoods casino) where the "classic" setting features cherry wood and leather booths; while some find the "resortlike" prices a bit dicey, the attached lounge offers a less expensive bar menu and often "less of a wait" than the dining room.

Central Steakhouse 🗷Ⓜ *Steak*   24 | 22 | 22 | $51

New Haven | 99 Orange St. (bet. Center & Chapel Sts.) | 203-787-7885 |
www.centralsteakhouse.com

"Fantastic" dry-aged steaks and a "wonderful wine selection" give Bentara's steakhouse sibling in Downtown New Haven a "big-time feel" (and, some say, so do the "high prices"), and the staff is "pleasant" and "helpful"; critics are cool to the modern decor, saying it "lacks warmth", but many recommend the "romantic wine cellar" as a "perfect date-night spot."

Centro Ristorante &   20 | 18 | 19 | $37
Bar *Italian/Mediterranean*

Fairfield | 1435 Post Rd. (bet. Sanford St. & Unquowa Rd.) |
203-255-1210

Greenwich | The Mill | 328 Pemberwick Rd. (Glenville Rd.) | 203-531-5514
www.centroristorante.com

This "modern" Med–Northern Italian duo "pleases everybody" with "basic", "reliable" fare at "reasonable prices", "accommodating" service and a "colorful, lively" setting, with crayons and paper tablecloths that are "as much fun for adults as for kids" and "alfresco" dining in the warmer months – "overlooking the mill stream" in Greenwich and near the town gazebo in Fairfield; though some "can't figure out why" it's so "popular", most consider it a "real find for informal dining."

	FOOD	DECOR	SERVICE	COST

Chaiwalla ⓂⒶ *Tearoom*   ▽ 25 | 23 | 24 | $25

Salisbury | 1 Main St. (Under Mountain Rd.) | 860-435-9758

Aficionados advise "don't miss" this "small, sweet" cozy teahouse in Salisbury offering "original, simple" lunch and brunch fare ("tomato pie to die for"), "made with love (and butter)" "on the premises" and served in the "owner's actual kitchen"; just "leave room for the exquisite desserts" and one of the "excellent" teas; open weekends only in the winter.

Char Koon *Pacific Rim*   ▽ 23 | 15 | 20 | $27

South Glastonbury | Nayaug Shopping Ctr. | 882 Main St. (Water St.) | 860-657-3656 | www.charkoon.com

The "authentic, high-quality" Pacific Rim cuisine is "always served fresh" at this shopping-mall eatery in South Glastonbury, including the aptly named volcano flank steak that's a "dish full of fire"; though some grouse about "waiters who hover" over tables and feel "cramped" in the "small" space, others insist the setting "oozes charm in its own way" – and, by the way, "takeout is great."

Chat 19 *American*   18 | 19 | 18 | $38

Larchmont | 19 Chatsworth Ave. (Boston Post Rd.), NY | 914-833-8871 | www.chat19.net

A pub "with flair" describes this clubby Larchmont standby offering a "broad", "something-for-everyone" American menu from burgers to "inventive" entrees, all "reasonably priced" and backed by "fun" drinks; it's "handy for parents" and their brood, but later on is "packed to the brim with nipped-and-tucked" "singles", when the "buzz" can be "deafening."

Chatterley's *American*   ▽ 21 | 21 | 22 | $29

New Hartford | 2 Bridge St. (Main St.) | 860-379-2428 | www.chatterleysct.com

A "pleasant place for lunch" and a "favorite" venue for business gatherings, this New Hartford New American delivers "solid pub food" in a "charming" Victorian-style space (think padded chairs, flowers and wall sconces) housed in a circa-1773 brick building, which also boasts a sidewalk patio; karaoke on Thursdays and live music Fridays are added pluses.

Cheesecake Factory *American*   17 | 17 | 17 | $30

Hartford | 71 Isham Rd. (Raymond Rd.) | 860-233-5588
White Plains | The Source | 1 Maple Ave. (Bloomingdale Rd.), NY | 914-683-5253
www.thecheesecakefactory.com

"Humongous portions and humongous lines" characterize these American chain links where the "textbook"-size menu offers "lots of choices" and a "broad price spectrum" to keep families "stuffed and happy"; the "herd 'em in, herd 'em out" feel isn't for everyone and critics knock "mass-produced" fare and "overdone" decor, but overall it's a "crowd-pleaser", especially when it comes to the "amazing" namesake dessert, even if you need to "take it home for much later."

	FOOD	DECOR	SERVICE	COST

Chef Antonio *Italian* — 20 | 14 | 22 | $34

Mamaroneck | 551 Halstead Ave. (Beach Ave.), NY | 914-698-8610

"Still solid" is the word on this 50-year-old Mamaroneck "workhorse" known for its "traditional" Southern Italian cooking in "generous" helpings and coddling staff that "treats everyone like a regular"; "reasonable prices" are a plus, but many find the "dated" decor (and "some of the clientele") "in desperate need of a face-lift."

Chef Luis 🅂 *American* — 25 | 18 | 23 | $46

New Canaan | 129 Elm St. (bet. Main & Park Sts.) | 203-972-5847 | www.chefluis.net

Fans swear "you never want to leave" "charming" chef-owner Luis Lopez's New American on New Canaan's main drag showcasing his "eclectic", "flavorful" Latin- and Med-inflected fare, which is served by a "friendly, efficient" staff in "tight quarters" where the tables are "close enough to hear your neighbors' conversation"; a few find his habit of naming dishes after regulars "silly" and "insular", but all "love the BYO"; P.S. a liquor license and an expansion into the next-door space are pending.

Chengdu *Chinese* — ▽ 20 | 13 | 17 | $25

West Hartford | 179 Park Rd. (Oakwood Ave.) | 860-232-6455

Sinophiles say West Hartford is "lucky" to have this "reliable" "staple" that turns out "consistently good" Chinese fare at "reasonable prices"; the service is "prompt and efficient" and "you can almost always find a seat" in the "no-frills family" setting, and it "does a brisk takeout as well."

Chestnut Grille at the Bee & Thistle Inn 🅂Ⓜ *American* — ▽ 26 | 26 | 23 | $57

Old Lyme | Bee & Thistle Inn | 100 Lyme St. (I-95, exit 70) | 860-434-1667 | www.beeandthistleinn.com

The "divine" setting at Old Lyme's "historic" Bee and Thistle Inn is matched by "creative" New American cuisine that's "well prepared and presented beautifully", and served by a "professional" staff in a "romantic, warm" atmosphere, and the "extensive" wine list offers "perfect pairings"; whether you "share it with your loved one or take your parents", cognoscenti tout it as a "do-not-miss" experience that's "worth every penny"; open Tuesdays–Saturdays, dinner only.

Chez Jean-Pierre *French* — 24 | 21 | 23 | $51

Stamford | 188 Bedford St. (Broad St.) | 203-357-9526 | www.chezjeanpierre.com

Aficionados advise "go for the classics" at this "charming" French bistro in Downtown Stamford, aka "Paris without the Seine" to fans who laud the "savory" cuisine, "charming" owner and "courteous, professional" servers, who are "helpful" in selecting from the "reasonable" wine list; a few feel the "smallish" room "could use an update", while others caution "bring a full wallet", though "awesome" half-price wines on Sundays and prix fixe lunches and dinners help lower the tab.

	FOOD	DECOR	SERVICE	COST

China Pavilion Chinese   23 | 17 | 20 | $24

Orange | 185 Boston Post Rd. (Lindy St.) | 203-795-3555 |
www.chinapavilion.net

In business "for ages", with a parking lot that's "always full", this
"steady" Orange Chinese is "doing something right" say Sinophiles
who cite "fresh", "better-than-average" Cantonese and Sichuan fare
served in a "pleasant" atmosphere; fans insist "you can't go wrong"
with the "consistent" cuisine that holds its own against "anything in
Manhattan" – and "for half the price."

Ching's Table Asian   24 | 17 | 19 | $37

New Canaan | 64 Main St. (Locust Ave.) | 203-972-8550

Wild Ginger Dumpling House Asian

Darien | 971 Post Rd. (Center St.) | 203-656-2225

"Classic items are given twists and added depth" at this Pan-Asian pair
that's "always jammed on weekends" thanks to "fresh", "inventive"
dishes at "reasonable prices" served in a "friendly environment", and
though the decor may be "nothing to write home about", at least it's
"not embarrassing"; the presence of "lots of families with kids", however, results in noise levels some liken "to the Apollo moon launch",
which is why "takeout, takeout, takeout" is the mantra of many.

Chocopologie Cafe Dessert   22 | 18 | 17 | $28

South Norwalk | 12 S. Main St. (Washington St.) | 203-854-4754 |
www.chocopologie.com

A "treat for kids and adults", it's "like going to Willie Wonka's real
factory" (albeit with "cocktails" and "wine dinners") at this Euro-
style cafe–cum–"chocolate nirvana" in SoNo where you can watch
"unique" truffles being made; while the "decadent" desserts are "to
die for", the "savory meal items" (crêpes, sandwiches) are "fantastic as well", which helps many overlook what critics describe as
"lackluster" service and "cramped" seating.

Christopher Martins ◗ Continental   20 | 15 | 19 | $36

New Haven | 860 State St. (bet. Clark & Humphrey Sts.) | 203-776-8835 |
www.christophermartins.com

"No fussy preparations", just "reliable", "fresh" Continental fare made
with "locally sourced" ingredients makes this New Haven eatery a
"good value"; a "friendly" staff helps foster a "welcoming atmosphere"
in the "pleasant" dining room, which is graced by the works of "local
artists", although a few gripe about "having to run the gamut of the
noisy, crowded bar" to enter, while others suggest the restrooms "need
to be updated" – still, most regard it as a "solid choice."

Chuck's Steak House Steak   18 | 14 | 18 | $36

Branford | 377 E. Main St. (I-95) | 203-483-7557 |
www.chucksbranford.com
Danbury | 20 Segar St. (bet. Lake & Park Aves.) | 203-792-5555 |
www.chucksssteakhouse.com
Darien | 1340 Boston Post Rd. (I-95) | 203-655-2254 |
www.chucksssteakhouse.com

(continued)

(continued)

Chuck's Steak House

Rocky Hill | 2199 Silas Deane Hwy. (I-91, exit 24) | 860-529-0222 |
www.chuckssteakhouse.com
Storrs | 1498 Stafford Rd./Rte. 32 (Rte. 44) | 860-429-1900 |
www.chuckssteakhouse.com
West Haven | 1003 Boston Post Rd. (Tuthill St.) | 203-934-5300 |
www.chuckssteakhouse.com Ⓜ

Loyalists of this "tried-and-true" steakhouse chain tout it as a
"much less expensive alternative to the overpriced" competition, offering "tender" beef "nicely cooked" and a "wonderful salad bar" in
a "casual", "family-type" setting; foes find the fare "forgettable",
describe the digs as a "dark and dreary" "flashback to the early
'70s", and warn that servers appear "overwhelmed" when "the place
gets full – which it usually is."

Churrascaria Braza Ⓜ *Brazilian*   16 | 15 | 18 | $38

Hartford | 488 Farmington Ave. (Sisson Ave.) | 860-882-1839 |
www.brazarestaurant.com

"Vegetarians beware", this Brazilian steakhouse in Hartford is a
"place for carnivores" where "friendly" "wandering waiters" deliver
an "endless parade of grilled meat and seafood served from swords"
and there's also a "well-stocked buffet of sides"; skeptics, though,
skewer it as a "shadow of its former self", describing the food and
service as "erratic."

🆕 Cienega Latin Cuisine *Nuevo Latino*   - | - | - | E

New Rochelle | 179 Main St. (Lispenard Ave.), NY | 914-632-4000 |
www.cienegarestaurant.com

Architects and Brooklyn restaurateurs Vivian Torres and Pedro Muñoz
(Luz in Ft. Greene) have transformed an awkward triangular-shaped
space in New Rochelle into this sleek Nuevo Latino eatery painted in
modern, muted browns with votives illuminating the bar; expect
dishes like Peruvian corn chowder and rum-and-sugar-cane-glazed
lamb chops matched with an ambitious cocktail list.

Cinzano's *Italian*   18 | 16 | 17 | $35

Fairfield | 1920 Black Rock Tpke. (Stillson Rd.) | 203-367-1199 |
www.cinzanosrestaurant.com

Sure, it's "not the fanciest around", but this strip-mall Italian in
Fairfield is a "staple" for many, dishing out "large portions" of
"hearty", "solid" dishes in a "white-tablecloth" setting, with a staff
that "excels" at handling "big crowds"; critics pan it as "pedestrian",
but the "reasonable prices" make it a popular haunt for "families"
who want to spend a "comfortable night out with grandma."

City Limits Diner *Diner*   19 | 15 | 18 | $27

Stamford | 135 Harvard Ave. (I-95, exit 6) | 203-348-7000
White Plains | 200 Central Ave. (bet. Harding Ave. & Tarrytown Rd.),
NY | 914-686-9000
www.citylimitsdiner.com

"You're sure to run into someone you know" at these "ever-popular"
"diners on steroids" in Stamford and White Plains dispensing "so-

phisticated takes" on "wholesome" "comfort-fare" classics like "breakfast 'round the clock" and "tempting", "made-from-scratch desserts"; if prices are relatively "high", so is the "quality", and a "cheerful" chrome-bedecked setting and "kid-friendly" service keep them "tried-and-true."

City Steam Brewery Café *American*

15 | 17 | 17 | $25

Hartford | 942 Main St. (Temple St.) | 860-525-1600 | www.citysteambrewerycafe.com

The "fantastic" handcrafted beers are what "set this place apart" boast boosters of this Hartford brewpub, and while its "fish 'n' chips should not be missed", the "regular" American pub grub leads some to sniff it's "not a foodie place"; the "casual" setting, which features cast-iron railings from the original circa-1877 building (the former Brown, Thomson department store), is a "good place to meet people", though it can get "noisy", and comedians perform at the adjacent club, Brew HA HA, on Fridays and Saturdays.

Claire's Corner Copia *Vegetarian*

21 | 12 | 15 | $17

New Haven | 1000 Chapel St. (College St.) | 203-562-3888 | www.clairescornercopia.com

Even the "carnivorously inclined" find the "diverse, tasty" fare "amazing" (the Lithuanian coffee cake alone is "worth stopping by for") at this kosher vegetarian "institution" located across the street from the Yale campus in New Haven; you serve yourself and bus your table in the "cozy", "cafeteria-style" setting, where "abstruse academic discussions fill the air", and while some foes decry the "surly counter help" and find the prices "higher than appropriate", it remains a "huge favorite" in town.

Clamp's Hamburger Stand *Burgers*

- | - | - | I

New Milford | Rte. 202 (Sawyer Hill Rd.)

There's no phone, signage or even an address at this iconic, circa-1939 New Milford stand, whose "roadside ambiance seals the deal" for some, though most are hooked by the burgers with a "nice char on them", which are "not fancy" and "probably not healthy", just "really good", especially when topped with "excellent sautéed onions"; be sure to "get there in the summer", for it's closed from September to April.

Cobble Stone ● *American*

15 | 13 | 16 | $26

Purchase | 620 Anderson Hill Rd. (bet. Lincoln Ave. & Purchase St.), NY | 914-253-9678 | www.cobblestone-thecreek.com

"Convenient to SUNY Purchase" and the PepsiCo Sculpture Gardens, this "old-fashioned" tavern attracts students and theatergoers for a "nothing-fancy" American lineup of "good burgers", "cold beer" and the like; judging from the scores, the "food needs work", but tabs are "low" and service "quick", so it's "fine for what it is."

Colony Grill ● *Pizza*

24 | 7 | 13 | $18

NEW **Fairfield** | 1520 Post Rd. (Miller St.) | 203-259-1989

(continued)

(continued)

Colony Grill

Stamford | 172 Myrtle Ave. (bet. Elm & Frederick Sts.) | 203-359-2184 ♉
www.colonygrill.com

People "drive for hours" and endure "long waits and crowds" and "surly service" at this "hole-in-the-wall" in an "industrial" area of Stamford for its "amazing", "addictive" thin-crust pizzas, which have earned it a "cult following", even if a few skeptics pan the pies as "overrated"; some say the "bar" setting is "not a great place to take the kids", but cognoscenti report the new Fairfield location has "much better atmosphere."

Columbus Park Trattoria ⑤ *Italian* | 25 | 20 | 23 | $47 |

Stamford | 205 Main St. (Washington Blvd.) | 203-967-9191 |
www.columbusparktrattoria.com

At this "always friendly Downtown Stamford gem", "authentic dishes not usually found outside Italy" and "divine homemade pastas" have been "consistently palate-pleasing for decades", and the "all-in-the-family operation" "bends over backwards trying to please its guests"; some complain of "New York" prices and "cramped" quarters that get "noisy" when "crowded", but most insist its "tasty perfection" is "not to be missed."

Community Table *American* | ▽ 27 | 20 | 21 | $51 |

Washington | 223 Litchfield Tpke. (Wilbur Rd.) | 860-868-9354 |
www.communitytablect.com

At this Washington New American, "inventive" chef Joel Viehland's "ever-changing menus" of "uniformly excellent" dishes emphasizing "fresh food from local farms" are "meant to entice knowing locavores"; opinions are split on the spare room made with green building materials ("original and attractive" vs. "charmless" and "noisy"), and many deplore the "Soviet system of queuing" (i.e. no reservations) as "misguided", but for most it's nonetheless a "splendid addition to the Litchfield County dining scene"; P.S. closed on Tuesdays and Wednesdays.

Confetti Ⓜ *Italian/Seafood* | 22 | 17 | 19 | $35 |

Plainville | 393 Farmington Ave. (Ashford Rd.) | 860-793-8809 |
www.idineconfetti.com

The fish is "always fresh" and the "portions are huge" at this Plainville Italian seafooder boasting a "large menu that covers all the bases" and offers "good value"; the "personable" owners always "welcome you" and the service is "professional", though a few feel the staff's on "autopilot", and while critics say the place "looks like an afterthought", many others appreciate the "comfortable, homey" ambiance and consider it their local "go-to" spot.

Consiglio's *Italian* | 23 | 17 | 24 | $45 |

New Haven | 165 Wooster St. (bet. Brown St. & Depalma Ct.) |
203-865-4489 | www.consiglios.com

Don't be surprised if the "funny", "friendly" servers "join in the conversation" at your table at this "well-established" "icon" in New

Haven's Little Italy, where *amici* insist "you can't go wrong" with the "well-done", "traditional" Italian cuisine; though a few sniff the "place needs a spruce up", and others find it a bit "pricey", most agree the "dependable" eats and "old-world family charm" make it a "consistent Wooster Street winner."

Cookhouse, The *BBQ*

22 | 16 | 19 | $31

New Milford | 31 Danbury Rd. (Sunny Valley Rd.) | 860-355-4111 | www.thecookhouse.com

"Mouthwatering pulled pork, brisket and ribs" draw 'cuennoisseurs to the "upbeat" "country" setting of this renovated barn in New Milford, where the "stick-to-your ribs" BBQ is "worth the hassles" of "noisy" crowds and "agonizingly slow" service when it's busy ("you could have smoked it quicker at home"); a few doubters say this old-timer "used to be a lot better", but few find fault with the "reasonable" prices for "large portions."

Copacabana ◩ *Brazilian*

21 | 17 | 22 | $43

Port Chester | 29 N. Main St. (Westchester Ave.), NY | 914-939-6894 | www.copacabanaportchester.com

"If quantity is your thing", you can't go wrong with this all-you-can-eat Brazilian in Port Chester offering an "excellent variety" of skewered meats and a "top-notch" salad bar; "reasonable" prices, a "friendly" staff and a wood-trimmed space good for groups are added perks, though some say it falls short on "quality."

Corner Bakery *Bakery*

▽ 23 | 17 | 21 | $24

Pawling | 10 Charles Colman Blvd. (Main St.), NY | 845-855-3707 | www.mckinneyanddoyle.com

A "wonderful bakery" attached to its parent eatery, McKinney & Doyle, this "quaint, crowded" Pawling cafe offers "great cakes and pastries" along with soups, salads and sandwiches in "hearty portions" at breakfast and brunch; in short: "there's not a bad item", which makes it easy to "splurge" if you fancy an "expensive dessert."

◪ Coromandel *Indian*

25 | 18 | 22 | $34

Darien | Goodwives Shopping Ctr. | 25 Old Kings Hwy. N. (Sedgewick Ave.) | 203-662-1213
Orange | 185 Boston Post Rd. (Diana St.) | 203-795-9055
South Norwalk | 86 Washington St. (bet. Main & Water Sts.) | 203-852-1213
NEW Southport | 17 Pease Ave. (Woodrow Ave.) | 203-259-1213
Stamford | 68 Broad St. (Summer St.) | 203-964-1010
New Rochelle | 30 Division St. (bet. Huguenot & Main Sts.), NY | 914-235-8390
www.coromandelcuisine.com

Fans of this "distinctive" Indian chain sing "Jai Ho!" over its "amazing", "aromatic" cuisine, including a "sensational lunch buffet" that's a "steal", as well as "courteous", "helpful" servers who are "always willing to educate" diners about the "authentic" menu that "traverses all of India's regions"; while a few feel the decorator needs to "tone it down" a bit, others find the interiors "charming."

	FOOD	DECOR	SERVICE	COST

Così *Sandwiches* — 16 | 12 | 12 | $15

Avon | 385 W. Main St. (bet. Bushy Hill & Dale Rds.) | 860-678-8989
Greenwich | 129 W. Putnam Ave. (Dayton Ave.) | 203-861-2373
West Hartford | 970 Farmington Ave. (bet. Lasalle Rd. & Main St.) |
860-521-8495
Larchmont | Ferndale Shopping Ctr. | 1298 Boston Post Rd. (Weaver St.),
NY | 914-834-9797
New Rochelle | North Ridge Shopping Ctr. | 77 Quaker Ridge Rd.
(North Ave.), NY | 914-637-8300
Rye | 50 Purchase St. (Elm Pl.), NY | 914-921-3322
www.getcosi.com

"Gotta love that bread" "just out of the stone oven" rave regulars of
this "reasonably priced" cafe chain turning out "creative", "up-to-
date" sandwiches and "flavorful" salads; despite some complaints
of "uneven" service and quality, it's a lunch "staple" for many, plus
the make-your-own s'mores are a "gooey treat."

Costa del Sol Ⓜ *Spanish* — 25 | 21 | 23 | $39

Hartford | Costa del Sol Plaza | 901 Wethersfield Ave. (Eaton St.) |
860-296-1714 | www.costadelsolhartford.com

The "paella rocks" and the seafood and meats are "beautifully prepared" at this family-run Spanish in an "out-of-the-way location" in
Hartford, which also offers a "wide-ranging" wine list and "respect-
able sangria"; the "wonderful staff provides "friendly, genuine service" in a setting that's "homey and elegant at the same time",
another reason many regard it as the "best value" in town.

Country Bistro *American/French* — - | - | - | I

Salisbury | 10 Academy St. (Rte. 41) | 860-435-9420 |
www.thecountrybistro.com

Run by an "adorable mom and daughter", this "wonderful bistro" in
Salisbury is "like a home away from home" for fans, serving "fresh",
"healthy" French–New American "comfort food" and "positively sinful" desserts for breakfast, lunch and Sunday brunch, as well as
weekend suppers on the terrace in the warmer months; the mood is
"casual", but the "cozy" space is often crowded, so large groups
should call ahead.

Coyote Blue
Tex Mex Cafe Ⓜ *Southwestern* — 20 | 19 | 21 | $29

Middletown | 1960 Saybrook Rd. (Aircraft Rd.) | 860-345-2403 |
www.coyoteblue.com

"Fun, loud and best geared to a college crowd", this "out-of-the-
way" Southwestern "roadhouse" in Middletown pours margaritas
that "pack a punch" ("max two per person" is recommended) and
the moderately priced menu has a "wide variety of choices for even
the pickiest eaters", though some cynics find "nothing special"
about the fare; the service is "friendly", but cognoscenti caution you
can "expect a wait" on weekends.

Coyote Flaco *Mexican* — 23 | 18 | 22 | $34

Bridgeport | 694 Brooklawn Ave. (Capitol Ave.) | 203-338-0808 Ⓜ

(continued)

Coyote Flaco

Hartford | 635 New Britain Ave. (Mountain St.) |
860-953-1299 Ⓜ
Mansfield Center | 50 Higgins Hwy. (Stafford Rd.) | 860-423-4414
New Rochelle | 273 North Ave. (Huguenot St.), NY | 914-636-7222 Ⓜ
Port Chester | 115 Midland Ave. (bet. Eldridge & Leonard Sts.), NY |
914-937-6969
www.mycoyoteflaco.com
See review in The Berkshires Directory.

Craftsteak *Steak*

24 | 25 | 24 | $76

Ledyard | MGM Grand at Foxwoods | 240 MGM Grand Dr.
(Norwich Westerly Rd.) | 860-312-7272 |
www.mgmatfoxwoods.com

"If you hit big" at the tables or slots, head to Tom Colicchio's steakhouse in the Foxwoods Resort Casino for "superb" steaks "like butta'", served in a "stunning" contemporary space with a "high-roller atmosphere" that's an "oasis of quiet" amid the "tourists and gamblers"; the "professional" service is "what you'd expect" for such "over-the-top prices", and while a few sneer "save your money for the craps tables", many agree that it'd be "hard to find a better all-around package" than this.

Croton Creek
Steakhouse & Wine Bar *Steak*

20 | 20 | 19 | $62

Croton Falls | 4 W. Cross St. (Rte. 22), NY | 914-276-0437 |
www.crotoncreek.com

"Very cozy, especially in winter", this "popular" Croton Falls steakhouse offers prime beef and Kobe burgers with "delicious" sides and "original" desserts in rustic-chic quarters; though critics claim it's "unremarkable" and "expensive", "friendly" service and the "loungey atmosphere" of the wine bar make it "a happy find" for those pining for a local place that's "open late."

Cuckoo's Nest *Cajun/Mexican*

17 | 18 | 17 | $25

Old Saybrook | 1712 Boston Post Rd. (Rte. 166) | 860-399-9060 |
www.cuckoosnest.biz

For more than 30 years, this Cajun-Mexican in Old Saybrook has been a "fun place to visit", where there's "always something to look at" in the "bright", antiques-filled space and the "bar is hopping with local singles"; fans laud the "delicious" margaritas and "consistently good" *comida,* but skeptics say it's "overpriced" and "nothing spectacular", and the service is "inconsistent at best."

Cuvee ●Ⓜ *American*

▽ 16 | 22 | 20 | $36

West Hartford | 37 Raymond Pl. (Isham Rd.) | 860-756-5590 |
www.cuveewesthartford.com

Cognoscenti recommend this "chill" West Hartford New American for "dates or a "girls' night out", where you can "cozy up" "with your sweetie" on plush couches in the lounge or "meet friends" and "share" "tasty" small plates in the "cool" wine bar; some critics say the food and service can vary from "excellent" to "below average", while others could do without the "marauding groups of singles"; there's live jazz on Wednesdays.

DaCapo's Italiano Ristorante *Italian* ▽ 19 | 17 | 17 | $29

Avon | 5 E. Main St. (bet. Old Farms Rd. & Rte. 44) | 860-677-5599 | www.dacaporestaurant.com

"You won't go away hungry" from this "yummy" Avon "pizza and pasta palace" where both the individual and family-sized portions are "huge"; "earnest" staffers patrol the "bright", brick-lined environment, and while it's often "crowded and noisy", most patrons don't mind because the price is right; P.S. deck dining in summer.

Da Giorgio Ⓜ *Italian* ▽ 25 | 18 | 21 | $42

New Rochelle | Quaker Ridge | 77 Quaker Ridge Rd. (North Ave.), NY | 914-235-2727 | www.dagiorgiorestaurant.com

"Tucked away in a nondescript shopping strip" is this "homey", "chef-owned" New Rochelle Italian where Giorgio himself whips up "delicious" fare with loads of daily specials; factor in moderate tabs and a "cheery" staff, and it's certainly "better than one would expect" considering the locale.

Dakota Steakhouse *Steak* 17 | 17 | 18 | $36

Avon | 225 W. Main St. (Lawrence Ave.) | 860-677-4311 | www.steakseafood.com

Rocky Hill | 1489 Silas Deane Hwy. (I-91) | 860-257-7752 | www.dakotarockyhill.com

See review in The Berkshires Directory.

DaPietro's Ⓩ *French/Italian* 27 | 20 | 25 | $64

Westport | 36 Riverside Ave. (Post Rd.) | 203-454-1213 | www.dapietros.com

Chef "Pietro Scotti knocks 'em dead with his brilliant cuisine" at this French–Northern Italian "favorite for milestone celebrations" in Downtown Westport, whose large wine list, "impeccable" service and "high" tabs abet its reputation as a merchant of "everlasting memories"; just try to "make reservations far in advance", because the "jewellike" setting is "Lilliputian"; P.S. "don't miss" the "reasonably priced" lunch prix fixe.

David Burke Prime *Steak* 26 | 24 | 25 | $70

Ledyard | Foxwoods Resort Casino | 39 Norwich Westerly Rd. (bet. Grand Pequot Ave. & Watson Rd.) | 860-312-8753 | www.davidburkeprime.com

Fans feel like they've "hit the jackpot" at this "nice-looking" ("if you like black-and-white cowhide") Foxwoods steakhouse where "terrific" dry-aged prime cuts come via "attentive" servers; of course, you might need a "platinum card" to pay for it, but go ahead, "treat yourself."

David Chen *Chinese* 18 | 15 | 19 | $27

Armonk | 85 Old Mt. Kisco Rd. (Rte. 128), NY | 914-273-6767 | www.davidchens.com

With its "fancy fish tanks" and "old pagoda" entrance, "kids love" this Armonk "standby" known for its "dependable", "if not stellar", "traditional" Chinese cuisine with "helpful" waiters to aid you in ordering; "affordable" prices and "generous portions" keep it crowded, and there's delivery too.

Denmo's *Hot Dogs*

⎸ - ⎸ - ⎸ - ⎸ I ⎸

Southbury | 346 S. Main St. (Old Field Rd.) | 203-264-4626
"There's almost always a line" at this "quintessential" roadside snack stop in Southbury, known for its "great" hot dogs as well as "fantastic onion rings, monstrous burgers", clams, shrimp and lobster rolls; milkshakes and other frozen treats satisfy sweet tooths, and everything's appropriately priced; P.S. in January and February, it's only open from 10 AM–4 PM.

DiNardo's Ⓜ *Italian*

⎸ 19 ⎸ 16 ⎸ 18 ⎸ $41 ⎸

Pound Ridge | 76 Westchester Ave. (Trinity Pass Rd.), NY | 914-764-4024 | www.dinardos.net
The "pizza is tops" at this "old-fashioned" "small-town" Italian in Pound Ridge where there's "family dining" in the front room and a "great patio in summer"; some surveyors grouse about "average" eats at "above-average prices" but concede "it's the only game in town."

Diorio Ⓩ *American/Italian*

⎸ 25 ⎸ 23 ⎸ 23 ⎸ $47 ⎸

Waterbury | 231 Bank St. (Grand St.) | 203-754-5111 | www.diorios.com
"A Waterbury classic", this New American–Northern Italian pairs "outstanding" fare with "superb service" in a "charming" setting bedecked with "vintage fixtures, tin ceilings", "black-and-white tiles" and acid-burnt mirrors behind the "great bar"; its standing as a "good ol' boys" club for "business lunches and dinners" is supported by tabs that are "a little pricey."

Dish Bar & Grill *American*

⎸ 20 ⎸ 21 ⎸ 19 ⎸ $42 ⎸

Hartford | 900 Main St. (Pratt St.) | 860-249-3474 | www.dishbarandgrill.com
"Unique twists" abound at this "not-typical"-for-Hartford New American with "hip", "contemporary decor", a bar scene and regularly scheduled live music; unfortunately, a few "odd combinations" and "deconstructed dishes" "freak some people out", which leads them to peg it as "overpriced for what you get", the "great 'complete dish' special" at lunchtime notwithstanding.

Dock & Dine *Seafood*

⎸ 14 ⎸ 17 ⎸ 16 ⎸ $34 ⎸

Old Saybrook | 145 College St. (Saybrook Pt.) | 860-388-4665 | www.dockdinect.com
"Fabulous views of the Connecticut River" "flowing into the sound" trump seafood that's "a little too expensive" for being "lackluster" at this "barn" in Old Saybrook; indeed, the vistas are what make it a "tradition" for many families, who recommend you "definitely sit outside" in summer, because the interior "looks a bit shopworn."

Doc's Trattoria Ⓜ *Italian*

⎸ 19 ⎸ 19 ⎸ 19 ⎸ $42 ⎸

Kent | 9 Maple St. (Main St.) | 860-927-3810 | www.docstrattoria.com
Though some stalwarts still lament this Italian's move from its former "tiny Lake Waramaug" location to its present Kent address,

it's still popular with many "locals and NYC-based second-homers" for its "consistently good" pastas and brick-oven pizzas, served by an "affable" staff in a "comfortable, contemporary setting" (the liquor license is also welcome); critics who find it merely "adequate" say they "could do without this checkup."

Dolly Madison Inn *American*   ▽ 13 | 13 | 16 | $29

Madison | 73 W. Wharf Rd. (Surf Club Rd.) | 203-245-7377 | www.thedollymadison.com

"A prime location squandered on subprime cuisine" and "tired" decor is the consensus about this Traditional American in an inn that's been around "forever" (well, since 1931); however, it remains a "local hangout" thanks to "reasonable" prices and proximity to the Madison Country Club – the "fun bar" is its "19th hole."

Dolphins Cove Marina *Seafood*   - | - | - | M

Bridgeport | Dolphins Cove Marina | 421 Seaview Ave. (bet. Dekalb & Newfield Aves.) | 203-335-3301 | www.dolphinscovect.com

"After a day on the boat", folks in "flip-flops" "relax" at this "not-fancy" harborside "old-time lobster shack" in Bridgeport by grabbing "a picnic table on the patio" and digging into "great" crustacean preparations; a few find it all a bit "dreary", but the prices make it "too good to pass up."

Don Coqui ● *Puerto Rican*   23 | 22 | 19 | $43

New Rochelle | 115 Cedar St. (Garden St.), NY | 914-637-3737 | www.doncoqui.com

There's a "fiesta" feel and "fabulous people-watching" at this "chic" New Rochelle canteen from Jimmy Rodriguez (Manhattan's Sofrito) specializing in "zesty" Puerto Rican cuisine "more elegant than mamma makes" and "amazing" cocktails; factor in "loungey" looks with "DJs and dancing", and it "fills a void", so "slow" service and parking woes hardly put a damper on the "party."

Donovan's *American*   ▽ 18 | 14 | 20 | $24
(fka Donovan's & Mackenzie)

South Norwalk | 138 Washington St. (bet. Main & Water Sts.) | 203-354-9451 | www.donovanssono.com

After an interlude under a different name and ownership, this "cozy" 1889 South Norwalk pub with a "friendly staff" is back slinging "good burgers" and other "no-nonsense" American vittles amid vintage photos and Victorian furnishings; a bunch of TVs around the bar means you should be prepared for a "noisy" time when there's a "major sporting event on."

Dottie's Diner *Diner*   ▽ 18 | 9 | 17 | $19

Woodbury | 740 Main St. S. (bet. Middle Quarter & Sherman Hill Rds.) | 203-263-2516

Many just "go for the doughnuts" at this "real old-fashioned diner" in Woodbury, but others are drawn by its "famous chicken pot pie" and "huge portions" of "breakfast classics"; if you're from around these parts "you're sure to see someone you know" in the "cheerful"

FOOD | DECOR | SERVICE | COST

"'50s" setting, and while some cynics shrug "ho-hum", others consider it a "good value for the price"; P.S. the kitchen closes at 4 PM Saturdays and Sundays.

Douro *Portuguese*   — | — | — | E

Greenwich | 28 W. Putnam Ave. (bet. Benedict Pl. & Greenwich Ave.) | 203-869-7622 | www.dourorestaurantbar.com

At this upscale spot in Downtown Greenwich, chef Rui Correia gives traditional Portuguese fare a modern Mediterranean flair with a menu of small plates, entrees and his signature paella (*paelha*), which comes in vegetarian, chicken or seafood versions, all complemented by a list of Iberian wines; colorful plates adorn the walls of the warm, dimly lit modern space where a curtain separates the small dining area from the long bar.

Dragonfly 🗷 🅼 *Eclectic*   ▽ 17 | 23 | 17 | $38

Stamford | 488 Summer St. (Spring St.) | 203-357-9800 | www.dragonfloungect.com

At this Eclectic in Downtown Stamford, the "cool Gothic" setting will "transport you back to an old church from Ireland" and serves as a backdrop to "delicious" tapas, a "wild drink menu" and "interesting" wines by the glass; live jazz on weekends also makes for "a nice night out", but some critics gripe that "small plates don't need to come with small service", while others warn that they "can get expensive."

Drescher's 🗷 *German*   ▽ 19 | 16 | 16 | $32

Waterbury | 25 Leavenworth St. (bet. Grand & Main Sts.) | 203-573-1743 | www.dreschers.com

Housed in a historic building listed on the National Registry, this Waterbury Continental-German dates back to 1868, and currently serves "good" *essen* and beers in a setting full of "old-world charm", graced with such features as Tiffany lamps, vaulted tin ceilings and fin de siècle murals; a few dismiss the fare as "unimaginative" and chide the staff for being "unaccommodating", however.

🅩 Dressing Room 🅼 *American*   24 | 24 | 23 | $55

Westport | 27 Powers Ct. (State St.) | 203-226-1114 | www.dressingroomhomegrown.com

"Paul Newman must be smiling" on the "upscale" New American he founded with chef Michel Nischan next to the Westport Country Playhouse, offering "fabulous", "farm-focused organic" cuisine on a "newly revamped menu with lots of small plates", backed by a "wonderful" wine list and an array of "rare" liquors; "unpretentious" service and the "down-home" setting of a "beautifully restored" barn also win applause, and while a few find it "overpriced", for many it's a "wonderful" experience that "creates memories, all good"; P.S. live music on Fridays.

East Side Restaurant 🅼 *German*   17 | 18 | 20 | $33

New Britain | 131 Dwight St. (bet. East & Fairview Sts.) | 860-223-1188 | www.eastsiderestaurant.com

The "beer hall experience" at this New Britain German is a "rousing good time" that includes a "singing accordion player", "large one liter"

	FOOD	DECOR	SERVICE	COST

beers and a *"gemütlich* atmosphere" in a Bavarian setting; *freunden* praise the "authentic schnitzel" and other dishes, but critics find the fare "very average" and "not worth what they charge."

East-West Grille Ⓜ *SE Asian* ∇ 23 | 13 | 20 | $22

West Hartford | 526 New Park Ave. (Oakwood Ave.) | 860-236-3287 | www.eastwestgrille.com

"Extremely fresh ingredients" and "exquisite" presentations are the keys to the "always reliable" Southeast Asian fare at this affordable "family favorite" in West Hartford that also serves American breakfasts; the "upbeat" staff is "available when you need it and out of the way when you don't", the mood is "casual" and the space – a "former diner in Asian retro chic" – is "kitschy but interesting."

Eclisse *Italian* 21 | 18 | 20 | $37

Stamford | Harbor Sq. | 700 Canal St. (bet. Henry & Market Sts.) | 203-325-3773 | www.eclissestamford.com

"Pile in the family, pile up the food and dig in" to the "large pass-around" platters of Italian "comfort food" served up at this family-style eatery "tucked away in an industrial section of Stamford" with a space "so huge" it's "perfect for a group" of "10 people or more"; not surprisingly, it can get "noisy and raucous on weekend nights", and while some report "spotty" service, others tout it as an "affordable" and "consistent" option for the "quantity-minded."

🆕 Eclisse 21 | 20 | 20 | $45

Mediterraneo Cucina *Mediterranean*

White Plains | 189 E. Post Rd. (Waller Ave.), NY | 914-761-1111 | www.eclissewp.com

An "unusual mix of Persian and Italian plates" characterizes this "attractive" White Plains newcomer that locals are lauding as a "lovely addition" thanks to its "delicious" midpriced Med fare; it's "still working" out some service kinks, but the vibe is "lively" and "pleasant", and it's certainly "something different" for the area.

Edo Japanese Steakhouse *Japanese/Steak* 20 | 16 | 21 | $37

Port Chester | Pathmark Shopping Ctr. | 140 Midland Ave. (Weber Dr.), NY | 914-937-3333 | www.edohibachi.com

It's all about the "twirling knives" at these "solid" teppanyaki-style Japanese steakhouses in Pelham and Port Chester whipping up fare that's "typical" for the genre, and "plenty of it"; even if the traditional decor "leaves something to be desired", they remain ultra-"popular" (especially for birthdays), so "call in advance", or prepare to "wait."

80 West *Seafood* ∇ 19 | 19 | 19 | $42

White Plains | Renaissance Hotel | 80 W. Red Oak Ln. (Westchester Ave.), NY | 914-696-2782 | www.80westrestaurant.com

"Upscale, high-quality" "hotel dining" is on hand for guests at the White Plains Renaissance Hotel where the "small menu" focuses on seafood but manages to cover all the basics, from a bang-up breakfast buffet to grilled steaks to small plates at the bar; an added benefit: "you can actually hear your tablemates" in the "lovely, quiet" room looking out onto "woodsy" views.

Elbow Room *American*

18 | 16 | 15 | $29

West Hartford | 986 Farmington Ave. (Main St.) | 860-236-6195 | www.theelbowroomct.com

Popular among "young professionals", this "crowded, hip" New American in West Hartford offers an "interesting eclectic menu of "jazzed-up down-home" comfort food in a "large" space befitting the name, which includes a "wacky" dining room, rooftop patio ("such a joy on a beautiful evening") and a sidewalk terrace; critics, though, are "just not impressed" by the fare and say the service varies from "earnest to exasperating."

Eli Cannon's ⬤Ⓜ *American*

▽ 21 | 17 | 17 | $21

Middletown | 695 Main St. (Grand St.) | 860-347-3547 | www.elicannons.com

The "amazing" suds selection, including 32 on tap and "lots of esoteric microbrews", makes this "local institution" in Middletown a "beer snob's dream", and the affordable American pub grub is "plentiful and good", albeit "typical"; barbers' chairs, theater seats and a beer garden with sand and beach chairs are some of the features of the "funky", "eclectic" space, and insiders advise it's "surprisingly kid-friendly" for a bar – "earlier in the evening", that is.

Elizabeth's Cafe at Perfect Parties *American*

25 | 19 | 23 | $36

Madison | 885 Boston Post Rd. (bet. Scotland Ave. & Wall St.) | 203-245-0250 | www.perfectparties.com

This "small neighborhood spot" in Madison stands "right up there with the best", boasting a "creative, eclectic menu" of "reliably scrumptious" New American cuisine (including an "excellent" weekend brunch) and an "affordable, varied" wine list; the staff "treats you well" in the "quaint, cozy" "cottage" with "quirky decor", and while some say service can get "a little confused" and the digs look "tired", many regard it as a "reliable standby" and a "real treat."

🇿 Elm Street Oyster House *Seafood*

24 | 18 | 22 | $46

Greenwich | 11 W. Elm St. (Greenwich Ave.) | 203-629-5795 | www.elmstreetoysterhouse.com

"Still steady and true" (albeit "pricey" to some), this longtime "favorite" seafooder in Greenwich has been dishing out some of the "best oysters" and "freshest fish around", with a "handsome wine list to match", since 1994; "personable" service contributes to the "convivial" atmosphere, and while many find the scene "way too cramped" and "noisy", others insist it's become "more accessible" since it started taking reservations.

El Tio *Mexican*

18 | 12 | 17 | $24

New Rochelle | 25 Anderson St. (bet. Le Count Pl. & North Ave.), NY | 914-633-8686

Port Chester | 143 Westchester Ave. (bet. Broad & Pearl Sts.), NY | 914-939-1494

"Very authentic", these bare-bones Mexicans in New Rochelle and Port Chester offer "simple", "basic" fare that's "better than

| | FOOD | DECOR | SERVICE | COST |

most in the Northeast"; there's almost "no atmosphere" (and no hard liquor), although service is "friendly" and tabs are "as cheap as they come."

Emilio Ristorante ⓜ *Italian* — 25 | 20 | 25 | $53

Harrison | 1 Colonial Pl. (bet. Harrison Ave. & Purdy St.), NY | 914-835-3100 | www.emilioristorante.com

"A throwback to the Italian restaurants of yesteryear", this "charming" Harrison "treasure" turns out "excellent" "classic" dishes (including "antipasti you can make a meal of") in a "cozy" warren of rooms in a restored Colonial home; yes, it's "expensive", but with such an "accommodating" staff, most agree it's "worth it" for "special occasions."

Emma's Ale House *Pub Food* — 18 | 16 | 18 | $32

White Plains | 68 Gedney Way (Mamaroneck Ave.), NY | 914-683-3662 | www.emmasalehouse.com

"It's basically a sports bar", but nonetheless this "solid neighborhood joint" in White Plains "doesn't disappoint" with "polished" American "pub grub", an "excellent beer selection" and gratis baskets of "warm pretzels" that are "worth the price of the meal"; factor in a "congenial" atmosphere with pictures of the owner's canine lining the walls, and it works for a "casual" night out.

Encore Bistro Français *French* — 23 | 19 | 22 | $43

Larchmont | 22 Chatsworth Ave. (Boston Post Rd.), NY | 914-833-1661 | www.encore-bistro.com

A "delightful taste of Paris", this "tiny" Larchmont "charmer" transports guests with "wonderful" French cuisine and "just enough snooty service to add the final touch of authenticity"; "ever-present crowds" mean its "teensy storefront" space done up with vintage posters has a tendency to be "much too noisy", but "value pricing" compensates; P.S. lunch is "quieter" and a downright "bargain."

Enzo's *Italian* — 20 | 15 | 21 | $45

Mamaroneck | 451 Mamaroneck Ave. (Halstead Ave.), NY | 914-698-2911

An "affable" staff "makes you feel at home" at this "old-world" Mamaroneck Italian that "hasn't changed in eons", offering "robust", if "not exactly original", fare in "portions ample enough to feed Pavarotti"; however, in light of the "high-end prices", a number of surveyors note the "tired" Tuscan-inspired setting "could use a little freshening" up.

Eos Greek Cuisine *Greek* — 24 | 19 | 22 | $39

Stamford | 490 Summer St. (bet. Broad & Spring Sts.) | 203-569-6250 | www.eosgreekcuisine.com

Fans cheer "*opa*" for the "modern" Greek fare ("you'll wish you could hold eight forks" when devouring the octopus) at this "family-run" midpriced taverna in Downtown Stamford's Restaurant Row; while the "Mykonos white" contemporary decor leaves a few cold, the staff "aims to please", plus there's "outdoor seating in warm weather."

	FOOD	DECOR	SERVICE	COST

Épernay Bistro ⊠ Ⓜ *American/French*

▽ 22 | 22 | 25 | $40

Bridgeport | 272 Fairfield Ave. (bet. Broad St. & Lafayette Circle) | 203-334-3000 | www.epernaybistro.com

"Don't be intimidated by the location" advise aficionados who insist this "lovely" French bistro is "worth the journey" to Downtown Bridgeport for "exquisite" cuisine and "wonderful" service from the "very sweet husband-and-wife owners" and their "well-informed, but not pretentious" staff; there are live jazz performances on Thursdays in the "comfortable" space that includes a "cute room" and "cozy bar", and the prices are "excellent", all of which make it a "true find."

Esca *Italian*

▽ 19 | 21 | 19 | $43

Middletown | 437 Main St. (Washington St.) | 860-316-2552 | www.escact.com

It's "like stepping into a marble palace" at this upscale Middletown Italian that appeals to a "stylish, hip" clientele with a "great wine list", "outstanding" offerings from a raw bar and "creative" cocktails; fans insist it "never disappoints" and laud it as a sign of the town's "gastronomic renaissance", but to cynics who find the fare "heavy-handed" and the decor "over the top", "that's not saying much."

España Ⓜ *Spanish*

20 | 19 | 21 | $42

Larchmont | 147 Larchmont Ave. (Boston Post Rd.), NY | 914-833-1331 | www.espanatapas.com

For something "different" in Larchmont, try this "inviting" Spaniard for "authentic" tapas, "fantastic wines" and a multitude of paellas served in a "lovely" space; an "attentive" staff is a perk, although critics complain of "hit-or-miss" fare ("choose carefully") and bills that "can add up quickly."

Euro Asian *Asian*

17 | 18 | 17 | $33

Port Chester | Waterfront at Port Chester | 30 Westchester Ave. (bet. Townsend St. & Traverse Ave.), NY | 914-937-3680 | www.euroasianrestaurant.com

A "mix" of traditional and "fusion" Asian dishes with "gorgeously presented" sushi characterizes this "lively" Port Chester eatery situated in a slick, wood-lined space that feels "cool" for the neighborhood; in spite of the "great location" near the multiplex, however, detractors decry the service as "lackluster", and the fare as inconsistent.

Eveready Diner ◗ *Diner*

20 | 19 | 20 | $21

Brewster | 90 Independence Way (Dykeman Rd.), NY | 845-279-9009 | www.theevereadydiner.com

Even "self-proclaimed food snobs" get "nostalgic" at this "chrome-and-neon" slice of "Americana" in Brewster, celebrating the diner's "glory days in spades" with "crammed menus" offering "piles" of "stick-to-your-ribs grub", malteds, egg creams and such; "cheerful service" and "gentle prices" add to the "consummate experience", while 24-hour service on weekends lives up to the name.

	FOOD	DECOR	SERVICE	COST

Fat Cat Pie Co. *Pizza* | 23 | 15 | 19 | $27 |

Norwalk | 9-11 Wall St. (bet. High & Knight Sts.) | 203-523-0389 | www.fatcatpie.com

"Civilized, artisan-style" pizzas featuring "local and organic ingredients" and "fantastic thin crusts", plus "healthy salads" and a "spectacular selection of wines in all prices ranges" leave piezani "in love" with this Norwalk pizzeria run by "hip" owners and a "knowledgeable" staff; the only knock is on the "sparsely decorated" "industrial space" where "voices and noise carry" too well for some.

Feng Asian Bistro *Asian* | 22 | 23 | 21 | $43 |

Canton | Shoppes at Farmington Valley | 110 Albany Tpke. (bet. Lovely St. & Secret Lake Rd.) | 860-693-3364
Hartford | 93 Asylum St. (bet. Main & Trumbull Sts.) | 860-549-3364
www.fengrestaurant.com

This "classy" Pan-Asian duo is an "amazing addition to dining in Hartford County", serving "tasty, beautifully plated" dishes, including "creative" sushi and, at the Canton sibling, teppanyaki (aka hibachi) offerings that "don't disappoint", in "trendy" settings; the service at both is "wonderful", though some say it can get "slow when crowded", and happy hour offers "delightful deals."

Ferme *American* | ▽ 21 | 21 | 20 | $43 |

Avon | Avon Old Farms Hotel | 279 Avon Mountain Rd. (Waterville Rd.) | 800-836-4000 | www.fermerestaurant.com

This "new incarnation" of what once was Seasons in the Avon Old Farms Hotel dishes out "innovative" New American farm-to-table cuisine made with the "freshest ingredients" from "local farmers", including a "top-notch Sunday brunch" in a "lovely dining room" and outdoor patio; the prices are "relatively modest", though some find the wine list "somewhat pricey", the service is "super" and there's live music Thursdays–Saturdays.

Ferrante *Italian* | 20 | 21 | 18 | $44 |

Stamford | 191 Summer St. (Broad St.) | 203-323-2000 | www.ferranterestaurant.com

For "*delizioso* dining" in a "great location", fans tout this Northern Italian in Downtown Stamford, which earns bravos for its "attractive" oak-pillared interior, highlighted by abundant fresh flowers and windows that open to the street in summer, "above-average" cuisine and "friendly" service; detractors demur, however, calling it "inconsistent" and "overpriced."

NEW **Fez, The** *Mediterranean/Moroccan* | ▽ 20 | 19 | 22 | $37 |

Stamford | 227 Summer St. (Broad St.) | 203-975-0479 | www.thefez1.com

"Inventive" Moroccan and Mediterranean tapas and an "eclectic" wine list are served in a "sexy" space that "looks like it was lifted from a Middle Eastern souk" at this "interesting, affordable addition to Downtown Stamford"; the "omnipresent" owner and "attentive" staff make sure "all diners have a good time", while belly dancers on Fridays, live jazz and bring-your-own-vinyl-record nights add to the "unusual, terrific" experience.

	FOOD	DECOR	SERVICE	COST

Fife 'n Drum *American*

18 | 18 | 21 | $44

Kent | 53 N. Main St. (Kent Green Blvd.) | 860-927-3509 |
www.fifendrum.com

At their "reliable favorite" in Kent, the Traymon family "really does treat you like one of them", offering a "comfortable" Traditional American menu, including duck and Caesar salad served tableside by "tuxedo-clad" waiters, and an "extensive wine list"; patriarch Dolph plays jazz piano in the "classic" "men's-club" setting, and while a few critics find it "overrated and overpriced", most consider this "step back in time" a real "treat."

Fifty Coins *American*

16 | 13 | 18 | $25

New Canaan | 26 Locust Ave. (bet. Forest & Main Sts.) | 203-972-3303
Ridgefield | 426 Main St. (Big Shop Ln.) | 203-438-1456
www.fiftycoinsrestaurant.com

"Local families" and "laid-back ladies who do casual lunch" flock to these "afforable", casual Americans, centrally located in New Canaan and Ridgefield, respectively, for a "quick bite" of "basic but tasty" "pub-style" eats, served by a "friendly" staff in a "horsey-theme" setting (they're named after a racehorse); neighsayers, though, knock the fare as merely "so-so" and bemoan the "noise" and "kids."

55° *Italian*

23 | 21 | 22 | $45

Fairfield | 55 Miller St. (bet. Boston Post Rd. & Carter Henry Dr.) |
203-256-0099 | www.55winebar.com

"The mmm's and oooh's are never-ending" at this "solid" Fairfield Northern Italian, a sibling to New Canaan's Cava that also offers a "great wine selection", "knowledgeable", "friendly" service and prices that many feel are "fair"; the "upscale", multilevel space is "beautiful", though the "noise level's a bit high", especially later in the evening when the "active bar" becomes a "hothouse" for "singles"; P.S. "nice patio" too.

59 Bank *American*

19 | 18 | 19 | $34

New Milford | 59 Bank St. (Railroad St.) | 860-350-5995 | www.59bank.com

A "comfortable" "locals' place", this New Milford American is a popular stop for "drinks" and "reliable", "down-home" eats such as panini, flatbread pizzas and salads at "moderate" prices; the staff is "friendly", though some say the service can be "spotty", and suggest that the menu and decor could both "use an update"; P.S. there's live music on weekends.

Fin *Japanese*

23 | 12 | 19 | $33

Fairfield | 1253 Post Rd. (bet. Beach & Unquowa Rds.) | 203-255-6788
Stamford | 219 Main St. (Washington Blvd.) | 203-359-6688
www.fin-sushi.com

"Fin fans" "cannot get enough" of the "beautifully presented", "super-fresh" sushi at this Japanese duo in Fairfield and Stamford, and declare it "one of the best buys" for a "simple meal without fuss"; "friendly", "helpful" service and "reasonable" prices are additional pluses, but critics carp over "cramped seating" and "no real decor", lamenting that the "pristine" fare "deserves grander surroundings."

	FOOD	DECOR	SERVICE	COST

Firebox *American*

24 | 24 | 21 | $46

Hartford | Billings Forge | 539 Broad St. (bet. Capitol Ave. & Russ St.) | 860-246-1222 | www.fireboxrestaurant.com

An "ever-changing menu" of "superb farm-to-table" New American cuisine featuring "CT-fresh" ingredients "keeps repeat diners from getting bored" at this upscale-casual in the renovated old Billings Forge in Downtown Hartford; service is "excellent" in the "elegant" space where there's occasional live music that's "not intrusive" (though some find the background noise "overwhelming"), and while a few balk at the "sketchy" location, others are glad to do their part for the ongoing "neighborhood renaissance."

Firehouse Deli *Deli*

21 | 11 | 16 | $15

Fairfield | 22 Reef Rd. (Post Rd.) | 203-255-5527 | www.firehousedelifairfield.com

A "crowded take-out paradise", this Fairfield deli dishes out "huge", "terrific" sandwiches and "fresh salads" from a menu with enough "variety to please almost everyone", including kids and collegians "feeding the freshman 15"; the staff is "obliging" but the queues can "get intense" in the otherwise "low-key" setting with a "tiny back room", so insiders recommend taking your order to the "park across the street."

First & Last Tavern *Italian*

19 | 17 | 17 | $26

Avon | 26 W. Main St. (Simsbury Rd.) | 860-676-2000
Hartford | 939 Maple Ave. (bet. Freeman & Linnmoore Sts.) | 860-956-6000
Middletown | 220 Main St. (College St.) | 860-347-2220
Plainville | 32 Cooke St. (New Britain Ave.) | 860-747-9100
www.firstandlasttavern.com

For a "predictable" "family meal in a nice setting" or a "weekend outing with friends", fans heads to these "familiar neighborhood" haunts for "*buono*" brick-oven pizzas with "interesting toppings", "fresh" salads and "solid pub food" served by "cheerful" staffers in "spacious" surroundings where there's a "likable" bar scene; critics find it a bit "expensive" for "basic" eats and wish that "some new offerings" would show up on the menu.

Flaggstead Smokehouse *BBQ*

- | - | - | M

Farmington | 1085 Farmington Ave. (Forest Park Dr.) | 860-674-6028 | www.flaggsteadsmokehouse.com

Run by a family whose "heart is in the South", this Farmington smokehouse turns out a "mean" Texas-style BBQ, including brisket that "especially shines"; while everything's "true to form", right down to the Lone Star beer and cowboy-themed digs, purists and Yankee fans alike wish the staff would "lose the Red Sox caps"; it's BYO for wine.

Flanders Fish Market & Restaurant *Seafood*

21 | 13 | 18 | $30

East Lyme | 22 Chesterfield Rd. (Rte. 1) | 860-739-8866 | www.flandersfish.com

"Always popular", but "especially in summer", this casual seafooder-cum-retailer in East Lyme offers "tasty presentations" of "fresh, fresh, fresh" fin fare, plus a Sunday brunch buffet, at "reasonable" prices; outdoor dining and "fast, friendly" service notwithstanding, some sniff that it has "all the charm of a cafeteria", and feel it's a "better fish market than restaurant", but others insist it's "everything you'd want in a New England fish place."

Flipside Burgers & Bar *Burgers*   17 | 15 | 18 | $22

Fairfield | 1125 Post Rd. (bet. Beach & Unquowa Rds.) | 203-292-8235 | www.flipsiderestaurant.com

For "cost-effective", "uncomplicated" dining, the "preppies of Fairfield" and others head to this "family-friendly" burgertory where you can "create your own" hamburger or order one of its "interesting combinations"; the staff is one of the "friendliest around" and there's a circular bar that's popular among the "college set", and while some critics don't give a flip for what they say is "middling" fare, others find it "satisfying" and the prices "reasonable."

Flood Tide *Continental/Eclectic*   ∇ 21 | 18 | 18 | $46

Mystic | Inn at Mystic | 3 Williams Ave. (Denison Ave.) | 860-536-8140 | www.innatmystic.com

"Beautiful water views" and "classical piano playing at the bar" help set the stage for some "sophisticated dining" at this "special-occasion" Continental-Eclectic at the Inn at Mystic, where the "sumptuous" fare is backed by a "great wine list", and the "large drinks" may leave you "napping by the fire"; "wonderful" service is another plus, but some feel this "local high-end favorite" has "slipped in the last few years" and "needs updating."

Foe, An American Bistro Ⓜ *American*   ∇ 19 | 18 | 19 | $41

Branford | 1114 Main St. (Veto St.) | 203-483-5896 | www.foebistro.com

When you "want something a bit more upscale and don't want to travel far", this Branford New American is a "dependable" choice according to fans who tout its "reliable", "well-crafted" cooking, "fast" service and "relaxed, romantic" setting; critics find the fare overly "cautious" and the space "lacking vivacity", while insiders hint that it's "more fun" if you "eat at the bar."

Fonda La Paloma *Mexican*   19 | 14 | 18 | $35

Cos Cob | 531 E. Putnam Ave. (Orchard St.) | 203-661-9395 | www.fondalapaloma.com

There's a "stuck-in-time charm" to this veteran Cos Cob Mexican serving "traditional" fare and an "excellent selection of margaritas" in a "pleasant", "family-friendly" setting where you can catch the "occasional mariachi band"; critics complain that the food "doesn't live up to the price" and the digs "need an update", but defenders counter by pointing out that the "parking lot is full every night."

Forbidden City Bistro *Chinese*   25 | 23 | 20 | $41

Middletown | 335 Main St. (Court St.) | 860-343-8288 | www.forbiddencitybistro.com

There are "no chow mein noodles" (or a "buffet in sight") at this "elegant" Middletown sibling of Glastonbury's Char Koon serving "fabulous", "attractively plated" Chinese cuisine and an "extensive wine list" in a "formal" setting; though some report service glitches "when it gets busy", many recommend this "unexpected find" for "dates" or "meeting friends for cocktails."

42 🗷 *American*   22 | 27 | 22 | $72

White Plains | Ritz-Carlton Westchester | 1 Renaissance Sq., 42nd fl. (Main St.), NY | 914-761-4242 | www.42therestaurant.com

"So very ritzy" with its "stunning views" and "sophisticated vibe", this "elegant" 42nd-floor dining room at the Ritz-Carlton in White Plains makes you want to "dress up" to celebrate "special occasions" and savor "talented" chef Anthony Goncalves' "inventive riffs" on New American cuisine; however, service "varies from visit to visit" (sometimes "personable", other times "snooty"), which can be irksome given the "sky-high prices."

NEW Frankie & Fanucci's   21 | 17 | 19 | $24
Wood Oven Pizzeria *Pizza*

Mamaroneck | 301 Mamaroneck Ave. (Palmer Ave.), NY | 914-630-4360 | www.fandfpizza.com

A "welcome addition" to the Westchester "pizza scene", this Hartsdale parlor puts out "terrific" Neapolitan-style thin-crust pies that are "a cut above" the competition (and prices are a step up too); it's "kid city" in the "casual" dining room most nights, so "noisy", "crowded" conditions should come as no surprise; P.S. the Mamaroneck branch is newer, and takeout-oriented.

Frankie & Johnnie's Steakhouse 🅼 *Steak*   24 | 22 | 22 | $66

Rye | 77 Purchase St. (Purdy Ave.), NY | 914-925-3900 | www.frankieandjohnnies.com

Boosters "bank on" this "top-notch" Rye steakhouse in a former savings and loan for "perfectly cooked" "prime" beef and "delicious" sides bolstered by a 650-label wine list; its "inviting" white-tablecloth setting and "attentive" service make it well suited to a "client" lunch, but you'll need to "bring the boss' credit card."

⚡ Frank Pepe Pizzeria *Pizza*   24 | 11 | 17 | $21

Danbury | 59 Federal Rd. (Morgan Ave.) | 203-790-7373
Fairfield | 238 Commerce Dr. (bet. Berwick Ct. & Brentwood Ave.) | 203-333-7373
Manchester | 233 Buckland Hills Dr. (bet. Buckland & Deming Sts.) | 860-644-7333
New Haven | 157 Wooster St. (Brown St.) | 203-865-5762
Uncasville | Mohegan Sun Casino | 1 Mohegan Sun Blvd. (bet. Rtes. 2 & 32) | 860-862-8888 ●

⚡ Frank Pepe's The Spot 🅼 *Pizza*

New Haven | 163 Wooster St. (Brown St.) | 203-865-7602
www.frankpepe.com

"There's magic in that coal-fired brick oven" swear fans of the New Haven pizzeria "mecca" and its newer outposts, voted Connecticut's Most Popular for what many claim is "the most memorable pie you'll ever inhale" – featuring thin, chewy crusts "with the right hint of smokiness" and toppings like "fresh shucked" clam – that are worth enduring "long waits" and "grumpy" service; while some find the

	FOOD	DECOR	SERVICE	COST

pies "overrated" and accuse the branches of "living on New Haven's reputation", most aver that "all the fussing and the buzz is true."

Fratelli *Italian* | 19 | 13 | 18 | $36 |

New Rochelle | East End Shopping Ctr. | 237 E. Main St. (Stephenson Blvd.), NY | 914-633-1990 | www.fratellirestaurantnewrochelle.com

Families frequent this "neighborhood" Italian in a New Rochelle shopping center for "better-than-average" cooking at "reasonable" rates; although the service is "warm", the "plain" peach-hued setting and fare are "underwhelming" to some.

Friends & Company *American*   ∇ | 18 | 18 | 19 | $31 |

Madison | 11 Boston Post Rd. (Rte. 77) | 203-245-0462 | www.friendsandcompanyrestaurant.com

A "Shoreline establishment" "you can count on", this Madison American serves "health-conscious" fare "simply prepared" and "served with a smile" by an "efficient" staff; a few are "underwhelmed" by what they call "ordinary" fare, but many regard it as a "reliable" option, with a "warm" atmosphere that "makes for a comfy evening."

Fuji Mountain *Japanese* | 15 | 15 | 18 | $37 |

Larchmont | 2375 Boston Post Rd. (Deane Pl.), NY | 914-833-3838

"The tricks at the grill never disappoint" at this midpriced Japanese in Larchmont that's the "quintessential birthday place" for neighborhood kids; no surprise, many report "the spectacle is better than the food", and the "loud", "hot" "atmosphere can be brutal."

Full Moon Asian Thai Restaurant *Thai*   ∇ | 24 | 24 | 23 | $30 |

White Plains | 124 E. Post Rd. (Court St.), NY | 914-328-7555 | www.fullmoonasianthairestaurant.com

Whether for a "quick lunch" or "quiet" dinner, this "delightful", "little" White Plains Thai satisfies with "wonderfully authentic" dishes in a room trimmed with imported sandstone and bamboo; prices are low and the staff is "eager to please", so even if some say the food "could use a little oomph", it's still a "find" for the area.

NEW Gabriele's Italian Steakhouse *Italian/Steak* | - | - | - | E |

Greenwich | 35 Church St. (Putnam Ave.) | 203-622-4223 | www.gabrielesofgreenwich.com

At this expensive Greenwich Italian steakhouse, suits loosen their ties around the clubby bar with a big stone fireplace, while in the packed dining room, coffered ceilings and white tablecloths don't muffle the roar of conversations as waiters deliver seafood towers, 44-ounce porterhouses and simple red-sauce dishes, and the sommelier guides diners through a 2,000-bottle wine list; reservations are required, even on a Tuesday.

Gabrielle's *American* | 25 | 21 | 24 | $47 |

Centerbrook | 78 Main St. (Westbrook Rd.) | 860-767-2440 | www.gabrielles.net

An "excellent choice" for "family dinners" or pre- and après-theater dining, this Centerbrook New American offers "delicious combinations" of "outstanding" small plates that "won't break the bank", and a Monday half-price special that ensures a "packed" house; the "pleasant" staff "works hard to please", and even if some think the restored Victorian is "nothing special", most declare this spot a "sure winner."

Gates Californian/Mediterranean

19 | 18 | 19 | $32

New Canaan | 10 Forest St. (East Ave.) | 203-966-8666

As "reliable as sunrise", this "reasonably priced" Cal-Med is a "family-friendly" fixture in New Canaan, where you can find a "hustle-bustle lunch and brunch scene" featuring a "wide variety" of "solid" (some say "undistinguished") dishes "served with a smile" in a "bright", "cheerful" environment that's "friendly to the little ones"; some grown-ups "prefer the quiet bar to the noisy dining room", however.

Gavi Italian

19 | 16 | 19 | $50

Armonk | 15 Old Rte. 22 (Rte. 22), NY | 914-273-6900 | www.gavirestaurant.com

"Basic" Italian fare is on the menu at this "comfortable" Armonk eatery hosting "cozy" dinners and a "nice bar for a late drink"; though "they aim to please", "service can be unpredictable" and the unimpressed find it "overpriced" for a "neighborhood place" delivering "so-so" comestibles.

Geronimo Southwestern

20 | 21 | 19 | $35

New Haven | 271 Crown St. (High St.) | 203-777-7700 | www.geronimobarandgrill.com

"Cold margaritas" plus a "hot crowd" equals a "destination spot" for fans of this New Haven Southwestern offering a "solid menu" of "tasty, satisfying" dishes at "modest prices" to complement the "amazing" beverages; the "bar area is terrific" and the "low lighting" in the dining room creates an "inviting" ambiance, and the service is, well, "satisfactory"; there are salsa lessons on Sundays and tequila tasting classes twice a month.

Gervasi's Italian

20 | 21 | 23 | $47

White Plains | 324 Central Ave. (Tarrytown Rd.), NY | 914-684-8855 | www.gervasis.com

"They treat you like royalty" at this White Plains Italian where chef John Gervasi (ex Mulino's) turns out "tasty" seafood and pastas plus a "terrific" mimosa-fueled Sunday brunch; its "unique" decor varies by room (with black chandeliers and exposed-brick walls among the elements), although in spite of an overall "enjoyable" experience, some find the prices "high" for the area.

Ginban Asian Bistro & Sushi Asian

23 | 21 | 20 | $33

Mamaroneck | 421 Mamaroneck Ave. (Spencer Pl.), NY | 914-777-8889 | www.ginbanasianbistro.com

Amid numerous options on Mamaroneck Avenue, this "hip", blue-lit canteen stands out with an "exhaustive" assortment of "out-of-the-ordinary" Asian items including ultra-"inventive" sushi rolls that are "not for the traditionalist"; "service can be spotty" ("especially when they're busy"), but tabs are modest, and delivery is a plus.

	FOOD	DECOR	SERVICE	COST

Ginger Man *Pub Food* | 18 | 19 | 17 | $33 |

Greenwich | 64 Greenwich Ave. (Lexington Ave.) | 203-861-6400 | www.gingermangreenwich.com
South Norwalk | 99 Washington St. (bet. Main & Water Sts.) | 203-354-0163 | www.gingermannorwalk.com
Lagerheads "go for the beers" at these tavern twins, whose "expansive" list of brews "from around the world" (52 on tap in SoNo, 26 in Greenwich, and more than 100 bottled labels at both) trump their menu of "traditional pub fare", which offers "no surprises" according to critics; the service is "friendly", and there's a "nice patio" at the former location, while the latter boasts a "warm, inviting" back room where you can warm up by a "roaring fire."

Globe Bar & Grill *American* | 17 | 18 | 18 | $37 |

Larchmont | 1879 Palmer Ave. (Chatsworth Ave.), NY | 914-833-8600 | www.globegrill.com
"Noisy and informal", this Larchmont New American is a "go-to" for "family" meals or a drink with friends; however, while the "lively" atmosphere with sidewalk seating and an active "bar scene" is "lots of fun", foes find the service uneven and the rather "basic" burgers and pizza "mediocre at best."

Gnarly Vine *American*   ∇ | 17 | 16 | 20 | $30 |

New Rochelle | 501 Main St. (bet. Lawton St. & Norman Rockwell Blvd.), NY | 914-355-2541 | www.thegnarlyvine.com
"For a glass of wine with the girls", "there aren't many places like this" New Rochelle American restaurant/bar offering "nice, inexpensive" vino (30 by the glass and 50 bottles) matched with "light snacks" like tuna tartare and Sicilian meatballs; its loungey looks, "relaxing" vibe and barkeeps that "know their stuff" further its rep as a place to "hang out", even if some suggest the food's only "so-so."

Go Fish *Seafood* | 22 | 20 | 21 | $35 |

Mystic | Olde Mistick Vill. | 26 Coogan Blvd. (Rte. 27) | 860-536-2662 | www.gofishct.com
Sure, this seafooder in a shopping mall across from the Mystic Aquarium "mostly caters to the tourist trade", but the fin fare is "always fresh" and the sushi bar offerings are "first-rate"; a "skilled" staff works the "spacious" ("charmless" to some) room, and while thrifty sorts find it a bit "pricey", most deem it a "solid choice."

Golden Rod *Asian* | 18 | 11 | 15 | $26 |

New Rochelle | 55 E. Main St. (Premium Point Rd.), NY | 914-235-6688
When you're "too tired to cook", this New Rochelle Pan-Asian is "perfectly adequate" for a "diverse" array of "choices for everyone" at "inexpensive" rates; just know that the "small", "sterile" dining room and occasionally "attitude"-laden staff have many opting for takeout.

Gold Roc Diner ◑ *Diner*   ∇ | 14 | 11 | 17 | $18 |

West Hartford | 61 Kane St. (Oakwood Ave.) | 860-236-9366
"Always convenient, always open, always reliable", this "classic" 24/7 "old-timer diner" in West Hartford is a "great stop" "just off

the freeway" for "middle-of-the-night road food" or a "sober-up place" for an "inebriated college crowd"; while many feel it's "nothing to write home about", defenders insist it "gets the job done."

NEW Goose American Bar & Bistro *American*

| - | - | - | M |

Darien | 972 Post Rd. (bet. Center St. & Corbin Dr.) | 203-656-2600 | www.thegoosedarien.com

Landing in the refurbished nest of the former Black Goose Grille in Downtown Darien, this midpriced New American bistro and watering hole offers updated comfort food – from simple lobster sliders to Nantucket bouillabaisse and classic boeuf bourguignon – in two dining rooms, which can get noisy when they fill up with families (and kids); the updated space also includes a vintage 19th-century walnut bar and a private dining room with skylights.

Grant's *American*

| 25 | 22 | 23 | $48 |

West Hartford | 977 Farmington Ave. (Main St.) | 860-236-1930 | www.billygrant.com

Chef Billy Grant "knows how to prepare delicious food" and "uses local fresh ingredients" in his "superb" New American cuisine at this West Hartford "mecca for foodies" (Bricco's sibling), though some declare the "excellent" desserts are the "real stars"; the "hardworking" staff provides "stellar" service, while "marvelously mixed" cocktails help fuel a "jumping bar scene at night", and calls for a "redo" of the Mediterranean-style decor notwithstanding, it's "highly recommended" by most for "special occasions" or "impressing that certain someone."

Graziellas *Italian*

| 19 | 16 | 18 | $40 |

White Plains | Esplanade White Plains Hotel | 95 S. Broadway (Post Rd.), NY | 914-761-5721 | www.graziellasny.com

An "oldie but goodie" on the red-sauce circuit, this White Plains Italian proffers "value"-priced fare like chicken parm, penne alla vodka and such; even if the rustic decor and "predictable" menu "could use a face-lift", at least service is "dependable."

Great Taste *Chinese*

| 20 | 18 | 20 | $26 |

New Britain | 597 W. Main St. (Corbin Ave.) | 860-827-8988 | www.greattaste.com

The "owner stands guard over everything" at this New Britain Chinese and the "attention to detail" is evident in the "well-prepared" fare (including tableside Peking duck that's a "show"), "efficient" service and a "nicely decorated", "white-tablecloth" setting; it's "reasonably priced", and while some sniff "don't take the name literally", many consider it a "great value."

NEW Green Gourmet to Go 🚫Ⓜ *Vegetarian*

| - | - | - | I |

Bridgeport | 2984 Fairfield Ave. (bet. Bennett & Fox Sts.) | 203-873-0057 | www.greengourmettogo.com

Vegetarian and vegan fare, plus gluten-free desserts (e.g. sweet potato blondies), made with locally sourced organic ingredients are prepared at this bright, spring-green storefront in the Black Rock section of Bridgeport offering takeout in earth-friendly packaging and counter service with limited seating; chef-owner Linda Soper-Kolton's healthful philosophy extends to the palate – the food is as tasty as it is vitamin and antioxidant-rich.

Greenwich Tavern *American*   21 | 20 | 20 | $44

Old Greenwich | 1392 E. Putnam Ave. (Ferris Dr.) | 203-698-9033 | www.greenwichtavern.net

Chef-owner Rafael Palomino (Sonora) has displayed a "magic touch" in transforming the former Palomino's in Old Greenwich into a Traditional American offering an "eclectic menu" suiting "every mood and budget", and "unobtrusive" service; cynics find it "a little pricey" for what they say is "not serious dining", but surveyors like the "beautiful space" and the "vibrant social scene."

NEW Greenwood's   ∇ 16 | 14 | 15 | $31
Grille & Ale House *American*

Bethel | 186 Greenwood Ave. (Depot Pl.) | 203-791-0408

A "full spectrum" of Traditional American eats are on offer at this newcomer housed in Bethel's Old Opera House that's "making a mark" as a "down-to-earth" "pre-theater dinner" option; exposed brick and a tin ceiling punctuate the "pub setting", though a few frown at the big-screen TVs, and wonder whether it's "more about sports than food"; Thursdays are open-mike nights, and there's live music every other Saturday.

Grist Mill *Continental*   23 | 23 | 22 | $43

Farmington | 44 Mill Ln. (Garden St.) | 860-676-8855 | www.thegristmill.net

A "wonderful spot for a romantic dinner", this Continental offers "fabulous views" of the Farmington River rapids and eponymous mill, the backdrop for "carefully prepared" "classic dishes" such as Dover sole, served by an "efficient" staff in a "warm, charming" atmosphere; the "lovely location" largely trumps complaints about "uninspired" cooking or a scene that's "stuck in the past."

Griswold Inn *American*   18 | 25 | 19 | $44

Essex | Griswold Inn | 36 Main St. (Scholes Ln.) | 860-767-1776 | www.griswoldinn.com

You "can't get much more New England" than this "beautiful old" inn in the "picture-perfect town" of Essex, a "legend since 1776", where the "warren of rooms" graced with an "incredible collection of marine art" have "charm to burn", and "knowledgeable" service is another plus; the Traditional American fare is almost an "afterthought", but many laud the "honest food at reasonable prices", including the "wonderful" Sunday hunt breakfast, and oenophiles extol the "creative" tapas and "fine-wine tastings" from the wine bar.

Gusano Loco *Mexican*   21 | 11 | 21 | $33

Mamaroneck | 1137 W. Boston Post Rd. (Richbell Rd.), NY | 914-777-1512 | www.gusanoloco.net

It's certainly "nothing fancy", but this Mamaroneck Mexican "joint" earns a loyal following with "tasty", "authentic" takes on the classics that hit "closer to the mark than most"; a "warm welcome" from the staff, low-cost margaritas and live music on weekends complete the picture.

Gus's Franklin Park Seafood   21 | 10 | 19 | $42

Harrison | 126 Halstead Ave. (1st St.), NY | 914-835-9804 | www.gusseafood.com

This "old-time" Harrison seafooder "hasn't changed much in 50 years", serving "simple Americana" like "fresh-from-Maine" lobsters, fried shrimp and prime rib in a "no-frills", "publike" space crammed with "regulars"; despite some whispers that "its time has passed", there are "long lines for a table" most nights.

G.W. Tavern American   20 | 22 | 21 | $38

Washington Depot | 20 Bee Brook Rd. (bet. Blackville Rd. & Calhoun St.) | 860-868-6633 | www.gwtavern.com

"It feels like George Washington just left" this "neighborhood haunt" in Washington Depot serving "solid" American "comfort food" at "palatable prices" in a "cozy tavern" (circa 1850) that's a "four-season delight" – "warm by the hearth" in winter, cool on the patio overlooking the Shepaug River in spring and summer, "full-throttle color in fall"; "friendly service" comes all-year-round, though a few think it "needs improvement" and find the fare "just ok."

Haiku Asian Bistro & Sushi Bar Asian   22 | 19 | 20 | $35

Mamaroneck | 265 Mamaroneck Ave. (Prospect Ave.), NY | 914-381-3200

White Plains | 149 Mamaroneck Ave. (bet. E. Post Rd. & Maple Ave.), NY | 914-644-8887 ●

www.haikuasianbistro.com

For sushi so "fresh" it's practically "still swimming" plus an array of "delicious" Pan-Asian plates, regulars rely on this "trendy", everexpanding chainlet that's "always busy", frequently "loud" and sometimes "turns the tables so quickly" you feel "hurried"; those who deem the tabs "a little spendy" will find "good value" in the "amazing lunch deals."

Hajime Ⓜ Japanese   25 | 14 | 20 | $42

Harrison | 267 Halstead Ave. (Harrison Ave.), NY | 914-777-1543

Like "Nobu" for "one-third of the price", this "mom-and-pop" Harrison Japanese slices up "sparkling"-fresh slabs of fish that are "nothing fancy", just "superb" "high-quality" fare; the "quiet" setting can be a little "intimidating to the uninitiated", so regulars recommend you "sit at the bar" and let the chef "graciously coach you through the selection process."

Halstead Avenue Bistro American   20 | 15 | 20 | $39

Harrison | 123 Halstead Ave. (1st St.), NY | 914-777-1181 | www.halsteadbistro.com

A "welcoming, neighborhood place", this Harrison bistro is where a "personable" staff proffers a "tasty", "if not adventurous", New American menu; even if a few find the fare and white-tablecloth setting "boring", it's a "civilized" option, and the midweek prix fixe for $19.95 is "unbeatable."

Harbor Lights *Mediterranean/Seafood*   20 | 23 | 20 | $44

Norwalk | 82 Sea View Ave. (bet. East Ave. & 1st St.) | 203-866-3364 | www.harborlightsrestaurant-ct.com

The "wall of windows" overlooking Norwalk's harbor "makes you feel like you're on a boat" gush fans of this white-tablecloth "treasure" whose "well-prepared" Med-inspired seafood "remains true to the view" and the service is "professional"; though a few cold fish find it "pricey" and "far from spectacular", for most, it's all about "location, location, location"; there's docking space for those who prefer to come by sea.

Hard Rock Cafe ● *American*   15 | 19 | 16 | $33

Ledyard | Foxwoods Resort Casino | 39 Norwich Westerly Rd. (bet. Grand Pequot Ave. & Watson Rd.) | 860-312-7625 | www.hardrock.com

"Rock memorabilia" is the claim to fame of this "noisy", "nostalgic", music-driven American chain link in the Foxwoods casino, and if the food doesn't exactly rock, it's fine for "enjoying a burger and a beer"; but those who deem the concept "so yesterday" ("does anyone still think this is cool?") feel it may be best left to "headbangers", "tourists" and youngsters who "love" those T-shirts.

Harney & Sons *Tearoom*   21 | 21 | 20 | $22

Millerton | Railroad Plaza | 13 Main St. (bet. Center St. & Elm Ave.), NY | 518-789-2121 | www.harney.com

"If you love tea", this "cute", "little" Millerton "salon" is "paradise", offering an "extensive variety of world-class" blends to buy or sip "freshly brewed" in the cafe along with "light sandwiches", "delicious soups", scones or other lunch and teatime eats; seating is "limited", but the terrace eases the crush when it's warm, while "browsing" in the adjacent shop is always a "fun diversion."

Harry's Bishops Corner Ⓜ *Pizza*   24 | 14 | 18 | $22

West Hartford | 732 N. Main St. (Albany Ave.) | 860-236-0400 | www.harrysbc.com

Run by two former employees of the original Harry's on Farmington Avenue (no longer affiliated), this "great little joint" in West Hartford's Bishops Corner serves up "outstanding" Napoletana-style thin-crust pizzas with "fresh, seasonal" toppings and salads with its "inimitable" house dressing (on sale by the bottle), and its "wine values beat everyone's"; fans praise the "community-oriented" owners and "efficient" staff, and while some say the dining room's "wooden booths leave a lot to be desired", for most, the pies are the "attraction here, pure and simple."

Harry's Pizza *Pizza*   26 | 13 | 19 | $22

West Hartford | West Hartford Ctr. | 1003 Farmington Ave. (bet. Lasalle Rd. & Woodrow St.) | 860-231-7166 | www.harryspizza.net

Piezani see a "vision of heaven" at this West Hartford "old reliable" – a "phenomenal selection" of "fabulous" thin-crust pizzas with "super-

FOOD | DECOR | SERVICE | COST

fresh ingredients" "you could eat everyday", served by a "friendly" staff; less sublime are the simple digs, which is why secular sorts "don't actually eat there", but rather "take the pie and run."

Harvest, The ⓜ Continental

▽ 21 | 25 | 22 | $54

Pomfret | 37 Putnam Rd. (Woodstock Rd.) | 860-928-0008 | www.harvestrestaurant.com

You "can't beat the setting" of this "beautiful" Pomfret Continental situated in a 1758 Colonial farmhouse in the state's "Quiet Corner", where a "friendly, punctual" staff "makes you feel special and taken care of" in the "pretty" space graced with fresh flowers and the works of local artists, while serving the "extensive" menu; opinions are split on the fare ("reliable" vs. "variable"), and some find the scene "a little touristy", but it's the "favorite" option of many for taking the family "out to celebrate."

☑ Harvest Supper ⓢⓜ American

27 | 21 | 25 | $55

New Canaan | 15 Elm St. (Main St.) | 203-966-5595

"Every bite is a delight" at this "refined" New American "gem" in New Canaan from owners Jack and Grace Lamb (of NYC's Jewel Bako); the "charming" Mrs. L. "ensures everyone feels welcome" in the "elegant" but "tiny" space, and if some grouse that the seating is "tight" and the chairs are "uncomfortable", almost all agree the "superb" "seasonal" dishes and "excellent service" "make up for that."

Hawthorne Inn American

20 | 15 | 19 | $39

Berlin | 2421 Berlin Tpke. (Toll Gate Rd.) | 860-828-3571 | www.hawthorne-inn.com

"Huge" portions of prime rib and "fantastic" seafood selections, including "lobster summer specials", are what make this Berlin American "famous", and fans praise the staff that's "wonderful to work with"; while some cynics find the fare "disappointing" and feel like they're "traveling back in time to the swinging '70s" due to decor "in desperate need of updating" and a mostly "older" clientele, others are hopeful that the "new owner may make some welcome changes."

Heirloom American/Continental

20 | 23 | 20 | $52

New Haven | Study at Yale Hotel | 1157 Chapel St. (bet. Park & York Sts.) | 203-503-3919 | www.studyhotels.com

"Refreshing in hot weather, cozy in cool weather", the space of this Continental–New American housed in the Study at Yale boutique hotel is "modern in every way", featuring hardwood floors, leather chairs and floor-to-ceiling windows; the staff is "welcoming" and the "uncomplicated", "locally sourced" cuisine "beats the expectations" of fans, though others find it "disappointing" and "overpriced."

Hopkins Inn ⓜ Austrian

19 | 22 | 21 | $51

New Preston | Hopkins Inn | 22 Hopkins Rd. (½ mi. west of Rte. 45 N.) | 860-868-7295 | www.thehopkinsinn.com

The "gorgeous" view of Lake Waramaug from the terrace of the 19th-century inn housing this New Preston Austrian may tempt you to sing "The Sound of Music", but its "well-mannered patrons" manage to resist the urge; a few think it "could use a little updating", right down to the "St. Pauli Girl waitress outfits", but for most, the "fabulous setting", "authentic" *essen* and "professional" service add up to an "incomparable experience"; P.S. closed January–March.

Horse & Hound Inn *American* 19 | 19 | 20 | $38
South Salem | 94 Spring St. (Main St.), NY | 914-763-3108 |
www.thehorseandhoundinn.com

Housed in a "historic" stagecoach stop in South Salem, this "comfortable" American offers "consistent" "neighborhood eats" and a "satisfying bar menu" served by a "well-meaning" staff; though "warm, inviting" and "perfect for a winter night", some feel the "unique setting" is "somewhat wasted" while others enjoy having "a local *Cheers*" with "fair prices."

Hot Basil Thai Café *Thai* ▽ 20 | 15 | 16 | $27
West Hartford | 565 New Park Ave. (Talcott Rd.) | 860-523-9554 |
www.hotbasilcafe.com

A "real find in an unlikely spot" in West Hartford, this moderately priced Thai dishes out "imaginative" fare "with a twist" that's "not dumbed down" for "unadventurous New Englanders", though critics say its "consistency" is a "question mark"; the digs may be "minimalist", but the atmosphere is "pleasant", and with a liquor store conveniently next door, "BYO makes it special."

Hot Tomato's 🗷 *Italian* 20 | 18 | 18 | $37
Hartford | 1 Union Pl. (Asylum St.) | 860-249-5100 |
www.hottomatos.net

After an ownership change in 2010, this Hartford "staple" "still attracts a fun crowd" with "huge" portions of "flavorful" Italian fare and "above-average" service; an outdoor patio with a "great view of Bushnell Park" offers a refuge to those who gripe that the "trattoria-type" interior can get so "loud" it "feels like the railroad station" where it's housed.

NEW Hudson Grille *American* 20 | 22 | 20 | $37
White Plains | 165 Mamaroneck Ave. (bet. E. Post Rd. & Maple Ave.),
NY | 914-997-2000 | www.hudsongrilleny.com

"More upscale" than your "average Mamaroneck Avenue pub", this "handsome" White Plains New American proffers an "expansive" lineup of "surprisingly good" fare, from crab cakes to rib-eyes; a "knowledgeable" staff is a plus, and there's also an "active" bar crowded with "singles"

Hunan Larchmont *Chinese/Japanese* 17 | 12 | 17 | $25
Larchmont | 1961 Palmer Ave. (West Ave.), NY | 914-833-0400 |
www.hunanlarchmont.com

A longtimer on the "suburban Chinese" circuit, this Larchmont Cantonese offers "predictable", "fairly average" cooking and sushi that fits the bill when you want a "quick dinner after catching a movie down the street"; "rushed" service "without a smile" and digs that could bear some "remodeling" prompt many to opt for takeout.

	FOOD	DECOR	SERVICE	COST

Z Ibiza *Ⓩ Spanish* — 27 | 21 | 23 | $49
New Haven | 39 High St. (bet. Chapel & Crown Sts.) | 203-865-1933 |
www.ibizanewhaven.com

Z Ibiza Tapas *Spanish*
Hamden | 1832 Dixwell Ave. (Robert St.) | 203-909-6512 |
www.ibizatapaswinebar.com

At this "classy" New Haven Spanish, the tapas and tasting menus
are "exotic and yet mainstream", complemented by an "ample" wine
list and served by an "attentive" staff in a "contemporary" setting;
meanwhile, its "non-tweedy" Hamden offspring is an "excellent addition" to an otherwise "run-down retail" district, offering the same
"fabulous" flavors as the mother ship with a "more casual flair" and
more affordable price points, though some caution it "does get
loud" and no reservations can mean "long lines on weekends."

Il Castello *Italian* — 24 | 19 | 25 | $54
Mamaroneck | 576 Mamaroneck Ave. (Waverly Ave.), NY |
914-777-2200 | www.ilcastellomenu.com

This "tiny" "jewel of a place" in Mamaroneck "packs a big punch"
with "delicious" "Northern Italian delicacies" and an "excellent wine
list" delivered via an "impeccable" staff; rich woods, chandeliers
and "civil sound levels" provide an "impress-a-date" setting at a cost
that's "not that expensive" for the neighborhood.

Il Palio *Ⓩ Italian* — 24 | 24 | 24 | $51
Shelton | Corporate Towers | 5 Corporate Dr. (Bridgeport Ave.) |
203-944-0770 | www.ilpalioct.com

Housed in a "magnificent building", this "luxe" Northern Italian
"makes you feel thousands of miles from" the Shelton "corporate
park" where it's located, and "often delivers" on its "grandiose
ambitions", with "excellent" cuisine, an "extensive wine list" and
"exceptional" service in a "warm, friendly" atmosphere; though
a few cynics sniff it's "not worth the money" unless it's "on
someone else's expense account", others hail it as a "special
place for special occasions."

Il Sogno *Italian/Mediterranean* — 24 | 19 | 23 | $49
Port Chester | 316 Boston Post Rd. (S. Regent St.), NY | 914-937-7200 |
www.ilsognony.com

Still somewhat under the radar, this Port Chester "sleeper" is an
"unexpected find" for "excellent" Italian-Med cuisine (including
"wonderful specials") set down in a "sleek", "subdued" interior
of stone and wood; given the "first-rate" service from a
"passionate" staff, many don't mind if it's "a few dollars more"
than the competition.

Imperial Wok *Chinese/Japanese* — 17 | 15 | 17 | $28
North White Plains | 736 N. Broadway (bet. McDougal Dr. & Palmer Ave.),
NY | 914-686-2700

"No surprises", just a "giant menu" of "typical" Chinese and Japanese
"favorites" served up in "large portions" keeps this North White
Plains "neighborhood" "standby" "bustling"; sure, the "decor could

use improvement" but "reasonable" prices make it "worth a visit" or a call for "speedy delivery."

Infinity Hall & Bistro 🅂 🅼 *American* ▽ 20 | 22 | 20 | $43

Norfolk | Infinity Music Hall | 20 Greenwoods Rd. W. (bet. John J. Curtis & Shepard Rds.) | 860-542-5531 | www.infinityhall.com

Fans sing the praises of this "surprisingly good" American bistro "attached to an incredible music venue" in a historic Norfolk building in a "bucolic setting in the North Litchfield Hills", where "pre-concert" dining is the default option, though insiders insist the menu offerings are "creative enough to warrant a visit on a non-show night"; but critics caution if you're there for a performance, "leave lots of time", for "slo-ow" service can lead to waits as "never-ending" as the name.

Inn at Newtown *American* 18 | 18 | 19 | $39

Newtown | Inn at Newtown | 19 Main St. (Church Hill Rd.) | 203-270-1876 | www.theinnatnewtown.com

Set in a "lovely country inn" in the center of Newtown, this New American offers "consistently fine food" featuring local and organic meats and produce that'll "fulfill your comfort food cravings" and "attentive, not intrusive" service, and you can have a "quiet dinner in the main dining room", "savor a drink by the fireplace in the lounge" or revel in the "hustle and bustle" of the taproom, where live music is performed; skeptics sniff it's a "decent dining experience, but not exceptional."

Irving Farm 19 | 12 | 16 | $17
Coffee House *Coffeehouse/Sandwiches*

Millerton | 44 Main St. (Dutchess Ave.), NY | 518-789-2020 | www.irvingfarm.com

"Everything you want a local coffeehouse to be", this "popular" Millerton "staple" serves "really nice sandwiches", soups, salads and "fine pastries", along with "excellent coffees" – even the "plain ol' joe is delightful"; it "fits the bill" whether you "snag a comfy couch" and "lounge" in the "eccentric space", "grab a bite" before a movie next door or opt for a light dinner on Friday or Saturday night.

🅩 Isabelle et Vincent 🅼 *Bakery/French* 27 | 22 | 22 | $19

Fairfield | 1903 Post Rd. (bet. Bungalow Ave. & Granville St.) | 203-292-8022 | www.isabelleetvincent.com

"Quiet your inner expat" at this "heavenly" patisserie that's a "virtual sensory voyage to Paris" with its "immense selection" of "exquisite" breads and pastries and "world-class" chocolates; Strasbourg natives Isabelle and Vincent Koenig "greet you with a warm smile" in the "tiny" bakery, and while it's "not cheap", most agree "France's loss is Fairfield's gain."

It's Only Natural *Health Food* 20 | 18 | 21 | $24

Middletown | Main Street Mkt. | 386 Main St. (bet. Court St. & Dingwall Dr.) | 860-346-9210 | www.ionrestaurant.com

This veteran health-fooder and "vegan heaven" in Middletown is "better than most" meatless eateries declare fans; somewhat "upscale" flesh- and fish-free fare is served in a "charming, eclectic" setting with a "soothing" vibe, and "even non-vegetarians" will appreciate the "nice" outdoor deck in the summer.

Jaipore Royal Indian *Indian*
23 | 19 | 21 | $33

Brewster | 280 Rte. 22 N. (3 mi. off I-684, exit 8), NY | 845-277-3549 | www.fineindiandining.com

"An oasis of fine Indian dining", this "elegant" Brewster "find" dispenses "well-spiced" "regional specialties" in a "charming" "Victorian house" that "adds to the experience"; a "gracious" staff that will "help newcomers" plus "moderate prices" and a "wow"-worthy buffet" add to the "good karma."

Jasper White's
Summer Shack *New England/Seafood*
21 | 16 | 19 | $40

Uncasville | Mohegan Sun Casino | 1 Mohegan Sun Blvd. (bet. Rtes. 2 & 32) | 860-862-9500 | www.summershackrestaurant.com

For finatics, the "fresh", "well-prepared" seafood (including a pan-fried lobster that's "heaven" on a plate) at this casino piscatorium is the "highlight of a trip to Mohegan Sun", and many who find the "loud", "cavernous" room "overwhelming" opt to dine at the "huge bar" – just "plan to fight for a seat" on weekends; critics, though, call the menu a "crapshoot" befitting a gambling house, with a "few winners and lots of losers."

🅩 Jean-Louis ⑤ *French*
28 | 24 | 25 | $75

Greenwich | 61 Lewis St. (bet. Greenwich Ave. & Mason St.) | 203-622-8450 | www.restaurantjeanlouis.com

"Food heaven" is what fans call chef-owner Jean-Louis Gerin's Greenwich French thanks to his "extraordinary" cuisine, "prepared with art, professionalism and love"; add an "excellent wine list", "impeccable" service and a "lovely", "sophisticated" setting, and it's a "superb" package; P.S. those who can "only afford to go there once a decade" will welcome the prix fixe lunch ($29) and dinner ($69).

Jeffrey's *American/Continental*
26 | 22 | 23 | $46

Milford | 501 New Haven Ave. (Old Gate Ln.) | 203-878-1910 | www.jeffreysofmilford.com

For a "special night out", fans head to this "awesome upscale" Milford establishment for "inventive", "well-executed" Continental-New American cuisine served by a staff that "aims to please" in "classy" surroundings; although some critics are cool to the "pseudo-Tuscan" decor, many say the outdoor deck overlooking a marsh is "dreamy in summertime."

Jeff's Cuisine ⓜ *BBQ/Southern*
25 | 9 | 19 | $21

South Norwalk | South Norwalk Plaza | 54 N. Main St. (bet. Ann & Marshall Sts.) | 203-852-0041 | www.jeffscuisine.com

"Bring your wet naps" to this South Norwalk joint where 'cuennoisseurs "end up stuffed, satisfied and sticky" after "gorging" on the "knockout", "real-deal" BBQ and Southern victuals; so maybe it's "not a place for a first date", but "jolly" owner Jeff "makes you feel like you're in his home" and "may even dance with you" when the "amazing blues band" is playing in the bar.

J. Gilbert's *Southwestern/Steak* | 25 | 22 | 23 | $46 |

Glastonbury | 185 Glastonbury Blvd. (Main St.) | 860-659-0409 | www.jgilberts.com

The "finely prepared" steaks that "melt in your mouth", "excellent" wine list, "efficient" service and "warm, upscale" surroundings at this Glastonbury Southwestern meatery link are "what you'd expect from a high-end steakhouse", and there's a "lively bar scene" to boot; a few find it "too expensive for a chain" and "a little heavy in the old-boy tradition", but many others regard it as a "go-to place" for "business dinners" and "special occasions."

Joe's American Bar & Grill *American* | 15 | 16 | 18 | $29 |

Fairfield | 750 Post Rd. (Eliot Pl.) | 203-319-1600 | www.joesamerican.com

You "always know what to expect" at this Fairfield American chain link: "reliable", "classic" "upscale pub food" (like "good burgers") doled out in "generous portions" and listed on a menu featuring "choices for the whole family" and "decent prices"; the "comfortable", "informal", usually "crowded" environs all offer "social" bars and service that "tries hard to be attentive and generally succeeds", and some even have "nice patios" too.

John Harvard's Brew House *Pub Food* | 16 | 17 | 17 | $25 |

Manchester | 1487 Pleasant Valley Rd. (Buckland Ave.) | 860-644-2739 | www.johnharvards.com

See review in The Berkshires Directory.

John-Michael's Ⓜ *European* | 24 | 25 | 23 | $62 |

North Salem | Purdys Homestead | 100 Titicus Rd. (Rte. 22), NY | 914-277-2301 | www.johnmichaelsrestaurant.com

"A special place" for "romantic" dining, this "charming, old" North Salem "farmhouse" (the historic Purdys Homestead) provides a "comfortable" setting for "innovative" chef John-Michael Hamlet's "exceptional" European repertoire, which comes "amazingly presented" and professionally served; factor in "blazing fireplaces", and it's a "winter delight" whose "high prices" are "well worth it."

Johnny Ad's ⵰ *American* | 21 | 9 | 10 | $20 |

Old Saybrook | 910 Boston Post Rd. (Ledge Rd.) | 860-388-4032 | www.johnnyads.com

"Nothing fancy" but "perfect for what it is", this "roadside stand" in Old Saybrook serves "tasty, fresh" seafood, including "buttery lobster rolls" and some of the "best fried clams in the area", on "paper plates" in the "double-wide" dining room or "picnic tables" outside; "fast" service adds to its "good value."

Johnny Rockets *Burgers* | 16 | 16 | 16 | $18 |

Milford | Connecticut Post Mall | 1201 Boston Post Rd. (Cedarhurst Ln.) | 203-878-4220

(continued)

(continued)

Johnny Rockets

South Windsor | Evergreen Walk | 101 Evergreen Way (Tamarack Ave.) | 860-432-0048

Uncasville | Mohegan Sun Casino | 1 Mohegan Sun Blvd. (bet. Rtes. 2 & 32) | 860-862-3797 ●

www.johnnyrockets.com

"Classic burgers", "malted milkshakes" and a "big helping of nostalgia" are the bait at these "'50s-style" diners where "singing waiters and waitresses" dole out "good old American food" to "children and the young at heart"; while "jukebox tunes are a bonus", critics call the offerings "so-so" and the prices "positively 21st-century."

John's Café   *American/Mediterranean*   23 | 18 | 21 | $45

Woodbury | 693 Main St. S. (Rte. 64) | 203-263-0188 | www.johnscafe.com

"Creative and fresh", but "not fussed up", the New American–Med cuisine "attracts new customers as well as regulars" to this "quaint New England" bistro in Woodbury, where a "friendly" staff provides "prompt" service in a "cozy", "at-home" setting; critics report that the "small" digs can get "loud", and others fret that it's "getting a little pricey", but most feel it's "definitely worth a trip."

Joseph's Steakhouse   *Steak*   24 | 21 | 25 | $62

Bridgeport | 360 Fairfield Ave. (Lafayette Blvd.) | 203-337-9944 | www.josephssteakhouse.com

Carnivores crow this steakhouse is "as close to Peter Luger's as you can get" in Bridgeport ("except they take plastic"), where "seasoned", "friendly" waiters deliver "terrific" porterhouse steaks and "huge" sides in a dark-wood, exposed-brick setting; a few cynics dismiss it as a "wannabe" that "isn't close" to the original, "except for its prices", but many tout it as their "favorite restaurant for entertaining."

Kalbi House   *Korean*   19 | 11 | 18 | $34

White Plains | 291 Central Ave. (Wilson St.), NY | 914-328-0251

"You don't have to travel to Queens" for Korean food, thanks to this White Plains canteen that "satisfies cravings for bulgogi, warming tofu stews" and other "traditional" dishes in a bare-bones setting; despite a "language barrier", the servers are "helpful", although the relatively "high" tabs are a sore spot for those who call it "pricey for what you get."

Karamba Café   *Cuban/Pan-Latin*   ∇ 22 | 11 | 18 | $20

White Plains | 185 Main St. (Court St.), NY | 914-946-5550 | www.karambacafe.com

"One of the great bargains of Westchester" is this "authentico" White Plains Cuban–Pan-Latin purveying "filling", "unfussy" fare like arroz con pollo and Cuban sandwiches in portions that ensure "you won't go home hungry"; yes, the setting is strictly "no-frills", but the counter staff is "courteous", even amid the lunchtime mob "scene."

	FOOD	DECOR	SERVICE	COST

Karuta *Japanese*
▽ 18 | 12 | 18 | $33

New Rochelle | North Ridge Shopping Ctr. | 77 Quaker Ridge Rd. (North Ave.), NY | 914-636-6688

"The owner is a delight" at this New Rochelle Japanese that's "nice to have in the neighborhood" thanks to its "reasonably priced" sushi and cooked items; it's a mainstay for takeout, even if some shrug the food and setting are "nothing special."

Kazu *Japanese*
25 | 20 | 21 | $37

South Norwalk | 64 N. Main St. (West Ave.) | 203-866-7492 | www.kazusono.com

To sate that "spicy tuna roll craving", fans head to this "hip" South Norwalk Japanese for what they say is the "best sushi in Fairfield County", from a "reasonably priced" menu that also includes "sashimi on steroids" and "fresh, delicious" entrees; the staff is "friendly" while the setting is "pleasant, if basic", and its location next to Sono Cinema makes it a popular "family scene", so couples counselors advise "make your date a late-night one."

Kelly's Corner *Pub Food*
▽ 17 | 12 | 19 | $22

Brewster | 1625 Rte. 22 (Rte. 312), NY | 845-278-4297 | www.kellyscorner.com

A "local watering hole" that "doesn't try to be something it's not", this "traditional", Irish-accented American pub in Brewster dishes up "better-than-average" grub in "abundant" amounts at good-"value" prices; "friendly" staffers and a "casual" setting make it "great for kids" too, but "go early, it fills up" fast "at prime time."

King & I Ⓜ *Thai*
24 | 16 | 19 | $30

Bridgeport | Beardsley Park Plaza | 545 Broadbridge Rd. (Huntington Tpke.) | 203-374-2081

Fairfield | 260 Post Rd. (Shoreham Village Dr.) | 203-256-1664 | www.kingandict.com

"Yul love" this Thai duo in Bridgeport and Fairfield for its "excellent" fare, including a "wonderful selection of curries", et cetera, and "friendly, helpful" service; their strip-mall locations notwithstanding, both are "nice-looking", and while a few fret that "prices have gone up", they still offer one of the "best lunch specials around."

Kira Sushi *Japanese*
23 | 14 | 20 | $35

Armonk | Armonk Town Ctr. | 575 Main St. (School St.), NY | 914-765-0800

The "wide range" of "original", "fantastically fresh" sushi and specialty rolls may just "spoil you for anywhere else" at this "casual" Armonk Japanese; service can be "brusque" and the strip-mall setting is "nothing to write home about", but the fare's "well priced" so it's about "as good as it gets in the 'burbs."

Kisco Kosher *Deli*
17 | 10 | 15 | $25

White Plains | 230 E. Post Rd. (bet. Mamaroneck Ave. & S. B'way), NY | 914-948-6600 | www.kiscokosher.com

"Overstuffed sandwiches", matzo-ball soup and other "traditional" kosher comestibles turn up at this "reliable" White Plains deli and catering outfit serving the area for over 30 years; decor is nonexistent and the food's "a few kreplach from perfection" (and not cheap either), but when you "need a fix", it's one of the "only games in town."

Kit's Thai Kitchen *Thai*   21 | 12 | 18 | $25

Stamford | Turn of the River Shopping Ctr. | 927 High Ridge Rd. (Cedar Heights Rd.) | 203-329-7800 | www.kitsthaikitchen.com

"When the Thai craving hits", aficionados head to this "fast and friendly" Stamford strip-maller, aka "Bangkok on a budget", turning out "plentiful" portions of "fresh", "addictive" fare that "packs a punch" ("if it says it's hot, it's hot!"); many find the space "cramped" and "not terribly inviting", and liken dining on the outdoor patio to "eating in a roadway", which may help explain why it does such "lively take-out business."

Kobis Japanese Steak House *Japanese*   22 | 21 | 21 | $30

Fairfield | 451 Kings Hwy. E. (bet. Jennings Rd. & Shepard St.) | 203-610-6888

Shelton | 514 Bridgeport Ave. (bet. Todd Rd. & Woodland Park) | 203-929-8666 | www.kobisrestaurant.com

"Kids love" these Japanese steakhouses in Fairfield and Shelton, where the teppanyaki chefs "always put on a good show" at the "hibachi" grills and indoor koi ponds also entertain; "friendly" service is another plus, but some purists demur at the "unusual" sushi combinations and find the fare in general "nothing special."

Kona Grill *American/Asian*   17 | 19 | 18 | $33

Stamford | Stamford Town Ctr. | 230 Tresser Blvd. (bet. Atlantic St. & Greyrock Pl.) | 203-324-5700 | www.konagrill.com

"Kids and parents love the big fish tank" behind the sushi bar in the "large", aquatic-themed space of this Stamford American-Asian chain link, which also boasts a "hopping" outdoor patio and an "unusually friendly" staff; happy hour offers "some of the best deals around", drawing a "professional crowd" into the mix, and while a few pan the fare as "uninspired" and overpriced", others deem the sushi "excellent" and the rest of the menu "better than expected."

Koo *Japanese*   23 | 18 | 19 | $47

Danbury | 29 E. Pembroke Rd. (Hayestown Rd.) | 203-739-0068 | www.koodanbury.com

Rye | 17 Purdy Ave. (2nd St.), NY | 914-921-9888 | www.koorestaurant.com

Acolytes insists there's "lots to coo about" at these separately owned Japanese jewel boxes in Rye and Danbury, from the "undeniably fresh", "exotic" sushi like "works of art" to the servers who "anticipate your needs"; given the "tony" addresses and "stylish" clientele, the "exceptionally high" prices should come as no surprise.

Kotobuki Ⓜ *Japanese*   24 | 12 | 21 | $36

Stamford | 457 Summer St. (bet. Broad & North Sts.) | 203-359-4747 | www.kotobukijapaneserestaurant.com

Chef-owner Masanori Sato "must have his own boat" to get such "fabulous fresh fish" marvel mavens of this Downtown Stamford spot serving some of the "most authentic sushi and Japanese food in the region"; sure, some find the digs "dreary" and "there are fancier places" around, but the owner and his family "treat you like family" and the "price is right", so "don't let the appearance put you off."

Kudeta *Asian*   21 | 25 | 20 | $41

New Haven | 27 Temple St. (N. Frontage Rd.) | 203-562-8844 |
www.kudetanewhaven.com

"Color-shifting mood light", "sexy decor" and a "techno beat" may set the tone at this New Haven Asian fusion (which morphs into a "nightclub after hours"), but its "large, varied menu" with "numerous vegetarian options" is a "pleasant surprise" to many; detractors, though, say the "snazzy" "Las Vegas atmosphere" can't disguise what they describe as "so-so" fare and "way too slow" service.

Kujaku *Japanese*   ▽ 18 | 14 | 18 | $36

Stamford | 84 W. Park Pl. (Summer St.) | 203-357-0281 |
www.kujakustamford.com

While the "hokey teppanyaki" show in the "back room" "can be fun for the kids" at this Downtown Stamford Japanese, many grown-ups opt for the front where they can order "very fresh" sushi, as well as "decent" cooked fare such as tempura; a few dismiss it as "mediocre", but to others the "more than reasonable" prices, "especially at lunch", make it "a place to recommend."

Kumo *Japanese*   ▽ 20 | 19 | 20 | $32

Hamden | 218 Skiff St. (Whitney Ave.) | 203-281-3166
New Haven | 7 Elm St. (State St.) | 203-562-6688
www.kumojapaneserestaurant.com

While "fresh sushi is the draw" for some, others "clamor for the 'hibachi' (teppanyaki) tables" at this Japanese duo in Hamden and New Haven, where "dirt-cheap" specials and "attentive" service add to its allure; skeptics, though, "wouldn't go out of their way" for what they deem "serviceable but undistinguished" eats.

La Bocca *Italian*   23 | 19 | 21 | $46

White Plains | Renaissance Corporate Ctr. | 8 Church St.
(bet. Hamilton Ave. & Main St.), NY | 914-948-3281 |
www.laboccaristorante.com

"Tucked away" inside the Renaissance Corporate Center in Downtown White Plains is this "cozy" Italian restaurant where an "attentive" staff ferries "authentic", "mouthwatering" fare, "much of it from the North"; it's not cheap, but pays off with a "warm, inviting" ambiance that's equally suited to "work lunches" and "date night."

La Bretagne ⊠ *French*   24 | 16 | 25 | $54

Stamford | 2010 W. Main St. (bet. Harvard Ave. & Havemeyer Ln.) |
203-324-9539 | www.labretagnerestaurant.com

"Just like the French restaurant your parents took you to", this country French in Stamford presents "well-prepared" classics such as duck à l'orange carved tableside and Dover sole "to die for", a "topnotch" wine selection, "attentive service" and a quiet setting that enables you to "carry on a conversation"; most agree the room looks "tired", but defenders declare "whiners should get past the age of the patrons" and appreciate what they call one of the "best deals in town."

🅩 La Crémaillère 🅜 *French*

27 | 26 | 26 | $81

Bedford | 46 Bedford-Banksville Rd. (Round House Rd.), NY | 914-234-9647 | www.cremaillere.com

"Memorable evenings" transpire at this "gold standard" of "fine dining" in Bedford, where "superb" "traditional" French cuisine is elevated by an "extensive wine cellar" and "outstanding" service in a "beautiful" farmhouse that "oozes charm"; "such excellence comes at a price", but for a "special treat" "you can't ask for much more"; P.S. jackets suggested.

La Herradura *Mexican*

18 | 18 | 18 | $26

Mamaroneck | 406 Mamaroneck Ave. (Spencer Pl.), NY | 914-630-2377
New Rochelle | 1323 North Ave. (Northfield Rd.), NY | 914-235-3769
New Rochelle | 563 Main St. (Center Ave.), NY | 914-235-2055

For "hearty plates" of "down-to-earth" Mexican cooking, devotees deem this "colorful", casual chainlet a downright "bargain"; "spiffy", "Aztec-inspired" digs and "service with a smile" seal the deal and make it a standby for families.

La Manda's ⊄ *Italian*

19 | 6 | 17 | $30

White Plains | 251 Tarrytown Rd. (Dobbs Ferry Rd./Rte. 100B), NY | 914-684-9228

There's a "homey, neighborhood feel" to this "old-fashioned, no-nonsense" "red-sauce joint" in White Plains that's been cooking up the "classics" – including "addictive", "thin-crust" pizzas – "with a practiced hand" since 1947; its longevity and low costs have most overlooking the "dumpy", "cafeteria"-style dining room and occasionally "attitude"-laden service; P.S. cash only.

La Paella 🅜 *Spanish*

25 | 19 | 22 | $44

Norwalk | 44 Main St. (Burnell Blvd.) | 203-831-8636 | www.lapaellatapaswinebarrestaurant.com

A "real find hiding in plain sight", this storefront Spanish in Norwalk's Wall Street area is "worth the trip" for "fantastic" tapas, "excellent" paella and a "reasonably priced" selection of Spanish wines; chef-owner Jaime Lopez is a "terrific host" and his "friendly" staff helps create a "warm, inviting" ambiance in the candlelit dining room; one caveat: the eponymous signature dish is priced per person.

🅩 La Panetière *French*

27 | 27 | 27 | $78

Rye | 530 Milton Rd. (Oakland Beach Ave.), NY | 914-967-8140 | www.lapanetiere.com

"Decidedly elegant", this "stately" Rye manor is "worth spiffing up for" thanks to its "divine" "haute" New French cuisine that's "exquisitely presented" and served with "wonderful wines" by a "flawless" staff; factor in a "fairy-book" setting that "transports you to Provence", and it's a perfect place to "drop a bundle", although the lunchtime prix fixe is an absolute "bargain"; P.S. jackets suggested.

La Piccola Casa *Italian*

∇ 21 | 15 | 20 | $46

Mamaroneck | James Fenimore Cooper Hse. | 410 W. Boston Post Rd. (Fenimore Rd.), NY | 914-777-3766 | www.lapiccolacasa.com

Occupying a "cute location overlooking the harbor", this Mamaroneck Italian delivers "good" Northern-style cuisine like veal chops and tortellini Bolognese; "attentive" servers who are "happy to accommodate" add to the appeal, although a few find tabs a touch "overpriced" for the area.

Larchmont Tavern *American*

17 | 14 | 19 | $26

Larchmont | 104 Chatsworth Ave. (bet. Boston Post Rd. & Palmer Ave.), NY | 914-834-9821 | www.larchmonttavern.com

A "longtime local tradition", this Larchmont tavern has been slinging "brews, burgers" and other "stick-to-your-ribs" American grub since 1933; it's "noisy, crowded" and perhaps the fare's "nothing special", but populist prices and a "warm", "family-friendly" atmosphere make it a "hometown favorite" nonetheless.

La Riserva *Italian*

21 | 18 | 22 | $43

Larchmont | 2382 Boston Post Rd. (Deane Pl.), NY | 914-834-5584 | www.lariservarestaurant.com

"Lots of customers" appreciate this Larchmont Northern Italian offering "solid", "classic" fare in "enormous portions"; it's not inexpensive, but the "gracious" owner "always makes you feel welcome", the staff "knows you by name" and it's an old NY Yankee favorite so "you might just run into Joe Torre" too.

NEW La Scarbitta Ristorante Ⓜ *Italian*

- | - | - | M

Mamaroneck | 215 Halstead Ave. (Ward Ave.), NY | 914-777-1667

Rosa Merenda left Spadaro in New Rochelle to open this midpriced Mamaroneck BYO Italian with a similarly homey vibe; the moderately priced menu focuses on regional peasant cuisine like ricotta gnocchi and wild boar capped with homemade desserts.

La Taverna Ⓜ *Italian*

21 | 13 | 21 | $38

Norwalk | Broad River Shopping Ctr. | 130 New Canaan Ave. (I-95, exit 15) | 203-849-8879

An "unexpected delight" in the Broad River section of Norwalk, this "quintessential" family-run Northern Italian is "popular with the neighborhood" thanks to "reliable", "well-priced" fare and "attentive owners" who "make you feel at home"; though some say the digs seem "a little run-down", the "good value" it offers makes it an "easy choice" for many.

La Tavola Ⓩ *Italian*

∇ 26 | 21 | 24 | $43

Waterbury | 702 Highland Ave. (bet. Bennett & Wilkenda Aves.) | 203-755-2211 | www.latavolaristorante.com

"Not your grandma's Italian restaurant", this "hip, happening" Waterbury Italian is "all the rage" among area foodies thanks to chef Nicola Mancini's "exceptional" cuisine with a "modern flair", which is served in a "cool", "trendy" space; while some report it "gets very

	FOOD	DECOR	SERVICE	COST

loud" "when it's busy", it's quickly become the "favorite" of many; there's live music on Wednesday nights.

La Villetta �’ *Italian* — 24 | 17 | 23 | $52

Larchmont | 7 Madison Ave. (N. Chatsworth Ave.), NY | 914-833-9416

On the scene for over a decade, this "clubby" Larchmont Italian from father-and-son team Francesco and Pasquale Coli is a find for "excellent", "expensive" cuisine "among the best in the area" set down by a staff that "makes you feel very much cared for"; perhaps the "tight" seating is "a little too cozy", although a recent redo may remedy that.

Layla's Falafel *Lebanese* — 22 | 7 | 18 | $16

Fairfield | 2088 Black Rock Tpke. (Stillson Rd.) | 203-384-0100
Stamford | 245 Main St. (bet. Atlantic St. & Washington Blvd.) | 203-316-9041 �’
Stamford | 936 High Ridge Rd. (Cedar Heights Rd.) | 203-461-8004
www.laylasfalafel.com

"Fresh, flavorful falafel", "shawarma that rocks" and other "authentic, homey dishes", including "plenty for vegetarians to choose from", make this trio of affordable Lebanese "holes-in-the-wall" an "outstanding find"; the "staff is extremely friendly", though some find the service "less than ebullient", and most consider the "no-frills" appearance "irrelevant", since it's "really a take-out place", and besides, "great decor would be asking too much for this price."

La Zingara *Italian* — 26 | 22 | 24 | $43

Bethel | 8 P.T. Barnum Sq. (Greenwood Ave.) | 203-744-7500 | www.lazingararistorante.com

Fans sing the praises of this Italian in "out-of-the-way" Bethel, where the "perfectly prepared" cuisine featuring produce from its own organic farm and local purveyors is backed by "superb wines by the glass"; insiders also tout the prix fixe brunch with live jazz and unlimited Bellinis or Bloody Marys, while "top-notch" service and a "relaxed", rustic setting seal the deal; closed Tuesdays.

Lazy Boy Saloon ☻ *Pub Food* — 19 | 13 | 15 | $27

White Plains | 154 Mamaroneck Ave. (bet. E. Post Rd. & Maple Ave.), NY | 914-761-0272 | www.lazyboysaloon.com

A "mecca for craft beer enthusiasts", this White Plains pub boasts 400 bottles, 40 draughts, plus wings and other "decent" bar bites; "spotty service" and "crowded, noisy" digs come with the territory, and unless you're meeting for a drink or watching "a big game", some diners declare it "not worth the trouble."

Le Château Ⓜ *French* — 25 | 27 | 25 | $69

South Salem | 1410 Rte. 35 (Rte. 123), NY | 914-533-6631 | www.lechateauny.com

An "elegant" mansion with "spectacular" Hudson Valley vistas forms the "amazing" setting for this South Salem French where supporters savor "exceptional" "classic haute cuisine" and selections from the "great wine list", all "impeccably served"; a minority is "underwhelmed" by the experience, but it remains a "special-occasion" standby that's "commensurately pricey"; P.S. jackets suggested.

⚡ Le Farm 🏷️Ⓜ *American* | 27 | 20 | 23 | $61 |

Westport | 256 Post Rd. E. (bet. Compo Rd. & Imperial Ave.) | 203-557-3701 | www.lefarmwestport.com

At his high-end Westport New American, chef-owner Bill Taibe "wows you from start to finish" with his "fantastic", "fresh, seasonal" cuisine that demonstrates his "dedication to local producers"; the staff is "friendly and helpful", and the "cozy" space has a "farmhouse feel", so while it may be "oh so trendy", most agree this "winner" "walks the walk."

Le Fontane Ristorante Ⓜ *Italian* | 22 | 20 | 20 | $43 |

Katonah | 137 Rte. 100 (Rte. 139), NY | 914-232-9619 | www.lefontane.net

This Katonah Italian "price performer" supplies "satisfying", "if predictable", Southern-style cooking in a "quiet", "relaxed" setting overseen by a "gracious host" who "remembers you by name"; the mood is "warm", and best of all, if you "score a table outside in summer" you'll "feel like you're in Venice."

Legal Sea Foods *Seafood* | 19 | 18 | 19 | $43 |

White Plains | City Ctr. | 5 Mamaroneck Ave. (bet. Main St. & Martine Ave.), NY | 914-390-9600 | www.legalseafoods.com

Enjoy some of "Boston's best seafood in your backyard" via this "high-quality" chain link in White Plains that's "deservedly popular" for its "always fresh" offerings, including "legendary New England clam chowder"; though it's a bit "basic" for the "upscale" prices and the "modern" decor isn't for everyone, the staff is "accommodating" and the gluten-free menu earns it "huge props."

Lenny & Joe's Fish Tale *Seafood* | 23 | 11 | 17 | $24 |

Madison | 1301 Boston Post Rd. (Hammonasset Connector) | 203-245-7289

Westbrook | 86 Boston Post Rd. (bet. Grove Beach Rd. & Linden Ave.) | 860-669-0767
www.ljfishtale.com

A pair of "Shoreline mainstays", these "basic fish shacks" serve "bangin' seafood", including the "gold standard" of lobster rolls; at the Madison BYO sibling, diners with "sand between their toes" "grab some clam strips" at the counter, bring their own beer or wine and sit outside, where kids can ride the carousel, while the larger and "slightly more upscale" Westbrook location has table service and serves alcohol.

Lenny's Indian Head Inn *Seafood* | 21 | 13 | 17 | $29 |

Branford | 205 S. Montowese St. (2 mi. south of Main St.) | 203-488-1500 | www.lennysnow.com

This "atmospheric shore tavern by the moor" in Branford serves "no-frills" "fresh seafood" in a "rustic" setting with a "large" dining room, cozy pub (where you'll find a "boisterous" "bar scene") and back

FOOD | DECOR | SERVICE | COST

porch overlooking Sybil Creek; though some report "unpredictable" service, the "kid-friendly" atmosphere finds favor with families.

Leon's *Italian*

18 | 21 | 17 | $42

New Haven | 501 Long Wharf Dr. (Water St.) | 203-562-5366 | www.leonsrestaurant.com

Fans of this "upscale" New Haven Italian "standby" laud its "new, beautiful location" overlooking Long Island Sound as a "splendid setting" for its "longtime favorite dishes" such as the gypsy chicken and other "red-sauce classics"; some stalwarts, though, lament it's "not the same as the original", calling the fare "variable" and the service "haphazard", and accuse it of "living on its reputation."

☑ Le Petit Cafe Ⓜ *French*

29 | 24 | 28 | $56

Branford | 225 Montowese St. (Main St.) | 203-483-9791 | www.lepetitcafe.net

"As good as it gets" in Connecticut, Roy Ip's "charming" Branford bistro was voted the state's No. 1 for Food thanks to his "brilliant" cuisine that'll "leave you speechless" on a four-course prix fixe menu "with plenty of choices"; the "delightful" toque "greets you at the door" and he and his "friendly, knowledgeable staff" make you "feel like a treasured guest" in the "attractive", "intimate" space, which is all the more reason many deem it one of the "best dining values in the U.S."; P.S. only two seatings per night.

Le Provençal Bistro *French*

23 | 19 | 22 | $51

Mamaroneck | 436 Mamaroneck Ave. (bet. Mt. Pleasant & Palmer Aves.), NY | 914-777-2324 | www.provencalbistro.com

Just like "your favorite Parisian bistro", this "warm", "cozy" French in Mamaroneck serves up "delicious", "authentic" cuisine in a "nicely appointed" dining room tended by a "lovely", "skillful" staff; tabs can be expensive and weekends are crowded, but on the whole it "never disappoints"; P.S. Thursday's mussels special is a "bargain."

L'Escale *French*

23 | 25 | 21 | $64

Greenwich | Delamar Hotel | 500 Steamboat Rd. (I-95, exit 3) | 203-661-4600 | www.lescalerestaurant.com

"Class distinction is alive and well" at this "gorgeous", "upscale" waterside French in Greenwich's Delamar Hotel, where "hedge-funders and wannabes" sit outside and "watch the yachts dock" in the harbor in the warmer months, and warm up by the wood-burning stove in the "elegant", candlelit dining room in winter; the "tasty", "inventive" fare is served by a "well-trained" staff, though some find it "aloof" and "pretentious", while others chafe at the "decibel level" and the "bumper-to-bumper" bar scene at night.

Lime *Health Food*

23 | 11 | 20 | $27

Norwalk | 168 Main Ave. (Center Ave.) | 203-846-9240 | www.limerestaurant.com

While meatless mavens call this "whole-earth" health-food institution in Norwalk a "vegetarian must" for its "fresh", "creative" flesh-free fare, carnivores can appreciate the signature steak Gorgonzola and "great" seafood offerings, all of which are backed by organic beers and wines; service is "friendly", but some report it can be "slow" when the "small" space gets "crowded" with "regulars", and others opine that the "old" digs "need a "face-lift."

Litchfield Saltwater Grille *American*   ▽ 20 | 19 | 16 | $47

Litchfield | 26 Commons Dr. (Rte. 202) | 860-567-4900 | www.litchfieldsaltwatergrille.org

"Although landlocked", this Litchfield American seafooder is a "keeper" for cognoscenti who commend its "well-prepared" fin fare and terra firma dishes that make "fine use of locally supplied products", complemented by a wine list of some 450 labels; the husband (chef)-and-wife (sommelier) team provides "above-average" service in a "lovely" setting with a "somewhat informal" vibe; P.S. the happy-hour menu offers some "great bargains", and there's also a dinner prix fixe on Tuesdays and Wednesdays.

Little Kitchen *Asian*   21 | 20 | 18 | $32

Westport | Compo Acres Shopping Ctr. | 423 Post Rd. E. (N. Compo Rd.) | 203-227-2547

Proving that "big flavors come from little kitchens", this Pan-Asian "polymath" in Westport turns out a "big choice" of "interesting, tasty" dishes "spanning sushi to massaman" in a "darkly lit", "dramatic black-and-red setting"; critics knock the "erratic" service and surmise "something was lost in translation" in the kitchen, but many others tout it as a "reliable standby" for a "casual dinner" and a "terrific lunch" option.

Little Mexican Cafe ● *Mexican*   21 | 13 | 19 | $27

New Rochelle | 581 Main St. (Centre Ave.), NY | 914-636-3926 | www.littlemexicancafe.com

"Never mind the bland decor" instruct enthusiasts of this "cute", "little" New Rochelle Mexican where the margaritas are "strong", the flavors are "authentic" and the "chunky" guacamole "couldn't be any fresher if you'd made it yourself"; on top of all that, prices are "very reasonable" too.

Little Pub *Pub Food*   23 | 20 | 20 | $27

Ridgefield | 59 Ethan Allen Hwy. (Rte. 102) | 203-544-9222 | www.littlepub.com

Since it opened in 2009, this public house in Ridgefield's Branchville section has been "packed from day one" thanks to an "extensive beer selection" that's a "joy" and pub grub that "rocks" ("awesome" burgers, "delectable" tuna tacos), although a few grouse that the "menu needs more British items" to keep it real; a "friendly" staff tends to a "happy" crowd in "cozy" digs with a fireplace and "heated porch", and while the "extremely small" space can mean long "waits" and a "packed" parking lot, most declare this one a "winner."

Little Thai Kitchen *Thai*   23 | 14 | 19 | $28

Darien | 4 West Ave. (Boston Post Rd.) | 203-662-0038

(continued)

(continued)
Little Thai Kitchen
Greenwich | 21 St. Roch Ave. (Gerry St.) | 203-622-2972
Little Buddha *Thai*
Stamford | 2270 Summer St. (Bridge St.) | 203-356-9166
Thai Spice *Thai*
Norwalk | 345 Main Ave. (Linden St.) | 203-846-3533
www.littlethaikitchen.com

The "go-to" to-go spots of many for "fresh", "tasty" Thai cusine at "reasonable" prices, these "teeny" "shoeboxes" are "big in flavor and value", with "great lunch specials" that are "perfect when you're not on an expense account"; the staff is "friendly", though seating is limited ("does this place have tables?"), and if you choose to dine in, caution cognoscenti, try to avoid "getting trampled to death by the evening take-out crowds"; Greenwich and Little Buddha in Stamford are BYO.

Liv's Oyster Bar *Seafood*
25 | 22 | 22 | $45

Old Saybrook | 166 Main St. (Maplewood St.) | 860-395-5577 | www.livsoysterbar.com

"Ooh-la-la oysters" from an "outstanding raw bar" highlight the menu at this "popular" "seafood-centric cafe" on Old Saybrook's main drag, which also offers plenty of "creative and expertly pre-pared" "fresh fish" specials at "reasonable prices" for those "not interested in sucking down a bivalve"; the owners keep a "watchful eye" on things while "cordial" servers provide "attentive" service in the "noisy" renovated movie theater setting that's "pleasant", "albeit not romantic."

Lolita Cocina & Tequila Bar ☽ *Mexican*
22 | 23 | 19 | $46

Greenwich | 230 Mill St. (bet. Henry & Water Sts.) | 203-813-3555 | www.lolitamexican.com

"Young hipsters" flock to Greenwich's Byram neighborhood to "see and be seen" (but not heard, with music at "dance-club noise level") at this "hoppin' spot" offering Mexican fare with "kitschy", "unusual twists"; a "fabulous tequila list" and an "intriguing bordello atmo-sphere" fuel the "dark", "sexy" vibe, so despite service that "can be spotty" and a check that's "pricey for what you get", most agree it's "so worth the trip."

Long Ridge Tavern *American*
14 | 19 | 16 | $38

Stamford | 2635 Long Ridge Rd. (Rte. 104) | 203-329-7818 | www.longridgetavern.com

This old converted barn on a Stamford back road with a "cozy fireplace" and "lots of antiques" just "screams out for some good down-home cooking", but while the American "tavern grub" "straight out of the '50s" "does the trick" for some, to others it seems as if "the chef is lost in the woods without a GPS"; still, "in an area with no restaurants" it's a "comfortable" "oasis" for many, with a "welcoming staff", live music on weekends and "pretty outdoor seating" in the warmer months.

Longwood Restaurant Ⓜ *American*   ▽ 18 | 22 | 21 | $48

Woodbury | Longwood Country Inn | 1204 Main St. S.
(bet. Mansion House Rd. & Woodside Circle) | 203-266-0800 |
www.longwoodcountryinn.com

Housed in a "romantic" circa-1789 inn graced with antiques and offering "nice rolling country views", this Traditional American in
Woodbury makes for a "pleasant dining" experience, offering "well-
prepared", though "not innovative" fare in a "pretty" room that's
"never crowded"; the service is "attentive" but some find the staff a
bit "overly casual and familiar" given the "upscale" tabs.

L'Orcio Ⓜ *Italian*   23 | 21 | 22 | $44

New Haven | 806 State St. (bet. Eld & Pearl Sts.) | 203-777-6670 |
www.lorcio.com

In a "town like New Haven", this Italian "stands out" with its "fabulous handmade pastas" and other "scrumptious" dishes, "interesting wines" and "ethereal desserts", served by a "gracious"
staff in a "cute" "townhouse" setting with a "cozy" bar; in summer, dining "under the trellis and hanging flowers" of the outdoor
patio is "heavenly."

Los Cabos *Mexican*   ▽ 15 | 12 | 18 | $28

Norwalk | 36 Westport Ave. (East Ave.) | 203-847-5711 |
www.loscabosmexicanfood.com

"Conveniently located" in Norwalk, this midpriced Mexican is a
"solid family-dining" option and a "fun after-work place" thanks to
"friendly" service, "standard" *comida* and "strong" drinks in a colorful, rustic setting; cynics sneer that the "franchisey" fare reminds
you you're a "long way from Cabo San Lucas."

Louis' Lunch Ⓧ Ⓜ ⊅ *Burgers*   22 | 11 | 12 | $12

New Haven | 261-263 Crown St. (bet. College & High Sts.) |
203-562-5507 | www.louislunch.com

Though the "brouhaha continues" over this New Haven cash-
only "landmark's" claim to being the "birthplace of the hamburger", most agree the taste of its "juicy" "works of art" (broiled on
a vertical spit and served on white toast) is "not to be contested";
seats are "sparse" in the "tiny" space where, insiders warn, you
"certainly don't get it your way" from the "sassy" staff ("do not dare
ask for ketchup"), and while some cynics sniff that the "lines are
longer than it deserves", they're clearly outvoted.

Luca Ristorante Italiano Ⓧ *Italian*   26 | 24 | 26 | $58

Wilton | 142 Old Ridgefield Rd. (Godfrey Pl.) | 203-563-9550 |
www.lucaristoranteitaliano.com

For "a little bit of Italy" in "sleepy" Downtown Wilton, *paesani* head
to Luca and Sandra Morrone's storefront "gem" where "sensational", "delectable delicacies" ("light, flavorful sauces", "superb
pastas"), "wonderful desserts" and a "strong wine list" are served
by a "friendly, professional" staff in an "attractive", "romantic" room
with "flattering lighting"; the tabs are "high-end" but most agree the
"quality justifies the cost."

| | FOOD | DECOR | SERVICE | COST |

Lucky's *Diner*
18 | 19 | 18 | $18

Stamford | 209 Bedford St. (bet. Broad & Spring Sts.) | 203-978-0268 | www.luckysrestaurant.net

"You'll feel like you jumped on Doc's time machine" and landed in the "'50s" at this "inexpensive" "burger joint of burger joints" in Downtown Stamford, slinging "juicy" hamburgers, "piping hot fries" and "thick, tasty" milkshakes in a "loud, bright" setting with juke-boxes "playing old-time rock 'n' roll"; the staff is "friendly", and though some dismiss the eats as "ordinary", others find it "fun for kids and unpretentious adults."

Luc's Café Ⓩ *French*
24 | 21 | 21 | $44

Ridgefield | 3 Big Shop Ln. (bet. Bailey Ave. & Main St.) | 203-894-8522 | www.lucscafe.com

For a "little bit of France" in Ridgefield, Francophiles head to this basement bistro for "authentic, rustic French cooking" served by a staff with "appropriately thick accents" (and, some say, "snotty" demeanors); once you get past the "long lines", you can rub elbows with celebs ("frequent Keith Richards sightings" are reported), but "don't stretch or you'll hit your neighbor" in the "noisy", "cavelike" space that makes the outdoor patio seem "especially nice in good weather."

Luigi's Ⓜ *Italian*
▽ 24 | 17 | 23 | $26

Old Saybrook | 1295 Boston Post Rd. (School House Rd.) | 860-388-9190

A "reliable winner", this "old-school" Italian in Old Saybrook "never disappoints" with its "superb", "traditional" fare served in a "re-laxed", "family-friendly" atmosphere; insiders report the "utilitar-ian" space is "always crowded", but the "warm" chef-owner and his "delightful" staff make sure "you will always get in."

Luna Pizza *Pizza*
21 | 11 | 18 | $19

Glastonbury | 88 Hebron Ave. (bet. Main St. & New London Tpke.) | 860-659-2135
Simsbury | Simsbury Commons | 530 Bushy Hill Rd. (Rte. 44) | 860-651-1820 | www.lunapizzasimsbury.com
West Hartford | 999 Farmington Ave. (Lasalle Rd.) | 860-233-1625 | www.lunapizzact.com

Piezani moon over the thin-crust pizzas with a "slight char" that gives them a "decidedly New Yawk air" at this "inexpensive" pizzeria trio run by "terrific owners"; expect to see "lots of small children" and "large parties" in the "casual" digs, which is why some prefer delivery, but a few homebodies complain of pies arriving "soggy and limp."

Lusardi's *Italian*
24 | 21 | 24 | $58

Larchmont | 1885 Palmer Ave. (bet. Chatsworth Ave. & Weaver St.), NY | 914-834-5555 | www.lusardislarchmont.com

"Still a standard-bearer for Westchester Italian", this "pricey" "class act" in Larchmont draws a "dressed-to-the-nines" crowd for "exem-plary", "modern" Med-inflected cooking backed by a 250-bottle wine list; even if the "elegant" environs can be "noisy and hectic", service is so "gracious" and "attentive" (especially if you're a regular) that it's "never a miss."

Mackenzie's Grill Room ● *Pub Food*

16 | **13** | **17** | **$29**

Old Greenwich | 148 Sound Beach Ave. (Webb Ave.) | 203-698-0223 | www.mackenziesgrillroom.com

A "throwback in chichi Old Greenwich", this public house close to the railroad station lures "weary commuters" and others with "enjoyable", "basic" American pub grub and a "wide range of beverages at the bar", all at "reasonable prices"; the staff is "friendly" and it's a "great place to watch the game", but critics carp at the "TVs blaring from all corners" and damn the digs as "dark and depressing"; P.S. live music on Thursdays is a plus.

Made In Asia *Asian*

21 | **17** | **20** | **$34**

Armonk | 454 Main St. (bet. Annadale St. & Orchard Dr.), NY | 914-730-3663 | www.madeinasiarestaurant.com

Once you get past the "unappealing" strip-mall exterior, you'll find a "consistent" kitchen at this "convenient" Armonk Pan-Asian proffering "fresh", "tasty" sushi rolls and cooked specialties; everyone likes the "reasonable" tabs and "efficient" service, and "tatami rooms" are a turn-on for groups too.

Maestro's *Italian*

▽ **20** | **13** | **21** | **$32**

New Rochelle | 1329 North Ave. (Quaker Ridge Rd.), NY | 914-636-6813

"Everyone should have a little trattoria like this" "red-sauce" standby in New Rochelle known for its "basic" Italian fare offering "very good bang for the buck"; "unpretentious" digs and a "warm" staff complete the package.

Mamma Francesca *Italian*

19 | **15** | **20** | **$31**

New Rochelle | 414 Pelham Rd. (bet. Meadow Ln. & Town Dock Rd.), NY | 914-636-1229 | www.mammafrancesca.com

The "quintessential local Italian", this "friendly" "little hideaway" in New Rochelle attracts lots of locals for their "weekly pasta fix" in portions "guaranteed" to ensure leftovers; its setting overlooking the marina affords water views, and you "can't beat the prices."

Mancuso's *Italian*

▽ **21** | **15** | **21** | **$29**

Fairfield | 601 Kings Hwy. E. (Fairchild Ave.) | 203-367-5359 | www.mancusos-restaurant.com

Proud "food snobs" and others overlook the "undistinguished" location in the "wrong part of Fairfield" and head to this "reasonably priced local favorite" for "stick-to-your-ribs" Italian fare "like mama used to make"; so maybe it's "not gourmet eating", but the "staff and owners treat you like family" and the "big portions" and weekday early-bird special offer "good value."

Manna Dew *Eclectic*

22 | **18** | **21** | **$42**

Millerton | 54 Main St. (Center St.), NY | 518-789-3570

Millerton locals convene at this "bustling bistro" for "imaginative", "well-prepared" Eclectic fare, whether in the "inviting bar", in the "cozy, country" dining room or on the "beautiful terrace" overlooking the garden, where many of the "fresh, local" ingredients are grown; a "welcoming" staff, "outstanding wines" and music on weekends help explain why it's so "popular."

Marc Charles Steakhouse ☒ *Steak*   20 | 18 | 19 | $72

Armonk | La Quinta Hotel | 94 Business Park Dr. (Bedford Rd.), NY | 914-273-2700 | www.marccharlessteakhouse.com

"Satisfactory" cuts come "cooked as requested" at this steakhouse in the Armonk La Quinta Hotel also putting out "decent" sides and "decadent" deserts in a white-tablecloth setting; a drop in ratings since the last Survey reveals it may be "a bit of a letdown" for some, and it's not inexpensive either.

Marianacci's ☒ *Italian*   ∇ 21 | 16 | 21 | $50

Port Chester | 24 Sherman St. (S. Regent St.), NY | 914-939-3450 | www.marianaccis.com

This circa-1950 Port Chester Italian "keeps on ticking" with "nicely prepared", "old-time" fare set down in a "comfortable" white linen-clad setting; tabs can feel a "little pricey", but service is "affable" and it fits the bill for an evening of "quiet dining."

Mario's Place *Italian/Steak*   19 | 12 | 18 | $34

Westport | 36 Railroad Pl. (Riverside Ave.) | 203-226-0308

This "old-school" Italian steakhouse across from the Westport train station is "always crowded" with "commuting regulars" and "characters" who tuck into "huge" steaks and "basic" eats in portions so big "you won't have to eat for a week"; if "you're not a regular, don't bother" caution critics, who also pan the "pedestrian cuisine" and "tired" decor, but defenders praise this "neighborhood clubhouse" where "all of life's problems and the modern world are left at the door."

Marisa's Ristorante *Italian*   18 | 16 | 21 | $34

Trumbull | 6540 Main St. (Governor Trumbull Way) | 203-459-4225 | www.marisastrumbull.com

The mood is "warm" and "boisterous" at this family-run Trumbull Italian where "service with a smile" and a menu of "reliable" "favorites" "keep the tables full" with "families" and groups of "friends"; critics, however, knock the "large" dining room's decor as "overstated" and the eats as "over the hill", while the "busy bar scene" prompts wags to warn "watch out for cougars" and other "prowling aged singles"; there's a DJ Thursdays–Saturdays.

Market Restaurant *American*   20 | 22 | 16 | $50

Stamford | 249 Main St. (bet. Clark St. & Washington Blvd.) | 203-348-8000 | www.marketstamford.com

Admirers aver this "sleek" and "sexy" New American is "as close to Manhattan as you're going to find" in Stamford, with its "flashy copper-and-earth-tone" interior boasting an open kitchen, a "seasonally changing menu" featuring "innovative dishes" and a 300-label wine list and creative cocktails that enable you to "get your drink on"; "overpriced" fume critics who describe the service as "uninspired" and the fare as just "ok", but many still recommend it for a "business lunch" or other "functional, workday-paced meal."

Mary Ann's *Tex-Mex*

| 15 | 12 | 16 | $26 |

Stamford | 184 Summer St. (bet. Broad St. & Tresser Blvd.) | 203-323-8900
Port Chester | 23½ N. Main St. (Westchester Ave.), NY | 914-939-8700
www.maryannsmexican.com

Families frequent these Tex-Mex cantinas in Port Chester and Stamford doling out "basic" eats with a moderately "healthy" bent in "kitschy", "pleasant-enough" environs; critics call the formula "tired" and the grub "generic at best", but at least "you won't be disappointed" by the "reasonable" prices; P.S. the Port Chester branch moved to new digs post-Survey.

Match *American*

| 26 | 22 | 23 | $50 |

South Norwalk | 98 Washington St. (bet. Main & Water Sts.) | 203-852-1088 | www.matchsono.com

Chef/co-owner "Matt Storch's creativity is unmatched" and it shows in his "superb" "seasonal" New American cuisine boasting "inventive food combinations" at this "happening" SoNo favorite, while "friendly, knowledgeable" service enhances the experience; the scene is "hip but cozy", and there's "lots of good people-watching" in the "loud, crowded" bar and outdoor patio, so while it's "pricey", many reckon it's "worth every penny."

Matthew's *American*

| ▽ 24 | 17 | 22 | $41 |

Unionville | 55 Mill St. (S. Main St.) | 860-673-7373 | www.matthews-restaurant.com

The seasonal menu featuring "fabulous" steaks, seafood "done to perfection" and more will "keep you interested" in this New American maritimer in historic Unionville on the Farmington River; though some find its location in a "small commercial building" "weird" and think the decor could "use some upgrading", "personalized" service, "reasonable prices" and live music on Wednesday nights help make up for it.

Max-a-Mia *Italian*

| 24 | 20 | 23 | $40 |

Avon | 70 E. Main St. (Waterville Rd.) | 860-677-6299 | www.maxrestaurantgroup.com

"The wood-fired oven makes fantastic pizzas and breads" and casts a "warm Tuscan glow" on the "lively" bistro setting of this Italian outpost of the Max empire in Avon that's "always crowded" (and "always noisy") thanks to "terrific food" and "solid" service; "families are accommodated well" and there's also a "great bar scene", and if some find it a bit "suburban bland", for many others it's a "terrific standby."

Max Amore Ristorante *Italian*

| 23 | 21 | 23 | $42 |

Glastonbury | Shops at Somerset Sq. | 140 Glastonbury Blvd. (Main St.) | 860-659-2819 | www.maxrestaurantgroup.com

"Cool Italian food with a chic twist" is the draw at this member of the Max chain in Glastonbury, a "great stopover if heading to Bradley Airport" and popular among "families" and "ladies who lunch"; though

FOOD | DECOR | SERVICE | COST

a few wince at the "noisy", "trendy" scene, most agree the "reliable, if not exciting" fare and "considerate" service are a "sure bet."

Max Burger *American*

| 25 | 19 | 21 | $28 |

West Hartford | 124 Lasalle Rd. (bet. Farmington Ave. & S. Main St.) | 860-232-3300 | www.maxrestaurantgroup.com

The Max group "gets creative without being crazy" with this "family-oriented" "raucous gourmet burger palace" in West Hartford whose "exotic", "plump and juicy" hamburgers, including the signature fatty melt (a patty between two grilled-cheese sandwiches), are "pieces of art", while "creative shakes" and a "beer selection that can't be beat" "keep the palate tingling"; the staff is "courteous", and despite grumblings about "ridiculous" waits, "weak" service and "overpriced" eats, it's become "quite the hot spot."

☑ Max Downtown *American/Steak*

| 27 | 25 | 27 | $57 |

Hartford | City Pl. | 185 Asylum St. (bet. Ann & Trumbull Sts.) | 860-522-2530 | www.maxrestaurantgroup.com

"Every meal is a celebration" at the "flagship" of the Max group located in Downtown Hartford, a "big-time", "big-city" New American offering "delectable" steaks, "top-shelf seafood" and other "creative offerings", with a spotlight on "locally grown" ingredients; "superb" service helps you feel "comfortable" in the "steakhouse" setting with "tasteful modern decor", and contributes to the satisfying sense that "you're in the right place at the right time."

Max Fish *Seafood*

| 23 | 23 | 23 | $46 |

Glastonbury | 110 Glastonbury Blvd. (bet. Main St. & Naubuc Ave.) | 860-652-3474 | www.maxrestaurantgroup.com

"Fresh fish, properly prepared", "without fussiness", finds favor with finatics at this "upscale" seafood Max outpost in Glastonbury, where the "raw bar is a beautiful thing to behold" and happy hour is "something special"; "personal" service helps excuse a sometimes "noisy" scene, and while a few critics "expected more, based on the name" and the "prices", others "can't wait to go back."

Max's Oyster Bar *Seafood*

| 26 | 24 | 24 | $47 |

West Hartford | 964 Farmington Ave. (S. Main St.) | 860-236-6299 | www.maxrestaurantgroup.com

While the "raw bar rocks" with "fresh, exotic" oysters at this "bivalve blowout" in the West Hartford Center, fish "cooked to perfection" and "fabulous steaks" also impress, as do the "excellent wines by the glass" and "professional, helpful" service; the ambiance is "divine" in the upscale setting with a "big-city feel", though some say it's "not a place for a romantic dinner", with "too much going on" (read: "noisy"), and it's "expensive", so take care not to max out your plastic.

☑ Mayflower Inn & Spa *American*

| 24 | 28 | 24 | $72 |

Washington | The Mayflower Inn & Spa | 118 Woodbury Rd. (Rte. 199) | 860-868-9466 | www.mayflowerinn.com

"Just setting foot in" this "elegant" Relais & Chateaux "country inn" and "destination restaurant" in Washington "will make you feel special" swoon surveyors smitten by the "heaven-on-earth" surroundings, "sophisticated" American cuisine "presented beautifully" and "caring, knowledgeable" service; while it's "outstanding in all regards for the money-is-no-object set", it may be "overpriced for the cost-conscious", some of whom recommend dining in the Tap Room as a "nicer", cheaper alternative to the main dining room.

McKinney & Doyle
Fine Foods Cafe Ⓜ American

| 25 | 18 | 23 | $41 |

Pawling | 10 Charles Colman Blvd. (Main St.), NY | 845-855-3875 | www.mckinneyanddoyle.com

"Rural Pawling's" "a lucky town" to have this "superior" New American "gem" where Shannon McKinney's "robust", "knockout" fare suits everyone, "from picky kids to fussy seniors" – he "even makes liver look good"; "divine breads" from the attached bakery, an "outstanding" brunch", "fair prices" and "wonderful, down-home service" to match the "tavernlike setting" lead to "long lines on weekends", though a new expansion should ease the wait.

Mediterranean Grill Mediterranean

| 18 | 17 | 19 | $45 |

Wilton | Stop & Shop Plaza | 5 River Rd. (Old Ridgefield Rd.) | 203-762-8484 | www.mediterraneangrillwilton.com

"Don't be discouraged by the shopping-center location" advise aficionados of this Wilton Mediterranean for the "attentive" hospitality from "eye-candy" servers, "unexpectedly pleasant ambiance" and "wonderful" outdoor patio will help you "soon forget about it"; critics, though, find the prices "too high" for what they call "average food", and feel this spot is "slipping."

Mediterraneo Mediterranean

| 21 | 19 | 19 | $49 |

Greenwich | 366 Greenwich Ave. (Grigg St.) | 203-629-4747 | www.mediterraneoofgreenwich.com

It's a "scene to sit outside" on the patio in summer with a "stylish crowd" at this "popular" Mediterranean "standby" in Downtown Greenwich where "great people-watching" comes with the "varied menu" that includes "fresh" seafood and "well-made" pizzas; but critics complain of "outrageous pricing", "rushed" service and "ear-splitting noise" that's tolerable only if you bring a "date you don't want to talk to."

Meetinghouse Food & Spirits Ⓜ American

| 20 | 15 | 17 | $40 |

Bedford Village | 635 Old Post Rd./Rte. 22 (Court Rd.), NY | 914-234-5656 | www.meetinghouserestaurant.com

"Conveniently located" near the Bedford Playhouse, this compact New American is the place to fuel up "before or after" a movie on usually "solid" eats (like burgers and ribs) that are sometimes "hit-or-miss"; though service can be spotty, and some say you're "paying for the village ambiance", it remains both "popular" and "crowded."

Meigas Spanish

| 24 | 21 | 22 | $54 |

Norwalk | 10 Wall St. (bet. High & Knight Sts.) | 203-866-8800 | www.meigasrestaurant.com

For "serene adult dining", fans tout this upscale Norwalk Spanish that works equally well for a "business dinner" or "two people in

FOOD | DECOR | SERVICE | COST

love", offering a "wonderful" tapas tasting menu and "bargain" prix fixe dinners (Mondays–Wednesdays), "graciously served" in a room with "well-spaced tables" (though some find the decor "a little too office park"); three years after ownership changed hands, some sigh that "it's not quite what it was", but to many others, it's a "good choice for that special night out."

Meli-Melo Crêperie *French*

25 | 12 | 20 | $23

Greenwich | 362 Greenwich Ave. (Fawcett Pl.) | 203-629-6153 | www.melimelogreenwich.com

You may no longer need to "go off hours" to get into this French fixture on lower Greenwich Avenue anymore thanks to a post-Survey expansion that added 55 new seats to the erstwhile "super-cramped" digs, where "amazing, authentic crêpes", "from savory to sweet", and a "huge selection" of "excellent" soups, "fresh" salads and more are served by a "friendly" staff; loyalists just "hope the expanded space doesn't change them."

Melting Pot *Fondue*

17 | 18 | 18 | $46

Darien | 14 Grove St. (bet. Brook & Day Sts.) | 203-656-4774
White Plains | 30 Mamaroneck Ave. (bet. Main St. & Martine Ave.), NY | 914-993-6358
www.meltingpot.com

"It's all about sharing" and "cooking your own food" at these outlets of the national chain serving "every kind of fondue", including "delicious" chocolate pots; while it's a "romantic" "treat" for "younger couples" and "fun to do with a group", critics contend it's "overpriced" and "pretentious", and would prefer a "more casual" setup; P.S. go with a large party if you want "two burners."

Métro Bis ☒ *American*

25 | 19 | 24 | $52

Simsbury | Simsburytown Shops | 928 Hopmeadow St. (bet. Massaco St. & Plank Hill Rd.) | 860-651-1908 | www.metrobis.com

Chef Chris Prosperi and wife Courtney Febbroriello have "got it together" at their New American bistro, "Simsbury's shining star" offering a seasonal menu of "consistently excellent" locally sourced fare, a "solid wine list" and "personal", "pleasantly unobtrusive" service; quibbles about "sparse" decor and the "odd strip-mall setting" notwithstanding, the experience enables many to feel like they've "escaped the suburbs for a couple of hours."

Michael Jordan's Steak House *Steak*

23 | 21 | 21 | $64

Uncasville | Mohegan Sun Casino | 1 Mohegan Sun Blvd. (bet. Rtes. 2 & 32) | 860-862-8600 | www.michaeljordansteakhouse.com

"Superb steaks and seafood" are a slam-dunk at No. 23's cow palace in the Mohegan Sun where "smiling servers do their best" and the setting's "so lovely you forget you're in a casino" – but don't expect quiet, for it's "always packed"; some may need a "big win at the tables" to afford the "pricey" affair, and while a few sniff their $$$ would've been better spent on a "pair of Air Jordans", others insist "you get what you pay for."

	FOOD	DECOR	SERVICE	COST

Michael's Trattoria ⬧ *Italian* — ▽ 24 | 21 | 22 | $40

Wallingford | 344 Center St. (Main St.) | 203-269-5303 |
www.michaelstrattoria.com

For a "little piece of Europe in Downtown Wallingford", those in the know recommend this "consistent" Northern Italian serving "sophisticated", "reasonably priced" fare, including "first-rate seafood", in a "plain-wrapper" of a space, where the "owner is always mingling with the crowd"; while a few decry "unbearable noise levels" and "spotty" service, it nonetheless "seems to have a lot of regulars."

ⓩ Mill at 2T ⬧Ⓜ *American* — 28 | 28 | 26 | $57

Tariffville | 2 Tunxis Rd. (Rte. 189) | 860-658-7890 |
www.themillat2T.com

Despite its bucolic location in the "woods by a river", Kelleanne and Ryan Jones' "elegant" New American, housed in a "beautiful", "inviting" converted mill in Tariffville, makes you "feel like you're in NYC" with Ryan's "consistently excellent, inventive" cuisine featuring "fresh, local" ingredients, which is backed by a "clever" wine list; husband and wife are "wonderful hosts" and their staff is "unfailingly pleasant and knowledgeable", and sure, it's "expensive", but most agree the experience is "worthy of the bill."

Mill on the River *Continental* — 20 | 22 | 19 | $39

South Windsor | 989 Ellington Rd. (Beldon Rd.) | 860-289-7929 |
www.themillontheriver.com

"Romantic to the max", "you won't find anywhere prettier" than this "charming", "rustic" Continental housed in a restored mill overlooking the Podunk River in South Windsor, a popular site for "big first dates", weddings and celebrations, with an outdoor gazebo that's a "treat in the right weather"; the kitchen turns out an "interesting variety of choices", including a "super" Sunday brunch, and the service is "prompt" – just "bring a fat wallet."

🆕 Millstone Café Ⓜ *American* — - | - | - | M

Kent | 14 N. Main St. (Bridge St.) | 860-592-0500

A "wonderful addition" to Kent, this New American arrival is also "well worth a trip from nearby towns or NY" attest those in the know who laud its "seasonal" dishes made with "very fresh" local ingredients served in a "convivial" space that's "charming without being pretentious"; though a few report "haphazard" service, others see "a lot of enthusiasm" from the staff; a bakery annex is scheduled to open in spring 2011.

Milonga *Argentinean/Italian* — 22 | 18 | 21 | $51

North White Plains | 577 N. Broadway (Fisher Ln.), NY | 914-358-1444 |
www.milongarestaurant.com

Habitués hail this "lively, lovely" North White Plains Argentinean, a "much-needed addition" to the area with "delicious" Angus steaks and Italian items served in a "clubby" wood-lined dining room with a tapas menu "ideal for sharing" available in the lounge; "welcoming" service overcomes "noisy" acoustics and tabs that can feel "pricey" to some.

	FOOD	DECOR	SERVICE	COST

Miso *Japanese*

23 | 21 | 22 | $42

New Haven | 15 Orange St. (bet. Crown & George Sts.) | 203-848-6472 | www.misorestaurant.com

"Succulent" seafood – in "creative" sushi rolls and cooked specials alike – reel in fans to this "upscale" Japanese in Downtown New Haven, where guests are welcomed into the "spacious dining room" by the "warm" owner and "friendly" staff; critics "don't know why" the "prices keep rising", though, and feel it "could be better" for the cost.

Miya's Sushi *Japanese*

25 | 15 | 21 | $34

New Haven | 68 Howe St. (Grand Ave.) | 203-777-9760 | www.miyassushi.com

At his New Haven establishment, "lovable free spirit" Bun Lai – chef, community activist and former wrestling coach – creates "fascinatingly eclectic", "creative" takes on Japanese cuisine (mitzvah roll, anyone?) featuring "sustainable" ingredients; a selection of house-infused sake helps many forgive the "crappy beer" choices, if not the "cramped" digs, and while some "just can't fathom" the "weird combinations", others insist it'll "change your view of what sushi can be."

Modern Apizza Ⓜ *Pizza*

25 | 11 | 18 | $20

New Haven | 874 State St. (Humphrey St.) | 203-776-5306 | www.modernapizza.com

In the "New Haven pizza hierarchy", loyalists declare this longtime "local favorite" (circa 1934) "just as good" as its two rivals, "but without the waits" or "undue hype", and fume that it "does not get the recognition it deserves" for the thin-crust, "charred, chewy goodness" that comes out of its brick oven; "polite" service is another plus, and though the decor may "leave much to be desired", "you come here for the pie, not the atmosphere."

NEW Moderne Barn *American*

22 | 26 | 21 | $55

Armonk | 430 Bedford Rd. (bet. Cox Ave. & Greenwich Rd.), NY | 914-730-0001 | www.modernebarn.com

"Manhattan comes north" via this "buzzing" Armonk newcomer from the Livanos family (City Limits, NYC's Abboccato, Molyvos and Oceana) courting the county's "glitterati" with an "enjoyable" globe-trotting New American menu served in a "stunning", "soaring" "equestrian-themed" space; service "kinks" and a "cacophonous" noise level "detract", although on the whole, it's clearly a "hit" with the masses.

Modern Restaurant & Pizzeria *Italian*

22 | 9 | 18 | $25

New Rochelle | 12 Russell Ave. (Main St.), NY | 914-633-9479 | www.modernrestaurantandpizzeria.com

Prepare to "fight the locals for a table" at this diminutive New Rochelle pizza parlor turning out "terrific" "brick-oven" pies alongside other "solid" Southern Italian eats; in spite of its beyond-"casual" "hole-in-the-wall" setting, it's a "reliable" pit stop for families and a fallback for delivery too.

	FOOD	DECOR	SERVICE	COST

Molly Spillane's *American*   `15` `17` `16` `$29`

Mamaroneck | 211 Mamaroneck Ave. (Prospect Ave.), NY | 914-899-3130 | www.mollyspillanespub.com

This his-and-hers sports bar in Mamaroneck may be "nothing to write home about", but it "gets the job done" with "traditional" grub with an Irish lilt served in "nicely appointed" settings with TVs blaring the big game; it's "loud" and often "packed", but the "hard-working" barkeeps keep the "pints of Guinness" flowing "even when they're busy."

Molto Wine Bar *Italian*   `21` `21` `17` `$36`

Fairfield | 1215 Post Rd. (bet. Beach & Unquowa Rds.) | 203-292-8288 | www.pizzeriamolto.com

The "scene is the star" at this "hip", "happening" Fairfield Italian enoteca that resembles a "1960s Roman trattoria" with a "bangin' bar", serving "tasty tapas-style" plates and "delicious designer pizzas" along with a "decent wine list" in a "loud" setting that's "always packed" with "young folks"; critics dismiss it as a "typical yuppie joint" – i.e. "annoying" and "overpriced" – but *amici* insist it lives "up to the hype."

Morello Bistro *Italian*   `22` `25` `21` `$53`

Greenwich | 253 Greenwich Ave. (W. Elm St.) | 203-661-3443 | www.morellobistro.com

Housed in a "beautifully renovated building" with "gorgeous vaulted ceilings" and an "elegant, airy feel", this Greenwich Avenue Italian is a "fantastic experience" according to fans, who cite the "varied", "well-executed" menu, "extensive, well-priced" wine list and "helpful" service in addition to the "impressive" surroundings; many say it's "expensive", but others consider it "reasonably priced for Greenwich" and a "good value" overall.

Morgans Fish House *Seafood*   `21` `20` `20` `$50`

Rye | 22 Elm Pl. (bet. Purchase St. & Theodore Fremd Ave.), NY | 914-921-8190 | www.morgansfishhouse.net

"Completely redone" by the folks behind Rye Grill and Ruby's Oyster Bar, this Rye seafooder now features a "broader, more pocketbook-friendly menu" of incredibly fresh" fare served in "cute", "casual" digs that recall a New England fish shack; it still pulls a "fashionable" local crowd, even if loyalists lament the "ordinary", "middle-of-the-road" grub (down three points from our last Survey) is "not as good as it used to be."

Morton's The Steakhouse *Steak*   `24` `21` `24` `$69`

Hartford | 852 Main St. (Asylum St.) | 860-724-0044
Stamford | UBS Investment Bank | 377 N. State St. (Elm St.) | 203-324-3939
White Plains | 9 Maple Ave. (Bloomingdale Rd.), NY | 914-683-6101 www.mortons.com

A steakhouse "standard-bearer", this "big-ticket" chain offers "excellently prepared" cuts of beef and "grand sides" "served professionally" amid an "ambiance of wealth and class"; some find it a bit

FOOD | DECOR | SERVICE | COST

"staid" and wish they'd "lose the raw-meat presentation" and "high" wine pricing, but the many who love its "traditional" ways consider it "one of the best."

Mo's New York Grill M *American*   18 | 21 | 19 | $48

New Rochelle | 14 Memorial Hwy. (bet. Huguenot & Main Sts.), NY | 914-632-1442 | www.mosnewyorkgrill.com

A "shrine to Yankees baseball", this New Rochelle grill from All-Star pitcher Mariano Rivera is "worth it for fans" thanks to its "fabulous photos and memorabilia throughout", plus the "chance to spot Mo himself"; its "solid" American menu spans from burgers to seafood to "excellent cuts of beef", although it still strikes some as "disappointing for the price."

Mulino's of Westchester ●⊠ *Italian*   24 | 23 | 24 | $66

White Plains | 99 Court St. (Quarropas St.), NY | 914-761-1818 | www.mulinosny.com

It "looks like a scene from *Goodfellas*" at this "outstanding", "old-line" White Plains Italian, a "favorite of local politicians" and "special-occasion" celebrants thanks to its "bountiful" feasts kicked off by a "never-ending procession" of antipasti; the "beautifully" designed room has "the feel of Little Italy with more class", and the "festive" holiday decorations are truly "over-the-top" – so "enjoy", and try not to "think about your wallet."

Murasaki *Japanese*   - | - | - | M

West Hartford | 23 Lasalle Rd. (Farmington Ave.) | 860-236-7622 | www.murasakijapaneserestaurant.com

The sushi is "always fresh" and the service is "always prompt and pleasant" at this compact Japanese stalwart in West Hartford, which also offers a full menu of cooked items such as broiled miso cod; though some find it "expensive", hard-core fans just "roll" with the prices for "delicious" eats that are "worth every penny."

Mystic Pizza *Pizza*   15 | 13 | 16 | $20

Mystic | 56 W. Main St. (Bank St.) | 860-536-3700

Mystic Pizza II *Pizza*

North Stonington | 209 Providence-New London Tpke. (Norwich Westerly Rd.) | 860-599-3111
www.mysticpizza.com

Still "popular tourist destinations" thanks to the 1988 film, this pizzeria in Downtown Mystic and its North Stonington spin-off dish out "enjoyable" pies in "nostalgic" settings full of movie memorabilia; though cynics snort "Julia Roberts could make better pizza than this" and warn of "long lines" and "less-than-friendly service", for some cineastes it's still "fun to say you've been there."

❷ Napa & Co. *American*   24 | 23 | 22 | $56

Stamford | 75 Broad St. (bet. Bedford & Summer Sts.) | 203-353-3319 | www.napaandcompany.com

Oenophiles "know they're going to have a great night" once they "see the wall of wine" at this "trendy" Stamford New American where "creative", "locally sourced" farm-to-table fare and "excellent pairings" are served by a "professional" staff; while some critics find it "too noisy" and "overpriced", claiming it's trying too hard "to be NYC", others promise a "memorable meal", whether it's a "casual dinner or more formal night out."

Nat Hayden's Real Pit Barbecue *BBQ*

— | — | — | M

Windsor | 226 Broad St. (Maple Ave.) | 860-298-8955 | www.haydensrealbbq.com

The "succulent" pulled pork and "outstanding smoked meats" at this Windsor pit are "as close to real BBQ as you'll find in these parts" swear 'cuennoisseurs who also praise "tempting" sides such as the pepper jack grits; the "small place will fill up quickly", so "be prepared for a long line, but don't worry – it moves fast."

Nautilus Diner ● *Diner*

16 | 13 | 17 | $23

Mamaroneck | 1240 W. Boston Post Rd. (bet. Richbell Rd. & Weaver St.), NY | 914-833-1320

An "impossibly long menu" of "old-style" American favorites is the hook at this "quintessential" Mamaroneck diner, a 24/7 mainstay set in "glossy" digs and manned by a "sweet" crew; even if the fare's rather "run-of-the-mill", it's a "local staple" – come on a weekend and you'll certainly "see someone you know."

Nessa *Italian*

21 | 18 | 19 | $50

Port Chester | 325 N. Main St. (Horton Ave.), NY | 914-939-0119 | www.nessarestaurant.com

Very "romantic", this "wonderful, little" midpriced Port Chester Italian puts out "simple", "modern" dishes and "standout wines" in a sultry space awash in candlelight; service can be hit-or-miss, and the "noise is incredible", so "bring earplugs", or try the patio (with a bocce court) "in the summer."

New Deal Steakplace *Steak*

▽ 14 | 10 | 15 | $31

Westbrook | 704 Boston Post Rd. (Eckford Ave.) | 860-399-0015

There's nothing to fear at this "family-friendly" meatery in Westbrook serving steaks that are "consistent", "simple and good", as well as a "wide menu for the pickiest of eaters" in a "pub-type" setting; "reasonable prices" make it a "good value"; it's dinner only in the winter.

Niko's Greek Taverna *Greek*

20 | 14 | 20 | $35

White Plains | 287 Central Ave. (Aqueduct Rd.), NY | 914-686-6456 | www.nikostaverna.com

"Like the Greek family you never knew you had", this modestly appointed White Plains kitchen coddles guests with "hearty" Hellenic fare and service that "bends over backwards to take care of you"; it's "always packed", although the "charming" outdoor tables ease the crush in summer.

Nino's *Italian*

▽ 20 | 14 | 20 | $37

South Salem | 355 Rte. 123 (Glen Dr.), NY | 914-533-2671 | www.ninos123.com

"Locals like" this "laid-back" South Salem Italian laying out a "wonderful variety" of "filling" "homestyle" fare, and several praise the

FOOD | DECOR | SERVICE | COST

brick-oven pizzas; the staff is "competent" but it's "not much on atmosphere" so some might prefer "takeout."

Nino's ⑤ *Italian*
21 | 18 | 20 | $46

Bedford Hills | 13 Adams St. (Rte. 117), NY | 914-864-0400
"Wood-fired pizzas" with "a little zest" plus "dependable" "old-school" Italian cuisine appeal to "families" and "couples" alike at this "popular" Bedford Hills storefront that manages to maintain a "cozy, warm atmosphere"; a lively "bar business" encourages those in the know to "opt for the back room" when they want "a quieter dinner."

Noah's Ⓜ *American*
24 | 18 | 20 | $37

Stonington | 113 Water St. (Church St.) | 860-535-3925 | www.noahsfinefood.com
You don't need to "bring two of everything" to "get on board" this Stonington regional American offering "terrific", "well-priced" New England comfort food "with an emphasis on local ingredients" and "friendly" service in a "warm", "cozy" atmosphere; though a few think the "whole place needs a face-lift", it nonetheless remains a "locals' favorite."

Noda's Japanese Steakhouse *Japanese*
19 | 14 | 20 | $35

White Plains | White Plains Mall | 200 Hamilton Ave. (Dr. Martin Luther King Ave.), NY | 914-949-0990 | www.nodarestaurant.com
All the usual "theatrics" turn up at this well-priced White Plains teppanyaki where the "entertaining", "knife-twirling" show makes it a magnet for birthday parties; the "filling" Japanese fare and sushi is "good" enough, although judging from the scores, the decor has "seen better days."

No. 9 ⑤Ⓜ *American*
27 | 23 | 25 | $49

Millerton | Simmons' Way Village Inn | 53 Main St. (bet. Dutchess & N. Maple Aves.), NY | 518-592-1299 | www.number9millerton.com
Ensconced in the dining room of Millerton's "luxury" Simmons' Way Inn, chef Tim Cocheo's "fantastic" two-year-old offers a "daring" French- and Austrian-accented New American menu and "pulls it off superbly", with "sublime", "mouthwatering" cooking that draws "fans from a 10-town radius"; the "congenial", "sophisticated country setting", "personal service" and "midweek prix fixe offering even greater value" have devotees declaring "its name is off by one - it should be a 10!"

NEW Norimaki ⑤ *Japanese*
- | - | - | M

Washington | 4 Green Hill Rd. (Titus Rd.) | 860-868-0555
Chef Makoto Sekikawa and his "charming" wife, Jinyi, have resurrected their former NYC Japanese in Washington Township, and sushi savants laud it as "an extraordinary addition to the Litchfield dining scene", serving "wonderfully fresh", "artfully presented" sushi, as well as a "consistently interesting" menu of cooked fare

that "shifts with the seasons"; cognoscenti whisper "do not tell anyone, but this is the real deal."

North Star *American*

20 | 18 | 21 | $47

Pound Ridge | 85 Westchester Ave. (Pine Dr.), NY | 914-764-0200 | www.northstarny.com

"Delivering on both taste and atmosphere", this "casual bistro" in Pound Ridge is a "hub of activity" where selections from a "creative" New American menu come via "friendly" servers; for some "it's all about the live music" on weeknights and the half-price "wine deal" on Tuesdays, but it's also "jammed on weekends."

Nuage *French/Japanese*

24 | 20 | 23 | $62

Cos Cob | Mill Pond Shopping Ctr. | 203 E. Putnam Ave. (bet. Sinawoy Rd. & Suburban Ave.) | 203-869-2339 | www.nuagerestaurant.com

"Deservedly popular" for its "beautifully prepared" French-Japanese cuisine, including "wonderful seafood", and "attentive" service, this "quiet gem" in Cos Cob is "highly underrated" according to fans; the "relaxed" atmosphere belies the "expense-account" prices, and some feel the strip-mall space is "not luxurious enough" to complement the "pricey" fare, though "sunset on the patio can be spectacular."

NEW Oakhurst Diner *Diner*

▽ 16 | 16 | 15 | $24

Millerton | 19 Main St. (Center St.), NY | 518-592-1313

"Not your everyday diner", this recently reopened "retro" Millerton coffee shop takes an "interesting approach" with its three squares a day, mixing "comfort" "classics" with "imaginative", "upmarket" eats like "venison chili" and "deftly spiced vegetable" dishes for "cheap"; new owners gave the 1950s "vintage" interior a cosmetic overhaul, so all that's "lacking" is service at times.

NEW Oaxaca Kitchen *Mexican*

- | - | - | M

New Haven | 228 College St. (bet. Chapel & Crown Sts.) | North Haven | 203-859-5774 | www.thali.com

Prasad Chirnomula of Thali fame steps outside of his comfort zone and delves into the regional cuisine of Oaxaca at his hip new Mexican located in the heart of New Haven, where moderate prices should especially appeal to Yale students and faculty; the dramatic bar has an outdoor feel, and the transporting dining room features cowhide banquettes.

Octagon *Seafood/Steak*

▽ 24 | 21 | 23 | $56

Groton | Mystic Marriott Hotel & Spa | 625 North Rd. (I-95) | 860-326-0360 | www.waterfordgrouprestaurants.com

"They know how to prepare a steak" at this high-end surf 'n' turf in Groton's Mystic Marriott, a "special place for a special evening" with "top-flight" beef, a "terrific" wine list that's "not too overpriced" and "knowledgeable, attentive" service in a "lovely", "upscale" setting; a few find the scene "stodgy", but for many others it's a "pleasant experience" that's "worth the price."

	FOOD	DECOR	SERVICE	COST

Old Heidelberg *German* | 21 | 18 | 20 | $33 |

Bethel | 55 Stony Hill Rd. (McNeil Rd.) | 203-797-1860 |
www.restauranttheidelberg.com

"Get your German on" at this Bethel Deutsch where *"schön gut" essen* such as the "obscenely huge pork shank" and (natch) an "extensive beer list" are "served with a smile" in an "authentic", rustic setting, with "nice outdoor dining" in the biergarten and bands in "requisite lederhosen" performing traditional "classics"; "tidy" prices are another plus, and while a few cynics find the fare "uneven" and attribute its "always packed" house to a "lack of competition", others insist it's "worth a visit."

Old Lyme Inn *American*   ▽ 22 | 22 | 23 | $56 |

Old Lyme | Old Lyme Inn | 85 Lyme St. (I-95) | 860-434-2600 |
www.oldlymeinn.com

Housed in a "wonderful Shoreline Colonial manor" in Old Lyme, this inn eatery offers seasonal Traditional American cuisine in a "lovely" Winslow dining room with chandeliers and 12-ft.-tall floor-to-ceiling windows, and a grill menu in the tap room; though a few feel it's getting "tired", others deem it "excellent" all around.

Olé Molé *Mexican* | 19 | 10 | 17 | $22 |

Darien | 1020 Post Rd. (bet. Brook & Day Sts.) | 203-202-7051
Stamford | 1030 High Ridge Rd. (Olga Dr.) | 203-461-9962 Ⓜ
www.olemole.net

"Reliable" and "relatively authentic" Mexican fare, "friendly" service and "affordable" prices make this duo a "great value in expensive towns", especially for families with "kids", but purists pan the offerings as "white-bread" eats for "people who don't like spices"; cognoscenti also caution "eat in at your own peril", for you may need a "shoehorn" to "squeeze in" to the "tiny storefronts", which is why many opt for "takeout."

Olio Bar & Restaurant *American*   ▽ 24 | 19 | 19 | $41 |

Groton | 33 Kings Hwy. (Rte. 1) | 860-445-6546 |
www.olioct.com

Foodies praise the "consistent quality" of the "above-average" New American cuisine at this Groton sibling of Mystic's Bravo Bravo; "cramped" claustrophobes complain of "limited space" in the candlelit room, while others grouse about "outlandish noise levels", but many regard it as an "excellent place to eat."

Oliva Cafe Ⓜ *Mediterranean* | 24 | 18 | 21 | $47 |

New Preston | 18 E. Shore Rd. (Church St.) | 860-868-1787 |
www.olivacafe.com

The Mediterranean fare is "spectacularly tasty, yet simple" at this "hidden gem in New Preston", where the atmosphere is "friendly" and "welcoming" in the "lovely setting" of an old Colonial with a balcony and terrace for outdoor dining; the prices are "so reasonable you want to eat there daily", and while some grouse that the "menu hasn't changed in ages", others reason that this is "as adventurous as it gets in the NW hills."

	FOOD	DECOR	SERVICE	COST

Olive Market Ⓜ *Spanish* — 24 | 20 | 22 | $30

Georgetown | 19 Main St. (Redding Rd.) | 203-544-8134 |
www.theolivemarket.net/olive

You can "shop while your garlic pizza cooks" at this "informal", mid-priced Spanish cafe housed in a cheese shop/gift store in the village of Georgetown serving "unique" South American–influenced breakfast fare, "zesty" sandwiches and more, plus "fabulous" tapas dinners Thursdays–Saturdays; chef-owner Fernando Pereyra "adds charm and warmth" to the "quaint", "casual" setting, and the rest of the staff is "friendly and attentive."

Oliver's Taverne *American* — ▽ 16 | 19 | 18 | $29

Essex | 124 Westbrook Rd. (Deep River Rd.) | 860-767-2633 |
www.oliverstavern.com

A "good selection of beers", "predictable" American pub grub, "reasonable" prices and lots of "camaraderie" make this "casual" Essex tavern a "comfortable, enjoyable" scene, albeit a "not-too-exciting" one according to some; sports fans can catch games upstairs, where critics carp that "too many TVs" make things "noisy", and there's live "Dixieland jazz" downstairs once a month.

Olive Tree Ⓜ *American* — ▽ 21 | 21 | 22 | $37

Southbury | 137 E. Hill Rd. (Hillhouse Rd.) | 203-263-4555 |
www.theolivetreesouthbury.com

Sure it's "not hip or trendy", but diehards declare "you can't go wrong" at this Southbury American overlooking the Heritage Village golf course, where a "friendly" staff serves "plentiful" portions of "steady" fare in a "lovely old house"; there's "fireside seating" in the "cozy bar" and the "beautiful patio" offers some of the "best views in the area", and while a few wags feel like they're dining in a "nursing home with nicer furniture", at least it's "not noisy."

Omanel *Portuguese* — ▽ 19 | 12 | 16 | $30

Bridgeport | 1909 Main St. (bet. Commercial & Grand Sts.) |
203-335-1676

Located in a "nothing section of Bridgeport", this Portuguese "hidden gem" offers "extremely big" portions of "authentic" "home cooking" at some of the "best prices in town"; though some describe the service as "so-so" and sniff "don't expect any decor", stalwarts say "bring it on" and "go anyway."

Ondine *French* — 26 | 23 | 26 | $70

Danbury | 69 Pembroke Rd. (Wheeler Dr.) | 203-746-4900 |
www.ondinerestaurant.com

At this French "classic" in Danbury, the "unpretentious" staff "gets good service right" while the kitchen creates "fabulous", "traditional" Gallic cuisine "the way it used to be", and the "creative, elegant" $59 dinner prix fixe and $39 Sunday afternoon dinner help keep the tabs from getting *trop chèr*; though some find the decor a bit "stodgy" and in need of an "update", others are "comfortable" in the "sophisticated" setting and declare it a "superior restaurant for special occasions."

	FOOD	DECOR	SERVICE	COST

O'Neill's
Pub & Restaurant ● *Pub Food*

▽ 19 | 18 | 20 | $27

South Norwalk | 93 N. Main St. (bet. Ann & Pine Sts.) |
203-838-0222 | www.oneillsono.com

Even after a short move around the corner from its previous location, this "authentic" South Norwalk Irish public house still "feels like home" to a "nice crowd" thanks to "amiable" service, an "excellent beer selection" and traditional English and Irish fare that "transcends" the usual pub grub; "reasonable" prices and live bands on weekends are additional reasons so many "love this local hangout."

116 Crown ● *Eclectic*

21 | 25 | 21 | $40

New Haven | 116 Crown St. (bet. Church & Orange Sts.) | 203-777-3116 |
www.116crown.com

It's easy to "forget you're in New Haven" at this "sophisticated" joint with a "drop-dead gorgeous, translucent bar" and "all the sexy, dark charm of a trendy NYC hot spot", where "exotic" – and "potent" – "handcrafted cocktails" are served with Eclectic small plates (aka 'American tapas') by a staff that "respects its customers"; a few say the service is a bit too "relaxed", though, while others warn "don't go hungry", for those "pricey" little portions can add up in a hurry.

121 Restaurant & Bar *American*

22 | 19 | 20 | $43

North Salem | 2 Dingle Ridge Rd. (Rte. 121), NY | 914-669-0121 |
www.121restaurant.com

A "perennial favorite" for North Salem "families and the horsey crowd", this "upscale pub" trots out "consistently good" New American fare, from "creative" wood-fired pizzas to braised short ribs; a "well-trained" staff, a "cozy fireplace" and "porch dining" make for a "congenial atmosphere", though an "energetic bar scene" gets "loud on weekends" and the "wait for a table" can be "frustrating."

121 Restaurant @ OXC Ⓜ *American*

21 | 21 | 19 | $36

Oxford | Waterbury-Oxford Airport | 7 Juliano Dr. (Christian St.) |
203-262-0121 | www.121atoxc.com

"The view, whether through the windows or outside on the deck", is the most "entertaining" part of this New American "next to the runway" at Waterbury-Oxford Airport, but the "innovative", "diverse menu" is its own draw, as everything "from pizzas to entrees" is of "high quality" and "not too pricey"; for being in the "countryside" "in the middle of nowhere", the decor is quite "city chic", with a "lovely bar area" that's "fun" when "full."

🆕 On the Way Café Ⓜ ⊅ *European*

- | - | - | I

Rye | 34 Ridgeland Terrace (bet. Forest Ave. & Playland Pkwy.), NY |
914-921-2233 | www.ontheway caferye.com

With polished lamps and a smooth white marble counter as focal points, this former luncheonette across from the entrance to Rye Playland has morphed into a sleek European-style cafe; the daytime menu is well priced and runs the gamut from frittatas to wraps to beef carpaccio with plenty of espresso to wash it all down; P.S. cash only.

O'Porto Ⓜ *Portuguese*   ▽ 23 | 19 | 20 | $41

Hartford | 2075 Park St. (bet. Bulkeley & Rowe Aves.) | 860-233-3184 | www.oportohartford.com

"O the Portuguese cuisine" at this "slicker incarnation of the old Casa Lisboa" in Hartford rhapsodize fans who credit it with "improving" on its predecessor's "rustic", "well-seasoned" fare; a few grumble that the "prices are steeper" as well, but "attentive" service and the "nicely designed quarters in a former warehouse" make it a "good value" for many.

Opus 465 *American*   18 | 17 | 17 | $42

Armonk | 465 Main St. (Orchard Dr.), NY | 914-273-4676 | www.opus465.com

There are "different rooms for different moods" at this "reliable" Armonk American providing a "loud" "after-work watering hole" downstairs and a "cozier" upstairs in which to enjoy "substantial" "comfort-food" classics; critics claim the decor's "a little tired", but weekend bands are a plus and patrons "love eating outside" in good weather.

Orem's Diner ◐ *Diner*   15 | 12 | 17 | $19

Wilton | 167 Danbury Rd. (Wolfpit Rd.) | 203-762-7370 | www.oremsdiner.com

The "definitive diner", this "Wilton institution" offers a "huge menu" and servings (forget "portion control") ferried by a "warm, friendly staff", all making it a "home away from home" for local families; it's also a "quick", "reliable" choice for business breakfasts, so just add in "reasonable prices" to answer the question: "why is this place so crowded?"

Oscar's *Deli*   18 | 8 | 13 | $18

Westport | 159 Main St. (bet. Elm St. & Parker Harding Plaza) | 203-227-3705

"When you can't get to Manhattan", this "fixture in Downtown Westport" will do for fans who kvell over the "overstuffed" sandwiches on "great rye bread", "mouthwatering matzo ball soup" and other "authentic Jewish deli" specialties, which make up for the "brusque" service; you can "kibitz" at one of the "jammed-together tables" inside or "watch shoppers" go by from one of the "sidewalk tables" on warm days.

Osetra Ⓜ *Eclectic/Seafood*   23 | 18 | 20 | $50

South Norwalk | 124 Washington St. (bet. Main & Water Sts.) | 203-354-4488 | www.osetrasono.com

Dishes such as "fried lobster with caramel sauce" "speak volumes about the imagination" of "talented" and "elaborately tattooed" chef-owner Dave Nevins of this SoNo Eclectic seafooder, where his "fresh, inventive creations" are backed by "exceptional cocktails" and a wine list that "kills"; opinions of the service vary ("attentive"

	FOOD	DECOR	SERVICE	COST

vs. "moody"), and some say "the room could use some help", but many regard it as a "neighborhood gem."

Osianna ⑤ Mediterranean
| 25 | 21 | 23 | $44 |

Fairfield | 70 Reef Rd. (Sherman St.) | 203-254-2070 | www.osianna.com

While "nothing is less than stellar" on the "varied" menu of this "wonderful" Fairfield Greek-Med, it's the aromas of "superbly grilled and sautéed" seafood (the name is derived from the mythical god of the sea) that elicit "Pavlovian responses" from finatics; service is "warm and gracious" and the "charming, inviting" setting includes a "nice" outdoor patio, and while some find it "pricey for what you get", the lunch prix fixe is an "amazing bargain" and the dinner prix fixe is "very reasonable" as well.

Osteria Applausi ⑤ Italian
| ▽ 24 | 19 | 22 | $48 |

Old Greenwich | 199 Sound Beach Ave. (Arcadia Rd.) | 203-637-4447 | www.osteriaapplausi.com

"Everything is freshly made", including mamma's "lovely" pasta, at this "authentic" Italian "mainstay" (sibling of Columbus Park) situated on the "small-town main street" of Old Greenwich; there's sleek new "darker" decor, and the staff's "personal attention is welcoming", just be sure to "get reservations", and don't be surprised if the tab's "a bit pricey."

Outback Steakhouse Steak
| 17 | 14 | 18 | $31 |

Danbury | 116 Newtown Rd. (I-84) | 203-790-1124
Manchester | 170 Hale Rd. (Slater St.) | 860-648-2900
Newington | 3210 Berlin Tpke. (Deming St.) | 860-666-0002
New London | 305 N. Frontage Rd. (bet. Briggs & Colman Sts.) | 860-447-9205
North Haven | Big Y Shopping Ctr. | 345 Washington Ave. (bet. Temple & Wadsworth Sts.) | 203-985-8282
Orange | 132 Marsh Hill Rd. (Rte. 95) | 203-795-0700
Shelton | 698 Bridgeport Ave. (Old Stratford Rd.) | 203-926-3900
Southington | 817 Queen St. (Aircraft Rd.) | 860-276-9585
Wilton | 14 Danbury Rd. (bet. Fawn Ridge Ln. & Heathcoate Rd.) | 203-762-0920
White Plains | 60 S. Broadway (Bloomingdale Rd.), NY | 914-684-1397
www.outback.com

"Reliable" (if "not prime") seasoned steaks provide "real value for the dollar" at this "Aussie-themed" "middle-of-the-road" chain where folks love to "overindulge in the bloomin' onion"; it's too "kitschy" and "packaged" for pickier patrons and the "cute" service is "hit-or-miss", but "you can take all of your kids and your neighbors too" since you'll blend right into the "noisy" surroundings.

Paci ⑤Ⓜ Italian
| 26 | 25 | 23 | $58 |

Southport | 96 Station St. (Pequot Ave.) | 203-259-9600 | www.pacirestaurant.com

Aficionados report a "fantastic dining experience" at this "long-standing gem at the Southport train station" in the form of "delectable", "expertly prepared" Italian cuisine served by a "knowledgeable" staff in an "interesting" room with a "high" cathedral ceiling and "challenging acoustics" (some "prefer to eat at the bar" rather than "shout to be heard"); sure, it's "expensive", but most agree it's "worth the high cost."

Pacifico   *Nuevo Latino/Seafood*   24 | 21 | 22 | $46

New Haven | 220 College St. (Crown St.) | 203-772-4002 | www.pacificorestaurants.com

An "energetic" "mix of Yale students and older folks", including lots of "theatergoers", gravitates to this "classy" Nuevo Latino seafooder across from the Shubert in Downtown New Haven for "amazing food that appeals to all the senses" and "fantastic" mojitos served by an "efficient, pleasant" staff in "cozy", "warm" environs; for a "quiet meal" advise insiders, "upstairs is a better choice."

Palmer's Crossing   *American*   21 | 20 | 21 | $38

Larchmont | 1957 Palmer Ave. (Larchmont Ave.), NY | 914-833-3505 | www.palmerscrossing.com

"Reliable" is the word on this white-tablecloth Larchmont American featuring a "solid", "something-for-everyone" menu in an "upscale" bi-level space with a "crowded" bar; perhaps it's "not a destination" restaurant, but tabs are moderate and service "accommodating", while live music on weekends "makes it all that much better."

Pantry, The ⊠ Ⓜ   *American*   24 | 14 | 19 | $24

Washington Depot | 5 Titus Rd. (Rte. 47) | 860-868-0258

A "long-standing favorite for breakfast" and the "see-and-be-seen lunch place" in "charming" Washington Depot, this "kind of pricey" American deli "run by lovely people" offers prepared dishes and baked goods that are "marvelous" enough to "blind one to the glam and glitz of the clientele"; "interesting" "gifts, chocolates and housewares" are "displayed on shelves right next to your table", and though the "small" space is "always crowded", most agree "it's hard not to love" this place.

Papacelle ⊠   *Italian*   ▽ 24 | 23 | 23 | $43

Avon | 152 Simsbury Rd. (Rte. 44) | 860-269-3121 | www.papacelle.com

At this "reasonably priced", family-run Italian in Avon, the "wonderful" dishes "made to order" show the "touch of a really fine chef", and are complemented by a "quality wine list", while the "professional" staff is "always there at the right time, but never in the way"; the Tuscan-style setting includes a "lovely outdoor patio", and there's live music on the weekends – in sum, it's a "delight to visit."

Papaya Thai & Asian BBQ   *Thai*   20 | 19 | 18 | $31

South Norwalk | 24 Marshall St. (N. Water St.) | 203-866-8424 | www.papayathai.com

An "interesting" menu of "well-prepared" Thai fare, including "really good" BBQ, is served against an "exotic" backdrop of thatched huts, palm trees and wood carvings at this SoNo spot, where the "outdoor seating is wonderful on a summer day"; a few purists pan the fare as "pedestrian" and "Americanized", but for many, the "super-friendly" service, "relaxed" vibe and "great" cocktails excuse any shortcomings.

	FOOD	DECOR	SERVICE	COST

Paradise Bar & Grille   *American*   ▽ 13 | 23 | 17 | $33

Stamford | Stamford Landing | 78 Southfield Ave. (I-95, exit 7) |
203-323-1116 | www.paradisebarandgrille.com

It's like a "mini-vacation" at this New American where you can "relax" and "watch the water, the boats and the birds" at the Stamford marina from a window seat or the deck in warm weather, and the "happening bar scene" provides "post-work stress relief"; while critics carp that "even the view does not compensate" for the "basic" eats ("hope you like it fried"), at least it's "reasonably priced" and the servers are "friendly."

Pascal's Ⓜ *French*   23 | 21 | 24 | $48

Larchmont | 141 Chatsworth Ave. (Palmer Ave.), NY |
914-834-6688

The "charming" owners "make you feel welcome" at this "lovely" Larchmont bistro offering "wonderful", "traditional" French cuisine including a weekday prix fixe that's a "value"; it caters to an "older" crowd that appreciates service that's "never rushed" and a "quiet" atmosphere that's "good for conversation."

Pasta Nostra Ⓩ Ⓜ *Italian*   25 | 16 | 21 | $56

South Norwalk | 116 Washington St. (bet. Main & Water Sts.) |
203-854-9700 | www.pastanostra.com

It's "all about the food" at Joe Bruno's upscale SoNo Italian, a "culinary extravaganza" featuring an "ever-changing" menu of "awesome" "fresh everything" and an "interesting" wine list, served in a "starkly decorated" storefront by a chef-owner and staff that "love what they do"; while Bruno's "unique" ways don't charm everyone, admirers insist he's "chilled out" and say his presence alone is "worth the price of a meal."

Pasta Vera   *Italian*   20 | 13 | 18 | $34

Greenwich | 48 Greenwich Ave. (W. Putnam Ave.) | 203-661-9705 |
www.pastavera.com

While this "convenient midpricer" Italian on Greenwich Avenue does a "booming counter business", it also offers a "nice sit-down menu" featuring "standard", "no-fuss, no-pretensions" dishes, which come in "ample portions", and "reasonably priced" wines; there's "always a table available" in the "airy", "sparse" digs, but some report that "service can be uneven."

Pastorale Bistro & Bar Ⓜ *French*   23 | 22 | 23 | $51

Lakeville | 223 Main St. (Lincoln City Rd.) | 860-435-1011 |
www.pastoralebistro.com

Weekenders call this Lakeville French bistro the "essential Friday night stop on the way to the country house", while locals laud it as a "perfect spot for a relaxing dinner"; "inventive" Gallic fare is served in the "rustically romantic" antique house with a "beautiful" outdoor deck, where management and staff offer a "warm welcome, whether or not they know your name", and while a few feel it's "slipping", many others consider it a "pleasant surprise in the middle of nowhere."

	FOOD	DECOR	SERVICE	COST

Patrias Restaurant *Peruvian/Spanish*
▽ 21 | 14 | 23 | $35

Port Chester | 35½ N. Main St. (bet. Adee St. & Westchester Ave.), NY | 914-937-0177

A "pleasant surprise" "in the heart of" Port Chester", this "cute, little" nook is a find for "novel" Spanish-Peruvian cuisine like "good paella" and a "variety of tapas"; in spite of a tight squeeze in the dining room, the mood is "friendly" and insiders insist it "shouldn't be missed."

Pat's Kountry Kitchen *American*
▽ 16 | 12 | 16 | $21

Old Saybrook | 70 Mill Rock Rd. E. (Boston Post Rd.) | 860-388-4784

Cognoscenti caution you may have "flashbacks" of "elementary school" after dining at this "old-time diner" in Old Saybrook serving "wonderful breakfasts" and Traditional American coffee-shop chow (including the "best chicken pot pie" and its signature clam hash) in a room stuffed with teddy bears, blue plates and local art under a red ceiling; "long waits" are to be expected.

Pellicci's *Italian*
19 | 12 | 18 | $30

Stamford | 96-98 Stillwater Ave. (bet. Alden & Spruce Sts.) | 203-323-2542 | www.pelliccis.com

Since 1947, this family-run "old-fashioned red-sauce house" on Stamford's West Side has been a veritable "Rock of Gibraltar", serving up "generous portions" ("always have leftovers") of "standard Italian fare", including "family-style" menus that "cannot be beat for taste or value" according to fans; though most agree the digs look a bit "tired", the owners are "nice to everyone", and while a few jibe that it's "past its prime", most are hopeful it "will continue forever."

Penang Grill *Asian*
22 | 15 | 20 | $28

Greenwich | 55 Lewis St. (Greenwich Ave.) | 203-861-1988

The "cute", "low-frills" digs are "too small for such gigantic flavor" say fans of this BYO Pan-Asian on a side street off Greenwich Avenue offering an "enjoyable" "Indo-Malay-Thai-Chinese-American mashup" with an "emphasis on vegetables"; while a few carp that the "food is not what it has been", "bargain prices" and a staff "so nice it's almost unreal" help make it a "great value" in the minds of many; P.S. cognoscenti counsel it "gets fairly crowded, so opt for takeout."

Penny Lane Pub *Pub Food*
19 | 19 | 20 | $33

Old Saybrook | 150 Main St. (bet. Elmwood St. & Maynard Rd.) | 860-388-9646 | www.pennylanepub.net

There's "lots of buzz" at this "down-home gastropub" on Main in Old Saybrook offering "fine burgers" plus English-style bar fare such as "shepherd's pie" and "fish 'n' chips" in a "cozy", "comfortable" setting, with outdoor seating that's a "plus on a warm evening"; while some find it "overpriced", others deem it a "good value."

Peppercorn's Grill ⊠ *Italian*
26 | 22 | 24 | $50

Hartford | 357 Main St. (bet. Buckingham St. & Capital Ave.) | 860-547-1714 | www.peppercornsgrill.com

Chef Dino Cialfi's "excellent, authentic" Italian cuisine is "always on the money" at this "pricey" Downtown Hartford establishment offering a "varied" menu; "politicos" and Bushnell theatergoers pack the "clubby, intimate" space, and the "friendly" staff makes sure you "get to the theater in time (without rushing)."

Peppino's Ristorante Italian
20 | 15 | 21 | $37

Katonah | 116 Katonah Ave. (Jay St.), NY | 914-232-3212 | www.peppinosristorante.com

"Popular with locals", this "comfy, casual" Katonan depends on a staff of "real pros" to deal out its "nice-sized portions" of "classic" Northern Italian specialties; after 20 years the converted train-station quarters "feel a little old", even with the Tuscan touches, but the "value for the money" compensates.

P.F. Chang's China Bistro Chinese
18 | 19 | 17 | $33

Stamford | Stamford Town Ctr. | 230 Tresser Blvd. (bet. Atlantic St. & Greyrock Pl.) | 203-363-0434

West Hartford | West Farms Mall | 322 W. Farms Mall (New Britain Ave.) | 860-561-0097

White Plains | Westchester Mall | 125 Westchester Ave. (Bloomingdale Rd.), NY | 914-997-6100
www.pfchangs.com

"Light, delicious", "Americanized" Chinese food keeps fans "coming back", especially for the "standout" lettuce wraps, to this "trendy", "stylish" chain; though not everyone is convinced ("overpriced", "ordinary", "loud"), the "consistent" service is a plus, as is the "smart" menu "catering to people with allergies" and other needs.

Piccolo Arancio ⌧ Italian
25 | 21 | 23 | $48

Farmington | 819 Farmington Ave. (Main St.) | 860-674-1224 | www.piccoloarancio.com

"Small and elegant", Peppercorn's "suburban sister" in Farmington is "good for quiet romantic dates, business groups or taking the parents out" thanks to "genuine" Italian cuisine with "subtle flavors", servers who are "attentive without hovering" and an "intimate", "upscale" setting; while oenophiles applaud the "reasonably priced wines", wallet-watchers sigh "be prepared to pay . . . and pay . . . and pay."

Piero's Ⓜ Italian
24 | 9 | 22 | $41

Port Chester | 44 S. Regent St. (bet. Ellendale Ave. & Franklin St.), NY | 914-937-2904

"Don't be deceived" by the "dive"-y digs, this "no-frills" Port Chester Italian is "an insider's favorite", garnering praise for its "outstanding" "red-sauce" repasts and a "wonderful" staff that sets it out in "huge portions"; a "personable" owner and "gently priced" menu make up for "eating on your neighbor's lap", and the many "regulars" attest it's "not to be missed."

🆕 Pine Social, The American
∇ 23 | 23 | 22 | $41
(fka Rocco's Italian Kitchen)

New Canaan | 36 Pine St. (bet. Grove & Park Sts.) | 203-966-5200 | www.roccosct.com

New Canaanites are "pleasantly surprised" by the "turnaround" of the former Rocco's into this "casual", "medium-priced" New American where "good, solid" fare is served by the "same welcoming staff"; there's live guitar Thursdays–Saturdays in the "clubby" setting with a "nice big bar", and some predict this "makeover" will "attract a younger, more social crowd" than its predecessor's.

NEW Piri-Q 🔖Ⓜ *Portuguese* ▽ 20 | 16 | 19 | $29

Mamaroneck | 360 Mamaroneck Ave. (bet. Maple & Mt. Pleasant Aves.), NY | 914-341-1443 | www.piri-q.com

Good ol'-fashioned barbecue gets a "tasty" Portuguese twist at this Mamaroneck newcomer from Rui Correia (of the shuttered Oporto) specializing in fire-roasted chicken and ribs doused in "delicious" signature piri-piri sauce; it's a "cute" spot done up in traditional terra-cotta tile, and "value"-priced takeout inspires "return visits."

Pizzeria Lauretano Ⓜ *Pizza* 22 | 13 | 18 | $25

Bethel | 291 Greenwood Ave. (Grassy Plain St.) | 203-792-1500

A "jewel" in a "barren landscape for foodies" is how fans describe this Bethel pizzeria for its "gourmet" Neapolitan-style pizzas featuring "top-notch, fresh ingredients" and "slightly charred, thin crusts"; live jazz "draws a full house" on Sunday nights, and though some say the "spare" strip-mall digs make you "always feel like you're there past closing time" and the service can be "hit-or-miss", others still exclaim *molto grazie."*

Plan B Burger Bar *Burgers* 22 | 17 | 18 | $23

Glastonbury | 120 Hebron Ave. (bet. Main St. & New London Tpke.) | 860-430-9737
Simsbury | 4 Railroad St. (bet. Phelps Ln. & Station St.) | 860-658-4477
West Hartford | 138 Park Rd. (bet. Beverly Rd. & Kingston St.) | 860-231-1199 ◗
www.planbburger.com

The "burgers, beer and bourbon" are the "bomb" at this hamburger trio where "impressive" patties of beef ground in-house are complemented by a "huge beer selection" and "incredibly well-stocked bar", with "friendly" service as a bonus; Simsbury is housed in a "cute" retrofitted train station with "nice" outdoor seating, while West Hartfordians warn of "long waits" due to limited seating.

Plates Ⓜ *American* 25 | 21 | 22 | $56

Larchmont | 121 Myrtle Blvd. (Murray Ave.), NY | 914-834-1244 | www.platesonthepark.com

This "pleasantly grown-up" Larchmont American "just keeps getting better" with "inventive, beautifully presented" seasonal cuisine (and "outstanding" desserts) courtesy of chef-owner Matthew Karp; it's set in a "lovely" "historic" home overlooking a "charming" park, so in spite of some service hiccups and "pricey" bills, most find it "well worth the cost", and the once-a-week BYO special is a steal.

Plum Tree *Japanese* 20 | 18 | 20 | $36

New Canaan | 70 Main St. (Locust Ave.) | 203-966-8050 | www.plumtreejapanese.com

Though it's "far from the sea", this "family-friendly" Japanese is "close to the hearts of New Canaan's sushi-starved folks" for its

	FOOD	DECOR	SERVICE	COST

"fine, fresh" fin fare served by an "attentive" staff in a "relaxing" setting that includes an "oasislike" outdoor rock garden, a private room decorated with hand-painted paper and an indoor fish pond that "keeps the kids occupied"; a few consider it merely "adequate", while others find it downright "delightful."

Polpo *Italian*   24 | 21 | 21 | $63

Greenwich | 554 Old Post Rd. (W. Putnam Ave.) | 203-629-1999 | www.polporestaurant.com

"Well-executed" Italian fare, "fresh" seafood and an "excellent" wine list "served with panache" are found at this "Greenwich power scene" where "hedge-fund managers" ("and the women who pretend to love them") and other "Ferrari-driving" sorts gather around a "wonderful 'old boys' piano bar" and revel in the "warm" setting full of "old-world style and charm" (and "noise", some complain); opinions are split on the service – "informative and friendly" vs. "arrogant" and "pretentious" – and "unless you are on expense account or a millionaire", the "prices can be excessive."

☒ PolytechnicON20 ☒ *American*   28 | 28 | 29 | $64

Hartford | Hartford Steam Boiler Bldg. | 1 State St., 20th fl. (Columbus Blvd.) | 860-722-5161 | www.ontwenty.com

While the "open, airy" 20th-floor setting with "spectacular views" of the Connecticut River and "exemplary", "sophisticated" service earn this Hartford New American Connecticut's No. 1 Decor and Service honors, respectively, "masterful" chef Noel Jones' "divine" cuisine and "well-thought-out pairings" from an "extensive wine list" make it "truly something special"; it's "expensive", but most feel the prices are "fair", so the "only downside" seems to be "limited hours" (lunch only Mondays–Fridays, happy hour and dinner on Fridays).

Pond House Café ☒ *American*   21 | 22 | 21 | $32

West Hartford | Elizabeth Pk. | 1555 Asylum Ave. (bet. Golf & Sycamore Rds.) | 860-231-8823 | www.pondhousecafe.com

A "favorite" among "ladies who lunch" and outdoor concert-goers, this pondside New American "smack-dab in the middle of Elizabeth Park" in West Hartford offers "breathtaking views" when the "park is in bloom"; "solid", "imaginative" fare and corkage-free BYO make it a "good value", and the "friendly" staff "really makes an effort", though some report "spotty" service "when it's full", which is almost "always the case at weekend brunch."

Ponte Vecchio *Italian*   18 | 18 | 19 | $33

Fairfield | The Brick Walk | 1275 Post Rd. (bet. Beach & Unquowa Rds.) | 203-256-1326 | www.pontevecchiofairfield.com

The "lovely" chef-owner is "always present" and gives a "warm welcome to those who enter" his Fairfield Italian offering "reliable" dishes from a "varied menu", including "incredible" lunch specials and a dinner prix fixe that's a "real deal"; outdoor seating is another plus, and while many suits praise it as a "pleasant" stop "after a day at the office", parents report it's "fine for kids" as well.

Porter House *American/Pub Food*

19 | 17 | 20 | $30

White Plains | 169 Mamaroneck Ave. (E. Post Rd.), NY | 914-831-5663 | www.porterhousebar.com

"When you're in the mood for a burger and a beer", this White Plains pub on the Mamaroneck Avenue strip comes through with "typical", well-priced Americana in "big" portions; it's "more of a bar than a restaurant", so expect a "lively" vibe with lots of "singles", especially "after work" and on weekends, while summertime sees a "hopping" crowd on the patio.

Portofino Pizza & Pasta *Italian/Pizza*

22 | 10 | 19 | $18

Goldens Bridge | A&P Shopping Ctr. | Rtes. 22 & 138 (Anderson Ln.), NY | 914-232-4363

"A bigger slice you will not find" swear fans of this "reasonably priced" Goldens Bridge pizza joint that's "been there forever" and is run by "some of the nicest guys around"; it's "not the most stylish" and counter service "can be slow", so some stick with "takeout."

Positano's *Italian*

22 | 22 | 22 | $52

Westport | 233 Hills Point Rd. (Compo Hill Ave.) | 203-454-4922 | www.positanoswestport.com

"Be transported" to a better place, thanks to "gorgeous views" of Westport's Old Mill Beach and Long Island Sound, "delectable" Italian cooking, an "extensive wine list" and "professional" service at this waterfront establishment; you "pay a high price for the setting" say critics who find the fare "unexciting", but many others declare it a "place to visit more than once"; P.S. insiders recommend lunch for "extremely reasonable" tabs and a room that's "not as crowded."

Post Corner Pizza *Pizza*

20 | 10 | 18 | $22

Darien | 847 Boston Post Rd. (Mansfield Ave.) | 203-655-7721 | www.postcornerpizza.com

"Families love" this casual Darien "tradition" that's been around "forever" offering "heavenly" Greek-style deep-dish pizza, along with other "good-value" salads, gyros and such; service is "quick", and "you can't hurt the furniture since it hasn't changed in years", ergo, it's "noisy and crowded" "when the kids' sports teams let out."

Posto 22 *Italian*

21 | 18 | 21 | $39

New Rochelle | 22 Division St. (bet. Huguenot & Main Sts.), NY | 914-235-2464 | www.posto22.com

This "cute" trattoria in Downtown New Rochelle recalls "Little Italy" with "solid" "home cooking" set down in a "tight" space that's "boisterous" on weekends; even if detractors declare it "nothing special", prices are "reasonable", the staff "pleasant" and it's just the kind of place that makes you "happy."

NEW Post Road Ale House *American*

- | - | - | M

New Rochelle | 11 Huguenot St. (bet. Jackson & Lincoln Sts.), NY | 914-633-4610 | www.postroadalehouse.com

Brian MacMenamin's latest is this New Rochelle entry offering a democratic American menu spanning wings, steaks and seafood

FOOD | DECOR | SERVICE | COST

(including raw-bar items) backed by microbrews and cocktails; the space evokes an updated tavern with exposed brick and other industrial touches, while moderate bills complete the package.

Pot-au-Pho ●⑧ *Vietnamese* ▽ 17 | 12 | 16 | $19

New Haven | 77 Whitney Ave. (bet. Grove & Trumbull Sts.) | 203-776-2248

A "very college kind of place", this New Haven Vietnamese offers "pleasant, if not thrilling" fare and "helpful" service at affordable prices, and "late-night" hours for the après–"parties and clubbing" Yale crowd; critics, though, pan the fare as "bland" and "overpriced", and lament that it's virtually the "only pho game in town."

Primavera *Italian* 24 | 23 | 21 | $50

Croton Falls | 592 Rte. 22 (bet. Birch Hill & Deans Corner Rds.), NY | 914-277-4580 | www.primaverarestaurantandbar.com

An "upscale" Croton Falls crowd convenes at this "inviting" Northern Italian–Med where choosing from a "vast" array of "delicious" specials is helped along by "willing", "on-target" servers; the major quibble is over the "Manhattan prices", which don't faze those who are "always impressed."

Prime 16 *Pub Food* ▽ 23 | 15 | 19 | $22

New Haven | 172 Temple St. (Chapel St.) | 203-782-1616 | www.prime16.com

This "modern burger joint" is "exactly what New Haven needed" exclaim enthusiasts, citing "creative", "well-prepared" burgers and "more good stuff on the menu", including "good choices for vegetarians", a "phenomenal" beer selection (20 taps) and specials like the $5 lunch burger (Tuesdays–Fridays) and half-price beer at happy hour; no wonder it's "always packed" with a "friendly" crowd.

Puket Café *Thai* ▽ 26 | 16 | 23 | $21

Rocky Hill | 945 Cromwell Ave. (Cold Spring Rd.) | 860-436-4366
Wethersfield | 1030 Silas Deane Hwy. (bet. Maple & Mill Sts.) | 860-529-6590
www.puketcafe.com

"Blink" and "you'll miss" this "unassuming" Wethersfield Thai and its new Rocky Hill spin-off, though the "savory, flavorful" fare, with "just the right amount of heat to keep your palate interested", will open your eyes; the "friendly, attentive" staff works "incredibly quickly" and the prices are "affordable"; Rocky Hill also serves Japanese and sushi.

Putnam House Restaurant & 19 | 18 | 20 | $36
Tap Room *American*

Bethel | 12 Depot Pl. (Greenwood Ave.) | 203-791-1852 | www.theputnamhouse.com

A "local favorite" in Bethel, this American offers a "broad menu" of "well-prepared", "reliable" fare in the Victorian-style dining room and casual taproom, and its outdoor patio "rocks during warm weather"; the staff is "friendly" and the "owner is always there and ready to help", adding to its "good value."

	FOOD	DECOR	SERVICE	COST

Q Restaurant & Bar *BBQ* — 22 | 12 | 17 | $26

Port Chester | 112 N. Main St. (bet. Adee St. & Willette Ave.), NY |
914-933-7427 | www.qrestaurantandbar.com

"Feasting" on "dream-worthy" barbecue is the order of the day at
this Port Chester portal for "fall-of-the-bone" ribs and other "down-
and-dirty" 'cue backed by an "excellent selection of craft and micro-
brew beers"; "bare-bones" decor and "cafeteria-style ordering" are
part of the "sloppy" "fun", and "kids love it", while adults chortle
over the "low prices."

Quattro Pazzi *Italian* — 23 | 18 | 20 | $37

Fairfield | 1599 Boston Post Rd. (bet. Reef Rd. & Ruane St.) |
203-259-7417

Norwalk | Oak Hills Park | 165 Fillow St. (Charles Marshall Dr.) |
203-855-1800 Ⓜ

NEW **Stamford** | 269 Bedford St. (Prospect St.) | 203-324-7000
www.quattropazzi.com

There's "lots of choices" on the menu of this "moderately priced"
Italian trio serving "reliable, quality dishes" in a "warm, friendly setting"; the "cafe-style" Downtown Fairfield location gets "crowded"
(many wish "they'd take reservations"), while Stamford's two-level
is roomier, and Norwalk boasts a terrace offering "great views" of
the Oak Hills Golf course.

Rainforest Cafe *American* — 12 | 24 | 15 | $29

Farmington | Westfarms Mall | 500 Westfarms Mall (New Britain Ave.) |
860-521-2002 | www.rainforestcafe.com

If the idea of "eating next to a robotic elephant that sprays water
every 30 minutes" appeals, head for this jungle-themed
Farmington chain link filled with "spellbinding" animatronic crea-
tures plus "families, families, families"; the American eats are
"bland" and "expensive for what you get", but the "concept works"
(despite being "slightly overwhelming"), so it's a "fun place to take
the kids once."

Ralph 'n' Rich's *Italian* — 23 | 21 | 23 | $42

Bridgeport | 815 Main St. (bet. N. Frontage Rd. & State St.) |
203-366-3597 | www.ralphnrichsct.com

An "old-school Italian joint that gets it right", this "classy" "classic"
in Downtown Bridgeport serves "huge portions" of "consistent"
"standards", including the "family-style 'Sunday Sauce' dinners that
leave *paesani* "happily stuffed"; the staff "makes you feel like family"
in the "well-designed" space (with free parking in back) that's "always busy" with a "lively crowd", leading many to conclude that
"Rich and Ralph know what they are doing."

Rani Mahal *Indian* — 23 | 14 | 21 | $32

Mamaroneck | 322-323 Phillips Park Rd. (bet. E. Prospect Ave. &
Spencer Pl.), NY | 914-835-9066 | www.ranimahalny.com

Curry-lovers praise the "wonderful" "variety" at this Mamaroneck
Indian doling out "dependably delicious" subcontinental fare with
"nice twists on traditional dishes"; most overlook the "odd" subter-

ranean locale since servers are "helpful" and the "weekday buffet is a foodie's delight and a bargain to boot."

Rasa *Indian* ▽ 24 | 18 | 20 | $29
(fka Chola)

Greenwich | 107 Greenwich Ave. (Lewis St.) | 203-869-0700 | www.rasagreenwich.com

The kitchen will "crank up the heat if you really want it" at this mid-priced Greenwich Indian that offers a "nice assortment" of "standard dishes done with flair", served by an "attentive" staff; though some appreciate the "vibrant, colorful" setting, takeout is the default option of many.

Ray's Cafe *Chinese* 19 | 8 | 17 | $26

Larchmont | 1995 Palmer Ave. (Parkway St.), NY | 914-833-2551 | www.rayscafeny.com

Rye Brook | Rye Ridge Shopping Ctr. | 176 S. Ridge St. (bet. Crescent Pl. & Ellendale Ave.), NY | 914-937-0747

Customers count on these Larchmont–Rye Brook siblings for relatively "healthy" Shanghainese dishes with a focus on "fresh" veggies and gluten-free offerings that are "better than most"; considering the "so-so service" and "dreary" settings that are "begging for a makeover", most opt for takeout.

Rebeccas ⊠Ⓜ *American* 26 | 21 | 23 | $80

Greenwich | 265 Glenville Rd. (bet. Pemberwick & Riversville Rds.) | 203-532-9270 | www.rebeccasgreenwich.com

The "superb", "tantalizing flavors" and "beautiful presentations" on chef/co-owner Reza Khorshidi's "imaginative menu" make this Greenwich New American a "culinary paradise", one that's "run like a well-oiled machine" by his "gracious" wife and partner, Rebecca, and their "professional" staff; "exquisite flowers" grace the "lovely environment", but some grouse that "regular customers" are favored, while wallet-watchers wince at the "*très* haute prices."

Red Barn *American* 16 | 19 | 18 | $38

Westport | 292 Wilton Rd. (Merritt Pkwy., exit 41) | 203-222-9549 | www.redbarnrestaurant.com

You almost expect to see "Paul Revere sitting next to you" at this "classic New England" spot in Westport, housed in a barn with "rustic decor", "inviting" working fireplaces and a lakeside dining area; the service is "accommodating" and the "reasonably priced", "generous portions" of Traditional American fare (including a Sunday brunch buffet) offer "good value", though critics find it "tired" ("even the shrimp cocktail is ready for an old-age home").

Red Lotus *Thai* 21 | 19 | 20 | $32

New Rochelle | 227 Main St. (Stephenson Blvd.), NY | 914-576-0444 | www.redlotusthai.com

Fans "frequent" this New Rochelle Thai for "flavorful" basic dishes "pleasantly served" "in a pretty red room"; "tight parking is a downside", but modest prices make up for it, and many "love it for takeout."

	FOOD	DECOR	SERVICE	COST

NEW Red Lulu Cocina & Tequila Bar *Mexican*

▽ 24 | 24 | 21 | $46

South Norwalk | 128 Washington St. (bet. Main & Water Sts.) | 203-939-1600 | www.redlulumexican.com

Lolita's "way-sexy" SoNo sibling is "no ordinary" Mexican but rather "dining theater" with a "Goth" flair, where creative *comida* is served in "dark" rooms ("bring candles to see") decorated with black and "red-flocked" wallpaper and "ornate chandeliers", while "one of the largest tequila bars in the county" turns out "awesome" drinks; insiders advise "be prepared for a wait" and note that you may find yourself "texting" your date due to the pumping music.

Red Plum *Asian*

21 | 22 | 22 | $33

Mamaroneck | 251 Mamaroneck Ave. (bet. Palmer & Prospect Aves.), NY | 914-777-6888 | www.redplumrestaurant.com

An "interesting" array of Pan-Asian specialties – from "unusually fresh" sushi to pad Thai – awaits at this "modern" Mamaroneck sib of Sushi Toyo also pouring specialty cocktails at a marble bar; even if prices are "higher" than its next-door neighbor, the vibe is "pleasant in a Zen kind of way", and it's something of a "go-to" in the area.

Red Rooster Drive-In ⊘ *Burgers*

18 | 11 | 15 | $13

Brewster | 1566 Rte. 22 (Rte. 312), NY | 845-279-8046

"Road food just as it should be" is the lure at this "nifty", 1960s Brewster drive-in dishing up "good burgers", "perfect dogs", "fresh, fried onion rings" and "frosty shakes" "like you remember from your childhood"; "kids love it" and grown-ups who enjoy the "retro vibe" "feel nostalgic" picnicking outside (seating's minimal) then taking "a whirl through the miniature golf course" next door.

Rein's NY Style Deli-Restaurant *Deli*

22 | 12 | 17 | $22

Vernon | Shops at 30 Plaza | 435 Hartford Tpke. (bet. Dobson & Merline Rds.) | 860-875-1344 | www.reinsdeli.com

For a "slice of the Lower East Side" in "nowheresville", locals and road-warriors shuttling "between New York and Boston" head to this "Jewish oasis" in Vernon for a "huge menu" of "gargantuan" sandwiches and other "top-notch" nosh, including "super" half-sour pickles and gluten-free items, served with "just the right bit of attitude"; though the space is "nothing to write home about" and it's "always packed" and "noisy", many insist it's "worth going out of your way."

Reka's *Thai*

19 | 15 | 20 | $34

White Plains | 2 Westchester Ave. (Main St.), NY | 914-949-1440 | www.rekasthai.com

A White Plains "fixture" since 1987, this modest but "welcoming" Thai features "classic", "authentic" cooking – and "plenty of it" – "spiced as you request"; most don't mind the distinctly "unfancy" basement digs, because prices are low, and the lunch specials "can't be beat."

Restaurant at Rowayton
Seafood *Seafood*

FOOD	DECOR	SERVICE	COST
22	20	19	$50

Rowayton | 89 Rowayton Ave. (bet. Crockett St. & Logan Pl.) |
203-866-4488 | www.rowaytonseafood.com

Only the "freshest possible seafood from the fish market next door"
could trump the "impressive seaside real estate" of this "fine purveyor" of fin fare in Rowayton with a "view of the Five Mile River and
marina"; "valet parking for your BMW" (unless you come by boat)
and an "*International Yachtsman* cover-boy" crowd highlight the
"Connecticut-chic" scene, but critics decry the "high prices" and
pervasive "attitude", while wondering "who do you have to bribe to
get a table on the porch?"

◪ Restaurant at Water's Edge *American*

FOOD	DECOR	SERVICE	COST
23	26	25	$47

Westbrook | Water's Edge Resort & Spa | 1525 Boston Post Rd.
(Knothe Hill) | 860-399-5901 | www.watersedge-resort.com

A "sweeping view of the Sound" is the backdrop at this "upscale"
New American at Westbrook's Water's Edge resort, where it's
"lovely" to "walk around the grounds" or retire to the "beautiful"
outdoor patio for "cocktails, live music or wedding peeping"; "excellent" service and "exceptional" fare, including a "fantastic" Sunday
brunch, are additional reasons many consider it "worth the money
and the drive."

Restaurant L&E and
French 75 Bar ⓜ *French*

FOOD	DECOR	SERVICE	COST
∇ 24	25	22	$63

Chester | 59 Main St. (Maple St.) | 860-526-5301 |
www.restaurantfrench75bar.com

A "welcome newcomer replacing an old favorite", this New French
in the former space of Restaurant du Village is "worth the drive" to
Chester for its monthly menu of "superlative" tapas-size dishes and
"superb" wine list, served by an "accommodating" staff in a "beautiful", "charming" antiques-filled room; though critics carp about
"small plates adding up to big tabs", for many others, it's a "real
find"; the 75 Bar offers bar bites.

ⓃⒺⓌ Restaurant North ⓈⓂ *American*

FOOD	DECOR	SERVICE	COST
26	22	25	$60

Armonk | 386 Main St. (bet. Bedford Rd. & Elm St.), NY | 914-273-8686 |
www.restaurantnorth.com

A "terrific new addition" to the Northern Westchester scene, this
"chic" "hot spot" from Union Square Cafe alums brings "destination
dining" to Armonk with "sublime" "farm-to-table" New American
fare, a "fantastic" wine list and a "sharp, solicitous" staff; it's
"pricey" and the din can be "deafening" (upstairs is more "serene"),
but the biggest hurdle may be scoring a reservation.

Ristorante Luce *Italian*

FOOD	DECOR	SERVICE	COST
∇ 22	19	19	$45

Hamden | Mt. Carmel Shopping Ctr. | 2987 Whitney Ave. (Ives St.) |
203-407-8000 | www.ristoranteluce.net

"Large portions" of "solid", "traditional" Italian fare at "reasonable
prices" and a large wine list make this family-run ristorante the "go-
to neighborhood eatery" for many Hamden inhabitants; the "dark",

"formal" interior somewhat belies its shopping-mall location, and while fans find the staff "very pleasant", others think the service could use a "fine-tune."

River House *American*

17 | 20 | 17 | $42

Westport | 299 Riverside Ave. (bet. River Ct. & Sylvan Ln.) | 203-226-5532 | www.riverhousewestport.com

Taking in "amazing" vistas of the Saugatuck River from the "bright, airy" interior or outdoor patio is "always a nice way to dine" say fans of this riverside Westport Traditional American, a "go-to brunch or lunch place", or "evening cocktails in the summer"; critics who knock the fare as "uneven", however, wonder whether the "lovely setting" is "worth the price", since "you can't eat the view."

River Tavern *American*

26 | 21 | 22 | $47

Chester | 23 Main St. (Rte. 148) | 860-526-9417 | www.rivertavernchester.net

An "excellent choice" in "delightful" Chester, this "cozy" "gem" is the showcase for Jonathan Rapp's "consistently fabulous" daily menus of "innovative" New American dishes made with the "freshest ingredients, almost all locally grown"; further assets: an "interesting", "fairly priced" wine list and a "friendly" staff that provides "efficient" service amid "informal", "elegantly sparse" surroundings; P.S. "save room for the date pudding" and be sure to "order it in advance."

Rizzuto's Wood-Fired Kitchen & Bar *Italian*

20 | 19 | 18 | $36

Bethel | 6 Stony Hill Rd. (Sky Edge Dr.) | 203-790-4444
West Hartford | 111 Memorial Rd. (S. Main St.) | 860-232-5000
Westport | 540 Riverside Ave. (Bridge St.) | 203-221-1002
www.rizzutos.com

The "aroma from the brick oven makes you hungry as soon as you enter" this Italian trio offering "something for everyone" "from low end to high", including "yummy pizzas", and in a setting that's "upscale without being stuffy", drawing lots of "families" as well as a "nice bar crowd"; calling the cooking "hit-or-miss" and the service "anything but professional", however, critics lament that it "looks like it wants to be a chain."

Roasted Peppers *American*

21 | 16 | 20 | $34

Mamaroneck | 320 Mamaroneck Ave. (Spencer Pl.), NY | 914-341-1140 | www.roastedpeppersny.com

This "welcome" addition along Mamaroneck Avenue's ever-expanding restaurant strip specializes in "creative" New American cooking with Tex-Mex "twists" (like their signature roast pepper); the "casual" space with exposed brick and sun-inspired tones is "comfortable" enough, and "inexpensive" prices complete the package.

Roger Sherman Inn Ⓜ *Continental*

24 | 25 | 23 | $59

New Canaan | Roger Sherman Inn | 195 Oenoke Ridge (Holmewood Ln.) | 203-966-4541 | www.rogershermaninn.com

A "big old historical country house" is the "luxurious, comfo~· setting for a "top-notch" dinner or "magnificent" brunch a.

nified" New Canaan Continental offering "wonderful" fare and "unobtrusive, watchful" service in a "beautiful", "white-tablecloth" space with a "lovely outdoor porch"; while a few sound the "snooze alert" for the "old-school" scene, a younger, "preppy" crowd ("Muffy? Is it really you?") gathers in the "casual" bar for a "well-done" menu of "small plates" and occasional "live music."

Ron Blacks ❶ *Pub Food* ▽ 16 | 19 | 18 | $32

White Plains | 181 Mamaroneck Ave. (bet. Maple Ave. & Rutherford St.), NY | 914-358-5811 | www.ronblacks.com

The many craft beers on tap "are a wonder to behold" at this "roomy" White Plains pub also proffering "bar-food" options – from nachos to steaks – in "comfortable" digs with lots of wood and walls full of antique clocks; so even if the grub's "underwhelming", it's still a "cool place to hang out."

Rouge Winebar *Mediterranean* ▽ 21 | 22 | 24 | $36

South Norwalk | 88 Washington St. (Main St.) | 203-354-4781 | www.rougewinebar-ct.com

Insiders insist you "must not miss" this "under-the-radar star" in SoNo or its "creative, tasty" Med small plates, which can be paired with "excellent" wines by the glass; the staff is "friendly and knowledgeable", and the cozy, exposed-brick setting is "quieter than many other spots" in town, making it a "good scene for a date or a drink."

Route 22 *Pub Food* 14 | 17 | 16 | $27

Armonk | 55 Old Rte. 22 (Kaysal Ct.), NY | 914-765-0022 | www.rt22restaurant.com

A "cross between a truck stop, a diner and Chuck E. Cheese", this Armonk watering hole is where parents "take the kids for a burger" "served in cute car boxes" amid "lots of distractions"; "erratic" service and "noisy" environs drive adults sans children to "go elsewhere."

Royal Palace *Chinese* 25 | 16 | 23 | $29

New Haven | 32 Orange St. (Crown St.) | 203-776-6663

"Excellent" and "incredibly affordable", this New Haven Chinese serves a "huge", bifurcated menu that includes both Sino-American "staples" and "exotic, more authentic" dishes, and the "friendly owners are happy to help you decipher the two"; though most dismiss the "mundane decor", the "large round tables with lazy Susans" are "great for tasting parties."

Royal Palace *Indian* 20 | 13 | 19 | $35

White Plains | 77 Knollwood Rd. (Dobbs Ferry Rd./Rte. 100B), NY | 914-289-1988 | www.royalpalacecuisines.com

"Lots" of "flavorful" choices – especially at the "limitless" buffets at both lunch and dinner – keep loyalists coming to this "friendly" White Plains Indian; its spare setting could likely use an "update", but at least it's "convenient to the movies", and priced well too.

Rraci ⊠ *Italian* | 26 | 22 | 25 | $50

Brewster | 3670 Rte. 6 (bet. Branch & Thomas Rds.), NY | 845-278-6695 | www.rracisrestaurant.com

"You can tell they care" at this "high-end" Brewster Italian offering a "bit of heaven" via "delicious, homemade pasta" and such "wow"-worthy seafood "they must own the boat"; those who find the "attractive" low-lit setting too "cave"-like and "deafening" at times can head to the "lovely garden", while practically "perfect" service and prices that are a "bargain for the quality" help make it "a winner."

RSVP ⊠⊅ *French* | ∇ 28 | 16 | 22 | $92

West Cornwall | 7 Railroad St. (Rte. 128) | 860-672-7787

It's "like dining at a friend's house" at this 20-seat BYO French bistro in West Cornwall – "in fact, you have to be a friend or a friend of a friend" of the "idiosyncratic" owners to snag a table for the weekend $75 prix fixe "multicourse extravaganza"; though some find the "claustrophic seating" and the hosts' "sense of their own importance" stifling, many declare it a "must-dine experience" and promise "you'll be surprised each time you go"; no credit cards accepted.

Ruby's Oyster Bar & Bistro *Seafood* | 23 | 20 | 21 | $48

Rye | 45 Purchase St. (Smith St.), NY | 914-921-4166 | www.rubysoysterbar.com

Locals "love" this "pearl" of an oyster bar in Rye, a "fashionable" stop for bivalves "galore", "wonderful" bistro-style seafood and "generous pours" on drinks; it owes its "sophisticated", "city" vibe to a "hopping bar" scene and a "yuppie" clientele, just know that "noisy" acoustics can make "earplugs" a necessity.

Rue des Crêpes *French* | 19 | 20 | 18 | $25

Harrison | 261 Halstead Ave. (Harrison Ave.), NY | 914-315-1631 | www.ruedescrepes.com

A "delightful hideaway", this "quaint, little" cafe in Harrison puts out "borderline-addictive" crêpes "prepared in every way imaginable" and other French fare in a "casual" muralled interior decked out with Parisian touches; modest prices are a perk, although service can be a sore spot and the "Epcot"-y decor is a little "overly cute" to some.

Ruth's Chris Steak House *Steak* | 25 | 22 | 24 | $65

Newington | 2513 Berlin Tpke. (Kitts Ln.) | 860-666-2202 | www.ruthschris.com

Newington Carnivores "love the sizzling platters" of "oh-so-good buttery steaks" at this "top-quality" chophouse chain link that comes through with "winning" sides too; delivering "old-style service" in a "traditional" setting, it's "expensive" (and "not for the dieter"), but "reliable", especially when you're "entertaining friends and clients."

Rye Grill & Bar *Eclectic* | 18 | 20 | 18 | $38

Rye | 1 Station Plaza (on 1st St., off Purdy Ave.), NY | 914-967-0332 | www.ryegrill.com

"Still a handy standby", there's "something for everyone" at this "renovated" Rye Eclectic whose "beautiful" three-level digs are "large" enough to accommodate diners looking for "solid" "high-end" pub grub as well as those interested in an "attractive young bar scene"; though service can be "haphazard" and the "noise is a deal-breaker" for some, there's "never a dull moment."

Rye Roadhouse *Cajun/Creole* | 18 | 12 | 18 | $33 |

Rye | 12 High St. (bet. Clinton & Maple Aves.), NY | 914-925-2668 | www.ryeroadhouse.com

You'll need a "good GPS" to track down this "deliberately seedy" Rye "roadhouse" "nestled into" a residential neighborhood and turning out "authentic" Cajun-Creole in a "laid-back" atmosphere; yes, it's "basically a bar", but the food's "a big step up from pub fare" and "friendly" staffers plus occasional live music make for a "fun night out."

Sage American Grill *Seafood/Steak* | 19 | 22 | 20 | $41 |

New Haven | 100 S. Water St. (Howard Ave.) | 203-787-3466 | www.sageamerican.com

"Lovely water views" of New Haven Harbor make this "bright, airy" surf 'n' turfer a "favorite on a warm sunny day", "especially for Sunday brunch", and the "long, varied" menu offers "plenty of choices" of "nicely done" steaks and seafood, in portions so "huge" you'll likely "take home half your meal"; the "convivial" atmosphere "invites lingering", though it may be just that "service lags a bit" when it's busy, as some report.

Sagi Ⓩ *Italian* | 23 | 19 | 23 | $40 |

Ridgefield | 23 Catoonah St. (Main St.) | 203-431-0200 | www.sagiofridgefield.com

The Occhino family "welcomes everyone with open arms" at their "lovely" trattoria "nestled" off Ridgefield's main drag where chef-owner Bianca DeMasi-Occhino "takes great pride" in her "well-prepared" and "well-presented" "homestyle" dishes, which can be paired with "incredibly reasonable" wines by the glass; though some report "no elbow room" in the "warm" cream-and-red interior, others find the atmosphere "relaxing" and the prices "amazing for the area."

𝗡𝗘𝗪 Sails American Grill Ⓜ *American* | - | - | - | M |

Norwalk | 148 Rowayton Ave. (bet. McKinley St. & Wilson Ave.) | 203-853-7245 | www.sailsamericangrill.com

Old salts and landlubbers squeeze aboard this smallish new boîte in Rowayton Village overlooking Five Mile River for affordable New American fare served up by a seasoned crew amid streamlined nautical decor (e.g. racing sails on the ceiling, boating cushions on the banquettes); a fireplace glows in cool weather, a patio beckons in warm and the lively bar promises good cheer in all seasons, but take warning: decibels can approach foghorn levels.

Saito ⓏⓂ *Eclectic/Japanese* | ∇ 27 | 22 | 24 | $57 |

Greenwich | 249 Railroad Ave. (bet. Arch St. & Field Point Rd.) | 203-557-0880

Those in the know report an "epiphany" at "genius" chef-owner Youichi Saito's "superb" Japanese-Eclectic in Greenwich, where he demonstrates his "rare gift" for "fusing together wondrous flavors" trom around the world; the service is "exceptional" and the space "elegant", though some find the latter "cold and loud", and while it's "expensive", most conclude it's "worth it."

Sakura *Japanese* | 21 | 18 | 21 | $38 |

Westport | 680 Post Rd. E. (Hills Point Rd.) | 203-222-0802 | www.sakurarestaurant.com

"Still a crowd-pleaser" after all these years, this Westport Japanese is "always mobbed" thanks to "endlessly entertaining" teppanyaki (aka hibachi) grills that are popular among "families with kids", "fresh, flavorful" sushi bar offerings and "pleasant" service; a few find the "chop-chop tables" "noisy" and "hokey", and the fare "overpriced", but others describe it as a "solid dining experience."

Sal e Pepe *Italian* | 24 | 19 | 21 | $43 |

Newtown | 975 Main St. (Swamp Rd.) | 203-426-0805 | www.salepeperestaurant.com

For "grown-up dining", *amici* endorse this "exceptional" Newtown Northern Italian serving "innovative", "well-prepared" dishes featuring "local, fresh" ingredients", including "fabulous pastas "made on-site"; owner Angelo Marini is "always ready to welcome" diners into the "attractive, comfortable" space that is "beyond the expectations" raised by its "storefront" facade, and though a few grouse about "NY prices", many consider it a "good value" overall.

Sally's Apizza Ⓜ⇚ *Pizza* | 25 | 9 | 11 | $21 |

New Haven | 237 Wooster St. (bet. Olive & Warren Sts.) | 203-624-5271 | www.sallysapizza.com

Wags liken this New Haven institution to a "private club that barely tolerates you", with a "famously rude" staff and "insiders breezing past you" on "ridiculous" lines "out of a Beckett play", but membership (plus the "patience of a stone") has its rewards – namely, what devotees call the "Holy Grail of pizza", i.e. "outstanding" thin-crust pies with "perfectly charred crusts" and the "freshest ingredients"; as long as you "don't expect ambiance", you'll "never leave disappointed."

Salsa Ⓜ⇚ *Southwestern* | ▽ 25 | 11 | 23 | $21 |

New Milford | 54 Railroad St. (Bank St.) | 860-350-0701

"The simple storefront" setting is "deceiving" say fans of this Southwestern specialist that's "not much in the way of decor", but a "must stop in Milford" for "fresh, tasty" fare at "bargain prices", served in a "casual", "laid-back" environment; it offers "good value for the buck", which is why it's "often quite busy."

Sal's Pizza ⇚ *Pizza* | 23 | 6 | 12 | $15 |

Mamaroneck | 316 Mamaroneck Ave. (Palmer Ave.), NY | 914-381-2022

The perpetual "lines" tell the story at this "authentic, gritty" "landmark" pizzeria in Mamaroneck putting out "superb", "cheesy" slices including a Sicilian slab "that will make you contemplate the meaning of life"; the "surly" service is "right out of central casting", but "by now that's part of the charm"; P.S. "top off your meal with gelato next door."

	FOOD	DECOR	SERVICE	COST

Saltwater Grille ⓜ *American*

| 17 | 23 | 16 | $46 |

Stamford | 183 Harbor Dr. (off Shippan Ave.) | 203-391-6500 |
www.saltwatergrille.net

"Location, location, location" is the mantra of fans of this harborside New American in Stamford that offers "lovely" vistas from a multi-level interior with a flagstone fireplace and "romantic" outdoor decks, and boosters praise the "modern, varied" seafood-centric menu and weekend brunch buffet; critics argue that the "water view is the only reason to go", dismissing the fare as "pedestrian" and the service as "disappointing", but others still recommend it as a "great place for drinks."

Sam's of Gedney Way *American*

| 19 | 16 | 20 | $36 |

White Plains | 52 Gedney Way (bet. Mamaroneck Ave. &
Old Mamaroneck Rd.), NY | 914-949-0978 |
www.samsofgedneyway.com

"Lots of repeat customers" laud this "easygoing" American "old-timer" in White Plains featuring a "no-surprises" traditional menu headlined by burgers that are "hard to top"; after 80 years on the scene, perhaps the "informal" "pubby" setting could use "refreshing", but prices are moderate and service "accommodating" (especially for parties) so you "can always count on" it.

Sardegna ⓜ *Italian*

| ▽ 19 | 15 | 22 | $37 |

Larchmont | 154 Larchmont Ave. (Addison St.), NY | 914-833-3399 |
www.sardegnany.com

"A pleasant change" from the usual, this "family-run" Larchmont Italian focuses on "carefully prepared" Sardinian specialties like malloreddus (a type of pasta) and wild game matched with "interesting" regional wines; factor in "attentive" service and prices that are "quite reasonable", and the consensus is it "should be busier."

Saybrook Fish House *Seafood*

| 22 | 16 | 20 | $37 |

Rocky Hill | 2165 Silas Deane Hwy. (bet. Harbor View Dr. & Joiners Rd.) |
860-721-9188 | www.saybrookfishhouserestaurants.com

Afishionados advise "go with a big appetite" to this "popular" Rocky Hill seafooder serving "solid preparations" of "fresh" fin fare that can be ordered with "family-size" salads; some critics carp about "bland" eats and a "chainlike" ambiance, but for others it remains a "dependable" option.

ⓩ Schoolhouse at Cannondale ⓜ *American*

| 27 | 23 | 24 | $59 |

Wilton | 34 Cannon Rd. (Seeley Rd.) | 203-834-9816 |
www.schoolhouseatcannondale.com

Fans would stay "after school any day of the week" to savor chef-owner Tim LaBant's "fabulous" weekly menu of "inspired" New American cuisine featuring "locally grown produce" at his "pricey" Wilton eatery, housed in a "charming former one-room schoolhouse" overlooking the Norwalk River; the toque "talks with every guest" while his "friendly" staff provides "attentive" service, and though some say they could use a hall pass from the "cramped" quarters, most give this "find" extra credit for a "delightful dining experience."

Scoozzi Trattoria & Wine Bar 🏧 *Italian* 22 | 22 | 21 | $41

New Haven | 1104 Chapel St. (York St.) | 203-776-8268 | www.scoozzi.com

At this New Haven Northern Italian that's "adjacent to Yale Rep", "uniformly good" cuisine is made with "fresh, locally sourced" ingredients and "attractively served" amid "comfortable, elegant" surroundings, with an outdoor patio that alfresco fans find "magical" on a "balmy evening"; the staff is "always on the ball", while Sunday brunch jumps with live jazz, all of which make it the "personal favorite" of many.

Scribner's *Seafood* 22 | 18 | 22 | $35

Milford | 31 Village Rd. (Hawley Ave.) | 203-878-7019 | www.scribnersrestaurant.com

"Off the beaten path", this Milford seafooder is "worth looking for" say "locals" who "recommend it to all out-of-town guests" as a "dependable" purveyor of "terrific", "fresh" (if "nothing fancy") fin fare, served in a nautically themed room full of "maritime novelties"; half-price wines on Tuesdays and Fridays and a "dirt-cheap" early-bird make it one of the "best bang for your bucks around."

Seaside Johnnie's *Seafood* 12 | 18 | 15 | $38

Rye | 94 Dearborn Ave. (Forest Ave.), NY | 914-921-6104 | www.seasidejohnnies.com

The "spectacular views" of Long Island Sound are the best things going for this "shack"-like seafooder on Rye's Oakland Beach; indeed the service is "slow" and the "pricey" "deep-fried" fare and "tropical drinks" are "ordinary" at best, but somehow, "sitting out on the patio makes it all ok"; P.S. open from April–October.

Seasons Japanese Bistro *Japanese* 23 | 16 | 20 | $35

White Plains | 105 Mamaroneck Ave. (Quarropas St.), NY | 914-421-1163 | www.seasonsjapanesebistro.com

"Exceptionally fresh fish" is the hook at this storefront sushi specialist in White Plains where there are "no frills", just "solid", "fairly priced" Japanese fare; its "simple", "calming" setting and "so-so" decor may not stand out, but it's certainly convenient, and "kid-friendly" too.

⊿ Serevan *Mediterranean* 27 | 23 | 25 | $54

Amenia | 6 Autumn Ln. (Rte. 44, west of Rte. 22), NY | 845-373-9800 | www.serevan.com

"A beacon amid the hayfields", this "outstanding" Amenia Mediterranean is a "gourmet paradise" where "gifted", "passionate" chef-owner Serge Madikians uses "top-quality ingredients" and "aromatic spices" to create "superb" "Middle Eastern–tinged" dishes so "scrumptious" you could "point at random" to the menu and have an "inspired" meal; slightly "pricey" tabs are trumped by the "quiet, welcoming farmhouse" setting, "polished" service and overall "convivial" experience.

	FOOD	DECOR	SERVICE	COST

Sesame Seed ⑤ *Mideastern*

21 | 16 | 18 | $24

Danbury | 68 W. Wooster St. (bet. Division & Pleasant Sts.) |
203-743-9850 | www.sesameseedrestaurant.com

The "quirky" "knickknacks" "cluttering" this "bohemian" "Danbury institution" are a "bit dated", but the "generous helpings" of Mideast eats are "always fresh"; a "relaxed attitude" from the staff and "reasonable prices" are two more features that render it "worth the wait" when it's "crowded" (usually around lunchtime).

Shack, The *American*
(fka Beach Café)

13 | 14 | 14 | $33

Fairfield | 2070 Post Rd. (Pine Creek Rd.) | 203-254-3606 |
www.theshackfairfield.com

Surveyors are split over the makeover of the former Beach Café in Fairfield into this "casual" American serving "bar crowd-pleasers" and "basic" comfort-food offerings in a "bright, airy" summer cottage setting; fans say it's "great for families" (the movie night is a "great bonus") and praise the "much improved layout", but foes blast the fare as "marginal" and the service as "weak", and fume over the "frat-party" atmosphere on weekends.

⚡ Shady Glen ⊘ *Diner*

21 | 15 | 21 | $14

Manchester | Manchester Parkade | 360 W. Middle Tpke. (Broad St.) |
860-643-0511
Manchester | 840 E. Middle Tpke. (bet. Lake & Westland Sts.) |
860-649-4245

"Step back in time" at this "classic" diner duo in Manchester (voted Connecticut's No. 1 Bang for the Buck), where "friendly", paper hat–wearing servers "right out of central casting" dish out "amazing" cheeseburgers and "wonderful homemade ice cream" in a "1950s" setting; all in all, fans boast "you won't find better value than this."

Sharpe Hill Vineyard Ⓜ *American*

- | - | - | E

Pomfret | 108 Wade Rd. (Rte. 97) | 860-974-3549 |
www.sharpehill.com

"Spectacular" views of the vineyards are the backdrop at this New American in Pomfret's Sharpe Hill winery, which offers "expertly prepared dishes" and "great wines" in a farmhouse setting that's "charming beyond belief", with a "lovely" outdoor patio; the "only caveat" – "very steep and narrow stairs" leading to the dining room; P.S. hours vary seasonally and reservations are required.

Shell Station *Continental/Seafood*

∇ 20 | 16 | 19 | $33

Stratford | 2520 Main St. (Broadbridge Ave.) | 203-377-1648 |
www.shellstationrestaurant.net

For "reliable" fin fare and sushi in a "wonderful strange location", afishionados in Stratford head to this Continental seafooder housed in the former train station; it's "nothing fancy" – some liken the setting to a "convenience store" – and you may have to "hold on to your plates as the trains roar by", but fans insist this "find" is on the right track for "decent food at a reasonable price."

	FOOD	DECOR	SERVICE	COST

Sherwood's ● *Pub Food* | 20 | 12 | 16 | $27 |

Larchmont | 2136 Boston Post Rd. (bet. Larchmont Ave. & Manor Pl.), NY | 914-833-3317 | www.sherwoodsrestaurant.com

"Stick to the burgers and ribs and you won't be disappointed" at this "dark", "noisy" Larchmont tavern, a "nice neighborhood" place also known for its "fine Buffalo wings"; perhaps the setting and service could use some work, but tabs are cheap, and the casual atmosphere is especially "good for kids."

Shish Kebab House of | ▽ 25 | 24 | 22 | $36 |
Afghanistan *Afghan*

West Hartford | 36 Lasalle Rd. (bet. Arapahoe Rd. & Farmington Ave.) | 860-231-8400 | www.afghancuisine.net

The eponymous skewers are "amazing" and "everything else is delish" at this "excellent"" West Hartford Afghan, a "treasure hidden in plain sight" where a "diverse", "interesting" menu is served in a "beautifully decorated" space with "oriental rugs on display" and a hookah lounge; live jazz in the bar and "traditional music" in the dining room round out the "unique dining experience."

Siena ☒ *Italian* | 23 | 19 | 21 | $53 |

Stamford | 519 Summer St. (bet. Broad & Spring Sts.) | 203-351-0898 | www.sienaristorante.net

"Wonderful" Tuscan dishes are complemented by "fine" Italian wines at this "expensive" destination in Downtown Stamford, where "regulars" are "treated like family" by a "knowledgeable staff" (indeed, some surveyors opine "it helps to be known here"); the setting is "pretty", though it would probably seem more "romantic" to more people if there weren't such a "loud", often "deafening" "noise level."

Solé Ristorante *Italian* | 21 | 18 | 20 | $48 |

New Canaan | 105 Elm St. (bet. Park St. & South Ave.) | 203-972-8887 | www.zhospitalitygroup.com

"Solid", "reliable" Northern Italian fare and "great pizzas" come via a mostly "friendly" "longtime staff" at this somewhat "pricey" New Canaan *cucina*; "incredibly loud" acoustics are "still an issue" (even when the "sparse" space "isn't full"), so "seek a corner" if you want to converse – or "grab a seat at the bar" overlooking the open kitchen instead and add to the "lively" proceedings.

SolToro Tequila Grill *Mexican* | ▽ 20 | 22 | 21 | $33 |

Uncasville | Mohegan Sun Casino | 1 Mohegan Sun Blvd. (bet. Rtes. 2 & 32) | 860-862-4800 | www.soltororestaurant.com

"Who knew Michael Jordan knows his authentic Mexican cuisine?" marvel admirers of MJ's cantina-style eatery at the Mohegan Sun casino in Uncasville where the south-of-the-border *comida* is "surprisingly good" and "friendly bartenders" mix cocktails with nearly 200 tequilas on display at the bar to complement "fantastic happy-hour specials"; still, some critics find it "expensive", while others wish it "stayed open later" than 10 PM (midnight Fridays and Saturdays).

	FOOD	DECOR	SERVICE	COST

SoNo Baking Company & Café *Bakery* 26 | 16 | 18 | $19

South Norwalk | 101 S. Water St. (Hanford Pl.) | 203-847-7666 | www.sonobaking.com

At John Barricelli's "outstanding" SoNo bakery/cafe, the "desserts taste as wonderful as they look" and are "made before your eyes", along with "extraordinary" breads and "excellent pastries", while the breakfast and lunch menus include "amazing omelets" and "wonderful sandwiches"; critics find the space a bit "awkward", and are "mystified" by the "attitude" of the counter help, while others caution that it'll cost you some "serious dough."

Sono Bana Japanese Restaurant *Japanese* ▽ 24 | 16 | 23 | $28

Hamden | 1206 Dixwell Ave. (Helen St.) | 203-281-9922 | www.sonobana.com

"Locals" ranging from "families with young children" to "Nobel laureates" can be found at this long-standing Japanese "gem" in Hamden, an "excellent everyday" option for "lovely, delicious sushi" and "reasonably priced" entrees, which are served by a "friendly" staff; the storefront space can get "busy in the evenings", so "calling for a reservation is recommended."

Sonora *Nuevo Latino* 24 | 22 | 22 | $49

Port Chester | 179 Rectory St. (Willett Ave.), NY | 914-933-0200 | www.sonorarestaurant.net

"Like a vacation in South America", this "festive" Port Chester "favorite" from Rafael Palomino charms guests with an "innovative" mix of "refined", "artistic" Nuevo Latino plates elevated by "fabulous" cocktails "that will knock you off your barstool"; a "knowledgeable" staff shows "attention to detail", now if only they could do something about the "incredibly noisy" acoustics.

Sono Seaport Seafood *Seafood* 15 | 12 | 13 | $29

South Norwalk | 100 Water St. (bet. Elizabeth St. & Hanford Pl.) | 203-854-9483 | www.sonoseaportseafood.com

A "classic summertime venue with outdoor picnic tables" on a deck overlooking Norwalk Harbor, this SoNo seafooder serves "honest" "New England–style" fin fare at "reasonable" prices in a "family-friendly" atmosphere; though critics find the interior downright "dismal", and warn of "rude" treatment from an "overworked" staff, the "alfresco dining continues to draw locals" nonetheless.

Soul de Cuba *Cuban* ▽ 25 | 18 | 20 | $30

New Haven | 283 Crown St. (bet. High & York Sts.) | 203-498-2822 | www.souldecuba.com

Amigos aver the "down-home, authentic" Cuban cuisine at this "tiny" joint on "New Haven's party street" is arguably the "best outside of Miami", served by a "hospitable" staff; though 'cramped', the space is "warm and vibrant", graced with memorabilia, family photos and religious artwork, and while cognoscenti counsel "be sure to make a reservation" to avoid "lines", even if you don't, most agree "it's worth the wait."

	FOOD	DECOR	SERVICE	COST

Southport Brewing Co. *Pub Food* | 16 | 15 | 16 | $27 |

Branford | 850 W. Main St. (Orchard Hill Rd.) | 203-481-2739
Hamden | 1950 Dixwell Ave. (Wilbur Cross Pkwy.) |
203-288-4677
Milford | 33 New Haven Ave. (bet. Prospect & River Sts.) |
203-874-2337
Southport | 2600 Post Rd. (River St.) | 203-256-2337
Stamford | 131 Summer St. (Broad St.) | 203-327-2337
www.southportbrewing.com

Though the pub grub is merely "routine" and the "sports-bar" decor is "nothing to get excited about" (except in Milford, which sits "next to scenic waterfalls"), this microbrewery chain draws sudsheads with "many beers of all hues and tastes"; it's also a magnet for parents who appreciate that it's "kid-friendly" ("magic shows on Sundays"), with a "patient" staff, "good portions" and "moderate prices."

Southwest Cafe *New Mexican* | 22 | 18 | 23 | $32 |

Ridgefield | Copps Hill Common | 109 Danbury Rd. (Farmingville Rd.) |
203-431-3398 | www.southwestcafe.com

Chef-owner Barbara Nevins "brings her love of Taos to your table" at this Ridgefield New Mexican where her "innovative" "take on Southwestern food" (served in small and large plates) strives for "gourmet-level" while remaining "moderately priced"; the "charming", "warm, cozy" spaces boasts "colorful" contemporary Navajo art and "attentive", "cheerful service", plus there's an "inviting" patio; P.S. it's a "must visit" when hatch chiles are in season.

Spadaro Ⓜ *Italian* | 26 | 14 | 22 | $51 |

New Rochelle | 211 E. Main St. (Stephenson Blvd.), NY |
914-235-4595

"Arthur Avenue comes to New Rochelle" via this "impossibly tiny", "family-run" Italian where there's no menu and the kitchen sends out "delicious" "multicourse" meals that would "enchant even the most jaded diner"; never mind the "hefty" bills, "noisy" acoustics and "strip-mall" digs, "if you can get in, you'll never want to leave."

Splash Ⓜ *Seafood* | 22 | 22 | 18 | $46 |

Westport | Inn at Longshore | 260 S. Compo Rd. (Julian Brodie Rd.) |
203-454-7798 | www.decarorestaurantgroup.com

On "warm evenings", the "magnificent waterfront views" are "to die for" at this "expensive" seafooder (a sibling of Greenwich's Baang) in Westport's Inn at Longshore serving "exceptional" Asian-accented fin fare, including a "fabulous", "extensive" brunch; some quip you'll need a "megaphone" "when it's crowded" or "bands are playing outside", while others chide the servers for being "too full of themselves", but for many it remains a "summer must."

Squire's Redding Roadhouse *Eclectic* | 16 | 19 | 19 | $35 |

Redding | 406 Redding Rd. (Rte. 107) | 203-938-3388 |
www.reddingroadhouse.com

A "friendly neighborhood place" that attracts "locals" ranging from "bikers" to "kids in soccer uniforms", this "reliable" Redding Eclectic boasts a "warm, inviting" "New England pub" setting, with "cozy fireplaces" in the dining room and "lively bar", where you can "imagine Mark Twain with a cigar and a whiskey"; the "extensive" menu offerings are "reliable" and, some say, "surprisingly expensive", but many consider it a "good value" overall.

Steak Loft Steak
18 | 15 | 18 | $33

Mystic | Olde Mistick Vill. | 27 Coogan Blvd. (Rte. 27) | 860-536-2661 | www.steakloftct.com

A "longtime favorite" among the "bus-tour" and "blue-haired" crowds, this "family"-oriented steakhouse off I-95 in Mystic is a "must-stop after the aquarium", serving "basic" beef and seafood along with an "astounding salad bar" in a barn of a space that's "so large, you almost never have to wait long"; still, it does get "loud and crowded during tourist season", and though "it's not a chain", some can't help sensing a "mass-production feeling."

Still River Café M American
▽ 28 | 26 | 27 | $67

Eastford | 134 Union Rd. (Centre Pike) | 860-974-9988 | www.stillrivercafe.com

A "destination in the beautiful Quiet Corner", this dinner-only (with lunch on Sundays) Eastford New American set on a 27-acre farm is where Kara Brooks "turns up the volume of taste full blast" in her "fabulous" cuisine prepared with "elegance, style" and "locally grown ingredients", including organic produce grown by husband Robert Brooks; "quietly competent" service and an "open, inviting" space in a refurbished barn also make it a "place to celebrate life."

Stonehenge 🅂 M Continental
22 | 23 | 22 | $59

Ridgefield | Stonehenge Inn | 35 Stonehenge Rd. (Rte. 7) | 203-438-6511 | www.stonehengeinn-ct.com

Since 1940, this "gorgeous old Colonial home" on many "idyllic" acres in Ridgefield has been serving "fine" Continental cuisine that's "expensive but not unreasonable" among "lovely", "elegant" adornments; some modernists "yawn" at the thought of it, but still, for a "formal" "special occasion", it "delivers."

Stone House M American/Seafood
18 | 20 | 19 | $38

Guilford | 506 Old Whitfield St. (Seaview Terrace) | 203-458-3700 | www.stonehouserestaurant.com

Set in a "lovely" "old stone house loaded with history", "located near the harbor" in Guilford, this "quaint" New American seafooder serves up "fresh, flavorful" fin fare at "reasonable prices"; for some, the "buzzy bar" is the "place to be", where bartenders "pour a mean drink", and in "warm weather", the "outdoor seating" at the adjacent Little Stone House cafe allows you to take full advantage of its "nice location on the water."

Strada 18 Italian
26 | 21 | 22 | $38

South Norwalk | 122 Washington St. (bet. Main & Water Sts.) | 203-853-4546 | www.strada18.com

There's a "perpetual crowd always waiting" at this SoNo Italian thanks to chef David Raymer's "superb" artisanal cuisine, including an "incredible selection" of thin-crust pizzas, complemented by a "first-rate wine list" and "wide selection of international beers"; "reasonable prices" and "friendly, knowledgeable" service are additional pluses, and while the "cramped" digs may be "nothing much to look at" for some, most agree it "never disappoints."

NEW Suburban, The 🅼 American/Mediterranean

▽ 24 | 22 | 19 | $50

Branford | 2 E. Main St. (Chestnut St.) | 203-481-1414 | www.thesuburbanrestaurant.com

Arturo and Suzette Franco-Camacho, former owners of New Haven's Bespoke and Roomba, "have done it again" with their "excellent new" American-Med gastropub in Branford, where there's "creativity in abundance" on the menu of small and large plates; the "charming ambiance" helps make up for what some say are "cramped" quarters and "slow" service.

Super Duper Weenie Hot Dogs

23 | 9 | 17 | $12

Fairfield | 306 Black Rock Tpke. (Commerce Dr.) | 203-334-3647 | www.superduperweenie.com

Devotees aver "you'll become a disciple" of this "hot-dog temple" in Fairfield after a taste of the "extraordinary" wieners with "innovative toppings" (all made "from scratch") and "superb" hand-cut fries; the "lines are long" in the "no-frills" space with "limited seating", but most agree it's "well worth the wait"; P.S. cognoscenti caution "don't ask for ketchup on your dog", or the owner "might show you the door."

🄏 Sushi Nanase Japanese

29 | 15 | 23 | $72

White Plains | 522 Mamaroneck Ave. (Shapham Pl.), NY | 914-285-5351

He may be "a man of few words", but chef Yoshimichi Takeda is a "true master" at this "tiny" 18-seat White Plains Japanese "secret" where he fashions "pristine" fish into "truly spectacular", "delectable" creations, voted No. 1 for Food in Westchester/Hudson Valley; the setting's spare and it's certainly not cheap, but if you "put yourself in their hands" you're in for an "unforgettable" experience; P.S. "reservations are a must."

Sushi 25 Chinese/Japanese (aka Hunan Taste)

- | - | - | M

New Canaan | 24 Elm St. (bet. Main St. & South Ave.) | 203-966-1009

This low key, "comfortable" Sino-Japanese on New Canaan's main drag serves "a wide variety" of sushi-bar selections and Chinese dishes, plus some Southeast Asian offerings, which surveyors deem "good but not excellent"; though the ambiance is "pleasant", some opt for takeout because dining in their "living room is even better."

Sycamore Drive-In 🏳 American

17 | 16 | 18 | $14

Bethel | 282 Greenwood Ave. (Diamond Ave.) | 203-748-2716 | www.sycamoredrivein.com

"Happy Days is alive and well" at the Austin family's "classic burger joint" in Bethel, which has been serving root beer "made on the premises", "amazing steak burgers", "lip-smacking" fries and more since 1948; other assets include "car-hop service" (sans roller skates) and the "incredibly popular" summer Cruise Nights, "when all the 1950s cars come to show off" – best of all, this "blast from the past" comes with "throwback prices."

Taberna ☑ Italian/Mediterranean ▽ 28 | 21 | 28 | $39

Bridgeport | 1439 Madison Ave. (Robin St.) | 203-338-0203 | www.tabernarestaurant.com

"Off the beaten path" in Bridgeport, this "wonderful" Italo-Med sibling of Norwalk's La Paella offers "outstanding" "Spanish and Italian delights" and an "excellent" wine list, "served in a personal way" by the "superb" owners and staff; "well-spaced tables" in the two dining rooms also add to a "very nice experience."

T&J Villaggio Trattoria ☑ Italian 21 | 12 | 19 | $34

Port Chester | 223-225 Westchester Ave. (bet. Grove & Oak Sts.), NY | 914-937-6665

"When you don't want to shell out for Tarry Lodge", this "enjoyable" Port Chester Italian is there with "huge helpings" of "old-style" "red-sauce" fare "better than your grandma made" backed by carafes of house wine; in spite of its "shabby", "nondescript" digs adjacent a pizzeria, supporters swear it feels "just like home."

Tandoori Taste of India Indian 21 | 15 | 18 | $33

Port Chester | 163 N. Main St. (bet. Highland & Mill Sts.), NY | 914-937-2727 | www.tandooritasteofindia.com

It's "nothing fancy", but this Port Chester Indian with a "solid lunchtime buffet" provides "reliable", "subtly flavored" takes on the classics and "the price is right" too; service is "prompt", and it doesn't hurt that it's the "only game in town" either.

Tango Grill Argentinean/Italian 21 | 20 | 21 | $59

White Plains | 128 E. Post Rd. (Court St.), NY | 914-946-6222 | www.tangogrillny.com

An "imaginative" array of Argentinean and Italian specialties characterizes this "upscale", "attractive" White Plains grill whose "lively vibe" is fueled by "killer sangria", "amazing mojitos" and "well-chosen wines"; a number note it's "slipped a bit" foodwise and service could use "beefing up", although the "NYC"-caliber bills remain intact.

Tapas Mediterranean 23 | 14 | 20 | $24

Bloomfield | 852 Cottage Grove Rd. (Bloomfield Ave.) | 860-882-0756

West Hartford | 1150 New Britain Ave. (Yale St.) | 860-521-4609

Tapas on Ann ☒ Mediterranean

Hartford | 126-130 Ann St. (bet. Asylum & Pearl Sts.) | 860-525-5988

www.tapasonline.com

"Well-crafted" Med entrees as well as "delectable" eponymous small plates served by a "caring" staff make for "superb dining" at this "inexpensive" trio; because they offer such "excellent value for money" they're "usually mobbed", and some report that "space is a problem", with diners "almost on top of one another."

NEW Tappo *Italian* — — — M

Stamford | 51 Bank St. (Atlantic St.) | 203-588-9870 | www.tapporestaurant.com

This newcomer in Downtown Stamford sets a "new standard for area Italian" according to fans who claim it's the "closest you can get to Italy without flying", offering authentic, local and organic ingredient-driven favorites and Neapolitan pizzas, which are backed by an "incredible" wine list; what's more, the owner and staff "aim to please" in the hip, contemporary space with a sidewalk patio.

Tarantino's ⑤ *Italian* 25 18 23 $47

Westport | 30 Railroad Pl. (bet. Franklin St. & Riverside Ave.) | 203-454-3188 | www.tarantinorestaurant.com

"Make a reservation and bring your appetite" to this high-end Westport Italian from the Marchetti-Tarantino family (Columbus Park Trattoria, Osteria Applausi) that's "always full of pretty people" enjoying "consistently well-prepared" "traditional" cuisine and a "top-notch" wine selection, served by a staff that makes you "feel like family"; some find the space "tight" and the "convivial" scene just plain "noisy", but for many others it's "wonderful in almost every regard."

Taro's ⊘ *Italian/Pizza* ▽ 19 11 22 $22

Millerton | 18 Main St. (N. Center St.), NY | 518-789-6630

It's "nothing flashy", but "you feel like family" at this "welcoming" Millerton Italian dispensing "excellent New York–style pizza" and "tasty" mains that "really satisfy"; "terrific service" and "affordable" rates add to the appeal, while its "proximity to the rail trail" is handy for hikers and it's practically "a must before or after a movie."

Tarry Lodge *Italian* 24 23 22 $53

Port Chester | 18 Mill St. (Abendroth Ave.), NY | 914-939-3111 | www.tarrylodge.com

"An absolute winner" cheer champions of this "foodie delight" in Port Chester from Mario Batali and Joe Bastianich, where chef Andy Nusser turns out "amazing", "chichi" pizzas and "sophisticated", "wonderfully prepared" pastas in a "casually elegant" marble-clad space that feels "unique for the 'burbs"; of course, it's "crazy crowded", "high decibel" and a "tough reservation", but the "pricey" tab is a "bargain if you choose wisely."

Taste of Charleston *Southern* — — — M

Norwalk | 195 Liberty Sq. (Goldstein Pl.) | 203-810-4075 | www.atasteofcharleston.net

"Just across the river from the action in SoNo", this Norwalk Southern "sleeper" is a "nice surprise in a strip mall", serving "tasty", "hands-on" Low Country fare and "cheap cheap drinks"; insiders overlook the "lack of decor" and find the experience "pleasant", and the "reasonable" prices are certainly cheaper than a "flight to Charleston."

	FOOD	DECOR	SERVICE	COST

Taste of China *Chinese*
22 | 14 | 22 | $30

Clinton | 233 E. Main St. (Meadow Rd.) | 860-664-4454 |
www.tasteofchinaus.com

"Not your typical local Chinese", this "gem along the Shoreline" in Clinton is a popular haunt of famous foodies and celebrity chefs for its "innovative", "high-quality" Sichuan and Chengdu dishes that "you won't find elsewhere", except "China proper", plus an "impressive beer menu" featuring Belgian ales; cognoscenti counsel ignore the "take-out decor" and "don't hesitate to ask for recommendations" for "something unusual" – but be sure to "ask the price" too.

Taste of India *Indian*
▽ 19 | 14 | 19 | $29

West Hartford | 139 S. Main St. (Sedgwick Rd.) | 860-561-2221 |
www.tasteofindiawh.com

"Solid" "takes on Indian basics" (including "terrific" tandoori dishes) and "friendly" service attract a "mostly local" crowd to this West Hartford spot; there's "no ambiance" to speak of, which may be why "takeout" is so popular, though value-seekers are happy to take a seat for the $8.95 weekday lunch buffet.

Tavern on Main *New England*
19 | 21 | 18 | $43

Westport | 150 Main St. (bet. Avery Pl. & Elm St.) | 203-221-7222 |
www.tavernonmain.com

This "lovely old tavern" in an "unparalleled location on Westport's Main Street" gets an "A for atmosphere" thanks to its "dark, pubby charm that's hard to rival", highlighted by a "roaring fireplace" in winter and a "pretty, cozy" patio in the summer; the regional American "comfort food" is "always reliable", but cynics sniff "don't expect to be wow'ed", while estimations of the service range from "average" to "overbearing."

⊠ Tawa *Indian*
27 | 22 | 23 | $34

Stamford | 211 Summer St. (bet. Broad & Main Sts.) | 203-359-8977 |
www.tawaonline.com

It's "worth the vertical trek" upstairs to the second-floor dining room of this Indian in Downtown Stamford offering a "unique menu" of dishes filled with "gorgeous flavors", including a daily lunch buffet; a subtly bejeweled setting, "solicitous staff" and "incredibly low prices for the quality" are further draws, as is the small-plate Bread Bar on the ground floor.

Ted's Montana Grill *American*
▽ 23 | 22 | 21 | $31

South Windsor | 500 Evergreen Way (Cedar Ave.) | 860-648-1100 |
www.tedsmontanagrill.com

Boosters "love the bison burgers" with the "best" pickles and "excellent" onion rings and also "applaud the eco-friendly practices" at this South Windsor link of Ted Turner's moderately priced grill chain; though it "looks like somebody's idea of a cleaned-up 1880s saloon" and a few guests grumble about "inconsistent" meals, service is generally "fast" and "accommodating", adding up to an overall "pleasant surprise."

	FOOD	DECOR	SERVICE	COST

Telluride *Southwestern* | 21 | 18 | 20 | $46

Stamford | 245 Bedford St. (bet. Forest & Spring Sts.) | 203-357-7679 |
www.telluriderestaurant.com

"Mosey on into" this Downtown Stamford Southwestern for what
partisans deem "delicious, inventive" victuals, "plentiful" wine options
and "attentive" service, all offered in a "rustic Western" ambiance;
however, a few habitués say it could use an "upgrade across the
board" – particularly "a menu makeover" and lower prices.

Temple Grill *American* | 17 | 15 | 16 | $30

New Haven | 152 Temple St. (bet. Chapel & Crown Sts.) | 203-773-1111 |
www.templegrill.com

"More-than-respectable food" in a "college-pub atmosphere" is
how surveyors describe this "casual" New Haven American that
appeals to the health-conscious with "half-size entrees" and a
"build-your-own-salad option" featuring an "incredible variety of ingredients"; the service is "friendly" and the outdoor patio is "terrific
for people-watching in the summer."

☑ Tengda Asian Bistro *Asian* | 22 | 18 | 19 | $37

Darien | Goodwives Shopping Ctr. | 25 Old Kings Hwy. N.
(Sedgewick Ave.) | 203-656-1688
Greenwich | 21 Field Point Rd. (bet. W. Elm St. & W. Putnam Ave.) |
203-625-5338
Milford | 1676 Boston Post Rd. (Woodruff Rd.) | 203-877-8888
Stamford | 235 Bedford St. (Forest St.) | 203-353-8005
Westport | 1330 Post Rd. E. (Old Rd.) | 203-255-6115
Katonah | Katonah Shopping Ctr. | 286 Katonah Ave. (Bedford Rd.),
NY | 914-232-3900 Ⓜ
www.asianbistrogroup.com

A "huge variety of interesting, tasty" Pan-Asian fare highlighting
"tricked-up rolls" and other "inventive sushi creations" means
there's "something for everyone" at this local chainlet that also
mixes "awesome" cocktails; the settings swing from "soothing" to
"sterile" and service is "variable" too, but prices are dependably
"reasonable", making it "suitable for families, business lunches and
anything in between" – and usually quite "hectic."

☑ Ten Twenty Post *French* | 21 | 21 | 20 | $46

Darien | 1020 Post Rd. (bet. Center St. & Corbin Dr.) | 203-655-1020 |
www.tentwentypost.com

"Very Darien", this "upscale" bistro is the "most happening place in
town", attracting a clientele of "preppy families and business types"
with its "seafood-centric" French-American menu and "friendly"
service, plus "cougars" and other "date-seeking missiles" with its
"large", "loud" bar scene; critics find the noise "unbearable" and the
fare "uneven", while others squirm at the *Revolutionary Road* vibe."

Tequila Mockingbird *Mexican* | 18 | 19 | 19 | $32

New Canaan | 6 Forest St. (East Ave.) | 203-966-2222

"Solid" "standards", "imaginative specials" and an array of "unusual tequilas" come at prices that are "reasonable" "for New

Canaan" at this "enduring" Mexican with a "friendly" staff; the "lively", "kid-friendly" atmosphere features colorful folk art, but it can be "way crowded", so regulars warn to make reservations "unless you want to wait in Margaritaville"; P.S. "go late to miss the family scene."

Tequila Sunrise *Mexican*   17 | 18 | 18 | $34

Larchmont | 145 Larchmont Ave. (bet. Addison St. & Boston Post Rd.), NY | 914-834-6378 | www.tequilasunriselarchmont.com

"Loud", "festive" and "fun", this Larchmont Mexican is the site of "celebrations" galore thanks to its feel-good atmosphere, enhanced by weekend mariachi bands and "delish" margaritas; "pretty-good" prices and "family-friendly" service are perks, even if some say the "Americanized" south-of-the-border cooking leaves "much to be desired."

Terra Mar *American*   ▽ 23 | 25 | 22 | $54

Old Saybrook | Saybrook Point Inn & Spa | 2 Bridge St. (College St.) | 860-388-1111 | www.saybrook.com

At the New American housed in the Saybrook Point Inn & Spa, recent renovations to the "elegant" dining room (which may outdate the Decor score) aim to enhance the "sensational" views of the Connecticut River, Long Island Sound and the marina; "fresh, beautifully presented" seasonal fare featuring local and organic ingredients and "accommodating" service make it a "great value" overall; P.S. "Sunday brunch is a special treat."

Terra Ristorante *Italian*   23 | 20 | 20 | $49

Greenwich | 156 Greenwich Ave. (bet. Elm & Lewis Sts.) | 203-629-5222 | www.zhospitalitygroup.com

"The smell of the wood-burning oven" draws shoppers on "super-luxe Greenwich Avenue" into this "expensive" Northern Italian where "reliable, simple", "yummy" pizzas and such are matched by "nice wines" with the aid of "friendly, knowledgeable" staffers; some feel that "loud" acoustics and "tables on top of each other" detract from the space and its "beautiful ceiling murals", so they ask for the "pleasant" patio when the weather allows.

Thali *Indian*   24 | 20 | 21 | $38

New Canaan | 87 Main St. (bet. East & Locust Aves.) | 203-972-8332

New Haven | 4 Orange St. (George St.) | 203-777-1177

Ridgefield | Ridgefield Motor Inn | 296 Ethan Allen Hwy. (Florida Hill Rd.) | 203-894-1080

NEW **Westport** | 376 Post Rd. E. (Compo Rd.) | 203-557-4848

www.thali.com

Thali Too *Indian*

New Haven | Yale University campus | 65 Broadway (Elm St.) | 203-776-1600 | www.thalitoo.com

"Sophisticated", "innovative" dishes and "generous" drinks are the specialties of these "decently priced" Indians; all branches boast "cool", "upscale" settings and generally "professional" service, but each offers its own distinct feature, among them an "aerial waterfall" in New Canaan, "creative" tapas in Westport, "well-prepared vegetarian" fare at Thali Too and a "no-tell motel setting" in Ridge-field ("don't be put off by" it).

Thataway Cafe *American*

| 17 | 14 | 18 | $29 |

Greenwich | 409 Greenwich Ave. (bet. Grigg St. & Railroad Ave.) | 203-622-0947 | www.thatawaycafe.com

With a "convenient location" near the train station and a "large" patio that's "great for people-watching", this Greenwich "insti-tution" with a "friendly, well-trained staff" remains "busy busy"; sure, the "not-fancy" American grub is merely "decent" and in-side sports the "same old drab" decor, but occasional live music livens things up, plus "it's one of the only affordable options" in the area.

Z Thomas Henkelmann ⊠Ⓜ *French*

| 28 | 28 | 28 | $90 |

Greenwich | Homestead Inn | 420 Field Point Rd. (bet. Bush Ave. & Mercia Ln.) | 203-869-7500 | www.thomashenkelmann.com

"Everything is simply exquisite" at this "destination restaurant" in a "beautiful Victorian mansion" in Greenwich, from the eponymous chef's "fabulous", "memorable" New French cuisine served by a "seasoned staff" that "treats you like royalty" to the "luxurious", "tasteful" decor; "expensive" tabs match the "formal" (ok, "a bit stuffy"), jackets-required atmosphere, but "for that special occa-sion", it's "worth it" – "you do indeed get what you pay for here."

Three Boys From Italy
Brick Oven Trattoria *Pizza*

| ▽ 23 | 8 | 18 | $21 |

White Plains | 206 Mamaroneck Ave. (Maple Ave.), NY | 914-358-1500 | www.gaudiosrestaurant.com

This White Plains pizzeria dishes out brick-oven slices with "fresh, unique" toppings, including an unusually large array of "crispy Sicilian" slabs that are worth "spending the calories on"; some find it "too small" or "swarmed with a young crowd", so "takeout" is popular.

3 Jalapeños *Tex-Mex*

| 17 | 15 | 18 | $28 |

Mamaroneck | 690 Mamaroneck Ave. (bet. Center & Waverly Aves.), NY | 914-777-1156 | www.3jalapenos.com

Even if fans "wouldn't do a hat dance" over this "kitschy" Mamaroneck Tex-Mex, they still relish the "solid", "plentiful" grub "served with a smile"; "friendly" service, "good drinks" – including "beers over and above the usual suspects' – and "reasonable prices" contribute to the "fiesta" feel.

Tiberio's ⊠Ⓜ *Italian*

| - | - | - | M |

Old Saybrook | 1395 Boston Post Rd. (Tompkins Rd.) | 860-388-2459 | www.tiberios-restaurant.com

Chef Antonio Barbi "brings his best from Naples" to the *tavola* at his low-key Old Saybrook "storefront", in the form of "well-prepared", "interesting interpretations of standard Italian" fare, and his "lovely wife", April, "adds to the charm"; those in the know tout it as an "outstanding experience" and "food value."

Tiger Bowl *Chinese*

`15` `6` `16` `$21`

Westport | Westport Shopping Ctr. | 1872 Boston Post Rd. E.
(bet. Buckley Ave. & Hulls Hwy.) | 203-255-1799 |
www.tigerbowlwestport.com

"Solid", if "not inspired", Chinese, "fast service" and "reasonable"
prices add up to a "packed" house at this Sino spot in Westport; many
demur at dining in a space with "zero decor" and a "great view of the
parking lot" and see it strictly as a "reliable take-out" option.

Todd English's Tuscany *Italian*

`22` `22` `20` `$58`

Uncasville | Mohegan Sun Casino | 1 Mohegan Sun Blvd. (bet. Rtes. 2 &
32) | 860-862-3236 | www.mohegansun.com

Todd English's Northern Italian in the Mohegan Sun casino serves
"impressive" "seasonal" cuisine at breakfast, lunch and dinner in a
"beautiful setting" under an indoor waterfall, where insiders advise
it's best to "dine inside the grotto" if you want to "talk to one another"; detractors find it "woefully overrated", however.

Toro *Chinese/Japanese*

`24` `25` `24` `$34`

Newtown | 28 Church Hill Rd. (bet. Queen St. & The Blvd.) |
203-364-0099 | www.toronewtown.com

"You feel like you're welcome" as soon as "you walk in" the "gorgeous"
space of this "convivial" "modern" Chinese-Japanese in Newtown
serving "excellent" sushi and "refreshing", "inventive" dishes from
the two East Asian neighbors; the "staff is a pleasure", and may even
fold origami "keepsakes" for the kids, while the tabs are "quite
reasonable" – the only complaint seems to be about the "acoustics."

Toscana *Italian*

`22` `22` `20` `$47`

Ridgefield | 43 Danbury Rd. (bet. Grove St. & Mountain View Ave.) |
203-894-8995 | www.toscanaridgefield.com

"Scrumptious" Tuscan dishes are served alongside "excellent"
wines in "delightful", upscale-casual, mural-bedecked surroundings
at this "high-end Ridgefield Italian"; a few complain that the fees are
too "pricey" and the acoustics "too loud", but with a "welcoming"
chef-owner and "pleasant" staff thrown into the mix, it's hard not to
have an "enjoyable evening" here.

Toshi Japanese *Japanese*

`∇ 21` `12` `17` `$38`

Avon | Riverdale Farms | 136 Simsbury Rd. (bet. Fisher Dr. &
Rosewood Rd.) | 860-677-8242 | www.toshirestaurant.com

Some regulars "never look at the menu" but "just have the sushi chef
create something" at this Avon Japanese that offers an all-you-can-
eat special of raw fin fare as well as a "wide selection" of cooked
dishes, complemented by an "interesting" sake selection; critics,
however, say the "so-so" digs "need redecorating" and report
"sometimes surly" service from a "woefully understaffed" crew.

Town Dock *American*

`19` `14` `20` `$32`

Rye | 15 Purdy Ave. (bet. 1st & 2nd Sts.), NY | 914-967-2497

Rye folks rely on this "trusty neighborhood spot", a "great place to
fall into" for American "comfort" food with a "New England" spin

(think burgers and chowder); expect "dark", "divey" seafaring digs, a "cheerful" staff and prices that "won't break the bank."

Towne Crier Cafe Ⓜ *American* ▽ 17 | 15 | 16 | $40

Pawling | 130 Rte. 22 (Chapin Ln.), NY | 845-855-1300 | www.townecrier.com

It's "lots of fun" at this veteran Pawling music venue where the New American menu is "not bad", the burritos are "better than ok" and the "desserts are very good"; "reasonable prices" compensate for "hurried service" and "old decor", but "you're really there to see the shows."

Toyo Sushi *Japanese* 21 | 16 | 18 | $34

Mamaroneck | 253 Mamaroneck Ave. (bet. Palmer & Prospect Aves.), NY | 914-777-8696 | www.toyosushi.com

Considered a "staple" for families, this "solid, but not remarkable", Japanese on Mamaroneck's "sushi row" slices up an "extensive" array of "fresh" fish in spare, modern surroundings; its popularity makes for "loud" acoustics and "officiously efficient" service, and some guests gripe "they're always rushing you out."

Trattoria Carl Anthony *Italian* 24 | 18 | 19 | $39

Monroe | Clock Tower Sq. | 477 Main St. (bet. Hubbell Dr. & Stanley Rd.) | 203-268-8486 | www.carlanthonys.com

While most agree this Monroe Italian's "well-priced", "excellent" cuisine is "never a letdown", opinions are split on the service, which fans say is "always fantastic", while foes grouse that it "gets in the way of a decent meal"; likewise, the dining room is either "quaint and comfortable" or "small and cramped", depending on whom you ask.

Trattoria Lucia *Italian* ▽ 18 | 19 | 18 | $37

Bedford | 454 Old Post Rd. (bet. Pea Pond & Stone Hill Rds.), NY | 914-234-7600 | www.ristorantelucia.com

"Dependable family dining" with pizza, pastas and "homemade gelato" is the thing in the "casual" portion of this Bedford Italian, while more ambitious "quiet, adult" repasts are served in a room reserved for "fine dining"; "lackluster" service is a damper, but the fireplaces are a draw, as is a take-out or delivery option.

Trattoria Vivolo *Italian* 25 | 17 | 25 | $42

Harrison | 301 Halstead Ave. (bet. Parsons & Purdy Sts.), NY | 914-835-6199 | www.trattoriavivolo.com

Though it "looks like an old-fashioned diner" from the outside, this Harrisonite is a "delightful surprise" dispensing "top-notch" Italian fare "lovingly" crafted by chef-owner Dean Vivolo and his "warm" staff; prices are deemed "fair for the quality", while the "elegantly refurbished" space is strung with "twinkle lights", and equally suited for jeans or a "dress-up" night on the town.

Tre Angelina Ⓢ *Italian* 21 | 18 | 23 | $49

White Plains | 478 Mamaroneck Ave. (bet. Marion & Shapham Pls.), NY | 914-686-0617 | www.treangelinany.com

Deemed a "cut above" the usual Italian, this Downtown White Plains trattoria rolls out "fine, Northern-style" specialties in "cozy" quarters chock-full of "politicos"; a "genteel" staff "aims to please" ("they'll make you anything you like") and may account for the "pricey" bills.

Tre Scalini *Italian* 24 | 21 | 22 | $43

New Haven | 100 Wooster St. (bet. Chestnut & Franklin Sts.) | 203-777-3373 | www.trescalinirestaurant.com

A "well-established" "winner" on Wooster Square in New Haven, this "upscale", "family-run" Italian is "worth the trip every time" for "authentic", "outstanding" cuisine and an "extraordinary wine list", served by a "responsive" staff; even though locals are pleased to find "no Yale students here", the "old-school", multilevel space can get "raucous", and some critics wince at the prices and "small portions", but for many it's a "place to return to again and again."

Trinity Grill & Bar *American* 20 | 16 | 20 | $34

Harrison | 7-9 Purdy St. (Halstead Ave.), NY | 914-835-5920 | www.trinitygrill.net

"A pleasant local option", this "family-oriented" Harrison tavern delivers "dependable" American fare (not unlike an "upscale diner") in roomy, recently refurbished digs with a "welcoming" bar up front; some say the "food could be better", but nevertheless it's a "quiet", "comfortable" place where "you always feel well cared for."

Trumbull Kitchen *Eclectic* 22 | 19 | 21 | $41
(aka TK)

Hartford | 150 Trumbull St. (bet. Asylum & Pearl Sts.) | 860-493-7412 | www.trumbullkitchen.com

At this "hip" Max outpost in Downtown Hartford, "everyone can find something that pleases" from the "very varied menu" of "inventive" Eclectic dishes, which includes happy-hour tapas, kids' offerings and gluten-free selections, at "good-value prices"; the service is "always solid" and there's a "lively bar scene" in the contemporary setting that some describe as "very dark and very noisy."

Turkish Cuisine Westchester *Turkish* 21 | 8 | 18 | $25

White Plains | 116 Mamaroneck Ave. (Quarropas St.), NY | 914-683-6111 | www.turkishcuisineny.com

"What a find!" marvel fans of this "quick-bite" Turk in White Plains offering "huge helpings" of "simple", "authentic" cooking in a "diminutive" storefront setting; perhaps the "drab" atmosphere's not unlike "eating in a lunchroom", but at least service is "caring" and "BYO keeps the price low"; P.S. the Decor score does not reflect a recent expansion.

Turkish Meze *Turkish* 23 | 16 | 21 | $37

Mamaroneck | 409 Mt. Pleasant Ave. (Stanley Ave.), NY | 914-777-3042 | www.turkishmeze.com

"Always packed", this "boisterous" Mamaroneck eatery is the place for "sensational", "exotic" Turkish cooking – from "soul-warming moussaka" and "incredible grilled fish" to "plentiful" meze – backed by "hard-to-find" beers and wines; a "genuinely friendly" staff keeps the mood "pleasant", and it "isn't too expensive" either.

Turquoise *Mediterranean/Turkish*

21 | 18 | 20 | $39

Larchmont | 1895 Palmer Ave. (bet. Chatsworth Ave. & Depot Way W.), NY | 914-834-9888 | www.turqmed.com

"Istanbul meets the suburbs" at this Larchmont Mediterranean-Turkish "transporting" diners with "fresh", "authentic" cuisine including "excellent grilled meats" and "tasty" meze "you can make a meal of"; although it's not cheap, service is "warm and welcoming" and the atmospheric setting with lanterns throughout is especially "fun for groups."

Tuscan Oven Trattoria *Italian*

20 | 18 | 19 | $39

Norwalk | 544 Main Ave. (bet. Glover Ave. & Valley View Rd.) | 203-846-4600 | www.tuscanoven.com

This "reliable" Northern Italian "may not knock your socks off", but it provides "homemade pastas", "crisp pizzas" and other "serviceably cooked" standards to its Norwalk clientele; with a "surprisingly cute" setting (indoors and alfresco on the patio), "cordial" service and "reasonably priced" tabs, it's "ideal for large, impromptu gatherings."

Tuscany Ⓜ *Italian*

▽ 24 | 20 | 23 | $40

Bridgeport | 1084 Madison Ave. (bet. Lincoln Ave. & Madison Terrace) | 203-331-9884

"What a find" in a "rough neighborhood" exclaim enthusiasts of this Tuscan specialist, a "great choice for authentic Italian cuisine in the heart of Bridgeport's Little Italy", where "experienced" servers bring out "unique displays of the day's selections" of "wonderful homemade pastas" to your table; the owners "welcome all guests like long-lost family members", and there's a private room that's "good for celebrations."

Two Boots Pizza *Pizza*

20 | 16 | 17 | $21

Bridgeport | 281 Fairfield Ave. (bet. Broad St. & Lafayette Circle) | 203-331-1377 | www.twoboots.com

A "great addition to a booming area of Bridgeport", this "relatively inexpensive" outpost of the NYC-based pizzeria chain offers a "hybrid pizza/Cajun" menu that includes "inventive", "eclectic" pies and "true jambalaya", "lubricated with cheap beer in cans" and served by a "friendly" staff; "fun for families earlier in the day", at night it's "hopping" with "live eclectic music" and a "younger crowd."

🄳 Union League Cafe 🄵 *French*

27 | 27 | 26 | $60

New Haven | 1032 Chapel St. (bet. College & High Sts.) | 203-562-4299 | www.unionleaguecafe.com

A "destination for that special event or celebration", this "New Haven landmark" across from the Yale campus is the showcase for chef Jean-Pierre Vuillermet's "masterful", "precisely prepared" French cuisine, backed by a "superior" wine list and served in the "elegant, yet comfortable" environs of a "historic brownstone" with a "wonderful old-school atmosphere"; the service is "impeccable" but "not snooty", and while many wince at the "bankers' prices", the $35 pre-theater prix fixe can give those who don't have "expense accounts" a taste of "what fine dining is meant to be."

	FOOD	DECOR	SERVICE	COST

U.S.S. Chowder Pot *Seafood*   `19` `15` `18` `$33`

Branford | 560 E. Main St. (School Ground Rd.) | 203-481-2356
Hartford | 165 Brainard Rd. (Murphy Rd.) | 860-244-3311
www.chowderpot.com

"Big portions" of "consistent", "basic" seafood for "not a lot of coin" and "easy, convenient locations" keep this "family-friendly" piscatorial pair "always busy", so "be prepared to wait"; the service is "friendly", though some find it "spotty", and while most agree the "fake waterfront" motif in the "big, barny" buildings is "kitschy", some insist "it works", creating a "casual, comfy" ambiance that's "good for big crowds"; there's live music and karaoke at Branford and dinner theater in Hartford.

☑ Valbella ⌧ *Italian*   `25` `23` `25` `$74`

Riverside | 1309 E. Putnam Ave. (Sound Beach Ave.) | 203-637-1155 | www.valbellact.com

"Porsche Turbos in the parking lot" and celebrities like "Regis or Frank Gifford" in the dining room generate a "glow" at this "way upscale" Italian in Riverside, a "posh playground" for a "chic crowd", where "exquisitely prepared" dishes and an "extensive wine list" are served by an "expert" staff in an "elegant" space that includes a "romantic" wine cellar; sure, the bill will "burn a hole in your pocket", but many say it's "worth it" for a "truly memorable evening."

☑ Valencia Luncheria ⌿ *Venezuelan*   `27` `10` `17` `$22`

Norwalk | 172 Main St. (bet. Center & Plymouth Aves.) | 203-846-8009 | www.valencialuncheria.com

"Let your taste buds become your primary sense" at this "inexpensive" Norwalk "hole-in-the-wall" serving "hearty, heaping portions" of "innovative, perfectly prepared" Venezuelan cuisine all day, including "incredible" arepas, "awesome" pernil (roast pork) and empanadas "thick with excellent fillings"; surveyors report "lines out the door" and "uncomfortable" seating in the "tiny", "storefront" space (though the works of local artists on the walls "can keep you interested"), but fans shrug "who cares?"; BYO and cash-only.

Vanilla Bean Cafe *American*   ▽ `22` `19` `18` `$26`

Pomfret | 450 Deerfield Rd. (Pomfret St.) | 860-928-1562 | www.thevanillabeancafe.com

A "'60s-style Alice's Restaurant vibe" permeates this "local institution" in "a lovely (if hard to find) country setting" in Pomfret serving a "cheap" all-day menu of American eats using local ingredients; the renovated barn is "biker heaven (but friendly biker)" on the weekends when there's also live music, and during the week it's a "great place to settle in with a laptop or a book."

Vazzy's *Italian*   `20` `15` `18` `$28`

Bridgeport | Beardsley Park Plaza | 513 Broadbridge Rd. (Huntington Tpke.) | 203-371-8046
NEW **Shelton** | 706 Bridgeport Ave. (bet. Old Strattford Rd.& Willow Dr.) | 203-944-7338
Stratford | 3355 Main St. (bet. Birch Pl. & Garden St. E.) | 203-375-2776

(continued)

Vazzy's 19th Hole *Italian*
Fairfield | Fairfield Wheeler Golf Course | 2390 Easton Tpke. (bet. Wellner Dr. & Wheeler Park Ave.) | 203-396-0147

Vazzy's Osteria *Italian*
Monroe | 415 Main St. (bet. Brook & Green Sts.) | 203-459-9800 www.vazzysrest.com

This quintet of "casual" Italian "standbys" serving up "decent" pizza and pasta are "fun for the family" and "won't kill your wallet"; sure, service can be "inconsistent" (from "first-class" to "glacial"), and the scene is often "crowded" and "loud" in digs that some describe as "ho-hum", but "huge goblets" of house Chianti can help drown out the din.

Venetian Restaurant *Italian*   18 | 15 | 22 | $42
Torrington | 52 E. Main St. (bet. Center & Franklin Sts.) | 860-489-8592 | www.venetian-restaurant.com

This "fancy", family-run Northern Italian has been a "neighborhood fixture" in Torrington for over 40 years (90 going back to the original owners), and if newbies declare it "a bit dated", longtime clientele defend its "nostalgic charm" – from the vintage 1930s art deco neon sign to the Caesar salad, "prepared tableside", it's "the real thing"; patrons "never feel rushed" in the dining room lined with murals of Venice, making it "always a satisfying evening."

Versailles *Bakery/French*   24 | 22 | 19 | $37
Greenwich | 339 Greenwich Ave. (Arch St.) | 203-661-6634 | www.versaillesgreenwich.com

Chef Jean-Pierre Bagnato has "revitalized" this "institution" by moving it to a "beautiful" new location "just a wee bit down Greenwich Avenue" and adding "sublime" seasonal French bistro dinners (in a "charming back area") to its roster of lunch and bakery fare, the latter starring "beautifully crafted", "decadent desserts"; best of all, prices are "affordable", a welcome surprise considering the level of "sophistication."

Viale Ristorante Bar & Grille Ⓜ *Italian*   ▽ 24 | 22 | 22 | $36
Bridgeport | 3171 Fairfield Ave. (bet. Davidson & Poland Sts.) | 203-610-6193 | www.vialeristorante.com

"Generous portions" of "fabulous" red-sauce fare are served up at this "comfortable" and "homey" "neighborhood" Italian in the Black Rock section of Bridgeport; loyal patrons point to a "moderately priced" wine list with a "wide selection", "friendly" owners and an outdoor patio as further pluses.

Via Sforza Trattoria *Italian*   22 | 21 | 21 | $41
Westport | 243 Post Rd. W. (Sylvan Rd.) | 203-454-4444 | www.viasforza.com

A stone-cottage-like exterior reveals a "Tuscan-farmhouse look inside" of this midpriced Italian "neighborhood" spot in Westport near the Norwalk border; the "pleasant" staff sets a "mellow mood" and makes you feel "like family", so while a no-reservations policy "may not assure you of an immediate table, the wait is worth it."

	FOOD	DECOR	SERVICE	COST

Village, The Pub Food
20	15	20	$32

Litchfield | 25 West St. (bet. Meadow St. & Rte. 63) | 860-567-8307 | www.village-litchfield.com

Fans say "every neighborhood needs" a "local hangout" like this Litchfield "tradition", which offers "dependable", "hearty" American pub grub and "more ambitious", "upscale" dishes in a "hopping bar area" and "cozy dining room"; the staff "tries hard to please", and while some critics find the surroundings a bit "boring", defenders insist the "fair fare at fair prices" makes up for "what it lacks in decor."

Village Square Bagels ⊘ Bakery
▽ 18	3	11	$12

Larchmont | 1262 Boston Post Rd. (Weaver St.), NY | 914-834-6969 | www.villagesquarebagel.com

"Basically a take-out place with just a few bare tables", this Larchmont bakery is the scene of "morning lines" for "great" bagels (hot all day long) and the usual "kosher" nosherie of lox, whitefish, spreads and salads; service "can be slow", but it's satisfactory "if they get your order right."

Vinny's Ale House Pizza/Pub Food
▽ 20	11	17	$21

NEW Fairfield | 93 Post Rd. (Grasmere Ave.) | 203-292-8730 | www.vinnysgrillandgrotto.com

Vinny's Backyard ◑ Pizza/Pub Food
Stamford | Springdale Shopping Ctr. | 1078 Hope St. (bet. Camp Ave. & Mulberry St.) | 203-461-9003 | www.vinnysbackyard.com

Catch the game on eight large-screen TVs while noshing on "home-run" pizzas, ribs, wings and other "great" grub at this "down-to-earth" Stamford strip-mall sports pub and pizzeria (and its younger Fairfield sibling); "away from the bar", there's a dining room whose "reasonable prices" and "kid-friendly" service make it appropriate for a "totally casual" family meal.

Vito's by the Park Italian
21	18	19	$36

Hartford | 26 Trumbull St. (Jewell St.) | 860-244-2200

Vito's by the Water Italian
Windsor | 1936 Blue Hills Ave. Ext. (bet. Griffin Rd. & Waterside Crossing) | 860-285-8660

Vito's Tavern & Pizzeria Italian
NEW New Britain | 136 Main St. (Chestnut St.) | 860-801-6800

Vito's Wethersfield Italian
(aka Vito's Pizzaria & Restaurant)
Wethersfield | 673 Silas Dean Hwy. (bet. Somerset St. & Wells Rd.) | 860-563-3333
www.vitosct.com

Now a quartet, these "good-value" "pizza-and-pasta joints" trade in "solid" Italian fare, including "Chicago-style" specialty pies that are welcome "in the land of thin crusts" (which they also offer); the Hartford original is perfect "when catching a show" at the nearby Bushnell, and the Windsor location, "overlooking the pond and geese", is an area "hot spot."

Viva Zapata *Mexican*
17 | 17 | 15 | $31

Westport | 530 Riverside Ave. (Bridge St.) | 203-227-8226 |
www.vivazapata.com

Westport's "eternal fraternity party" rages on at this "hacienda" dispensing cheap, "serviceable" Mexican vittles to soak up the star attraction: "delicious margaritas in mason jars"; service "fluctuates" but it's still "tons of fun" according to the "lively", "younger" crowds that throng the "awesome" outdoor patio in warmer months.

Vox Ⓜ *American/French*
21 | 20 | 20 | $55

North Salem | 721 Titicus Rd. (Peach Lake Rd.), NY | 914-669-4199 |
www.voxnorthsalem.com

A "highly enjoyable" oasis of "Gallic charm" "in the middle of nowhere", this "lovely" North Salem bistro serves a "clever" mix of French–New American dishes, "from burgers to cassoulet", with a "warm greeting" and "professional" attention; take your pick of a "spacious dining room" or, weather permitting, a patio with "beautiful views" that most believe is "worth the trip" and the "high prices."

V Restaurant & Wine Bar *Californian*
18 | 17 | 18 | $35

Westport | 1460 Boston Post Rd. E. (Maple Ave.) | 203-259-1160 |
www.vrestaurantandwinebar.com

With a Californian menu offering "something for everyone" (salads, pasta, wraps, pizza) this "casual" Westport cafe is "an easy place to take children" yet retains enough "class" to "hang with the girls" over a glass of vino (there are 21 by the glass from an "interesting, well-priced list"); despite "cheesy" vineyard murals it's "always crowded", perhaps because the "tenured" staff makes it so "warm and inviting."

Walter's ⊅ *Hot Dogs*
22 | 9 | 13 | $10

Mamaroneck | 937 Palmer Ave. (bet. Fulton & Richbell Rds.), NY |
www.waltershotdogs.com

The "cars are double parked" all the way down the block at this "iconic" Mamaroneck hot dog stand set in a circa-1928 "art deco" pagoda turning out "decadent" butter-griddled franks, "thick, creamy shakes" and "curly fries with a nice zing"; there are only a few picnic tables and "you'll need patience" for the "lines", even still, it's a "national treasure" that "shouldn't be missed on a warm day."

Wandering Moose Café Ⓜ *American*
▽ 16 | 11 | 15 | $26

West Cornwall | 421 Sharon Goshen Tpke. (Lower River) | 860-672-0178 |
www.thewanderingmoosecafe.com

This "homey" American next to West Cornwall's famous covered bridge is a "relaxed" place to wander for "good, simple country food" at breakfast, lunch and dinner; service can be "hit-or-miss" but overall it's a "good value" – and, yes, "you may see a moose."

Wasabi *Japanese*
▽ 25 | 13 | 24 | $30

Orange | 350 Boston Post Rd. (bet. Lambert & Orange Center Rds.) |
203-795-5856 | www.wasabiorange.com

"Try everything!" advise devotees of this "unassuming" Japanese joint in a "small, out-of-the-way strip mall" in Orange because the "artfully presented" sushi and other dishes are all "perfection"; the "owner is a doll" and her "always smiling" servers "go out of their way to make customers happy" (that it's "less pricey than" similar places doesn't hurt, either).

Wasabi Chi ⓜ *Asian* | 23 | 22 | 20 | $44 |

South Norwalk | 2 S. Main St. (Washington St.) | 203-286-0181 | www.wasabichi.com

Doug Nguyen's "trendy", little spot on the edge of SoNo offers a "creative and deep menu" of "light" Pan-Asian bites, including "innovative" sushi; modern "NYC decor", a "techno beat" soundtrack and a rollicking bar add up to a "fun" evening, and nobody complains about the "reasonable", midpriced tabs.

Watercolor Cafe ➋ *American* | 18 | 16 | 18 | $39 |

Larchmont | 2094 Boston Post Rd. (bet. Chatsworth & Larchmont Aves.), NY | 914-834-2213 | www.watercolorcafe.net

"Live music" fans are "in for a big treat" at this "arty" "little hideaway" in Larchmont whose "cozy" digs provide an "intimate setting" for "remarkably high-caliber" jazz, pop and folk talent; service is "attentive" and the New American cooking is "more than good enough", but it's really about the "vibrant scene" here.

Watermoon *Asian* | 23 | 19 | 18 | $39 |

Rye | 66 Purchase St. (bet. Elm Pl. & W. Purdy Ave.), NY | 914-921-8880

An "ample" array of "fresh-tasting" Pan-Asian offerings – from sushi to pad Thai – is served at this "chic" canteen "in the heart" of Rye boasting an indoor waterfall; moderate prices are a perk, although service can be "slow" and locals lament "if only it weren't so noisy."

Water's Edge at Giovanni's *Italian/Steak* | 19 | 17 | 19 | $45 |
(fka Giovanni's)

Darien | 2748 Post Rd. (I-95, exit 9) | 203-325-9979 | www.giovannis.com

"Great bang for the buck" is found in the prix fixes available at this "old-fashioned" Italian steakhouse in Darien, and though tabs can be a bit "pricey" if you go à la carte, "huge portions" ensure there's "always enough for leftovers"; detractors liken it to a "tired catering hall", but with "beautiful" water views and "great" service, they'd still RSVP 'yes' to a "wedding reception" here.

Water Street Cafe *American* | 26 | 17 | 23 | $40 |

Stonington | 143 Water St. (bet. Grand & Pearl Sts.) | 860-535-2122 | www.waterst-cafe.com

"Popular with locals" and a "destination" for seaside tourists, this "creative" New American cafe in Stonington serves "absolutely wonderful food" that's "priced right" (including a "great oyster bar"); if some see the "dark" interior and "thrift-shop" trappings as a "drawback", most find the "cozy" space quintessentially "New England", deeming it "a classic – if you can get in the door."

	FOOD	DECOR	SERVICE	COST

Westbrook Lobster *Seafood* — 19 | 13 | 18 | $30

Clinton | 346 E. Main St. (Bluff Ave.) | 860-664-9464
Wallingford | 300 Church St. (Main St.) | 203-265-5071
www.westbrooklobster.com

"Large portions" of "delectable, fresh" seafood cooked "the right way" are the draw at this shellfish-centric pair run by "friendly", "energetic" crews; "if you want fancy these aren't the places", but, despite "bare-bones" decor, folks who love a "good value" "keep coming back for more"; P.S. the Wallingford location sports a covered outdoor terrace overlooking the river, while Clinton has an on-site seafood market.

NEW **Westchester Burger Co.** *American* — 20 | 15 | 17 | $25

White Plains | 106 Westchester Ave. (Bloomingdale Rd.), NY | 914-358-9399 | www.westchesterburger.com

"Damn-good" burgers "to satisfy just about every hankering" await at this "impressive" White Plains newcomer grilling 19 different "juicy" versions as well as offering "vegetarian alternatives" on its "inventive" American menu; though the "boring" brick-lined setting's akin to an "upscale Applebee's" and "service issues" still need to be worked out, it's "always crowded" with a "nice bar for drinks" while you wait.

West Street Grill *American* — 24 | 21 | 23 | $57

Litchfield | 43 West St. (North St.) | 860-567-3885 |
www.weststreetgrill.com

Mixing "upscale dining with relaxed Connecticut countryside" "works very well" for this "iconic" Litchfield New American that offers "inventive", "high-quality" fare and an "excellent" wine list in a "lovely" setting, garnering a "loyal following" that includes "locals and celebs"; while the service is "top-notch" and the owners "pay attention that all goes well", a few are put off by the "'in' crowd" vibe.

When Pigs Fly 🚫 *BBQ* — ∇ 21 | 16 | 19 | $26
(aka When Pigs Fly Southern BBQ)

Sharon | 29 W. Main St. (bet. Main & New Sts.) | 860-492-0000 |
www.hudsonvalleybbq.com

At his BBQ joint in Sharon, "accomplished chef" Bennett Chinn "explores his passion for Southern cooking", incorporating Texas, North Carolina and St. Louis styles, as well as organic meats and local produce, into his "finger-licking" fare; an open kitchen highlights the space housed in a renovated circa-1940s barbershop; there's a sibling in Mabbettsville, NY.

White Horse Country Pub *Pub Food* — 19 | 23 | 20 | $32

New Preston | 258 New Milford Tpke. (Findley Rd.) | 860-868-1496 |
www.whitehorsecountrypub.com

"Snuggle up near the fireplace" or "get a seat on the patio overlooking the river" at this "quintessential country pub" in New Preston, housed in a "tastefully updated" building decorated with "historical pieces from England" and boasting a patio "overlooking the river", where the "congenial" owner and "friendly" staff foster an atmo-

	FOOD	DECOR	SERVICE	COST

sphere that encourages "hanging around"; critics find the fare merely "average", but others point out that "on this stretch of 202, there ain't many choices."

Wild Rice *Asian*

20	15	18	$29

Norwalk | 370 Main Ave. (Merritt Pkwy., exit 40A) | 203-849-1688 | www.wildrice999.com

"When you want sushi, your wife wants Thai and the kids want General Tso's chicken", this "family-friendly" "standby" in Norwalk covers all the bases with its "decent", "affordable" Pan-Asian fare; service is "swift" and "courteous", and they offer takeout and delivery within a five-mile radius.

Willett House *Steak*

24	21	23	$67

Port Chester | 20 Willett Ave. (Abendroth Ave.), NY | 914-939-7500 | www.thewilletthouse.com

Dubbed "the Peter Luger of Westchester" by its devotees, this "expensive" Port Chester "warhorse" set in a "historic" turn-of-the-century grain building channels the "old-school" chophouses of yore with "superior" cuts and "wonderful" sides "all done right" and ferried by an "experienced", "top-notch" staff; detractors declare it a little "tired", but "there's a reason it's been here so long."

Wilson's Barbeque Ⓜ *BBQ*

20	10	14	$24

Fairfield | 1851 Post Rd. (bet. Bungalow Ave. & Granville St.) | 203-319-7427 | www.wilsons-bbq.com

Pit master Ed Wilson's "tribute BBQ" pays homage to many regional styles (e.g. Carolina pulled pork that "melts in your mouth", "meaty" St. Louis ribs) at this Fairfield 'cuefeteria; "informal doesn't begin to describe" the "tiny, ramshackle" joint with just a few seats or the sometimes "lackadaisical" pace of service, but most just "grab and go", anyway; P.S. open Thursdays–Sundays.

Winvian Ⓜ *American*

▽ 27	28	26	$87

Morris | Winvian Resort | 155 Alain White Rd. (bet. County & E. Shore Rds.) | 860-393-3004 | www.winvian.com

"Feel like landed gentry" in what seems like "your own private 18th-century dining room" on an "idyllic" country estate in the Litchfield Hills that specializes in seasonal, locally driven American cuisine; the "innovative" menu is a "delight to the senses" and the service is "sophisticated" (i.e. "attentive but not intrusive"), but "cash in your stocks before going" and consider trying to "stay the night in one of the very special cottages" on this Relais & Châteaux property, which many agree is also "out of this world."

Woodland, The Ⓜ *American/Continental*

22	19	22	$45

Lakeville | 192 Sharon Rd. (bet. Lake & Wells Hill Rds.) | 860-435-0578

"Something for everyone and then some" is found on the "almost unbelievably varied" American-Continental menu at this "lively" Lakeville "old faithful" where even the "yummy sushi" is doled out in "large portions", and for "fair" prices too; the "wonderful, rustic" setting "feels like home" to its droves of devotees, who further appreciate the many wine "values", "big bar scene" and "efficient" service; P.S. "don't think of going without a reservation, even in the dead of winter."

Wood-n-Tap ● _Pub Food_ | 17 | 14 | 17 | $24 |

Farmington | 1274 Farmington Ave. (bet. Brickyard Rd. & Lakeshore Dr.) | 860-773-6736
Hartford | 99 Sisson Ave. (Capitol Ave.) | 860-232-8277
NEW **Orange** | 311 Boston Post Rd. (Racebrook Rd.) | 203-799-9663
Rocky Hill | 12 Town Line Rd. (bet. Mountain Laurel Dr. & Silas Deane Hwy.) | 860-571-9444
Southington | 420 Queen St. (bet. Laning & Loper Sts.) | 860-329-0032
Vernon | 236 Hartford Tpke. (bet. Green Circle & Talcottville Rds.) | 860-872-6700
www.woodntap.com

This "friendly" Hartford-area chain (with a new outpost down south in Orange) is a "blend of a pub and family restaurant", serving cheap, "basic" American "comfort food" in "so-so" digs; with "plenty of big screens" and a "decent beer selection", it can get "loud on weekends", but at other times it does duty as a "lunch stop" for the "local workforce", a place to "grab a drink with friends" or a late-night dining option "for those whose schedules vary."

Wood's Pit BBQ & Mexican Cafe Ⓜ _BBQ/Mexican_ | 21 | 13 | 18 | $28 |

Bantam | 123 Bantam Lake Rd. (Roosevelt Ave.) | 860-567-9869 | www.woodspitbbq.com

"Where else can you get BBQ pulled pork with a side of guacamole?" ask fans of this combination joint next to the Bantam Cinema offering "scrumptious" 'cue "with all the traditional sides" plus Mexican bites; the "families and locals" that "pack" this "happy", "laid-back" place attest to "good prices, better booze" and "pre-movie"–meal ease.

ⓩ Woodward House Ⓜ _American_ | 27 | 27 | 26 | $63 |

Bethlehem | 4 The Green (West Rd.) | 203-266-6902 | www.thewoodwardhouse.com

Each of the four distinctly and "beautifully appointed" rooms in this restored Colonial-era saltbox in Bethlehem is an "intimate" and "memorable" setting for "exquisitely prepared" New American cuisine that most agree is "never less than wonderful"; though the departure of the original chef-owner puts the Food score in question, the remaining owner, Adele Reveron, is as "gracious" a host as ever, treating the whole enterprise like an "only child: lovingly and with great care"; P.S. the "special-occasion" tabs can be beat by a $28 three-course prix fixe (a "great buy").

Yorkside ● _Greek/Pizza_ | ▽ 15 | 9 | 18 | $18 |

New Haven | Yale University campus | 288 York St. (bet. Elm & Wall Sts.) | 203-787-7471 | www.yorksidepizza.com

This "been-there-forever" family-owned Greek diner in New Haven is a "certified "Yale hangout" thanks to its proximity to campus, late-night hours and "reasonable" tabs; "zero ambiance" isn't an issue for most – including those rolling out of Toad's Place next door – who are just looking for "fast" service and "substantial" salads, pizza and other grub that "will fill you up."

Zhang's *Chinese/Japanese*　　16 | 13 | 17 | $24

Madison | 44 Boston Post Rd. (Old Post Rd.) | 203-245-3300
Mystic | 12 Water St. (bet. New London Rd. & W. Main St.) | 860-572-5725
Old Saybrook | 455 Boston Post Rd. (Stage Rd.) | 860-388-3999
www.zhangsrestaurant.com

An "efficient", "accommodating" staff presides over this Chinese-Japanese trio providing "reliable" fare, including "creative" sushi, at rock-bottom prices, but the nothing-special decor may be the reason so many "only get takeout"; purists pan the eats as "Asian food for Americans", but for others it's an "oasis" in an area where even "finding a bowl of properly cooked rice is a challenge."

Zinc 🗷 *American*　　24 | 21 | 23 | $47

New Haven | 964 Chapel St. (bet. College & Temple Sts.) | 203-624-0507 | www.zincfood.com

At this New Haven eatery, chef/co-owner Denise Appel "knows what she's doing and it shows" in her "delightful" "farm-to-table" New American cuisine, which includes some dishes with a "Pacific Rim touch"; some grouse that it's a "bit expensive", but the "young, dedicated" staff keeps the vibe "upbeat" in the "chic" "urban" space that "belies its location" across from the Green.

Zitoune Ⓜ *Moroccan*　　19 | 21 | 19 | $42

Mamaroneck | 1127 W. Boston Post Rd. (Richbell Rd.), NY | 914-835-8350 | www.zitounerestaurant.com

"Lovely for a date", this "dark, mysterious" Moroccan in Mamaroneck "transports you to Marrakesh" with "nicely spiced" tagines and couscous served by an "attentive" staff in an "exotic" pillow-strewn setting; it can be "expensive", although the early-bird special offers "great value."

CONNECTICUT AND NEARBY NEW YORK TOWNS INDEXES

Cuisines

Includes names, locations and Food ratings.

AFGHAN

Shish Kebab	**W Hartford**	25

AMERICAN

Adrienne	**New Milford**	25
AJ's Burgers	**New Roch**	20
American Pie	**Sherman**	22
Apricots	**Farmington**	23
Archie Moore's	**multi.**	18
Ash Creek	**multi.**	17
Aspen	**Old Saybrook**	20
@ the Corner	**Litchfield**	20
Atticus	**New Haven**	18
Aux Délices	**multi.**	24
Azu	**Mystic**	23
Bailey's	**Ridgefield**	21
Bar Americain	**Uncasville**	26
Beach House	**Milford**	22
Beach Hse. Café	**Old Greenwich**	18
Bedford Post/Barn	**Bedford**	23
Bedford Post/Farm	**Bedford**	25
Beehive	**Armonk**	21
Bespoke	**New Haven**	24
Bistro 22	**Bedford**	24
B.J. Ryan's	**Norwalk**	20
Blue	**White Pl**	20
Blue Lemon	**Westport**	24
Boathouse	**Lakeville**	17
NEW Boathse./Saugatuck	**Westport**	25
Bobby Valentine	**Stamford**	15
Bogey's Grille	**Westport**	17
Bombay Olive	**W Hartford**	19
Bonda	**Fairfield**	27
Booktrader Café	**New Haven**	18
Boom	**multi.**	22
Boulders Inn	**New Preston**	21
Brasserie Pip	**Ivoryton**	-
Brazen Fox	**White Pl**	17
Brewhouse	**S Norwalk**	19
Bull's Bridge	**Kent**	16
Z Carole Peck's	**Woodbury**	26
NEW Cask Republic	**New Haven**	-
Chat	**Larch**	18
Chatterley's	**New Hartford**	21
Cheesecake Fac.	**multi.**	17
Chef Luis	**New Canaan**	25
Chestnut Grille	**Old Lyme**	26
City Steam	**Hartford**	15
Cobble Stone	**Purchase**	15
Community Table	**Washington**	27
Country Bistro	**Salisbury**	-
Cuvee	**W Hartford**	16
Diorio	**Waterbury**	25
Dish B&G	**Hartford**	20
Dolly Madison Inn	**Madison**	13
Donovan's	**S Norwalk**	18
Z Dressing Room	**Westport**	24
Elbow Room	**W Hartford**	18
Eli Cannon's	**Middletown**	21
Elizabeth's Cafe	**Madison**	25
Emma's Ale House	**White Pl**	18
Épernay	**Bridgeport**	22
Ferme	**Avon**	21
Fife 'n Drum	**Kent**	18
Fifty Coins	**multi.**	16
59 Bank	**New Milford**	19
Firebox	**Hartford**	24
Foe	**Branford**	19
42	**White Pl**	22
Friends & Co.	**Madison**	18
Gabrielle's	**Centerbrook**	25
Ginger Man	**multi.**	18
Globe B&G	**Larch**	17
Gnarly Vine	**New Roch**	17
NEW Goose	**Darien**	-
Grant's	**W Hartford**	25
Greenwich Tav.	**Old Greenwich**	21
NEW Greenwood's Grille	**Bethel**	16
Griswold Inn	**Essex**	18
G.W. Tavern	**Wash Depot**	20
Halstead Ave.	**Harrison**	20

Hard Rock | **Ledyard**	15
🅩 Harvest Supper | **New Canaan**	27
Hawthorne Inn | **Berlin**	20
Heirloom | **New Haven**	20
Horse/Hound | **S Salem**	19
NEW Hudson Grille | **White Pl**	20
Infinity Hall/Bistro | **Norfolk**	20
Inn/Newtown | **Newtown**	18
Jeffrey's | **Milford**	26
Joe's American | **Fairfield**	15
Johnny Rockets | **multi.**	16
John's Café | **Woodbury**	23
Kelly's Corner | **Brewster**	17
Kona Grill | **Stamford**	17
Larchmont Tav. | **Larch**	17
🅩 Le Farm | **Westport**	27
Litchfield/Grille | **Litchfield**	20
Long Ridge Tav. | **Stamford**	14
Longwood | **Woodbury**	18
Market | **Stamford**	20
Match | **S Norwalk**	26
Matthew's | **Unionville**	24
Max Burger | **W Hartford**	25
🅩 Max Downtown | **Hartford**	27
🅩 Mayflower Inn | **Washington**	24
McKinney/Doyle | **Pawling**	25
Meetinghouse | **Bedford Vill**	20
Métro Bis | **Simsbury**	25
Mickey/Molly Spill. | **Mamaro**	15
🅩 Mill/2T | **Tariffville**	28
NEW Millstone Café | **Kent**	-
NEW Moderne Barn | **Armonk**	22
Mo's NY | **New Roch**	18
🅩 Napa & Co. | **Stamford**	24
Noah's | **Stonington**	24
No. 9 | **Millerton**	27
North Star | **Pound Ridge**	20
NEW Oakhurst Diner | **Millerton**	16
Old Lyme Inn | **Old Lyme**	22
Olio | **Groton**	24
Oliver's Taverne | **Essex**	16
Olive Tree | **Southbury**	21
121 Rest./Bar | **N Salem**	22
121 Rest./OXC | **Oxford**	21

Opus 465 | **Armonk**	18
Palmer's Crossing | **Larch**	21
Pantry | **Wash Depot**	24
Paradise B&G | **Stamford**	13
Pat's Kountry | **Old Saybrook**	16
NEW Pine Social | **New Canaan**	23
Plan B Burger | **multi.**	22
Plates | **Larch**	25
🅩 PolytechnicON20 | **Hartford**	28
Pond Hse. Café | **W Hartford**	21
Porter Hse. | **White Pl**	19
NEW Post Rd. Ale | **New Roch**	-
Putnam Hse. | **Bethel**	19
Rainforest Cafe | **Farmington**	12
Rebeccas | **Greenwich**	26
Red Barn | **Westport**	16
🅩 Rest./Water's Edge | **Westbrook**	23
NEW Rest. North | **Armonk**	26
River House | **Westport**	17
River Tavern | **Chester**	26
Roasted Peppers | **Mamaro**	21
NEW Sails | **Norwalk**	-
Saltwater Grille | **Stamford**	17
Sam's/Gedney | **White Pl**	19
🅩 Schoolhouse | **Wilton**	27
Shack | **Fairfield**	13
🅩 Shady Glen | **Manchester**	21
Sharpe Hill/Vineyard | **Pomfret**	-
Southport Brew. | **multi.**	16
Still River | **Eastford**	28
Stone House | **Guilford**	18
Ted's Montana | **S Windsor**	23
Temple Grill | **New Haven**	17
Terra Mar | **Old Saybrook**	23
Thataway Cafe | **Greenwich**	17
Town Dock | **Rye**	19
Towne Crier | **Pawling**	17
Trinity Grill | **Harrison**	20
Vanilla Bean | **Pomfret**	22
Village | **Litchfield**	20
Vox | **N Salem**	21
Wandering Moose | **W Cornwall**	16

Watercolor Cafe | **Larch**	18
Water St. Cafe | **Stonington**	26
NEW Westchester Burger | **White Pl**	20
West St. Grill | **Litchfield**	24
Winvian | **Morris**	27
Woodland | **Lakeville**	22
Wood-n-Tap | **multi.**	17
Z Woodward Hse. | **Bethlehem**	27
Zinc | **New Haven**	24

ARGENTINEAN

Milonga | **N White Plains**	22
Tango Grill | **White Pl**	21

ASIAN

Asiana Cafe | **Greenwich**	21
Asian Tempt. | **White Pl**	20
Baang Cafe | **Riverside**	23
Bambou | **Greenwich**	21
Bond Grill | **Norwalk**	21
Ching's/Wild Ginger | **multi.**	24
East-West Grille | **W Hartford**	23
Euro Asian | **Port Chester**	17
Ginban Asian | **Mamaro**	23
Golden Rod | **New Roch**	18
Kudeta | **New Haven**	21
Little Kitchen | **Westport**	21
Penang Grill | **Greenwich**	22
Red Plum | **Mamaro**	21
Watermoon | **Rye**	23
Wild Rice | **Norwalk**	20

AUSTRIAN

Hopkins Inn | **New Preston**	19

BAKERIES

American Pie | **Sherman**	22
Bedford Post/Barn | **Bedford**	23
Corner Bakery | **Pawling**	23
Z Isabelle/Vincent | **Fairfield**	27
NEW Millstone Café | **Kent**	-
SoNo Baking Co. | **S Norwalk**	26
Versailles | **Greenwich**	24
Village Sq. Bagels | **Larch**	18

BARBECUE

Big W's | **Wingdale**	26
Black-Eyed Sally | **Hartford**	20
Boathouse/Smokey | **Stamford**	19
Bobby Q's | **Westport**	21
Cookhouse | **New Milford**	22
Flaggstead | **Farmington**	-
Jeff's Cuisine | **S Norwalk**	25
Nat Hayden's BBQ | **Windsor**	-
Q Rest. | **Port Chester**	22
When Pigs Fly | **Sharon**	21
Wilson's BBQ | **Fairfield**	20
Wood's Pit BBQ | **Bantam**	21

BRAZILIAN

Churrasc. Braza | **Hartford**	16
Copacabana | **Port Chester**	21

BURGERS

AJ's Burgers | **New Roch**	20
Blazer Pub | **Purdys**	22
Brooklyn's Famous | **White Pl**	17
Burger Bar | **S Norwalk**	22
Burgers/Shakes | **multi.**	22
Clamp's | **New Milford**	-
Cobble Stone | **Purchase**	15
Croton Creek | **Crot Falls**	20
Donovan's | **S Norwalk**	18
Flipside Burgers | **Fairfield**	17
Johnny Rockets | **multi.**	16
Larchmont Tav. | **Larch**	17
Louis' Lunch | **New Haven**	22
Lucky's | **Stamford**	18
Max Burger | **W Hartford**	25
Meetinghouse | **Bedford Vill**	20
NEW Oakhurst Diner | **Millerton**	16
Oliver's Taverne | **Essex**	16
Plan B Burger | **multi.**	22
Porter Hse. | **White Pl**	19
Prime 16 | **New Haven**	23
Red Rooster | **Brewster**	18
Route 22 | **Armonk**	14
Sam's/Gedney | **White Pl**	19
Sherwood's | **Larch**	20
Sycamore Drive-In | **Bethel**	17

Town Dock	**Rye**	19
Towne Crier	**Pawling**	17
NEW Westchester Burger	**White Pl**	20

CAJUN

Black-Eyed Sally	**Hartford**	20
Cuckoo's Nest	**Old Saybrook**	17
Rye Roadhse.	**Rye**	18

CALIFORNIAN

| Gates | **New Canaan** | 19 |
| V Rest. | **Westport** | 18 |

CARIBBEAN

| **NEW** Alvin/Friends | **New Roch** | 26 |

CHINESE

(* dim sum specialist)
Aberdeen*	**White Pl**	23
Bao's	**White Pl**	20
Butterfly Chinese	**W Hartford**	19
Chengdu	**W Hartford**	20
China Pavilion	**Orange**	23
David Chen	**Armonk**	18
Forbidden City	**Middletown**	25
Great Taste	**New Britain**	20
Hunan Larchmont	**Larch**	17
Imperial Wok	**N White Plains**	17
P.F. Chang's	**multi.**	18
Ray's Cafe	**multi.**	19
Royal Palace	**New Haven**	25
Sushi 25	**New Canaan**	-
Taste/China	**Clinton**	22
Tiger Bowl	**Westport**	15
Toro	**Newtown**	24
Zhang's	**multi.**	16

COFFEEHOUSES

Atticus	**New Haven**	18
Booktrader Café	**New Haven**	18
Cafe Mozart	**Mamaro**	17
Irving Farm	**Millerton**	19

COFFEE SHOPS/DINERS

| Brooklyn's Famous | **White Pl** | 17 |
| City Limits | **multi.** | 19 |

Dottie's Diner	**Woodbury**	18
Eveready Diner	**Brewster**	20
Gold Roc	**W Hartford**	14
Lucky's	**Stamford**	18
Nautilus	**Mamaro**	16
NEW Oakhurst Diner	**Millerton**	16
Orem's Diner	**Wilton**	15
Z Shady Glen	**Manchester**	21
Sycamore Drive-In	**Bethel**	17

CONTINENTAL

Altnaveigh Inn	**Storrs**	23
Christopher Martins	**New Haven**	20
Drescher's	**Waterbury**	19
Flood Tide	**Mystic**	21
Grist Mill	**Farmington**	23
Harvest/Pomfret	**Pomfret**	21
Heirloom	**New Haven**	20
Jeffrey's	**Milford**	26
Mill/River	**S Windsor**	20
Roger Sherman	**New Canaan**	24
Shell Station	**Stratford**	20
Stonehenge	**Ridgefield**	22
Woodland	**Lakeville**	22

CREOLE

| Rye Roadhse. | **Rye** | 18 |

CUBAN

| Karamba | **White Pl** | 22 |
| Soul de Cuba | **New Haven** | 25 |

DELIS

Firehouse Deli	**Fairfield**	21
Kisco Kosher	**White Pl**	17
Oscar's	**Westport**	18
Rein's NY Deli	**Vernon**	22

DESSERT

American Pie	**Sherman**	22
Aux Délices	**multi.**	24
Cafe Mozart	**Mamaro**	17
Cheesecake Fac.	**multi.**	17
Chocopologie	**S Norwalk**	22
City Limits	**multi.**	19

Corner Bakery | **Pawling**	23
McKinney/Doyle | **Pawling**	25
Pantry | **Wash Depot**	24
SoNo Baking Co. | **S Norwalk**	26
Versailles | **Greenwich**	24

ECLECTIC

☑ Arch | **Brewster**	27
Ballou's | **Guilford**	18
NEW Bank St. Tavern | **New Milford**	18
Beehive | **Armonk**	21
Bin 100 | **Milford**	26
Bonda | **Fairfield**	27
Cafe Mirage | **Port Chester**	22
Capt. Daniel Packer | **Mystic**	21
Caseus | **New Haven**	25
Dragonfly | **Stamford**	17
Flood Tide | **Mystic**	21
Manna Dew | **Millerton**	22
116 Crown | **New Haven**	21
Osetra | **S Norwalk**	23
Rye Grill | **Rye**	18
Saito | **Greenwich**	27
Squire's | **Redding**	16
Trumbull Kitchen | **Hartford**	22

EUROPEAN

John-Michael's | **N Salem**	24
NEW On the Way Café | **Rye**	-

FONDUE

Melting Pot | **multi.**	17

FRENCH

Aux Délices | **multi.**	24
☑ Bernard's | **Ridgefield**	27
☑ Bistro Basque | **Milford**	26
Brasserie Pip | **Ivoryton**	-
Brix | **Cheshire**	21
Cafe Lola | **Fairfield**	24
Cavey's | **Manchester**	26
DaPietro's | **Westport**	27
☑ Isabelle/Vincent | **Fairfield**	27
☑ Jean-Louis | **Greenwich**	28
La Bretagne | **Stamford**	24
☑ La Crémaillère | **Bedford**	27

☑ La Panetière | **Rye**	27
Le Château | **S Salem**	25
L'Escale | **Greenwich**	23
Meli-Melo | **Greenwich**	25
Nuage | **Cos Cob**	24
Ondine | **Danbury**	26
Rest. L&E | **Chester**	24
RSVP | **W Cornwall**	28
☑ Thomas Henkelmann | **Greenwich**	28
Vox | **N Salem**	21

FRENCH (BISTRO)

NEW Bar Bouchée | **Madison**	28
Bistro Bonne Nuit | **New Canaan**	25
Bistro 22 | **Bedford**	24
☑ Café Routier | **Westbrook**	27
Chez Jean-Pierre | **Stamford**	24
Country Bistro | **Salisbury**	-
Encore Bistro | **Larch**	23
Épernay | **Bridgeport**	22
☑ Le Petit Cafe | **Branford**	29
Le Provençal | **Mamaro**	23
Luc's Café | **Ridgefield**	24
Pascal's | **Larch**	23
Pastorale | **Lakeville**	23
Rue/Crêpes | **Harrison**	19
☑ Ten Twenty Post | **Darien**	21
☑ Union League | **New Haven**	27
Versailles | **Greenwich**	24

FRENCH (BRASSERIE)

NEW Brasserie | **Fairfield**	24

GASTROPUB

NEW Suburban | **Amer./Med.** | **Branford**	24

GERMAN

Drescher's | **Waterbury**	19
East Side | **New Britain**	17
Old Heidelberg | **Bethel**	21

GREEK

Eos Greek | **Stamford**	24
Niko's Greek | **White Pl**	20

Osianna	**Fairfield**	25
Post Corner Pizza	**Darien**	20
Yorkside	**New Haven**	15

HOT DOGS

Denmo's	**Southbury**	-
Red Rooster	**Brewster**	18
Super/Weenie	**Fairfield**	23
Walter's	**Mamaro**	22

INDIAN

Bangalore	**Fairfield**	23
Bombay	**Westport**	22
Bombay Olive	**W Hartford**	19
Z Coromandel	**multi.**	25
Jaipore Indian	**Brewster**	23
Rani Mahal	**Mamaro**	23
Rasa	**Greenwich**	24
Royal Palace	**White Pl**	20
Tandoori Taste	**Port Chester**	21
Taste/India	**W Hartford**	19
Z Tawa	**Stamford**	27
Thali	**multi.**	24

IRISH

Mickey/Molly Spill.	**Mamaro**	15
O'Neill's	**S Norwalk**	19

ITALIAN

(N=Northern; S=Southern)

Abatino's	**N White Plains**	20
Abruzzi Tratt.	**Patterson**	21
Adriana's	**New Haven**	22
Alba's	N	**Port Chester**	23
Alforno	N	**Old Saybrook**	22
Angelina's Tratt.	**Westport**	17
Anna Maria's	**Larch**	21
NEW Arrosto	**Port Chester**	23
Assaggio	N	**Branford**	24
Aurora	N	**Rye**	21
Avellino's	**Fairfield**	20
Aversano's	**Brewster**	21
Bacchus	N	**S Norwalk**	-
NEW Bar Rosso	**Stamford**	-
Basta	**New Haven**	25
Bellizzi	**Larch**	15

Bertucci's	**multi.**	16
Bin 228	**Hartford**	22
Blue Dolphin	S	**Katonah**	23
Bravo Bravo	**Mystic**	26
Z Bricco	**W Hartford**	27
Brix	**Cheshire**	21
Buon Amici	**White Pl**	22
Buon Appetito	N	**Canton**	26
Cafe Allegre	**Madison**	23
Cafe Giulia	**Lakeville**	22
Cafe Goodfellas	S	**New Haven**	20
Cafe Livorno	N	**Rye**	19
Café/Green	N	**Danbury**	22
Cafe Silvium	**Stamford**	26
Carbone's	N	**Hartford**	24
Carrabba's	**Manchester**	18
Cava Wine	N	**New Canaan**	22
Cavey's	N	**Manchester**	26
Centro	N	**multi.**	20
Chef Antonio	S	**Mamaro**	20
Cinzano's	**Fairfield**	18
Columbus Park	**Stamford**	25
Confetti	**Plainville**	22
Consiglio's	**New Haven**	23
DaCapo's	**Avon**	19
Da Giorgio	**New Roch**	25
DaPietro's	N	**Westport**	27
DiNardo's	**Pound Ridge**	19
Diorio	N	**Waterbury**	25
Doc's Tratt.	**Kent**	19
Eclisse	**Stamford**	21
Emilio Rist.	**Harrison**	25
Enzo's	**Mamaro**	20
Esca	**Middletown**	19
Ferrante	N	**Stamford**	20
55°	N	**Fairfield**	23
59 Bank	**New Milford**	19
First/Last	**multi.**	19
Fratelli	**New Roch**	19
NEW Gabriele's	**Greenwich**	-
Gavi	**Armonk**	19
Gervasi's	**White Pl**	20
Graziellas	**White Pl**	19

Hot Tomato's | **Hartford**	20
Il Castello | **Mamaro**	24
Il Palio | N | **Shelton**	24
Il Sogno | **Port Chester**	24
La Bocca | **White Pl**	23
La Manda's | **White Pl**	19
La Piccola Casa | N | **Mamaro**	21
La Riserva | N | **Larch**	21
NEW La Scarbitta | **Mamaro**	-
La Taverna | N | **Norwalk**	21
La Tavola | **Waterbury**	26
La Villetta | **Larch**	24
La Zingara | **Bethel**	26
Le Fontane | S | **Katonah**	22
Leon's | **New Haven**	18
L'Orcio | **New Haven**	23
Luca Rist. | **Wilton**	26
Luigi's | **Old Saybrook**	24
Lusardi's | **Larch**	24
Maestro's | **New Roch**	20
Mamma Francesca | **New Roch**	19
Mancuso's | **Fairfield**	21
Marianacci's | **Port Chester**	21
Mario's Pl. | **Westport**	19
Marisa's | **Trumbull**	18
Max-a-Mia | **Avon**	24
Max Amore | N | **Glastonbury**	23
Michael's | N | **Wallingford**	24
Milonga | **N White Plains**	22
Modern Rest. | S | **New Roch**	22
Molto Wine | **Fairfield**	21
Morello | **Greenwich**	22
Mulino's | **White Pl**	24
Nessa | **Port Chester**	21
Nino's | **S Salem**	20
Nino's | **Bedford Hills**	21
Osteria Applausi | **Old Greenwich**	24
Paci | **Southport**	26
Papacelle | **Avon**	24
Pasta Nostra | **S Norwalk**	25
Pasta Vera | **Greenwich**	20
Pellicci's | **Stamford**	19
Peppercorn's Grill | **Hartford**	26
Peppino's | N | **Katonah**	20
Piccolo Arancio | **Farmington**	25
Piero's | **Port Chester**	24
Polpo | **Greenwich**	24
Ponte Vecchio | **Fairfield**	18
Portofino Pizza | **Goldens Br**	22
Positano's | S | **Westport**	22
Posto 22 | **New Roch**	21
Primavera | N | **Crot Falls**	24
Quattro Pazzi | **multi.**	23
Ralph/Rich's | **Bridgeport**	23
Rist. Luce | **Hamden**	22
Rraci | **Brewster**	26
Sagi | **Ridgefield**	23
Sal/Pepe | N | **Newtown**	24
Sardegna | **Larch**	19
Scoozzi Tratt. | N | **New Haven**	22
Siena | N | **Stamford**	23
Solé Rist. | N | **New Canaan**	21
Spadaro | **New Roch**	26
Strada 18 | **S Norwalk**	26
Taberna | **Bridgeport**	28
T&J Villaggio | **Port Chester**	21
Tango Grill | **White Pl**	21
NEW Tappo | **Stamford**	-
Tarantino's | **Westport**	25
Taro's | **Millerton**	19
Tarry Lodge | **Port Chester**	24
Terra Rist. | N | **Greenwich**	23
Tiberio's | **Old Saybrook**	-
Todd English's | N | **Uncasville**	22
Toscana | N | **Ridgefield**	22
Tratt. Carl Anthony | **Monroe**	24
Tratt. Lucia | **Bedford**	18
Tratt. Vivolo | **Harrison**	25
Tre Angelina | N | **White Pl**	21
Tre Scalini | **New Haven**	24
Tuscan Oven | **Norwalk**	20
Tuscany | N | **Bridgeport**	24
⊠ Valbella | **Riverside**	25
Vazzy's | **multi.**	20
Venetian | N | **Torrington**	18
Viale Rist. | **Bridgeport**	24
Via Sforza | **Westport**	22
Vito's | **multi.**	21

Vote at ZAGAT.com

Waters Edge at Giovanni's | **Darien**	19
Yorkside | **New Haven**	15

JAPANESE
(* sushi specialist)

Abis* | **Greenwich**	19
Akasaka* | **New Haven**	21
Edo | **Port Chester**	20
Feng Asian* | **multi.**	22
Fin/Fin II* | **multi.**	23
Fuji Mtn. | **Larch**	15
Haiku* | **multi.**	22
Hajime* | **Harrison**	25
Hunan Larchmont | **Larch**	17
Imperial Wok | **N White Plains**	17
Karuta* | **New Roch**	18
Kazu* | **S Norwalk**	25
Kira* | **Armonk**	23
Kobis | **multi.**	22
Kona Grill* | **Stamford**	17
Koo* | **multi.**	23
Kotobuki* | **Stamford**	24
Kujaku* | **Stamford**	18
Kumo* | **multi.**	20
Made In Asia* | **Armonk**	21
Miso | **New Haven**	23
Miya's Sushi* | **New Haven**	25
Murasaki* | **W Hartford**	-
Noda's Steak* | **White Pl**	19
NEW Norimaki* | **Washington**	-
Nuage | **Cos Cob**	24
Plum Tree* | **New Canaan**	20
Saito | **Greenwich**	27
Sakura* | **Westport**	21
Seasons Japanese* | **White Pl**	23
Sono Bana* | **Hamden**	24
Z Sushi Nanase* | **White Pl**	29
Sushi 25* | **New Canaan**	-
Z Tengda* | **multi.**	22
Toro | **Newtown**	24
Toshi Japanese* | **Avon**	21
Toyo Sushi* | **Mamaro**	21
Wasabi* | **Orange**	25

Wasabi Chi* | **S Norwalk**	23
Zhang's* | **multi.**	16

KOREAN
(* barbecue specialist)

Kalbi Hse.* | **White Pl**	19

KOSHER/ KOSHER-STYLE

Claire's Corner | **New Haven**	21
Kisco Kosher | **White Pl**	17
Village Sq. Bagels | **Larch**	18

LEBANESE

Layla's Falafel | **multi.**	22

MACROBIOTIC

It's Only Natural | **Middletown**	20

MALAYSIAN

Bentara | **New Haven**	24

MEDITERRANEAN

Acqua | **Westport**	22
Arugula | **W Hartford**	23
Z Basso Café | **Norwalk**	28
NEW Café d'Azur | **Darien**	-
Café Manolo | **Westport**	23
Centro | **multi.**	20
Douro | **Greenwich**	-
NEW Eclisse Med. | **White Pl**	21
NEW Fez | **Stamford**	20
Gates | **New Canaan**	19
Harbor Lights | **Norwalk**	20
Il Sogno | **Port Chester**	24
John's Café | **Woodbury**	23
Lusardi's | **Larch**	24
Mediterranean Grill | **Wilton**	18
Mediterraneo | **Greenwich**	21
Oliva Cafe | **New Preston**	24
Osianna | **Fairfield**	25
Primavera | **Crot Falls**	24
Rouge Winebar | **S Norwalk**	21
Z Serevan | **Amenia**	27
Taberna | **Bridgeport**	28
Tapas/Ann | **multi.**	23
Turquoise | **Larch**	21

MEXICAN

Agave Grill	**Hartford**	20
NEW Bartaco	**Port Chester**	-
Besito	**W Hartford**	22
Coyote Flaco	**multi.**	23
Cuckoo's Nest	**Old Saybrook**	17
El Tio	**multi.**	18
Fonda La Paloma	**Cos Cob**	19
Gusano Loco	**Mamaro**	21
La Herradura	**multi.**	18
Little Mex. Cafe	**New Roch**	21
Lolita Cocina	**Greenwich**	22
Los Cabos	**Norwalk**	15
NEW Oaxaca Kitchen	**New Haven**	-
Olé Molé	**multi.**	19
NEW Red Lulu	**S Norwalk**	24
SolToro	**Uncasville**	20
Tequila Mock.	**New Canaan**	18
Tequila Sunrise	**Larch**	17
Viva Zapata	**Westport**	17
Wood's Pit BBQ	**Bantam**	21

MIDDLE EASTERN

Aladdin	**Hartford**	-
Sesame Seed	**Danbury**	21

MOROCCAN

NEW Fez	**Stamford**	20
Zitoune	**Mamaro**	19

NEW ENGLAND

Back Porch	**Old Saybrook**	18
Jasper White's	**Uncasville**	21
Noah's	**Stonington**	24
Tavern/Main	**Westport**	19

NEW MEXICAN

Southwest Cafe	**Ridgefield**	22

NUEVO LATINO

NEW Cienega	**New Roch**	-
Pacifico	**New Haven**	24
Sonora	**Port Chester**	24

PACIFIC RIM

Char Koon	**S Glastonbury**	23

PAN-LATIN

Ay! Salsa	**New Haven**	-
Z Brasitas	**multi.**	25
Karamba	**White Pl**	22

PERUVIAN

Patrias	**Port Chester**	21

PIZZA

Abatino's	**N White Plains**	20
Aladdin	**Hartford**	-
Alforno	**Old Saybrook**	22
Angelina's Tratt.	**Westport**	17
NEW Anthony's Pizza	**White Pl**	22
Aurora	**Rye**	21
Bellizzi	**Larch**	15
Bertucci's	**multi.**	16
Bru Room/BAR	**New Haven**	25
California Pizza	**multi.**	17
Colony Grill	**multi.**	24
DiNardo's	**Pound Ridge**	19
Doc's Tratt.	**Kent**	19
Fat Cat Pie	**Norwalk**	23
First/Last	**multi.**	19
NEW Frankie/Fanucci's	**Mamaro**	21
Z Frank Pepe	**multi.**	24
Harry's Bishops	**W Hartford**	24
Harry's Pizza	**W Hartford**	26
La Manda's	**White Pl**	19
Luna Pizza	**multi.**	21
Maestro's	**New Roch**	20
Mancuso's	**Fairfield**	21
Modern Apizza	**New Haven**	25
Modern Rest.	**New Roch**	22
Molto Wine	**Fairfield**	21
Mystic Pizza	**multi.**	15
Nino's	**Bedford Hills**	21
Pizzeria Lauretano	**Bethel**	22
Portofino Pizza	**Goldens Br**	22
Post Corner Pizza	**Darien**	20
Rizzuto's	**multi.**	20
Sally's Apizza	**New Haven**	25
Sal's Pizza	**Mamaro**	23
Taro's	**Millerton**	19

Vote at ZAGAT.com

Tarry Lodge	**Port Chester**	24
Terra Rist.	**Greenwich**	23
3 Boys/Italy	**White Pl**	23
Tuscan Oven	**Norwalk**	20
Two Boots	**Bridgeport**	20
Vazzy's	**multi.**	20
Vinny's	**multi.**	20
Yorkside	**New Haven**	15

PORTUGUESE

Douro	**Greenwich**	-
Omanel	**Bridgeport**	19
O'Porto	**Hartford**	23
NEW Piri-Q	**Mamaro**	20

PUB FOOD

Archie Moore's	**multi.**	18
Blazer Pub	**Purdys**	22
Brazen Fox	**White Pl**	17
Brewhouse	**S Norwalk**	19
Bru Room/BAR	**New Haven**	25
Eli Cannon's	**Middletown**	21
Emma's Ale House	**White Pl**	18
Ginger Man	**multi.**	18
NEW Goose	**Darien**	-
John Harvard's	**Manchester**	16
Kelly's Corner	**Brewster**	17
Larchmont Tav.	**Larch**	17
Lazy Boy Saloon	**White Pl**	19
Little Pub	**Ridgefield**	23
Mackenzie's	**Old Greenwich**	16
O'Neill's	**S Norwalk**	19
Penny Lane Pub	**Old Saybrook**	19
Prime 16	**New Haven**	23
Ron Blacks	**White Pl**	16
Route 22	**Armonk**	14
Sherwood's	**Larch**	20
Southport Brew.	**multi.**	16
Village	**Litchfield**	20
Vinny's	**multi.**	20
White Horse	**New Preston**	19
Wood-n-Tap	**multi.**	17

PUERTO RICAN

Don Coqui	**New Roch**	23

SANDWICHES

Brooklyn's Famous	**White Pl**	17
Corner Bakery	**Pawling**	23
Cosi	**multi.**	16
Firehouse Deli	**Fairfield**	21
Harney/Sons	**Millerton**	21
Irving Farm	**Millerton**	19
Kisco Kosher	**White Pl**	17
Oscar's	**Westport**	18
Pantry	**Wash Depot**	24
Rein's NY Deli	**Vernon**	22

SEAFOOD

Abbott's Lobster	**Noank**	23
Atlantic Seafood	**Old Saybrook**	23
Beach House	**Milford**	22
Bill's Seafood	**Westbrook**	19
Boathouse/Smokey	**Stamford**	19
Carmen Anthony Fish.	**multi.**	22
Confetti	**Plainville**	22
Dock/Dine	**Old Saybrook**	14
Dolphins Cove	**Bridgeport**	-
80 West	**White Pl**	19
Z Elm St. Oyster	**Greenwich**	24
Flanders Fish	**E Lyme**	21
Gervasi's	**White Pl**	20
Go Fish	**Mystic**	22
Gus's Franklin Pk.	**Harrison**	21
Harbor Lights	**Norwalk**	20
Jasper White's	**Uncasville**	21
Johnny Ad's	**Old Saybrook**	21
Legal Sea Foods	**White Pl**	19
Lenny/Joe's	**multi.**	23
Lenny's Indian	**Branford**	21
Litchfield/Grille	**Litchfield**	20
Liv's Oyster	**Old Saybrook**	25
Matthew's	**Unionville**	24
Max Fish	**Glastonbury**	23
Max's Oyster	**W Hartford**	26
Morgans Fish	**Rye**	21
Octagon	**Groton**	24
Osetra	**S Norwalk**	23
Pacifico	**New Haven**	24
Rest./Rowayton Sea.	**Rowayton**	22

☑ Rest./Water's Edge | **Westbrook**	23
Ruby's Oyster | **Rye**	23
Sage | **New Haven**	19
Saltwater Grille | **Stamford**	17
Saybrook Fish | **Rocky Hill**	22
Scribner's | **Milford**	22
Seaside Johnnie's | **Rye**	12
Shack | **Fairfield**	13
Shell Station | **Stratford**	20
Sono Seaport | **S Norwalk**	15
Splash | **Westport**	22
Stone House | **Guilford**	18
☑ Ten Twenty Post | **Darien**	21
Town Dock | **Rye**	19
U.S.S. Chowder | **multi.**	19
Westbrook Lobster | **multi.**	19

SMALL PLATES

(See also Spanish tapas specialist)

NEW Bar Rosso | Italian | **Stamford**	–
Douro | Portug. | **Greenwich**	–
Dragonfly | Eclectic | **Stamford**	17
NEW Fez | Med./Moroccan | **Stamford**	20
Gabrielle's | Amer. | **Centerbrook**	25
Gnarly Vine | Amer. | **New Roch**	17
Milonga | Argent./Italian | **N White Plains**	22
116 Crown | Eclectic | **New Haven**	21
Osetra | Eclectic/Seafood | **S Norwalk**	23
Osianna | Med. | **Fairfield**	25
Southwest Cafe | New Mex. | **Ridgefield**	22
Tapas/Ann | Med. | **multi.**	23

SOUTHERN

NEW Alvin/Friends | **New Roch**	26
Jeff's Cuisine | **S Norwalk**	25
Taste/Charleston | **Norwalk**	–

SOUTHWESTERN

Boxcar Cantina | **Greenwich**	21
Coyote Blue | **Middletown**	20

Geronimo | **New Haven**	20
J. Gilbert's | **Glastonbury**	25
Salsa | **New Milford**	25
Telluride | **Stamford**	21

SPANISH

(* tapas specialist)

Barça* | **Hartford**	20
☑ Barcelona* | **multi.**	24
NEW Bellota/42* | **White Pl**	–
☑ Bistro Basque | **Milford**	26
Costa del Sol | **Hartford**	25
España* | **Larch**	20
☑ Ibiza* | **multi.**	27
La Paella | **Norwalk**	25
Meigas* | **Norwalk**	24
Olive Mkt.* | **Georgetown**	24
Patrias | **Port Chester**	21
Tapas/Ann* | **W Hartford**	23

STEAKHOUSES

Bacchus | **S Norwalk**	–
NEW Benjamin Steak | **White Pl**	24
Blackstones | **Norwalk**	25
BLT Steak | **White Pl**	23
☑ Capital Grille | **Stamford**	25
Carmen Anthony Steak | **multi.**	22
Cedars | **Ledyard**	28
Central Steak | **New Haven**	24
Chuck's Steak | **multi.**	18
Churrasc. Braza | **Hartford**	16
Craftsteak | **Ledyard**	24
Croton Creek | **Crot Falls**	20
Dakota Steak | **multi.**	17
David Burke | **Ledyard**	26
Edo | **Port Chester**	20
Frankie/Johnnie's | **Rye**	24
NEW Gabriele's | **Greenwich**	–
J. Gilbert's | **Glastonbury**	25
Joseph's | **Bridgeport**	24
Kobis | **multi.**	22
Marc Charles | **Armonk**	20
Mario's Pl. | **Westport**	19
☑ Max Downtown | **Hartford**	27
Michael Jordan's | **Uncasville**	23

Morton's	**multi.**	24
Mo's NY	**New Roch**	18
New Deal Steak	**Westbrook**	14
Octagon	**Groton**	24
Outback Steak	**multi.**	17
Ruth's Chris	**Newington**	25
Sage	**New Haven**	19
Steak Loft	**Mystic**	18
Waters Edge at Giovanni's	**Darien**	19
Willett House	**Port Chester**	24

TEAROOMS

Chaiwalla	**Salisbury**	25
Harney/Sons	**Millerton**	21

TEX-MEX

Mary Ann's	**multi.**	15
3 Jalapeños	**Mamaro**	17

THAI

Bangkok Gdns.	**New Haven**	19
Bangkok Thai	**Mamaro**	20
Full Moon	**White Pl**	24
Hot Basil	**W Hartford**	20
King & I	**multi.**	24
Kit's Thai	**Stamford**	21
Thai/Buddha/Spice	**multi.**	23
Papaya Thai	**S Norwalk**	20
Puket Café	**Wethersfield**	26
Red Lotus	**New Roch**	21
Reka's	**White Pl**	19

TURKISH

Turkish Cuisine	**White Pl**	21
Turkish Meze	**Mamaro**	23
Turquoise	**Larch**	21

VEGETARIAN

(* vegan)

Bloodroot*	**Bridgeport**	23
Claire's Corner	**New Haven**	21
NEW Green Gourmet	**Bridgeport**	-
It's Only Natural*	**Middletown**	20
Lime	**Norwalk**	23
Z Tawa	**Stamford**	27

VENEZUELAN

Z Valencia Lunch.	**Norwalk**	27

VIETNAMESE

Bamboo Grill	**Canton**	-
Pot-au-Pho	**New Haven**	17

CT/NEARBY NY

CUISINES

Locations

Includes names, cuisines and Food ratings.

Connecticut

AVON

Bertucci's	*Italian*	16
Carmen Anthony Fish.	*Seafood*	22
Così	*Sandwiches*	16
DaCapo's	*Italian*	19
Dakota Steak	*Steak*	17
Ferme	*Amer.*	21
First/Last	*Italian*	19
Max-a-Mia	*Italian*	24
Papacelle	*Italian*	24
Toshi Japanese	*Japanese*	21

BANTAM

Wood's Pit BBQ | *BBQ/Mex.* 21

BERLIN

Hawthorne Inn | *Amer.* 20

BETHEL

NEW Greenwood's Grille	*Amer.*	16
La Zingara	*Italian*	26
Old Heidelberg	*German*	21
Pizzeria Lauretano	*Pizza*	22
Putnam Hse.	*Amer.*	19
Rizzuto's	*Italian*	20
Sycamore Drive-In	*Amer.*	17

BETHLEHEM

Z Woodward Hse. | *Amer.* 27

BLOOMFIELD

Tapas/Ann | *Med.* 23

BRANFORD

Assaggio	*Italian*	24
Chuck's Steak	*Steak*	18
Foe	*Amer.*	19
Lenny's Indian	*Seafood*	21
Z Le Petit Cafe	*French*	29
Southport Brew.	*Pub*	16
NEW Suburban	*Amer./Med.*	24
U.S.S. Chowder	*Seafood*	19

BRIDGEPORT

Ash Creek	*Amer.*	17
Bloodroot	*Vegan/Veg.*	23
Coyote Flaco	*Mex.*	23
Dolphins Cove	*Seafood*	-
Épernay	*Amer./French*	22
NEW Green Gourmet	*Veg.*	-
Joseph's	*Steak*	24
King & I	*Thai*	24
Omanel	*Portug.*	19
Ralph/Rich's	*Italian*	23
Taberna	*Italian/Med.*	28
Tuscany	*Italian*	24
Two Boots	*Pizza*	20
Vazzy's	*Italian*	20
Viale Rist.	*Italian*	24

CANTON

Bamboo Grill	*Viet.*	-
Buon Appetito	*Italian*	26
Feng Asian	*Asian*	22

CENTERBROOK

Gabrielle's | *Amer.* 25

CHESHIRE

Brix | *French/Italian* 21

CHESTER

Rest. L&E	*French*	24
River Tavern	*Amer.*	26

CLINTON

Taste/China	*Chinese*	22
Westbrook Lobster	*Seafood*	19

COS COB

Fonda La Paloma	*Mex.*	19
Nuage	*French/Japanese*	24

DANBURY

Bertucci's	*Italian*	16
Café/Green	*Italian*	22
Chuck's Steak	*Steak*	18

Vote at ZAGAT.com

CONNECTICUT

LOCATIONS

Bambou | *Asian*	21
☑ Barcelona | *Spanish*	24
Boxcar Cantina | *SW*	21
Burgers/Shakes | *Burgers*	22
Centro | *Italian/Med.*	20
Così | *Sandwiches*	16
Douro | *Portug.*	-
☑ Elm St. Oyster | *Seafood*	24
NEW Gabriele's | *Italian/Steak*	-
Ginger Man | *Pub*	18
☑ Jean-Louis | *French*	28
L'Escale | *French*	23
Thai/Buddha/Spice | *Thai*	23
Lolita Cocina | *Mex.*	22
Mediterraneo | *Med.*	21
Meli-Melo | *French*	25
Morello | *Italian*	22
Pasta Vera | *Italian*	20
Penang Grill | *Asian*	22
Polpo | *Italian*	24
Rasa | *Indian*	24
Rebeccas | *Amer.*	26
Saito | *Eclectic/Japanese*	27
☑ Tengda | *Asian*	22
Terra Rist. | *Italian*	23
Thataway Cafe | *Amer.*	17
☑ Thomas Henkelmann | *French*	28
Versailles | *Bakery/French*	24

GROTON

Octagon | *Seafood/Steak*	24
Olio | *Amer.*	24

GUILFORD

Ballou's | *Eclectic*	18
Stone House | *Amer./Seafood*	18

HAMDEN

☑ Ibiza | *Spanish*	27
Kumo | *Japanese*	20
Rist. Luce | *Italian*	22
Sono Bana | *Japanese*	24
Southport Brew. | *Pub*	16

HARTFORD

Agave Grill | *Mexican*	20
Aladdin | *Mideast.*	-

Barça | *Spanish*	20
Bin 228 | *Italian*	22
Black-Eyed Sally | *BBQ*	20
Carbone's | *Italian*	24
Cheesecake Fac. | *Amer.*	17
Churrasc. Braza | *Brazilian*	16
City Steam | *Amer.*	15
Costa del Sol | *Spanish*	25
Coyote Flaco | *Mex.*	23
Dish B&G | *Amer.*	20
Feng Asian | *Asian*	22
Firebox | *Amer.*	24
First/Last | *Italian*	19
Hot Tomato's | *Italian*	20
☑ Max Downtown | *Amer./Steak*	27
Morton's | *Steak*	24
O'Porto | *Portug.*	23
Peppercorn's Grill | *Italian*	26
☑ PolytechnicON20 | *Amer.*	28
Tapas/Ann | *Med.*	23
Trumbull Kitchen | *Eclectic*	22
U.S.S. Chowder | *Seafood*	19
Vito's | *Italian*	21
Wood-n-Tap | *Pub*	17

IVORYTON

Brasserie Pip | *Amer.*	-

KENT

Bull's Bridge | *Amer.*	16
Doc's Tratt. | *Italian*	19
Fife 'n Drum | *Amer.*	18
NEW Millstone Café | *Amer.*	-

LAKEVILLE

Boathouse | *Amer.*	17
Cafe Giulia | *Italian*	22
Pastorale | *French*	23
Woodland | *Amer./Continental*	22

LEDYARD

California Pizza | *Pizza*	17
Cedars | *Steak*	28
Craftsteak | *Steak*	24
David Burke | *Steak*	26
Hard Rock | *Amer.*	15

LITCHFIELD

@ the Corner	*Amer.*	20
Litchfield/Grille	*Amer.*	20
Village	*Pub*	20
West St. Grill	*Amer.*	24

MADISON

NEW Bar Bouchée	*French*	28
Cafe Allegre	*Italian*	23
Dolly Madison Inn	*Amer.*	13
Elizabeth's Cafe	*Amer.*	25
Friends & Co.	*Amer.*	18
Lenny/Joe's	*Seafood*	23
Zhang's	*Chinese/Japanese*	16

MANCHESTER

Carrabba's	*Italian*	18
Cavey's	*French/Italian*	26
☑ Frank Pepe	*Pizza*	24
John Harvard's	*Pub*	16
Outback Steak	*Steak*	17
☑ Shady Glen	*Diner*	21

MANSFIELD CENTER

Coyote Flaco	*Mex.*	23

MIDDLETOWN

Coyote Blue	*SW*	20
Eli Cannon's	*Amer.*	21
Esca	*Italian*	19
First/Last	*Italian*	19
Forbidden City	*Chinese*	25
It's Only Natural	*Health*	20

MILFORD

Archie Moore's	*Pub*	18
Beach House	*Seafood*	22
Bin 100	*Eclectic*	26
☑ Bistro Basque	*French/Spanish*	26
Jeffrey's	*Amer./Continental*	26
Johnny Rockets	*Burgers*	16
Scribner's	*Seafood*	22
Southport Brew.	*Pub*	16
☑ Tengda	*Asian*	22

MONROE

Tratt. Carl Anthony	*Italian*	24
Vazzy's	*Italian*	20

MORRIS

Winvian	*Amer.*	27

MYSTIC

Azu	*Amer.*	23
Bravo Bravo	*Italian*	26
Capt. Daniel Packer	*Eclectic*	21
Flood Tide	*Continental/Eclectic*	21
Go Fish	*Seafood*	22
Mystic Pizza	*Pizza*	15
Steak Loft	*Steak*	18
Zhang's	*Chinese/Japanese*	16

NEW BRITAIN

East Side	*German*	17
Great Taste	*Chinese*	20
Vito's	*Italian*	21

NEW CANAAN

Bistro Bonne Nuit	*French*	25
Cava Wine	*Italian*	22
Chef Luis	*Amer.*	25
Ching's/Wild Ginger	*Asian*	24
Fifty Coins	*Amer.*	16
Gates	*Calif./Med.*	19
☑ Harvest Supper	*Amer.*	27
NEW Pine Social	*Amer.*	23
Plum Tree	*Japanese*	20
Roger Sherman	*Continental*	24
Solé Rist.	*Italian*	21
Sushi 25	*Chinese/Japanese*	-
Tequila Mock.	*Mex.*	18
Thali	*Indian*	24

NEW HARTFORD

Chatterley's	*Amer.*	21

NEW HAVEN

Adriana's	*Italian*	22
Akasaka	*Japanese*	21
Archie Moore's	*Pub*	18
Atticus	*Amer.*	18
Ay! Salsa	*Pan-Latin*	-
Bangkok Gdns.	*Thai*	19
☑ Barcelona	*Spanish*	24
Basta	*Italian*	25

Bentara	*Malaysian*	24
Bespoke	*American*	24
Booktrader Café	*Coffeehouse*	18
Bru Room/BAR	*Pizza*	25
Cafe Goodfellas	*Italian*	20
Carmen Anthony Steak	*Steak*	22
Caseus	*Eclectic*	25
NEW Cask Republic	*Amer.*	-
Central Steak	*Steak*	24
Christopher Martins	*Cont.*	20
Claire's Corner	*Veg.*	21
Consiglio's	*Italian*	23
☒ Frank Pepe	*Pizza*	24
Geronimo	*SW*	20
Heirloom	*Amer./Continental*	20
☒ Ibiza	*Spanish*	27
Kudeta	*Asian*	21
Kumo	*Japanese*	20
Leon's	*Italian*	18
L'Orcio	*Italian*	23
Louis' Lunch	*Burgers*	22
Miso	*Japanese*	23
Miya's Sushi	*Japanese*	25
Modern Apizza	*Pizza*	25
NEW Oaxaca Kitchen	*Mex.*	-
116 Crown	*Eclectic*	21
Pacifico	*Nuevo Latino/Seafood*	24
Pot-au-Pho	*Viet.*	17
Prime 16	*Pub*	23
Royal Palace	*Chinese*	25
Sage	*Seafood/Steak*	19
Sally's Apizza	*Pizza*	25
Scoozzi Tratt.	*Italian*	22
Soul de Cuba	*Cuban*	25
Temple Grill	*Amer.*	17
Thali	*Indian*	24
Tre Scalini	*Italian*	24
☒ Union League	*French*	27
Yorkside	*Greek/Pizza*	15
Zinc	*Amer.*	24

NEWINGTON

Bertucci's	*Italian*	16
Outback Steak	*Steak*	17
Ruth's Chris	*Steak*	25

NEW LONDON

Outback Steak	*Steak*	17

NEW MILFORD

Adrienne	*Amer.*	25
NEW Bank St. Tavern	*Eclectic*	18
Clamp's	*Burgers*	-
Cookhouse	*BBQ*	22
59 Bank	*Amer.*	19
Salsa	*SW*	25

NEW PRESTON

Boulders Inn	*Amer.*	21
Hopkins Inn	*Austrian*	19
Oliva Cafe	*Med.*	24
White Horse	*Pub*	19

NEWTOWN

Inn/Newtown	*Amer.*	18
Sal/Pepe	*Italian*	24
Toro	*Chinese/Japanese*	24

NOANK

Abbott's Lobster	*Seafood*	23

NORFOLK

Infinity Hall/Bistro	*Amer.*	20

NORTH HAVEN

Outback Steak	*Steak*	17

NORTH STONINGTON

Mystic Pizza	*Pizza*	15

NORWALK

Ash Creek	*Amer.*	17
☒ Basso Café	*Med.*	28
B.J. Ryan's	*Amer.*	20
Blackstones	*Steak*	25
Bond Grill	*Asian*	21
☒ Brasitas	*Pan-Latin*	25
Fat Cat Pie	*Pizza*	23
Harbor Lights	*Med./Seafood*	20
La Paella	*Spanish*	25
La Taverna	*Italian*	21
Lime	*Health*	23
Thai/Buddha/Spice	*Thai*	23

Los Cabos	*Mex.*	15
Meigas	*Spanish*	24
Quattro Pazzi	*Italian*	23
NEW Sails	*Amer.*	-
Taste/Charleston	*Southern*	-
Tuscan Oven	*Italian*	20
Z Valencia Lunch.	*Venez.*	27
Wild Rice	*Asian*	20

OLD GREENWICH

Beach Hse. Café	*Amer.*	18
Greenwich Tav.	*Amer.*	21
Mackenzie's	*Pub*	16
Osteria Applausi	*Italian*	24

OLD LYME

Boom	*Amer.*	22
Chestnut Grille	*Amer.*	26
Old Lyme Inn	*Amer.*	22

OLD SAYBROOK

Alforno	*Italian*	22
Aspen	*Amer.*	20
Atlantic Seafood	*Seafood*	23
Back Porch	*New Eng.*	18
Cuckoo's Nest	*Cajun/Mex.*	17
Dock/Dine	*Seafood*	14
Johnny Ad's	*Amer.*	21
Liv's Oyster	*Seafood*	25
Luigi's	*Italian*	24
Pat's Kountry	*Amer.*	16
Penny Lane Pub	*Pub*	19
Terra Mar	*Amer.*	23
Tiberio's	*Italian*	-
Zhang's	*Chinese/Japanese*	16

ORANGE

Bertucci's	*Italian*	16
China Pavilion	*Chinese*	23
Z Coromandel	*Indian*	25
Outback Steak	*Steak*	17
Wasabi	*Japanese*	25
Wood-n-Tap	*Pub*	17

OXFORD

| 121 Rest./OXC | *Amer.* | 21 |

PLAINVILLE

| Confetti | *Italian/Seafood* | 22 |
| First/Last | *Italian* | 19 |

POMFRET

Harvest/Pomfret	*Continental*	21
Sharpe Hill/Vineyard	*Amer.*	-
Vanilla Bean	*Amer.*	22

REDDING/REDDING RIDGE

| Squire's | *Eclectic* | 16 |

RIDGEFIELD

Bailey's	*Amer.*	21
Z Bernard's	*French*	27
Fifty Coins	*Amer.*	16
Little Pub	*Pub*	23
Luc's Café	*French*	24
Sagi	*Italian*	23
Southwest Cafe	*New Mex.*	22
Stonehenge	*Continental*	22
Thali	*Indian*	24
Toscana	*Italian*	22

RIVERSIDE

Aux Délices	*Amer./French*	24
Baang Cafe	*Asian*	23
Z Valbella	*Italian*	25

ROCKY HILL

Chuck's Steak	*Steak*	18
Dakota Steak	*Steak*	17
Puket Café	*Thai*	26
Saybrook Fish	*Seafood*	22
Wood-n-Tap	*Pub*	17

ROWAYTON

| Rest./Rowayton Sea. | *Seafood* | 22 |

SALISBURY

| Chaiwalla | *Tearoom* | 25 |
| Country Bistro | *Amer./French* | - |

SHARON

| When Pigs Fly | *BBQ* | 21 |

SHELTON

Bertucci's | *Italian*	16
Il Palio | *Italian*	24
Kobis | *Japanese*	22
Outback Steak | *Steak*	17
Vazzy's | *Italian*	20

SHERMAN

American Pie | *Amer.*	22

SIMSBURY

Luna Pizza | *Pizza*	21
Métro Bis | *Amer.*	25
Plan B Burger | *Burgers*	22

SOUTHBURY

Denmo's | *Hot Dogs*	-
Olive Tree | *Amer.*	21

SOUTH GLASTONBURY

Char Koon | *Pac. Rim*	23

SOUTHINGTON

Bertucci's | *Italian*	16
Outback Steak | *Steak*	17
Wood-n-Tap | *Pub*	17

SOUTH NORWALK

Bacchus | *Tuscan/Steak*	-
Z Barcelona | *Spanish*	24
Brewhouse | *Amer.*	19
Burger Bar | *Burgers*	22
Chocopologie | *Dessert*	22
Z Coromandel | *Indian*	25
Donovan's | *Amer.*	18
Ginger Man | *Pub*	18
Jeff's Cuisine | *BBQ/Southern*	25
Kazu | *Japanese*	25
Match | *Amer.*	26
O'Neill's | *Pub*	19
Osetra | *Eclectic/Seafood*	23
Papaya Thai | *Thai*	20
Pasta Nostra | *Italian*	25
NEW Red Lulu | *Mex.*	24
Rouge Winebar | *Med.*	21
SoNo Baking Co. | *Bakery*	26

Sono Seaport | *Seafood*	15
Strada 18 | *Italian*	26
Wasabi Chi | *Asian*	23

SOUTHPORT

Z Coromandel | *Indian*	25
Paci | *Italian*	26
Southport Brew. | *Pub*	16

SOUTH WINDSOR

Johnny Rockets | *Burgers*	16
Mill/River | *Continental*	20
Ted's Montana | *Amer.*	23

STAMFORD

Z Barcelona | *Spanish*	24
NEW Bar Rosso | *Italian*	-
Boathouse/Smokey | *BBQ/Seafood*	19
Bobby Valentine | *Amer.*	15
Z Brasitas | *Pan-Latin*	25
Cafe Silvium | *Italian*	26
California Pizza | *Pizza*	17
Z Capital Grille | *Steak*	25
Chez Jean-Pierre | *French*	24
City Limits | *Diner*	19
Colony Grill | *Pizza*	24
Columbus Park | *Italian*	25
Z Coromandel | *Indian*	25
Dragonfly | *Eclectic*	17
Eclisse | *Italian*	21
Eos Greek | *Greek*	24
Ferrante | *Italian*	20
NEW Fez | *Med./Moroccan*	20
Fin/Fin II | *Japanese*	23
Kit's Thai | *Thai*	21
Kona Grill | *Amer./Asian*	17
Kotobuki | *Japanese*	24
Kujaku | *Japanese*	18
La Bretagne | *French*	24
Layla's Falafel | *Lebanese*	22
Thai/Buddha/Spice | *Thai*	23
Long Ridge Tav. | *Amer.*	14
Lucky's | *Diner*	18
Market | *Amer.*	20

Mary Ann's	*Tex-Mex*	15
Morton's	*Steak*	24
🛚 Napa & Co.	*Amer.*	24
Olé Molé	*Mex.*	19
Paradise B&G	*Amer.*	13
Pellicci's	*Italian*	19
P.F. Chang's	*Chinese*	18
Quattro Pazzi	*Italian*	23
Saltwater Grille	*Amer.*	17
Siena	*Italian*	23
Southport Brew.	*Pub*	16
NEW Tappo	*Italian*	-
🛚 Tawa	*Indian*	27
Telluride	*SW*	21
🛚 Tengda	*Asian*	22
Vinny's	*Pizza/Pub*	20

STONINGTON

Noah's	*Amer.*	24
Water St. Cafe	*Amer.*	26

STORRS

Altnaveigh Inn	*Continental*	23
Chuck's Steak	*Steak*	18

STRATFORD

Shell Station	*Continental/Seafood*	20
Vazzy's	*Italian*	20

TARIFFVILLE

🛚 Mill/2T	*Amer.*	28

TORRINGTON

Venetian	*Italian*	18

TRUMBULL

Marisa's	*Italian*	18

UNCASVILLE

Bar Americain	*American*	26
🛚 Frank Pepe	*Pizza*	24
Jasper White's	*New Eng./Seafood*	21
Johnny Rockets	*Burgers*	16
Michael Jordan's	*Steak*	23
SolToro	*Mex.*	20
Todd English's	*Italian*	22

UNIONVILLE

Matthew's	*Amer.*	24

VERNON

Rein's NY Deli	*Deli*	22
Wood-n-Tap	*Pub*	17

WALLINGFORD

Archie Moore's	*Pub*	18
Michael's	*Italian*	24
Westbrook Lobster	*Seafood*	19

WASHINGTON

Community Table	*Amer.*	27
🛚 Mayflower Inn	*Amer.*	24
NEW Norimaki	*Japanese*	-

WASHINGTON DEPOT

G.W. Tavern	*Amer.*	20
Pantry	*Amer.*	24

WATERBURY

Bertucci's	*Italian*	16
Carmen Anthony Steak	*Steak*	22
Diorio	*Amer./Italian*	25
Drescher's	*German*	19
La Tavola	*Italian*	26

WESTBROOK

Bill's Seafood	*Seafood*	19
Boom	*Amer.*	22
🛚 Café Routier	*French*	27
Lenny/Joe's	*Seafood*	23
New Deal Steak	*Steak*	14
🛚 Rest./Water's Edge	*Amer.*	23

WEST CORNWALL

RSVP	*French*	28
Wandering Moose	*Amer.*	16

WEST HARTFORD

Arugula	*Med.*	23
🛚 Barcelona	*Spanish*	24
Besito	*Mex.*	22
Bombay Olive	*Amer./Indian*	19
🛚 Bricco	*Italian*	27
Butterfly Chinese	*Chinese*	19

Chengdu | Chinese	20
Così | Sandwiches	16
Cuvee | Amer.	16
East-West Grille | SE Asian	23
Elbow Room | Amer.	18
Gold Roc | Diner	14
Grant's | Amer.	25
Harry's Bishops | Pizza	24
Harry's Pizza | Pizza	26
Hot Basil | Thai	20
Luna Pizza | Pizza	21
Max Burger | Amer.	25
Max's Oyster | Seafood	26
Murasaki | Japanese	-
P.F. Chang's | Chinese	18
Plan B Burger | Burgers	22
Pond Hse. Café | Amer.	21
Rizzuto's | Italian	20
Shish Kebab | Afghan	25
Tapas/Ann | Med.	23
Taste/India | Indian	19

WEST HAVEN

Chuck's Steak | Steak	18

WESTPORT

Acqua | Med.	22
Angelina's Tratt. | Italian	17
Bertucci's | Italian	16
Blue Lemon | Amer.	24
NEW Boathse./Saugatuck | Amer.	25
Bobby Q's | BBQ	21
Bogey's Grille | Amer.	17
Bombay | Indian	22
Café Manolo | Med.	23
DaPietro's | French/Italian	27
Z Dressing Room | Amer.	24
Z Le Farm | Amer.	27
Little Kitchen | Asian	21
Mario's Pl. | Italian/Steak	19
Oscar's | Deli	18
Positano's | Italian	22
Red Barn | Amer.	16
River House | Amer.	17
Rizzuto's | Italian	20

Sakura | Japanese	21
Splash | Seafood	22
Tarantino's | Italian	25
Tavern/Main | New Eng.	19
Z Tengda | Asian	22
Thali | Indian	24
Tiger Bowl | Chinese	15
Via Sforza | Italian	22
Viva Zapata | Mex.	17
V Rest. | Calif.	18

WETHERSFIELD

Carmen Anthony Fish. | Seafood	22
Puket Café | Thai	26
Vito's | Italian	21

WILTON

Luca Rist. | Italian	26
Mediterranean Grill | Med.	18
Orem's Diner | Diner	15
Outback Steak | Steak	17
Z Schoolhouse | Amer.	27

WINDSOR

Nat Hayden's BBQ | BBQ	-
Vito's | Italian	21

WOODBURY

Carmen Anthony Fish. | Seafood	22
Z Carole Peck's | Amer.	26
Dottie's Diner | Diner	18
John's Café | Amer./Med.	23
Longwood | Amer.	18

Hudson Valley

AMENIA

Z Serevan | Med.	27

BREWSTER

Z Arch | Eclectic	27
Aversano's | Italian	21
Eveready Diner | Diner	20
Jaipore Indian | Indian	23
Kelly's Corner | Pub	17
Red Rooster | Burgers	18
Rraci | Italian	26

MILLERTON

Harney/Sons | *Tea*	21
Irving Farm | *Coffee/Sandwiches*	19
Manna Dew | *Eclectic*	22
No. 9 | *Amer.*	27
NEW Oakhurst Diner | *Diner*	16
Taro's | *Italian/Pizza*	19

PATTERSON

Abruzzi Tratt. | *Italian*	21

PAWLING

Corner Bakery | *Bakery*	23
McKinney/Doyle | *Amer.*	25
Towne Crier | *Amer.*	17

WINGDALE

Big W's | *BBQ*	26

Westchester County

ARMONK

Beehive | *Amer./Eclectic*	21
David Chen | *Chinese*	18
Gavi | *Italian*	19
Kira | *Japanese*	23
Made In Asia | *Asian*	21
Marc Charles | *Steak*	20
NEW Moderne Barn | *Amer.*	22
Opus 465 | *Amer.*	18
NEW Rest. North | *Amer.*	26
Route 22 | *Pub*	14

BEDFORD

Bedford Post/Barn | *Amer.*	23
Bedford Post/Farm | *Amer.*	25
Bistro 22 | *Amer./French*	24
Z La Crémaillère | *French*	27
Tratt. Lucia | *Italian*	18

BEDFORD HILLS

Nino's | *Italian*	21

BEDFORD VILLAGE

Meetinghouse | *Amer.*	20

CROTON FALLS

Croton Creek | *Steak*	20
Primavera | *Italian*	24

GOLDENS BRIDGE

Portofino Pizza | *Italian/Pizza*	22

HARRISON

Emilio Rist. | *Italian*	25
Gus's Franklin Pk. | *Seafood*	21
Hajime | *Japanese*	25
Halstead Ave. | *Amer.*	20
Rue/Crêpes | *French*	19
Tratt. Vivolo | *Italian*	25
Trinity Grill | *Amer.*	20

KATONAH

Blue Dolphin | *Italian*	23
Le Fontane | *Italian*	22
Peppino's | *Italian*	20
Z Tengda | *Asian*	22

LARCHMONT

Anna Maria's | *Italian*	21
Bellizzi | *Italian*	15
Chat | *Amer.*	18
Così | *Sandwiches*	16
Encore Bistro | *French*	23
España | *Spanish*	20
Fuji Mtn. | *Japanese*	15
Globe B&G | *Amer.*	17
Hunan Larchmont | *Chinese/Japanese*	17
Larchmont Tav. | *Amer.*	17
La Riserva | *Italian*	21
La Villetta | *Italian*	24
Lusardi's | *Italian*	24
Palmer's Crossing | *Amer.*	21
Pascal's | *French*	23
Plates | *Amer.*	25
Ray's Cafe | *Chinese*	19
Sardegna | *Italian*	19
Sherwood's | *Pub*	20
Tequila Sunrise | *Mex.*	17
Turquoise | *Med./Turkish*	21
Village Sq. Bagels | *Bakery*	18
Watercolor Cafe | *Amer.*	18

MAMARONECK

Bangkok Thai | *Thai*	20
Cafe Mozart | *Coffee*	17

Chef Antonio | *Italian*	20
Enzo's | *Italian*	20
NEW Frankie/Fanucci's | *Pizza*	21
Ginban Asian | *Asian*	23
Gusano Loco | *Mex.*	21
Haiku | *Asian*	22
Il Castello | *Italian*	24
La Herradura | *Mex.*	18
La Piccola Casa | *Italian*	21
NEW La Scarbitta | *Italian*	-
Le Provençal | *French*	23
Mickey/Molly Spill. | *Amer.*	15
Nautilus | *Diner*	16
NEW Piri-Q | *Portug.*	20
Rani Mahal | *Indian*	23
Red Plum | *Asian*	21
Roasted Peppers | *Amer.*	21
Sal's Pizza | *Pizza*	23
3 Jalapeños | *Tex-Mex*	17
Toyo Sushi | *Japanese*	21
Turkish Meze | *Turkish*	23
Walter's | *Hot Dogs*	22
Zitoune | *Moroccan*	19

NEW ROCHELLE

AJ's Burgers | *Amer.*	20
NEW Alvin/Friends | *Carib./Southern*	26
NEW Cienega | *Nuevo Latino*	-
Z Coromandel | *Indian*	25
Così | *Sandwiches*	16
Coyote Flaco | *Mex.*	23
Da Giorgio | *Italian*	25
Don Coqui | *Puerto Rican*	23
El Tio | *Mex.*	18
Fratelli | *Italian*	19
Gnarly Vine | *Amer.*	17
Golden Rod | *Asian*	18
Karuta | *Japanese*	18
La Herradura | *Mex.*	18
Little Mex. Cafe | *Mex.*	21
Maestro's | *Italian*	20
Mamma Francesca | *Italian*	19
Modern Rest. | *Italian*	22
Mo's NY | *Amer.*	18

Posto 22 | *Italian*	21
NEW Post Rd. Ale | *Amer.*	-
Red Lotus | *Thai*	21
Spadaro | *Italian*	26

NORTH SALEM

John-Michael's | *Euro.*	24
121 Rest./Bar | *Amer.*	22
Vox | *Amer./French*	21

PORT CHESTER

Alba's | *Italian*	23
NEW Arrosto | *Italian*	23
NEW Bartaco | *Mex.*	-
Cafe Mirage | *Eclectic*	22
Copacabana | *Brazilian*	21
Coyote Flaco | *Mex.*	23
Edo | *Japanese/Steak*	20
El Tio | *Mex.*	18
Euro Asian | *Asian*	17
Il Sogno | *Italian/Med.*	24
Marianacci's | *Italian*	21
Mary Ann's | *Tex-Mex*	15
Nessa | *Italian*	21
Patrias | *Peruvian/Spanish*	21
Piero's | *Italian*	24
Q Rest. | *BBQ*	22
Sonora | *Nuevo Latino*	24
T&J Villaggio | *Italian*	21
Tandoori Taste | *Indian*	21
Tarry Lodge | *Italian*	24
Willett House | *Steak*	24

POUND RIDGE

DiNardo's | *Italian*	19
North Star | *Amer.*	20

PURCHASE

Cobble Stone | *Amer.*	15

PURDYS

Blazer Pub | *Pub*	22

RYE

Aurora | *Italian*	21
Cafe Livorno | *Italian*	19
Così | *Sandwiches*	16

Vote at ZAGAT.com

Frankie/Johnnie's | *Steak* 24

Koo | *Japanese* 23

Z La Panetière | *French* 27

Morgans Fish | *Seafood* 21

NEW On the Way Café | *Euro.* -

Ruby's Oyster | *Seafood* 23

Rye Grill | *Eclectic* 18

Rye Roadhse. | *Cajun/Creole* 18

Seaside Johnnie's | *Seafood* 12

Town Dock | *Amer.* 19

Watermoon | *Asian* 23

RYE BROOK

Ray's Cafe | *Chinese* 19

SOUTH SALEM

Horse/Hound | *Amer.* 19

Le Château | *French* 25

Nino's | *Italian* 20

WHITE PLAINS/ N. WHITE PLAINS

Abatino's | *Italian* 20

Aberdeen | *Chinese* 23

NEW Anthony's Pizza | *Pizza* 22

Asian Tempt. | *Asian* 20

Bao's | *Chinese* 20

NEW Bellota/42 | *Spanish* -

NEW Benjamin Steak | *Steak* 24

BLT Steak | *Steak* 23

Blue | *Amer.* 20

Brazen Fox | *Pub* 17

Brooklyn's Famous | *Diner* 17

Buon Amici | *Italian* 22

Cheesecake Fac. | *Amer.* 17

City Limits | *Diner* 19

NEW Eclisse Med. | *Med.* 21

80 West | *Seafood* 19

Emma's Ale House | *Pub* 18

42 | *Amer.* 22

Full Moon | *Thai* 24

Gervasi's | *Italian* 20

Graziellas | *Italian* 19

Haiku | *Asian* 22

NEW Hudson Grille | *Amer.* 20

Imperial Wok | *Chinese/Japanese* 17

Kalbi Hse. | *Korean* 19

Karamba | *Cuban/Pan-Latin* 22

Kisco Kosher | *Deli* 17

La Bocca | *Italian* 23

La Manda's | *Italian* 19

Lazy Boy Saloon | *Pub* 19

Legal Sea Foods | *Seafood* 19

Melting Pot | *Fondue* 17

Milonga | *Argent./Italian* 22

Morton's | *Steak* 24

Mulino's | *Italian* 24

Niko's Greek | *Greek* 20

Noda's Steak | *Japanese* 19

Outback Steak | *Steak* 17

P.F. Chang's | *Chinese* 18

Porter Hse. | *Amer./Pub* 19

Reka's | *Thai* 19

Ron Blacks | *Pub* 16

Royal Palace | *Indian* 20

Sam's/Gedney | *Amer.* 19

Seasons Japanese | *Japanese* 23

Z Sushi Nanase | *Japanese* 29

Tango Grill | *Argent./Italian* 21

3 Boys/Italy | *Pizza* 23

Tre Angelina | *Italian* 21

Turkish Cuisine | *Turkish* 21

NEW Westchester Burger | *Amer.* 20

Special Features

Listings cover the best in each category and include names, locations and Food ratings. Multi-location restaurants' features may vary by branch.

BREAKFAST

(See also Hotel Dining)

American Pie	**Sherman**	22
Aux Délices	**multi.**	24
Cafe Mozart	**Mamaro**	17
City Limits	**White Pl**	19
Claire's Corner	**New Haven**	21
Corner Bakery	**Pawling**	23
Così	**multi.**	16
Irving Farm	**Millerton**	19
Karamba	**White Pl**	22
Meli-Melo	**Greenwich**	25
NEW Oakhurst Diner	**Millerton**	16
Orem's Diner	**Wilton**	15
Pantry	**Wash Depot**	24
Pat's Kountry	**Old Saybrook**	16
Rein's NY Deli	**Vernon**	22
Ruby's Oyster	**Rye**	23
SoNo Baking Co.	**S Norwalk**	26
☑ Valencia Lunch.	**Norwalk**	27
Vanilla Bean	**Pomfret**	22
Versailles	**Greenwich**	24

BRUNCH

☑ Arch	**Brewster**	27
Bedford Post/Barn	**Bedford**	23
Beehive	**Armonk**	21
☑ Bernard's	**Ridgefield**	27
Brewhouse	**S Norwalk**	19
City Limits	**White Pl**	19
Dakota Steak	**Avon**	17
Gates	**New Canaan**	19
Griswold Inn	**Essex**	18
Jaipore Indian	**Brewster**	23
La Zingara	**Bethel**	26
Le Provençal	**Mamaro**	23
McKinney/Doyle	**Pawling**	25
Paradise B&G	**Stamford**	13
Red Barn	**Westport**	16
☑ Rest./Water's Edge	**Westbrook**	23
Roger Sherman	**New Canaan**	24

Ruby's Oyster	**Rye**	23
Sage	**New Haven**	19
Splash	**Westport**	22
Tavern/Main	**Westport**	19
Terra Mar	**Old Saybrook**	23
Thataway Cafe	**Greenwich**	17
Watercolor Cafe	**Larch**	18

BUFFET

(Check availability)

Abis	**Greenwich**	19
Bangalore	**Fairfield**	23
Bombay	**Westport**	22
Bombay Olive	**W Hartford**	19
Brewhouse	**S Norwalk**	19
Confetti	**Plainville**	22
☑ Coromandel	**multi.**	25
Cuckoo's Nest	**Old Saybrook**	17
Dakota Steak	**multi.**	17
80 West	**White Pl**	19
Flanders Fish	**E Lyme**	21
Griswold Inn	**Essex**	18
Jaipore Indian	**Brewster**	23
Old Heidelberg	**Bethel**	21
Rani Mahal	**Mamaro**	23
Red Barn	**Westport**	16
☑ Rest./Water's Edge	**Westbrook**	23
Royal Palace	**White Pl**	20
Saltwater Grille	**Stamford**	17
Spadaro	**New Roch**	26
Splash	**Westport**	22
Squire's	**Redding**	16
Tandoori Taste	**Port Chester**	21
Taste/India	**W Hartford**	19
Thali	**multi.**	24
Todd English's	**Uncasville**	22
Vito's	**Wethersfield**	21

BUSINESS DINING

Acqua	**Westport**	22
Adriana's	**New Haven**	22

Vote at ZAGAT.com

CT/NEARBY NY

SPECIAL FEATURES

Waters Edge at Giovanni's | **Darien**	19
Willett House | **Port Chester**	24
Wood-n-Tap | **Hartford**	17

BYO

Abis | **Greenwich**	19	Thai/Buddha/Spice | **multi.**	23
Atticus | **New Haven**	18	Market | **Stamford**	20
Bacchus | **S Norwalk**	–	Meli-Melo | **Greenwich**	25
Bamboo Grill | **Canton**	–	Miya's Sushi | **New Haven**	25
☑ Basso Café | **Norwalk**	28	Morgans Fish | **Rye**	21
Beach Hse. Café | **Old Greenwich**	18	☑ Napa & Co. | **Stamford**	24
Big W's | **Wingdale**	26	Nat Hayden's BBQ | **Windsor**	–
Bin 100 | **Milford**	26	Nino's | **Bedford Hills**	21
Bond Grill | **Norwalk**	21	Olé Molé | **Stamford**	19
☑ Brasitas | **Stamford**	25	121 Rest./OXC | **Oxford**	21
Buon Appetito | **Canton**	26	Opus 465 | **Armonk**	18
Burgers/Shakes | **Greenwich**	22	Osianna | **Fairfield**	25
☑ Capital Grille | **Stamford**	25	Pascal's | **Larch**	23
Chef Luis | **New Canaan**	25	Pasta Nostra | **S Norwalk**	25
Community Table | **Washington**	27	Patrias | **Port Chester**	21
Copacabana | **Port Chester**	21	Penang Grill | **Greenwich**	22
☑ Coromandel | **multi.**	25	Penny Lane Pub | **Old Saybrook**	19
David Chen | **Armonk**	18	Peppino's | **Katonah**	20
Elbow Room | **W Hartford**	18	Piero's | **Port Chester**	24
Elizabeth's Cafe | **Madison**	25	☑ PolytechnicON20 | **Hartford**	28
☑ Elm St. Oyster | **Greenwich**	24	Pond Hse. Café | **W Hartford**	21
Emilio Rist. | **Harrison**	25	Puket Café | **Rocky Hill**	26
Encore Bistro | **Larch**	23	Q Rest. | **Port Chester**	22
Épernay | **Bridgeport**	22	Red Plum | **Mamaro**	21
España | **Larch**	20	RSVP | **W Cornwall**	28
55° | **Fairfield**	23	Rue/Crêpes | **Harrison**	19
Firebox | **Hartford**	24	Sal/Pepe | **Newtown**	24
Flaggstead | **Farmington**	–	Scoozzi Tratt. | **New Haven**	22
NEW Green Gourmet | **Bridgeport**	–	Scribner's | **Milford**	22
Hot Basil | **W Hartford**	20	Solé Rist. | **New Canaan**	21
John-Michael's | **N Salem**	24	Splash | **Westport**	22
Kira | **Armonk**	23	Stone House | **Guilford**	18
Kobis | **Shelton**	22	Strada 18 | **S Norwalk**	26
Le Château | **S Salem**	25	Telluride | **Stamford**	21
☑ Le Farm | **Westport**	27	☑ Ten Twenty Post | **Darien**	21
Lenny/Joe's | **Madison**	23	Tiberio's | **Old Saybrook**	–
Litchfield/Grille | **Litchfield**	20	Toscana | **Ridgefield**	22
		Tre Scalini | **New Haven**	24
		Turkish Cuisine | **White Pl**	21
		Turkish Meze | **Mamaro**	23
		Two Boots | **Bridgeport**	20
		☑ Union League | **New Haven**	27
		☑ Valencia Lunch. | **Norwalk**	27
		Viale Rist. | **Bridgeport**	24

Via Sforza | **Westport**	22
Village | **Litchfield**	20
Vox | **N Salem**	21
Water St. Cafe | **Stonington**	26
West St. Grill | **Litchfield**	24
Willett House | **Port Chester**	24
Winvian | **Morris**	27
Woodland | **Lakeville**	22
☑ Woodward Hse. | **Bethlehem**	27
Zinc | **New Haven**	24

CATERING

Acqua | **Westport**	22
Aux Délices | **multi.**	24
☑ Bernard's | **Ridgefield**	27
Blue | **White Pl**	20
Cafe Mirage | **Port Chester**	22
☑ Carole Peck's | **Woodbury**	26
Christopher Martins | **New Haven**	20
Claire's Corner | **New Haven**	21
☑ Coromandel | **New Roch**	25
Elizabeth's Cafe | **Madison**	25
Firehouse Deli | **Fairfield**	21
Golden Rod | **New Roch**	18
It's Only Natural | **Middletown**	20
Jeff's Cuisine | **S Norwalk**	25
Kira | **Armonk**	23
Koo | **Rye**	23
Match | **S Norwalk**	26
Max Amore | **Glastonbury**	23
☑ Max Downtown | **Hartford**	27
McKinney/Doyle | **Pawling**	25
Olé Molé | **Stamford**	19
Omanel | **Bridgeport**	19
Opus 465 | **Armonk**	18
Pantry | **Wash Depot**	24
Plates | **Larch**	25
Q Rest. | **Port Chester**	22
Quattro Pazzi | **Fairfield**	23
Sonora | **Port Chester**	24
Tango Grill | **White Pl**	21
Telluride | **Stamford**	21
Thali | **multi.**	24
Tratt. Carl Anthony | **Monroe**	24

☑ Valencia Lunch. | **Norwalk**	27
Vanilla Bean | **Pomfret**	22
Vazzy's | **multi.**	20
Willett House | **Port Chester**	24

CHILD-FRIENDLY

(Alternatives to the usual fast-food places; * children's menu available)

Abatino's* | **N White Plains**	20
Abbott's Lobster* | **Noank**	23
Abis* | **Greenwich**	19
American Pie* | **Sherman**	22
Archie Moore's* | **multi.**	18
Arugula | **W Hartford**	23
Ash Creek* | **Norwalk**	17
Asiana Cafe | **Greenwich**	21
Avellino's | **Fairfield**	20
Bailey's* | **Ridgefield**	21
Beach House | **Milford**	22
Beehive* | **Armonk**	21
Bellizzi* | **Larch**	15
Bertucci's* | **multi.**	16
Bill's Seafood* | **Westbrook**	19
Blazer Pub | **Purdys**	22
Blue Dolphin | **Katonah**	23
Boxcar Cantina | **Greenwich**	21
Brewhouse* | **S Norwalk**	19
Brooklyn's Famous* | **White Pl**	17
Carmen Anthony Fish.* | **multi.**	22
Carmen Anthony Steak* | **Waterbury**	22
Centro* | **multi.**	20
Chat | **Larch**	18
Cheesecake Fac.* | **White Pl**	17
Chuck's Steak* | **multi.**	18
City Limits* | **multi.**	19
Claire's Corner | **New Haven**	21
Corner Bakery | **Pawling**	23
Cosi* | **multi.**	16
Coyote Flaco* | **multi.**	23
Dakota Steak* | **Avon**	17
David Chen | **Armonk**	18
DiNardo's* | **Pound Ridge**	19
Dolphins Cove* | **Bridgeport**	–
East-West Grille | **W Hartford**	23

Fifty Coins*	multi.	16	Tequila Mock.*	New Canaan	18
Firehouse Deli*	Fairfield	21	Thali*	multi.	24
☑ Frank Pepe	New Haven	24	Tiger Bowl	Westport	15
Fuji Mtn.*	Larch	15	Town Dock*	Rye	19
Gates*	New Canaan	19	Turkish Meze*	Mamaro	23
Golden Rod	New Roch	18	Tuscan Oven	Norwalk	20
Gus's Franklin Pk.*	Harrison	21	☑ Valencia Lunch.	Norwalk	27
Harry's Pizza	W Hartford	26	Vazzy's*	multi.	20
Hot Tomato's	Hartford	20	Vinny's*	Stamford	20
Hunan Larchmont	Larch	17	Viva Zapata*	Westport	17

Fifty Coins* | multi. — 16
Firehouse Deli* | Fairfield — 21
☑ Frank Pepe | New Haven — 24
Fuji Mtn.* | Larch — 15
Gates* | New Canaan — 19
Golden Rod | New Roch — 18
Gus's Franklin Pk.* | Harrison — 21
Harry's Pizza | W Hartford — 26
Hot Tomato's | Hartford — 20
Hunan Larchmont | Larch — 17
It's Only Natural* | Middletown — 20
Jeff's Cuisine | S Norwalk — 25
Kazu | S Norwalk — 25
Kit's Thai | Stamford — 21
Kobis* | Fairfield — 22
Legal Sea Foods* | White Pl — 19
Lime* | Norwalk — 23
Little Kitchen | Westport — 21
Luna Pizza | multi. — 21
Mancuso's | Fairfield — 21
Mary Ann's* | Port Chester — 15
Meetinghouse* | Bedford Vill — 20
Melting Pot | Darien — 17
Modern Rest.* | New Roch — 22
Mystic Pizza* | multi. — 15
Nino's | S Salem — 20
Olé Molé | Stamford — 19
Omanel | Bridgeport — 19
Orem's Diner* | Wilton — 15
Pantry | Wash Depot — 24
P.F. Chang's | White Pl — 18
Portofino Pizza | Goldens Br — 22
Q Rest.* | Port Chester — 22
Ray's Cafe | multi. — 19
Red Barn* | Westport — 16
Route 22* | Armonk — 14
Rye Grill* | Rye — 18
Sally's Apizza | New Haven — 25
Saybrook Fish* | Rocky Hill — 22
Sesame Seed | Danbury — 21
SoNo Baking Co. | S Norwalk — 26
Sono Seaport* | S Norwalk — 15
Southport Brew.* | multi. — 16
Tavern/Main* | Westport — 19

Tequila Mock.* | New Canaan — 18
Thali* | multi. — 24
Tiger Bowl | Westport — 15
Town Dock* | Rye — 19
Turkish Meze* | Mamaro — 23
Tuscan Oven | Norwalk — 20
☑ Valencia Lunch. | Norwalk — 27
Vazzy's* | multi. — 20
Vinny's* | Stamford — 20
Viva Zapata* | Westport — 17

DANCING

Back Porch | Old Saybrook — 18
Chat | Larch — 18
Cuvee | W Hartford — 16
Don Coqui | New Roch — 23
NEW Fez | Stamford — 20
Geronimo | New Haven — 20
Gervasi's | White Pl — 20
Globe B&G | Larch — 17
Hawthorne Inn | Berlin — 20
Molto Wine | Fairfield — 21
☑ Rest./Water's Edge | Westbrook — 23
Saltwater Grille | Stamford — 17
Squire's | Redding — 16
Two Boots | Bridgeport — 20
U.S.S. Chowder | Branford — 19

DELIVERY

Abatino's | N White Plains — 20
Angelina's Tratt. | Westport — 17
Aux Délices | multi. — 24
Bamboo Grill | Canton — -
Bertucci's | multi. — 16
Black-Eyed Sally | Hartford — 20
Boathouse/Smokey | Stamford — 19
Bobby Valentine | Stamford — 15
Bogey's Grille | Westport — 17
Bombay | Westport — 22
Brooklyn's Famous | White Pl — 17
Coyote Flaco | multi. — 23
Golden Rod | New Roch — 18
Imperial Wok | N White Plains — 17
Kit's Thai | Stamford — 21

Kotobuki | **Stamford**	24
Kujaku | **Stamford**	18
Luna Pizza | **Simsbury**	21
Modern Rest. | **New Roch**	22
Noda's Steak | **White Pl**	19
Pellicci's | **Stamford**	19
Polpo | **Greenwich**	24
Post Corner Pizza | **Darien**	20
Royal Palace | **New Haven**	25
Royal Palace | **White Pl**	20

DINING ALONE

(Other than hotels and places with counter service)

AJ's Burgers | **New Roch**	20
Aladdin | **Hartford**	-
American Pie | **Sherman**	22
NEW Anthony's Pizza | **White Pl**	22
Aux Délices | **multi.**	24
Ay! Salsa | **New Haven**	-
Bacchus | **S Norwalk**	-
Bamboo Grill | **Canton**	-
Bangalore | **Fairfield**	23
Bangkok Gdns. | **New Haven**	19
Basta | **New Haven**	25
Big W's | **Wingdale**	26
Bloodroot | **Bridgeport**	23
Boathouse/Smokey | **Stamford**	19
Bull's Bridge | **Kent**	16
Burger Bar | **S Norwalk**	22
Butterfly Chinese | **W Hartford**	19
Cafe Mirage | **Port Chester**	22
Café/Green | **Danbury**	22
Chaiwalla | **Salisbury**	25
Char Koon | **S Glastonbury**	23
Chat | **Larch**	18
City Limits | **White Pl**	19
Claire's Corner | **New Haven**	21
Clamp's | **New Milford**	-
Corner Bakery | **Pawling**	23
Country Bistro | **Salisbury**	-
Coyote Flaco | **multi.**	23
David Chen | **Armonk**	18
Denmo's | **Southbury**	-
Dottie's Diner | **Woodbury**	18

Drescher's | **Waterbury**	19
East-West Grille | **W Hartford**	23
El Tio | **Port Chester**	18
Épernay | **Bridgeport**	22
Eveready Diner | **Brewster**	20
Fat Cat Pie | **Norwalk**	23
Fife 'n Drum | **Kent**	18
Fifty Coins | **multi.**	16
Fin/Fin II | **multi.**	23
Flaggstead | **Farmington**	-
Z Frank Pepe | **Manchester**	24
Friends & Co. | **Madison**	18
Great Taste | **New Britain**	20
NEW Greenwood's Grille | **Bethel**	16
Irving Farm | **Millerton**	19
Z Isabelle/Vincent | **Fairfield**	27
It's Only Natural | **Middletown**	20
Jeff's Cuisine | **S Norwalk**	25
Johnny Ad's | **Old Saybrook**	21
Karamba | **White Pl**	22
Kelly's Corner | **Brewster**	17
Kit's Thai | **Stamford**	21
Koo | **Danbury**	23
Larchmont Tav. | **Larch**	17
Layla's Falafel | **multi.**	22
Lenny/Joe's | **multi.**	23
Lenny's Indian | **Branford**	21
Leon's | **New Haven**	18
Lime | **Norwalk**	23
Little Kitchen | **Westport**	21
Little Pub | **Ridgefield**	23
Thai/Buddha/Spice | **multi.**	23
Louis' Lunch | **New Haven**	22
Mackenzie's | **Old Greenwich**	16
Max Burger | **W Hartford**	25
Meli-Melo | **Greenwich**	25
Michael's | **Wallingford**	24
Mystic Pizza | **multi.**	15
Nat Hayden's BBQ | **Windsor**	-
Nino's | **Bedford Hills**	21
Noah's | **Stonington**	24
NEW Oakhurst Diner | **Millerton**	16
Olé Molé | **multi.**	19

NEW On the Way Café | **Rye**	–
Oscar's | **Westport**	18
Pantry | **Wash Depot**	24
Pasta Vera | **Greenwich**	20
Pat's Kountry | **Old Saybrook**	16
Post Corner Pizza | **Darien**	20
Pot-au-Pho | **Nèw Haven**	17
Red Rooster | **Brewster**	18
Rein's NY Deli | **Vernon**	22
River House | **Westport**	17
Salsa | **New Milford**	25
Sardegna | **Larch**	19
Scribner's | **Milford**	22
SoNo Baking Co. | **S Norwalk**	26
Super/Weenie | **Fairfield**	23
Sycamore Drive-In | **Bethel**	17
Z Tengda | **Westport**	22
3 Boys/Italy | **White Pl**	23
Two Boots | **Bridgeport**	20
Z Valencia Lunch. | **Norwalk**	27
Venetian | **Torrington**	18
Viale Rist. | **Bridgeport**	24
Village | **Litchfield**	20
Village Sq. Bagels | **Larch**	18
Wasabi | **Orange**	25
Wilson's BBQ | **Fairfield**	20
Yorkside | **New Haven**	15
Zinc | **New Haven**	24

ENTERTAINMENT

(Call for days and times of performances)

Z Bernard's | varies | **Ridgefield**	27
Bill's Seafood | live music | **Westbrook**	19
Bobby Valentine | karaoke | **Stamford**	15
Luc's Café | jazz | **Ridgefield**	24
O'Neill's | varies | **S Norwalk**	19
Opus 465 | bands/karaoke | **Armonk**	18
Pizzeria Lauretano | jazz | **Bethel**	22
Ralph/Rich's | piano | **Bridgeport**	23
Southport Brew. | varies | **multi.**	16
Squire's | live music | **Redding**	16

Thataway Cafe | varies | **Greenwich**	17
Towne Crier | live music | **Pawling**	17
Vanilla Bean | live music | **Pomfret**	22
Watercolor Cafe | live music | **Larch**	18

FIREPLACES

Adrienne | **New Milford**	25
Alba's | **Port Chester**	23
Altnaveigh Inn | **Storrs**	23
Z Arch | **Brewster**	27
Back Porch | **Old Saybrook**	18
Ballou's | **Guilford**	18
NEW Bank St. Tavern | **New Milford**	18
Z Barcelona | **New Haven**	24
Beach House | **Milford**	22
Bedford Post/Barn | **Bedford**	23
Bedford Post/Farm | **Bedford**	25
NEW Benjamin Steak | **White Pl**	24
Z Bernard's | **Ridgefield**	27
Boathouse | **Lakeville**	17
Boom | **Westbrook**	22
Boulders Inn | **New Preston**	21
Boxcar Cantina | **Greenwich**	21
Bull's Bridge | **Kent**	16
Capt. Daniel Packer | **Mystic**	21
Carmen Anthony Fish. | **Woodbury**	22
Chaiwalla | **Salisbury**	25
Chestnut Grille | **Old Lyme**	26
Chuck's Steak | **multi.**	18
Cinzano's | **Fairfield**	18
Coyote Flaco | **New Roch**	23
Dakota Steak | **multi.**	17
Doc's Tratt. | **Kent**	19
Dolly Madison Inn | **Madison**	13
Z Dressing Room | **Westport**	24
Fife 'n Drum | **Kent**	18
Firebox | **Hartford**	24
Flood Tide | **Mystic**	21
Foe | **Branford**	19

Fonda La Paloma | **Cos Cob**	19
Frankie/Johnnie's | **Rye**	24
Friends & Co. | **Madison**	18
NEW Gabriele's | **Greenwich**	–
Geronimo | **New Haven**	20
Gervasi's | **White Pl**	20
Ginger Man | **Greenwich**	18
NEW Goose | **Darien**	–
Griswold Inn | **Essex**	18
G.W. Tavern | **Wash Depot**	20
Hopkins Inn | **New Preston**	19
Horse/Hound | **S Salem**	19
Il Palio | **Shelton**	24
Inn/Newtown | **Newtown**	18
Irving Farm | **Millerton**	19
☑ Isabelle/Vincent | **Fairfield**	27
J. Gilbert's | **Glastonbury**	25
John-Michael's | **N Salem**	24
☑ La Crémaillère | **Bedford**	27
Le Château | **S Salem**	25
Lenny's Indian | **Branford**	21
L'Escale | **Greenwich**	23
Litchfield/Grille | **Litchfield**	20
Little Pub | **Ridgefield**	23
Long Ridge Tav. | **Stamford**	14
Longwood | **Woodbury**	18
Lusardi's | **Larch**	24
☑ Mayflower Inn | **Washington**	24
Mill/River | **S Windsor**	20
New Deal Steak | **Westbrook**	14
Old Lyme Inn | **Old Lyme**	22
Oliva Cafe | **New Preston**	24
Oliver's Taverne | **Essex**	16
Olive Tree | **Southbury**	21
Ondine | **Danbury**	26
O'Neill's | **S Norwalk**	19
121 Rest./Bar | **N Salem**	22
Paradise B&G | **Stamford**	13
Pat's Kountry | **Old Saybrook**	16
Porter Hse. | **White Pl**	19
Red Barn | **Westport**	16
Rest./Rowayton Sea. | **Rowayton**	22
River House | **Westport**	17
Roger Sherman | **New Canaan**	24

Rye Grill | **Rye**	18
Sage | **New Haven**	19
NEW Sails | **Norwalk**	–
Sakura | **Westport**	21
Saltwater Grille | **Stamford**	17
☑ Serevan | **Amenia**	27
Sharpe Hill/Vineyard | **Pomfret**	–
Splash | **Westport**	22
Squire's | **Redding**	16
Stone House | **Guilford**	18
Tango Grill | **White Pl**	21
Tavern/Main | **Westport**	19
☑ Thomas Henkelmann | **Greenwich**	28
3 Jalapeños | **Mamaro**	17
Town Dock | **Rye**	19
Tratt. Lucia | **Bedford**	18
Tuscan Oven | **Norwalk**	20
☑ Union League | **New Haven**	27
☑ Valbella | **Riverside**	25
Vanilla Bean | **Pomfret**	22
Via Sforza | **Westport**	22
Vito's | **Hartford**	21
Wandering Moose | **W Cornwall**	16
White Horse | **New Preston**	19
Winvian | **Morris**	27
Wood-n-Tap | **multi.**	17

GAME IN SEASON

Adrienne | **New Milford**	25
☑ Bernard's | **Ridgefield**	27
NEW Boathse./Saugatuck | **Westport**	25
☑ Carole Peck's | **Woodbury**	26
DaPietro's | **Westport**	27
☑ Harvest Supper | **New Canaan**	27
☑ Jean-Louis | **Greenwich**	28
☑ Le Farm | **Westport**	27
☑ Napa & Co. | **Stamford**	24
Omanel | **Bridgeport**	19
Ondine | **Danbury**	26
Pastorale | **Lakeville**	23
☑ PolytechnicON20 | **Hartford**	28
Rebeccas | **Greenwich**	26
Rest. L&E | **Chester**	24

Still River | **Eastford**	28
Tarantino's | **Westport**	25
☑ Thomas Henkelmann | **Greenwich**	28
Versailles | **Greenwich**	24
Winvian | **Morris**	27
☑ Woodward Hse. | **Bethlehem**	27

GREEN/LOCAL/ ORGANIC

Aspen | **Old Saybrook**	20
Basta | **New Haven**	25
Bedford Post/Barn | **Bedford**	23
Bedford Post/Farm | **Bedford**	25
NEW Boathse./Saugatuck | **Westport**	25
Boxcar Cantina | **Greenwich**	21
Café Manolo | **Westport**	23
☑ Carole Peck's | **Woodbury**	26
☑ Dressing Room | **Westport**	24
Fat Cat Pie | **Norwalk**	23
Firebox | **Hartford**	24
☑ Harvest Supper | **New Canaan**	27
☑ Le Farm | **Westport**	27
Manna Dew | **Millerton**	22
Métro Bis | **Simsbury**	25
☑ Napa & Co. | **Stamford**	24
Pasta Nostra | **S Norwalk**	25
Rest. L&E | **Chester**	24
Still River | **Eastford**	28
NEW Tappo | **Stamford**	-
☑ Thomas Henkelmann | **Greenwich**	28
West St. Grill | **Litchfield**	24
Winvian | **Morris**	27
Zinc | **New Haven**	24

HISTORIC PLACES

(Year opened; * building)

1600 | Westbrook Lobster* | **Wallingford**	19
1640 | Grist Mill* | **Farmington**	23
1734 | Altnaveigh Inn* | **Storrs**	23
1740 | Woodward Hse.* | **Bethlehem**	27
1749 | Horse/Hound* | **S Salem**	19
1750 | La Crémaillère* | **Bedford**	27
1750 | Long Ridge Tav.* | **Stamford**	14
1756 | Capt. Daniel Packer* | **Mystic**	21
1756 | Chestnut Grille* | **Old Lyme**	26
1758 | Harvest/Pomfret* | **Pomfret**	21
1760 | Pastorale* | **Lakeville**	23
1762 | Bull's Bridge* | **Kent**	16
1773 | Chatterley's* | **New Hartford**	21
1774 | Adrienne* | **New Milford**	25
1775 | John-Michael's* | **N Salem**	24
1775 | Mill/River* | **S Windsor**	20
1775 | Winvian* | **Morris**	27
1776 | Griswold Inn* | **Essex**	18
1783 | Roger Sherman* | **New Canaan**	24
1789 | Longwood* | **Woodbury**	18
1790 | Bedford Post/Barn* | **Bedford**	23
1790 | Bedford Post/Farm* | **Bedford**	25
1792 | La Piccola Casa* | **Mamaro**	21
1793 | Elizabeth's Cafe* | **Madison**	25
1799 | Thomas Henkelmann* | **Greenwich**	28
1800 | Gabrielle's* | **Centerbrook**	25
1800 | Plan B Burger* | **Simsbury**	22
1810 | Tavern/Main* | **Westport**	19
1830 | Wandering Moose* | **W Cornwall**	16
1840 | Old Lyme Inn* | **Old Lyme**	22
1848 | Olive Tree* | **Southbury**	21
1850 | G.W. Tavern* | **Wash Depot**	20
1850 | La Panetière* | **Rye**	27
1850 | L'Orcio* | **New Haven**	23
1850 | Vanilla Bean* | **Pomfret**	22
1852 | Putnam Hse.* | **Bethel**	19
1868 | Drescher's | **Waterbury**	19

1870 | Paci* | **Southport** 26

1871 | Emilio Rist.* | **Harrison** 25

1872 | Schoolhouse* | **Wilton** 27

1880 | Donovan's* | **S Norwalk** 18

1880 | Mayflower Inn* | 24
Washington

1881 | Q Rest.* | **Port Chester** 22

1882 | Harney/Sons* | **Millerton** 21

1890 | Boulders Inn* | 21
New Preston

1890 | Brasserie Pip* | **Ivoryton** –

1890 | Flood Tide* | **Mystic** 21

1890 | Lime* | **Norwalk** 23

1890 | Red Barn* | **Westport** 16

1890 | Village* | **Litchfield** 20

1890 | Vito's* | **Hartford** 21

1890 | Water St. Cafe* | 26
Stonington

1893 | Feng Asian* | **Hartford** 22

1895 | Louis' Lunch | **New Haven** 22

1898 | Archie Moore's* | 18
New Haven

1899 | Basso Café* | **Norwalk** 28

1900 | Koo* | **Rye** 23

1900 | Piero's* | **Port Chester** 24

1900 | Polpo* | **Greenwich** 24

1900 | Rest./Rowayton Sea.* | 22
Rowayton

1900 | Rye Roadhse.* | **Rye** 18

1900 | Union League* | 27
New Haven

1900 | West St. Grill* | **Litchfield** 24

1902 | Plates* | **Larch** 25

1903 | Willett House* | 24
Port Chester

1905 | Old Heidelberg* | **Bethel** 21

1907 | Le Château* | **S Salem** 25

1915 | Arch* | **Brewster** 27

1915 | Épernay* | **Bridgeport** 22

1917 | Cobble Stone* | **Purchase** 15

1919 | Walter's | **Mamaro** 22

1920 | Brewhouse* | **S Norwalk** 19

1920 | Modern Rest.* | **New Roch** 22

1921 | Orem's Diner | **Wilton** 15

1921 | Venetian | **Torrington** 18

1925 | Frank Pepe | **New Haven** 24

1925 | Frank Pepe* | **New Haven** 24

1927 | Reka's* | **White Pl** 19

1930 | Liv's Oyster* | 25
Old Saybrook

1930 | Route 22* | **Armonk** 14

1931 | Dolly Madison Inn | 13
Madison

1931 | Gus's Franklin Pk. | 21
Harrison

1932 | Sam's/Gedney | 19
White Pl

1933 | Cavey's | **Manchester** 26

1933 | Larchmont Tav. | **Larch** 17

1934 | Blazer Pub | **Purdys** 22

1934 | Modern Apizza | 25
New Haven

1935 | Colony Grill | **Stamford** 24

1935 | East Side | **New Britain** 17

1935 | Post Rd. Ale* | **New Roch** –

1936 | First/Last | **Hartford** 19

1938 | Carbone's | **Hartford** 24

1938 | Consiglio's | **New Haven** 23

1938 | Leon's | **New Haven** 18

1938 | Sally's Apizza | **New Haven** 25

1939 | Clamp's | **New Milford** –

1940 | Blue Dolphin | **Katonah** 23

1940 | Stonehenge | **Ridgefield** 22

1940 | When Pigs Fly* | **Sharon** 21

1945 | Hawthorne Inn | **Berlin** 20

1946 | Hopkins Inn | **New Preston** 19

1947 | La Manda's | **White Pl** 19

1947 | Pellicci's | **Stamford** 19

1948 | Abbott's Lobster | **Noank** 23

1948 | Oscar's | **Westport** 18

1948 | Shady Glen | **Manchester** 21

1948 | Sycamore Drive-In | 17
Bethel

1949 | Stone House* | **Guilford** 18

1950 | Marianacci's | **Port Chester** 21

1955 | Made In Asia* | **Armonk** 21

1956 | Luigi's | **Old Saybrook** 24

1957 | Johnny Ad's | **Old Saybrook** 21

1960 | Chef Antonio | **Mamaro** 20

HOTEL DINING

Altnaveigh Inn
Altnaveigh Inn | **Storrs** 23

Avon Old Farms Hotel
Ferme | **Avon** 21

Bedford Post
Bedford Post/Barn | **Bedford** 23
Bedford Post/Farm | **Bedford** 25

Bee & Thistle Inn
Chestnut Grille | **Old Lyme** 26

Boulders Inn
Boulders Inn | **New Preston** 21

Copper Beech Inn
Brasserie Pip | **Ivoryton** -

Delamar Hotel
L'Escale | **Greenwich** 23

Esplanade White Plains Hotel
Graziellas | **White Pl** 19

Foxwoods Resort Casino
California Pizza | **Ledyard** 17
Cedars | **Ledyard** 28
David Burke | **Ledyard** 26
Hard Rock | **Ledyard** 15

Griswold Inn
Griswold Inn | **Essex** 18

Hi Ho Motel
Z Barcelona | **Fairfield** 24

Homestead Inn
Z Thomas Henkelmann | **Greenwich** 28

Hopkins Inn
Hopkins Inn | **New Preston** 19

Inn at Lafayette
Cafe Allegre | **Madison** 23

Inn at Longshore
Splash | **Westport** 22

Inn at Mystic
Flood Tide | **Mystic** 21

Inn at Newtown
Inn/Newtown | **Newtown** 18

La Quinta Hotel
Marc Charles | **Armonk** 20

Longwood Country Inn
Longwood | **Woodbury** 18

Marriott Residence Inn
Aberdeen | **White Pl** 23

Mayflower Inn & Spa
Z Mayflower Inn | **Washington** 24

MGM Grand at Foxwoods
Craftsteak | **Ledyard** 24

Mohegan Sun Casino
Bar Americain | **Uncasville** 26
Z Frank Pepe | **Uncasville** 24
Jasper White's | **Uncasville** 21
Johnny Rockets | **Uncasville** 16
Michael Jordan's | **Uncasville** 23
SolToro | **Uncasville** 20
Todd English's | **Uncasville** 22

Mystic Marriott Hotel & Spa
Octagon | **Groton** 24

Old Lyme Inn
Old Lyme Inn | **Old Lyme** 22

Renaissance Hotel
80 West | **White Pl** 19

Ridgefield Motor Inn
Thali | **Ridgefield** 24

Ritz-Carlton Westchester
NEW Bellota/42 | **White Pl** -
BLT Steak | **White Pl** 23
42 | **White Pl** 22

Roger Sherman Inn
Roger Sherman | **New Canaan** 24

Saybrook Point Inn & Spa
Terra Mar | **Old Saybrook** 23

Simmons' Way Village Inn
No. 9 | **Millerton** 27

Stonehenge Inn
Stonehenge | **Ridgefield** 22

Study at Yale Hotel
Heirloom | **New Haven** 20

Water's Edge Resort & Spa
Z Rest./Water's Edge | **Westbrook** 23

Whaler's Inn
Bravo Bravo | **Mystic** 26

Winvian Resort
Winvian | **Morris** 27

JACKET REQUIRED

☒ Thomas Henkelmann | Greenwich — 28

MEET FOR A DRINK

Agave Grill | Hartford — 20
NEW Anthony's Pizza | White Pl — 22
Archie Moore's | multi. — 18
Asian Tempt. | White Pl — 20
Aspen | Old Saybrook — 20
@ the Corner | Litchfield — 20
Azu | Mystic — 23
Baang Cafe | Riverside — 23
Bacchus | S Norwalk — ‑
Ballou's | Guilford — 18
NEW Bank St. Tavern | New Milford — 18
Bar Americain | Uncasville — 26
☒ Barcelona | multi. — 24
NEW Bartaco | Port Chester — ‑
Beach House | Milford — 22
NEW Bellota/42 | White Pl — ‑
NEW Benjamin Steak | White Pl — 24
Besito | W Hartford — 22
Bespoke | New Haven — 24
Bin 100 | Milford — 26
Bin 228 | Hartford — 22
Black-Eyed Sally | Hartford — 20
Blackstones | Norwalk — 25
BLT Steak | White Pl — 23
Boathouse | Lakeville — 17
Bobby Q's | Westport — 21
Bobby Valentine | Stamford — 15
Bogey's Grille | Westport — 17
Bond Grill | Norwalk — 21
Boxcar Cantina | Greenwich — 21
Brazen Fox | White Pl — 17
Brewhouse | S Norwalk — 19
☒ Bricco | W Hartford — 27
Bru Room/BAR | New Haven — 25
Burger Bar | S Norwalk — 22
Cafe Goodfellas | New Haven — 20
Capt. Daniel Packer | Mystic — 21
NEW Cask Republic | New Haven — ‑

Chat | Larch — 18
Christopher Martins | New Haven — 20
City Steam | Hartford — 15
Croton Creek | Crot Falls — 20
Cuckoo's Nest | Old Saybrook — 17
Cuvee | W Hartford — 16
Dish B&G | Hartford — 20
Dock/Dine | Old Saybrook — 14
Dolly Madison Inn | Madison — 13
Don Coqui | New Roch — 23
Donovan's | S Norwalk — 18
Elbow Room | W Hartford — 18
Emma's Ale House | White Pl — 18
Euro Asian | Port Chester — 17
Fat Cat Pie | Norwalk — 23
Feng Asian | Hartford — 22
NEW Fez | Stamford — 20
Fife 'n Drum | Kent — 18
Fifty Coins | multi. — 16
Firebox | Hartford — 24
First/Last | multi. — 19
Flipside Burgers | Fairfield — 17
Forbidden City | Middletown — 25
42 | White Pl — 22
Frankie/Johnnie's | Rye — 24
Full Moon | White Pl — 24
NEW Gabriele's | Greenwich — ‑
Geronimo | New Haven — 20
Ginger Man | multi. — 18
NEW Goose | Darien — ‑
Graziellas | White Pl — 19
NEW Greenwood's Grille | Bethel — 16
Gusano Loco | Mamaro — 21
Haiku | multi. — 22
Harbor Lights | Norwalk — 20
Horse/Hound | S Salem — 19
Hot Tomato's | Hartford — 20
NEW Hudson Grille | White Pl — 20
J. Gilbert's | Glastonbury — 25
John Harvard's | Manchester — 16
Kobis | Fairfield — 22
Kona Grill | Stamford — 17

Kudeta	**New Haven**	21
Lazy Boy Saloon	**White Pl**	19
Lenny's Indian	**Branford**	21
Leon's	**New Haven**	18
Little Pub	**Ridgefield**	23
Lolita Cocina	**Greenwich**	22
Long Ridge Tav.	**Stamford**	14
L'Orcio	**New Haven**	23
Los Cabos	**Norwalk**	15
Mackenzie's	**Old Greenwich**	16
Marc Charles	**Armonk**	20
Mario's Pl.	**Westport**	19
Market	**Stamford**	20
Match	**S Norwalk**	26
Max-a-Mia	**Avon**	24
Max Amore	**Glastonbury**	23
Max Burger	**W Hartford**	25
∎ Max Downtown	**Hartford**	27
Max Fish	**Glastonbury**	23
Mediterraneo	**Greenwich**	21
Melting Pot	**Darien**	17
Mickey/Molly Spill.	**Mamaro**	15
Milonga	**N White Plains**	22
Miya's Sushi	**New Haven**	25
NEW Moderne Barn	**Armonk**	22
Molto Wine	**Fairfield**	21
Mulino's	**White Pl**	24
∎ Napa & Co.	**Stamford**	24
Nino's	**Bedford Hills**	21
NEW Oaxaca Kitchen	**New Haven**	-
Oliver's Taverne	**Essex**	16
O'Neill's	**S Norwalk**	19
116 Crown	**New Haven**	21
121 Rest./Bar	**N Salem**	22
Osetra	**S Norwalk**	23
Palmer's Crossing	**Larch**	21
Papaya Thai	**S Norwalk**	20
Paradise B&G	**Stamford**	13
NEW Pine Social	**New Canaan**	23
Plan B Burger	**multi.**	22
Porter Hse.	**White Pl**	19
Putnam Hse.	**Bethel**	19
Ralph/Rich's	**Bridgeport**	23
NEW Red Lulu	**S Norwalk**	24
Red Plum	**Mamaro**	21
NEW Rest. North	**Armonk**	26
Ron Blacks	**White Pl**	16
Rouge Winebar	**S Norwalk**	21
Rye Grill	**Rye**	18
Rye Roadhse.	**Rye**	18
Sage	**New Haven**	19
NEW Sails	**Norwalk**	-
Saito	**Greenwich**	27
Sal/Pepe	**Newtown**	24
Saltwater Grille	**Stamford**	17
Scoozzi Tratt.	**New Haven**	22
Shack	**Fairfield**	13
Shell Station	**Stratford**	20
SolToro	**Uncasville**	20
Sonora	**Port Chester**	24
Southport Brew.	**Hamden**	16
Southwest Cafe	**Ridgefield**	22
Strada 18	**S Norwalk**	26
Tango Grill	**White Pl**	21
Tapas/Ann	**Bloomfield**	23
NEW Tappo	**Stamford**	-
Tarry Lodge	**Port Chester**	24
Telluride	**Stamford**	21
∎ Tengda	**Darien**	22
Tequila Mock.	**New Canaan**	18
Thali	**multi.**	24
Tratt. Carl Anthony	**Monroe**	24
Two Boots	**Bridgeport**	20
Viale Rist.	**Bridgeport**	24
Vinny's	**Stamford**	20
Vito's	**multi.**	21
Viva Zapata	**Westport**	17
Vox	**N Salem**	21
Wasabi Chi	**S Norwalk**	23
NEW Westchester Burger	**White Pl**	20
Wood-n-Tap	**multi.**	17

MICROBREWERIES

Bru Room/BAR	**New Haven**	25
City Steam	**Hartford**	15
John Harvard's	**Manchester**	16
Southport Brew.	**multi.**	16

NEWCOMERS

Alvin/Friends	**New Roch**	26
Anthony's Pizza	**White Pl**	22
Arrosto	**Port Chester**	23
Bank St. Tavern	**New Milford**	18
Bar Bouchée	**Madison**	28
Bartaco	**Port Chester**	-
Bellota/42	**White Pl**	-
Benjamin Steak	**White Pl**	24
Boathse./Saugatuck	**Westport**	25
Brasserie	**Fairfield**	24
Café d'Azur	**Darien**	-
Cask Republic	**New Haven**	-
Cienega	**New Roch**	-
Community Table	**Washington**	27
Eclisse Med.	**White Pl**	21
Fez	**Stamford**	20
Frankie/Fanucci's	**Mamaro**	21
Gabriele's	**Greenwich**	-
Goose	**Darien**	-
Green Gourmet	**Bridgeport**	-
Greenwood's Grille	**Bethel**	16
Hudson Grille	**White Pl**	20
La Scarbitta	**Mamaro**	-
Millstone Café	**Kent**	-
Moderne Barn	**Armonk**	22
Norimaki	**Washington**	-
Oakhurst Diner	**Millerton**	16
Oaxaca Kitchen	**New Haven**	-
On the Way Café	**Rye**	-
Pine Social	**New Canaan**	23
Piri-Q	**Mamaro**	20
Post Rd. Ale	**New Roch**	-
Red Lulu	**S Norwalk**	24
Rest. North	**Armonk**	26
Sails	**Norwalk**	-
Suburban	**Branford**	24
Tappo	**Stamford**	-
Thali	**Westport**	24
Westchester Burger	**White Pl**	20

OFFBEAT

Abbott's Lobster	**Noank**	23
Aladdin	**Hartford**	-
Aux Délices	**multi.**	24

Ay! Salsa	**New Haven**	-
Ballou's	**Guilford**	18
Bangkok Gdns.	**New Haven**	19
Barça	**Hartford**	20
🆕 Bartaco	**Port Chester**	-
Basta	**New Haven**	25
Bloodroot	**Bridgeport**	23
Boathouse/Smokey	**Stamford**	19
Cafe Goodfellas	**New Haven**	20
Cafe Lola	**Fairfield**	24
Cafe Mirage	**Port Chester**	22
🅩 Carole Peck's	**Woodbury**	26
Chaiwalla	**Salisbury**	25
Churrasc. Braza	**Hartford**	16
Claire's Corner	**New Haven**	21
Clamp's	**New Milford**	-
Country Bistro	**Salisbury**	-
Denmo's	**Southbury**	-
Dottie's Diner	**Woodbury**	18
Drescher's	**Waterbury**	19
Épernay	**Bridgeport**	22
Fat Cat Pie	**Norwalk**	23
🆕 Fez	**Stamford**	20
Flanders Fish	**E Lyme**	21
Friends & Co.	**Madison**	18
🆕 Green Gourmet	**Bridgeport**	-
Gusano Loco	**Mamaro**	21
Haiku	**multi.**	22
Infinity Hall/Bistro	**Norfolk**	20
🅩 Isabelle/Vincent	**Fairfield**	27
It's Only Natural	**Middletown**	20
Johnny Ad's	**Old Saybrook**	21
Kit's Thai	**Stamford**	21
Kobis	**Fairfield**	22
🅩 Le Farm	**Westport**	27
Lenny/Joe's	**multi.**	23
Lime	**Norwalk**	23
Louis' Lunch	**New Haven**	22
Lucky's	**Stamford**	18
Melting Pot	**multi.**	17
🅩 Mill/2T	**Tariffville**	28
Miya's Sushi	**New Haven**	25

Noah's	**Stonington**	24
Old Heidelberg	**Bethel**	21
121 Rest./OXC	**Oxford**	21
Pantry	**Wash Depot**	24
Pasta Nostra	**S Norwalk**	25
Pasta Vera	**Greenwich**	20
Pat's Kountry	**Old Saybrook**	16
⚡ PolytechnicON20	**Hartford**	28
Ray's Cafe	**multi.**	19
Rein's NY Deli	**Vernon**	22
Rouge Winebar	**S Norwalk**	21
Rue/Crêpes	**Harrison**	19
Rye Roadhse.	**Rye**	18
Salsa	**New Milford**	25
Scribner's	**Milford**	22
Sesame Seed	**Danbury**	21
Super/Weenie	**Fairfield**	23
Sycamore Drive-In	**Bethel**	17
Taste/Charleston	**Norwalk**	-
Thali	**multi.**	24
Tratt. Vivolo	**Harrison**	25

OUTDOOR DINING

(G=garden; P=patio; S=sidewalk;
T=terrace; W=waterside)

Abbott's Lobster	T, W	**Noank**	23
Adrienne	P	**New Milford**	25
Apricots	P, W	**Farmington**	23
⚡ Arch	P	**Brewster**	27
⚡ Barcelona	P	**multi.**	24
NEW Bartaco	P	**Port Chester**	-
Bill's Seafood	T, W	**Westbrook**	19
Bloodroot	G, P, W	**Bridgeport**	23
Boulders Inn	P	**New Preston**	21
Café/Green	P, T	**Danbury**	22
⚡ Carole Peck's	P	**Woodbury**	26
Chatterley's	P	**New Hartford**	21
Chez Jean-Pierre	S	**Stamford**	24
Confetti	T	**Plainville**	22
Dock/Dine	P, W	**Old Saybrook**	14
Dolphins Cove	P, W	**Bridgeport**	-
Elbow Room	T	**W Hartford**	18
Eli Cannon's	P	**Middletown**	21
Encore Bistro	S	**Larch**	23

Fin/Fin II	P	**Fairfield**	23
Flood Tide	T, W	**Mystic**	21
Grist Mill	P, W	**Farmington**	23
G.W. Tavern	T, W	**Wash Depot**	20
Hopkins Inn	T	**New Preston**	19
It's Only Natural	P	**Middletown**	20
Jeffrey's	G	**Milford**	26
La Zingara	P	**Bethel**	26
Lazy Boy Saloon	S	**White Pl**	19
Le Fontane	G	**Katonah**	22
Lenny/Joe's	G, P	**multi.**	23
L'Escale	T, W	**Greenwich**	23
Longwood	G	**Woodbury**	18
⚡ Mayflower Inn	P	**Washington**	24
Mediterranean Grill	P	**Wilton**	18
Mediterraneo	P	**Greenwich**	21
Meigas	P	**Norwalk**	24
Mill/River	P, W	**S Windsor**	20
Niko's Greek	P	**White Pl**	20
Nuage	P	**Cos Cob**	24
Old Heidelberg	G	**Bethel**	21
Oliva Cafe	T	**New Preston**	24
121 Rest./Bar	P, T	**N Salem**	22
Opus 465	P	**Armonk**	18
Oscar's	S	**Westport**	18
Pastorale	T	**Lakeville**	23
Pond Hse. Café	P	**W Hartford**	21
⚡ Rest./Water's Edge	T, W	**Westbrook**	23
River House	P, W	**Westport**	17
Roasted Peppers	S	**Mamaro**	21
Roger Sherman	P	**New Canaan**	24
Sage	P, W	**New Haven**	19
⚡ Schoolhouse	P, W	**Wilton**	27
Scoozzi Tratt.	P	**New Haven**	22
Seaside Johnnie's	T, W	**Rye**	12
SoNo Baking Co.	S	**S Norwalk**	26
Sono Seaport	P, W	**S Norwalk**	15
Splash	T, W	**Westport**	22
Squire's	P	**Redding**	16
Stone House	T, W	**Guilford**	18
Tarry Lodge	T	**Port Chester**	24
Tavern/Main	T	**Westport**	19

Terra Mar | P, W | **Old Saybrook** 23
Terra Rist. | P | **Greenwich** 23
Thataway Cafe | P | **Greenwich** 17
Vito's | S | **Hartford** 21
Viva Zapata | P | **Westport** 17
Vox | G, P, T | **N Salem** 21
West St. Grill | S | **Litchfield** 24

PEOPLE-WATCHING

Acqua | **Westport** 22
Arugula | **W Hartford** 23
Asian Tempt. | **White Pl** 20
Azu | **Mystic** 23
Baang Cafe | **Riverside** 23
Bar Americain | **Uncasville** 26
NEW Bar Bouchée | **Madison** 28
Ƨ Barcelona | **New Haven** 24
NEW Bartaco | **Port Chester** -
Bedford Post/Barn | **Bedford** 23
Bedford Post/Farm | **Bedford** 25
NEW Bellota/42 | **White Pl** -
NEW Benjamin Steak | **White Pl** 24
Bespoke | **New Haven** 24
BLT Steak | **White Pl** 23
Blue | **White Pl** 20
Boathouse | **Lakeville** 17
Bravo Bravo | **Mystic** 26
Brazen Fox | **White Pl** 17
Ƨ Bricco | **W Hartford** 27
Cafe Goodfellas | **New Haven** 20
Ƨ Carole Peck's | **Woodbury** 26
Community Table | 27
   Washington
Craftsteak | **Ledyard** 24
Don Coqui | **New Roch** 23
Ƨ Dressing Room | **Westport** 24
Elbow Room | **W Hartford** 18
Euro Asian | **Port Chester** 17
Feng Asian | **Hartford** 22
Ferrante | **Stamford** 20
NEW Fez | **Stamford** 20
Fife 'n Drum | **Kent** 18
Firebox | **Hartford** 24
42 | **White Pl** 22
Frankie/Johnnie's | **Rye** 24

NEW Gabriele's | **Greenwich** -
Ginban Asian | **Mamaro** 23
Ginger Man | **Greenwich** 10
Grant's | **W Hartford** 25
Griswold Inn | **Essex** 18
G.W. Tavern | **Wash Depot** 20
Haiku | **multi.** 22
Hot Tomato's | **Hartford** 20
NEW Hudson Grille | **White Pl** 20
Ƨ Ibiza | **New Haven** 27
Ƨ Jean-Louis | **Greenwich** 28
Koo | **Rye** 23
Lolita Cocina | **Greenwich** 22
Lusardi's | **Larch** 24
Market | **Stamford** 20
Match | **S Norwalk** 26
Max Burger | **W Hartford** 25
Ƨ Max Downtown | **Hartford** 27
Max Fish | **Glastonbury** 23
Max's Oyster | **W Hartford** 26
Ƨ Mayflower Inn | **Washington** 24
Michael Jordan's | **Uncasville** 23
Mickey/Molly Spill. | **Mamaro** 15
NEW Moderne Barn | **Armonk** 22
Molto Wine | **Fairfield** 21
Mulino's | **White Pl** 24
North Star | **Pound Ridge** 20
Nuage | **Cos Cob** 24
NEW Oaxaca Kitchen | -
   New Haven
Oliva Cafe | **New Preston** 24
116 Crown | **New Haven** 21
Paci | **Southport** 26
Pastorale | **Lakeville** 23
NEW Pine Social | **New Canaan** 23
Polpo | **Greenwich** 24
Porter Hse. | **White Pl** 19
Rebeccas | **Greenwich** 26
NEW Red Lulu | **S Norwalk** 24
Rist. Luce | **Hamden** 22
River House | **Westport** 17
Ron Blacks | **White Pl** 16
Ruby's Oyster | **Rye** 23
NEW Sails | **Norwalk** -

Saito | **Greenwich**	27
Scoozzi Tratt. | **New Haven**	22
SolToro | **Uncasville**	20
Sonora | **Port Chester**	24
Strada 18 | **S Norwalk**	26
Tango Grill | **White Pl**	21
NEW Tappo | **Stamford**	-
Tarry Lodge | **Port Chester**	24
Tavern/Main | **Westport**	19
Z Tengda | **multi.**	22
Todd English's | **Uncasville**	22
Z Union League | **New Haven**	27
Wasabi Chi | **S Norwalk**	23
West St. Grill | **Litchfield**	24
Winvian | **Morris**	27
Zinc | **New Haven**	24

POWER SCENES

Alba's | **Port Chester**	23
Baang Cafe | **Riverside**	23
Bedford Post/Farm | **Bedford**	25
NEW Bellota/42 | **White Pl**	-
NEW Benjamin Steak | **White Pl**	24
BLT Steak | **White Pl**	23
Boathouse | **Lakeville**	17
Z Capital Grille | **Stamford**	25
Carbone's | **Hartford**	24
Cavey's | **Manchester**	26
Central Steak | **New Haven**	24
Christopher Martins | **New Haven**	20
Craftsteak | **Ledyard**	24
Diorio | **Waterbury**	25
Z Dressing Room | **Westport**	24
Ferrante | **Stamford**	20
Firebox | **Hartford**	24
42 | **White Pl**	22
NEW Gabriele's | **Greenwich**	-
Graziellas | **White Pl**	19
Z Jean-Louis | **Greenwich**	28
Jeffrey's | **Milford**	26
Joseph's | **Bridgeport**	24
Koo | **Rye**	23
La Tavola | **Waterbury**	26
Lusardi's | **Larch**	24
Max-a-Mia | **Avon**	24

Z Max Downtown | **Hartford**	27
Max Fish | **Glastonbury**	23
Z Mayflower Inn | **Washington**	24
Meigas | **Norwalk**	24
NEW Moderne Barn | **Armonk**	22
Morton's | **multi.**	24
Mulino's | **White Pl**	24
O'Porto | **Hartford**	23
Peppercorn's Grill | **Hartford**	26
Polpo | **Greenwich**	24
Ralph/Rich's | **Bridgeport**	23
Tango Grill | **White Pl**	21
Z Thomas Henkelmann | **Greenwich**	28
Tre Scalini | **New Haven**	24
Z Union League | **New Haven**	27
Z Valbella | **Riverside**	25
West St. Grill | **Litchfield**	24
Willett House | **Port Chester**	24

PRIVATE ROOMS

(Restaurants charge less at off times; call for capacity)

Acqua | **Westport**	22
Bedford Post/Farm | **Bedford**	25
Z Bernard's | **Ridgefield**	27
Bru Room/BAR | **New Haven**	25
Z Carole Peck's | **Woodbury**	26
NEW Cask Republic | **New Haven**	-
Centro | **Greenwich**	20
Chatterley's | **New Hartford**	21
Chestnut Grille | **Old Lyme**	26
Dakota Steak | **Avon**	17
Eclisse | **Stamford**	21
Elbow Room | **W Hartford**	18
42 | **White Pl**	22
Ginger Man | **Greenwich**	18
NEW Goose | **Darien**	-
Graziellas | **White Pl**	19
Grist Mill | **Farmington**	23
Joseph's | **Bridgeport**	24
Kujaku | **Stamford**	18
Z La Panetière | **Rye**	27
Max Amore | **Glastonbury**	23
Z Max Downtown | **Hartford**	27
Max's Oyster | **W Hartford**	26

Mayflower Inn | **Washington** — 24
Meigas | **Norwalk** — 24
Michael Jordan's | **Uncasville** — 23
Morello | **Greenwich** — 22
116 Crown | **New Haven** — 21
Paci | **Southport** — 26
Plum Tree | **New Canaan** — 20
Polpo | **Greenwich** — 24
Primavera | **Crot Falls** — 24
Putnam Hse. | **Bethel** — 19
Roger Sherman | **New Canaan** — 24
Ruby's Oyster | **Rye** — 23
Scoozzi Tratt. | **New Haven** — 22
Scribner's | **Milford** — 22
Stonehenge | **Ridgefield** — 22
Tengda | **Greenwich** — 22
Thali | **New Canaan** — 24
Thomas Henkelmann | **Greenwich** — 28
Todd English's | **Uncasville** — 22
Toshi Japanese | **Avon** — 21
Tuscany | **Bridgeport** — 24
Union League | **New Haven** — 27
U.S.S. Chowder | **Hartford** — 19
Woodward Hse. | **Bethlehem** — 27

PRIX FIXE MENUS

(Call for prices and times)

Arch | **Brewster** — 27
Bernard's | **Ridgefield** — 27
Bin 100 | **Milford** — 26
DaPietro's | **Westport** — 27
Emilio Rist. | **Harrison** — 25
Firebox | **Hartford** — 24
Halstead Ave. | **Harrison** — 20
Jean-Louis | **Greenwich** — 28
La Crémaillère | **Bedford** — 27
La Panetière | **Rye** — 27
Meigas | **Norwalk** — 24
Mill/River | **S Windsor** — 20
Ondine | **Danbury** — 26
Pascal's | **Larch** — 23
Rest./Rowayton Sea. | **Rowayton** — 22
Shish Kebab | **W Hartford** — 25
Sonora | **Port Chester** — 24

Toshi Japanese | **Avon** — 21
Turkish Meze | **Mamaro** — 23

QUIET CONVERSATION

Altnaveigh Inn | **Storrs** — 23
American Pie | **Sherman** — 22
Apricots | **Farmington** — 23
Arch | **Brewster** — 27
Bacchus | **S Norwalk** — ⌐
Bailey's | **Ridgefield** — 21
Ballou's | **Guilford** — 18
Bangalore | **Fairfield** — 23
Bedford Post/Farm | **Bedford** — 25
NEW Bellota/42 | **White Pl** — ⌐
Bernard's | **Ridgefield** — 27
Bin 228 | **Hartford** — 22
Bistro Basque | **Milford** — 26
Bistro 22 | **Bedford** — 24
Blackstones | **Norwalk** — 25
Bloodroot | **Bridgeport** — 23
NEW Boathse./Saugatuck | **Westport** — 25
Brasserie Pip | **Ivoryton** — ⌐
Brix | **Cheshire** — 21
Bull's Bridge | **Kent** — 16
Burger Bar | **S Norwalk** — 22
Cafe Allegre | **Madison** — 23
Cafe Lola | **Fairfield** — 24
Cafe Mozart | **Mamaro** — 17
Carole Peck's | **Woodbury** — 26
Chaiwalla | **Salisbury** — 25
Chet Luis | **New Canaan** — 25
Chestnut Grille | **Old Lyme** — 26
NEW Cienega | **New Roch** — ⌐
Coromandel | **multi.** — 25
DaCapo's | **Avon** — 19
David Burke | **Ledyard** — 26
Diorio | **Waterbury** — 25
Drescher's | **Waterbury** — 19
NEW Eclisse Med. | **White Pl** — 21
Épernay | **Bridgeport** — 22
Esca | **Middletown** — 19
Ferme | **Avon** — 21
Fife 'n Drum | **Kent** — 18

Fin/Fin II | **Stamford**	23
Flood Tide | **Mystic**	21
Foe | **Branford**	19
Gabrielle's | **Centerbrook**	25
Gervasi's | **White Pl**	20
Graziellas | **White Pl**	19
NEW Green Gourmet | **Bridgeport**	–
Grist Mill | **Farmington**	23
G.W. Tavern | **Wash Depot**	20
Hopkins Inn | **New Preston**	19
Il Palio | **Shelton**	24
Il Sogno | **Port Chester**	24
Inn/Newtown | **Newtown**	18
⊠ Jean-Louis | **Greenwich**	28
John-Michael's | **N Salem**	24
John's Café | **Woodbury**	23
La Bocca | **White Pl**	23
La Bretagne | **Stamford**	24
⊠ La Crémaillère | **Bedford**	27
⊠ La Panetière | **Rye**	27
La Piccola Casa | **Mamaro**	21
Le Château | **S Salem**	25
⊠ Le Farm | **Westport**	27
Leon's | **New Haven**	18
⊠ Le Petit Cafe | **Branford**	29
Thai/Buddha/Spice | **Darien**	23
Longwood | **Woodbury**	18
L'Orcio | **New Haven**	23
Marc Charles | **Armonk**	20
Matthew's | **Unionville**	24
⊠ Mayflower Inn | **Washington**	24
Melting Pot | **Darien**	17
Métro Bis | **Simsbury**	25
Michael's | **Wallingford**	24
Milonga | **N White Plains**	22
Noah's | **Stonington**	24
No. 9 | **Millerton**	27
Nuage | **Cos Cob**	24
Old Lyme Inn | **Old Lyme**	22
Olive Tree | **Southbury**	21
Ondine | **Danbury**	26
Ošetra | **S Norwalk**	23
Papacelle | **Avon**	24

Pascal's | **Larch**	23
Patrias | **Port Chester**	21
⊠ PolytechnicON20 | **Hartford**	28
Puket Café | **Wethersfield**	26
Rani Mahal | **Mamaro**	23
Reka's | **White Pl**	19
Rest. L&E | **Chester**	24
River Tavern | **Chester**	26
Roger Sherman | **New Canaan**	24
Rouge Winebar | **S Norwalk**	21
RSVP | **W Cornwall**	28
Salsa | **New Milford**	25
Scribner's | **Milford**	22
Stonehenge | **Ridgefield**	22
Taste/Charleston | **Norwalk**	–
⊠ Tawa | **Stamford**	27
Town Dock | **Rye**	19
Turkish Meze | **Mamaro**	23
⊠ Union League | **New Haven**	27
Venetian | **Torrington**	18
Watercolor Cafe | **Larch**	18
Wild Rice | **Norwalk**	20
Winvian | **Morris**	27
⊠ Woodward Hse. | **Bethlehem**	27

RAW BARS

Bar Americain | **Uncasville**	26
David Burke | **Ledyard**	26
Dish B&G | **Hartford**	20
80 West | **White Pl**	19
⊠ Elm St. Oyster | **Greenwich**	24
First/Last | **Middletown**	19
Flanders Fish | **E Lyme**	21
42 | **White Pl**	22
Ginger Man | **Greenwich**	18
Go Fish | **Mystic**	22
Grant's | **W Hartford**	25
Jasper White's | **Uncasville**	21
Legal Sea Foods | **White Pl**	19
Lenny/Joe's | **Westbrook**	23
Litchfield/Grille | **Litchfield**	20
Liv's Oyster | **Old Saybrook**	25
⊠ Max Downtown | **Hartford**	27
Max Fish | **Glastonbury**	23
Max's Oyster | **W Hartford**	26

Morgans Fish | **Rye**	21
116 Crown | **New Haven**	21
121 Rest./Bar | **N Salem**	22
Osetra | **S Norwalk**	23
Pacifico | **New Haven**	24
Q Rest. | **Port Chester**	22
Ralph/Rich's | **Bridgeport**	23
Rest./Rowayton Sea. | **Rowayton**	22
Z Rest./Water's Edge | **Westbrook**	23
Rizzuto's | **Westport**	20
Ruby's Oyster | **Rye**	23
Sage | **New Haven**	19
Saybrook Fish | **Rocky Hill**	22
Seaside Johnnie's | **Rye**	12
Shell Station | **Stratford**	20
Splash | **Westport**	22
Town Dock | **Rye**	19
Tratt. Carl Anthony | **Monroe**	24
Z Union League | **New Haven**	27
U.S.S. Chowder | **multi.**	19
Vito's | **multi.**	21
Vox | **N Salem**	21
Water St. Cafe | **Stonington**	26
Westbrook Lobster | **multi.**	19
West St. Grill | **Litchfield**	24

ROMANTIC PLACES

Acqua | **Westport**	22
Adriana's | **New Haven**	22
Adrienne | **New Milford**	25
Apricots | **Farmington**	23
Z Arch | **Brewster**	27
Ballou's | **Guilford**	18
Bambou | **Greenwich**	21
Bedford Post/Farm | **Bedford**	25
NEW Bellota/42 | **White Pl**	-
Z Bernard's | **Ridgefield**	27
Besito | **W Hartford**	22
Bespoke | **New Haven**	24
Bistro Bonne Nuit | **New Canaan**	25
Bistro 22 | **Bedford**	24
Boom | **Old Lyme**	22
Boulders Inn | **New Preston**	21
Brasserie Pip | **Ivoryton**	-

NEW Café d'Azur | **Darien**	-
Cafe Lola | **Fairfield**	24
Carbone's | **Hartford**	24
Cavey's | **Manchester**	26
Chestnut Grille | **Old Lyme**	26
Chez Jean-Pierre | **Stamford**	24
NEW Cienega | **New Roch**	-
Cuvee | **W Hartford**	16
DaCapo's | **Avon**	19
Z Dressing Room | **Westport**	24
NEW Eclisse Med. | **White Pl**	21
Emilio Rist. | **Harrison**	25
Encore Bistro | **Larch**	23
Esca | **Middletown**	19
Flood Tide | **Mystic**	21
Frankie/Johnnie's | **Rye**	24
Gervasi's | **White Pl**	20
Grist Mill | **Farmington**	23
Griswold Inn | **Essex**	18
Harbor Lights | **Norwalk**	20
Z Harvest Supper | **New Canaan**	27
Hopkins Inn | **New Preston**	19
Horse/Hound | **S Salem**	19
Z Ibiza | **New Haven**	27
Inn/Newtown | **Newtown**	18
Z Jean-Louis | **Greenwich**	28
John-Michael's | **N Salem**	24
La Bretagne | **Stamford**	24
Z La Crémaillère | **Bedford**	27
Z La Panetière | **Rye**	27
La Piccola Casa | **Mamaro**	21
NEW La Scarbitta | **Mamaro**	-
La Zingara | **Bethel**	26
Le Château | **S Salem**	25
Z Le Farm | **Westport**	27
Z Le Petit Cafe | **Branford**	29
Le Provençal | **Mamaro**	23
Longwood | **Woodbury**	18
L'Orcio | **New Haven**	23
Z Mayflower Inn | **Washington**	24
Meigas | **Norwalk**	24
Melting Pot | **White Pl**	17
Métro Bis | **Simsbury**	25
Mill/River | **S Windsor**	20

Mulino's | **White Pl**	24
☑ Napa & Co. | **Stamford**	24
Nessa | **Port Chester**	21
No. 9 | **Millerton**	27
Old Lyme Inn | **Old Lyme**	22
Oliva Cafe | **New Preston**	24
Ondine | **Danbury**	26
121 Rest./Bar | **N Salem**	22
Opus 465 | **Armonk**	18
Pascal's | **Larch**	23
Pastorale | **Lakeville**	23
Peppercorn's Grill | **Hartford**	26
☑ PolytechnicON20 | **Hartford**	28
Ponte Vecchio | **Fairfield**	18
Positano's | **Westport**	22
Posto 22 | **New Roch**	21
Rest. L&E | **Chester**	24
Rist. Luce | **Hamden**	22
River House | **Westport**	17
River Tavern | **Chester**	26
Roger Sherman | **New Canaan**	24
Rouge Winebar | **S Norwalk**	21
Sardegna | **Larch**	19
Sonora | **Port Chester**	24
Still River | **Eastford**	28
Stonehenge | **Ridgefield**	22
Stone House | **Guilford**	18
Tango Grill | **White Pl**	21
☑ Thomas Henkelmann | **Greenwich**	28
Tratt. Vivolo | **Harrison**	25
Tre Scalini | **New Haven**	24
Trinity Grill | **Harrison**	20
☑ Union League | **New Haven**	27
Venetian | **Torrington**	18
Water St. Cafe | **Stonington**	26
White Horse | **New Preston**	19
Winvian | **Morris**	27
☑ Woodward Hse. | **Bethlehem**	27
Zinc | **New Haven**	24
Zitoune | **Mamaro**	19

SENIOR APPEAL

Adriana's | **New Haven**	22
Altnaveigh Inn | **Storrs**	23

American Pie | **Sherman**	22
Apricots | **Farmington**	23
Bedford Post/Farm | **Bedford**	25
Bistro 22 | **Bedford**	24
B.J. Ryan's | **Norwalk**	20
Bombay Olive | **W Hartford**	19
NEW Brasserie | **Fairfield**	24
Brasserie Pip | **Ivoryton**	-
Bravo Bravo | **Mystic**	26
Brix | **Cheshire**	21
Bull's Bridge | **Kent**	16
Cafe Allegre | **Madison**	23
Cafe Giulia | **Lakeville**	22
Carbone's | **Hartford**	24
Carrabba's | **Manchester**	18
Chestnut Grille | **Old Lyme**	26
Chuck's Steak | **Branford**	18
Consiglio's | **New Haven**	23
DaCapo's | **Avon**	19
David Burke | **Ledyard**	26
Dock/Dine | **Old Saybrook**	14
Dolly Madison Inn | **Madison**	13
Dolphins Cove | **Bridgeport**	-
Dottie's Diner | **Woodbury**	18
Encore Bistro | **Larch**	23
Eveready Diner | **Brewster**	20
Fife 'n Drum | **Kent**	18
Flanders Fish | **E Lyme**	21
Foe | **Branford**	19
Fonda La Paloma | **Cos Cob**	19
☑ Frank Pepe | **Manchester**	24
Friends & Co. | **Madison**	18
Go Fish | **Mystic**	22
Graziellas | **White Pl**	19
Grist Mill | **Farmington**	23
Griswold Inn | **Essex**	18
☑ Harvest Supper | **New Canaan**	27
Hawthorne Inn | **Berlin**	20
Il Castello | **Mamaro**	24
Inn/Newtown | **Newtown**	18
Kisco Kosher | **White Pl**	17
Kumo | **multi.**	20
☑ La Crémaillère | **Bedford**	27
☑ La Panetière | **Rye**	27

La Tavola | **Waterbury**	26
Le Château | **S Salem**	25
Lenny/Joe's | **multi.**	23
Lenny's Indian | **Branford**	21
Leon's | **New Haven**	18
Le Provençal | **Mamaro**	23
Little Pub | **Ridgefield**	23
Long Ridge Tav. | **Stamford**	14
Longwood | **Woodbury**	18
Louis' Lunch | **New Haven**	22
Matthew's | **Unionville**	24
Melting Pot | **Darien**	17
Mill/River | **S Windsor**	20
Milonga | **N White Plains**	22
Mulino's | **White Pl**	24
Nino's | **S Salem**	20
Nino's | **Bedford Hills**	21
Old Lyme Inn | **Old Lyme**	22
Olio | **Groton**	24
Pantry | **Wash Depot**	24
Papacelle | **Avon**	24
Pascal's | **Larch**	23
Pat's Kountry | **Old Saybrook**	16
Pellicci's | **Stamford**	19
Portofino Pizza | **Goldens Br**	22
Putnam Hse. | **Bethel**	19
Red Barn | **Westport**	16
☑ Rest./Water's Edge | **Westbrook**	23
Roger Sherman | **New Canaan**	24
Rue/Crêpes | **Harrison**	19
☑ Shady Glen | **Manchester**	21
Stonehenge | **Ridgefield**	22
T&J Villaggio | **Port Chester**	21
Taste/Charleston | **Norwalk**	-
Tavern/Main | **Westport**	19
☑ Tawa | **Stamford**	27
☑ Thomas Henkelmann | **Greenwich**	28
Vazzy's | **Bridgeport**	20
Venetian | **Torrington**	18
Wandering Moose | **W Cornwall**	16
Waters Edge at Giovanni's | **Darien**	19
West St. Grill | **Litchfield**	24

White Horse | **New Preston**	19
Winvian | **Morris**	27
Woodland | **Lakeville**	22
☑ Woodward Hse. | **Bethlehem**	27
Yorkside | **New Haven**	15

SINGLES SCENES

Archie Moore's | **multi.**	18
Asian Tempt. | **White Pl**	20
Azu | **Mystic**	23
Baang Cafe | **Riverside**	23
☑ Barcelona | **multi.**	24
NEW Bartaco | **Port Chester**	-
NEW Bellota/42 | **White Pl**	-
Bespoke | **New Haven**	24
Black-Eyed Sally | **Hartford**	20
Blue | **White Pl**	20
Boathouse | **Lakeville**	17
Bobby Q's | **Westport**	21
Bobby Valentine | **Stamford**	15
Bogey's Grille | **Westport**	17
Bond Grill | **Norwalk**	21
Brewhouse | **S Norwalk**	19
Bru Room/BAR | **New Haven**	25
City Steam | **Hartford**	15
Cobble Stone | **Purchase**	15
Cuckoo's Nest | **Old Saybrook**	17
Cuvee | **W Hartford**	16
Euro Asian | **Port Chester**	17
Feng Asian | **Hartford**	22
Firebox | **Hartford**	24
First/Last | **multi.**	19
Flipside Burgers | **Fairfield**	17
Forbidden City | **Middletown**	25
Frankie/Johnnie's | **Rye**	24
Ginger Man | **S Norwalk**	18
Haiku | **multi.**	22
Hot Tomato's | **Hartford**	20
NEW Hudson Grille | **White Pl**	20
It's Only Natural | **Middletown**	20
J. Gilbert's | **Glastonbury**	25
John Harvard's | **Manchester**	16
Kona Grill | **Stamford**	17
Kudeta | **New Haven**	21
Lazy Boy Saloon | **White Pl**	19

Lolita Cocina | **Greenwich**	22
Long Ridge Tav. | **Stamford**	14
Mackenzie's | **Old Greenwich**	16
Market | **Stamford**	20
Mary Ann's | **Port Chester**	15
Match | **S Norwalk**	26
Max Burger | **W Hartford**	25
Max Fish | **Glastonbury**	23
Mediterraneo | **Greenwich**	21
Melting Pot | **White Pl**	17
Mickey/Molly Spill. | **Mamaro**	15
Molto Wine | **Fairfield**	21
Oliver's Taverne | **Essex**	16
116 Crown | **New Haven**	21
121 Rest./Bar | **N Salem**	22
Paradise B&G | **Stamford**	13
Porter Hse. | **White Pl**	19
NEW Red Lulu | **S Norwalk**	24
Ron Blacks | **White Pl**	16
Rye Grill | **Rye**	18
Sage | **New Haven**	19
Saito | **Greenwich**	27
Saltwater Grille | **Stamford**	17
Shack | **Fairfield**	13
SolToro | **Uncasville**	20
Sono Seaport | **S Norwalk**	15
Southport Brew. | **multi.**	16
Splash | **Westport**	22
Strada 18 | **S Norwalk**	26
Telluride | **Stamford**	21
Ⓩ Tengda | **Katonah**	22
Tequila Sunrise | **Larch**	17
Terra Rist. | **Greenwich**	23
Thataway Cafe | **Greenwich**	17
Two Boots | **Bridgeport**	20
Viva Zapata | **Westport**	17
Wasabi Chi | **S Norwalk**	23
Wood-n-Tap | **Hartford**	17

SLEEPERS

(Good food, but little known)

Altnaveigh Inn | **Storrs**	23
Azu | **Mystic**	23
Buon Appetito | **Canton**	26
Cafe Giulia | **Lakeville**	22
Cedars | **Ledyard**	28
Chaiwalla | **Salisbury**	25
Char Koon | **S Glastonbury**	23
Chestnut Grille | **Old Lyme**	26
Corner Bakery | **Pawling**	23
Da Giorgio | **New Roch**	25
East-West Grille | **W Hartford**	23
Épernay | **Bridgeport**	22
Full Moon | **White Pl**	24
Karamba | **White Pl**	22
La Tavola | **Waterbury**	26
Luigi's | **Old Saybrook**	24
Matthew's | **Unionville**	24
Michael's | **Wallingford**	24
Octagon | **Groton**	24
Old Lyme Inn | **Old Lyme**	22
Olio | **Groton**	24
O'Porto | **Hartford**	23
Osteria Applausi | **Old Greenwich**	24
Papacelle | **Avon**	24
Prime 16 | **New Haven**	23
Puket Café | **multi.**	26
Rasa | **Greenwich**	24
Rest. L&E | **Chester**	24
Rist. Luce | **Hamden**	22
RSVP | **W Cornwall**	28
Saito | **Greenwich**	27
Salsa | **New Milford**	25
Shish Kebab | **W Hartford**	25
Sono Bana | **Hamden**	24
Soul de Cuba | **New Haven**	25
Still River | **Eastford**	28
Taberna | **Bridgeport**	28
Terra Mar | **Old Saybrook**	23
3 Boys/Italy | **White Pl**	23
Tuscany | **Bridgeport**	24
Vanilla Bean | **Pomfret**	22
Viale Rist. | **Bridgeport**	24
Wasabi | **Orange**	25
Winvian | **Morris**	27

TEEN APPEAL

Abatino's | **N White Plains**	20
Abbott's Lobster | **Noank**	23
Abis | **Greenwich**	19

Alforno | **Old Saybrook**	22
Altnaveigh Inn | **Storrs**	23
Angelina's Tratt. | **Westport**	17
Archie Moore's | **Derby**	18
Ash Creek | **Bridgeport**	17
Asian Tempt. | **White Pl**	20
Bangkok Gdns. | **New Haven**	19
Bentara | **New Haven**	24
Bertucci's | **multi.**	16
Big W's | **Wingdale**	26
Boathouse | **Lakeville**	17
Boathouse/Smokey | **Stamford**	19
Boxcar Cantina | **Greenwich**	21
Bravo Bravo | **Mystic**	26
Butterfly Chinese | **W Hartford**	19
Chuck's Steak | **multi.**	18
Churrasc. Braza | **Hartford**	16
City Limits | **multi.**	19
Claire's Corner | **New Haven**	21
Cookhouse | **New Milford**	22
Coyote Blue | **Middletown**	20
Dakota Steak | **Avon**	17
Denmo's | **Southbury**	-
Dolphins Cove | **Bridgeport**	-
Dottie's Diner | **Woodbury**	18
Eclisse | **Stamford**	21
Euro Asian | **Port Chester**	17
Eveready Diner | **Brewster**	20
Fifty Coins | **multi.**	16
Firehouse Deli | **Fairfield**	21
Flipside Burgers | **Fairfield**	17
Fonda La Paloma | **Cos Cob**	19
☑ Frank Pepe | **multi.**	24
Gates | **New Canaan**	19
Go Fish | **Mystic**	22
Great Taste | **New Britain**	20
Haiku | **multi.**	22
Harry's Pizza | **W Hartford**	26
Hawthorne Inn | **Berlin**	20
Kobis | **multi.**	22
Kumo | **multi.**	20
La Taverna | **Norwalk**	21
Lenny/Joe's | **multi.**	23
Little Kitchen | **Westport**	21
Louis' Lunch | **New Haven**	22
Lucky's | **Stamford**	18
Luigi's | **Old Saybrook**	24
Luna Pizza | **multi.**	21
Marisa's | **Trumbull**	18
Mary Ann's | **Port Chester**	15
Melting Pot | **Darien**	17
Mo's NY | **New Roch**	18
Mystic Pizza | **multi.**	15
Nautilus | **Mamaro**	16
Noda's Steak | **White Pl**	19
NEW Oakhurst Diner | **Millerton**	16
Oliver's Taverne | **Essex**	16
Olive Tree | **Southbury**	21
Orem's Diner | **Wilton**	15
Oscar's | **Westport**	18
Pat's Kountry | **Old Saybrook**	16
Pellicci's | **Stamford**	19
P.F. Chang's | **White Pl**	18
Pizzeria Lauretano | **Bethel**	22
Portofino Pizza | **Goldens Br**	22
Post Corner Pizza | **Darien**	20
Red Rooster | **Brewster**	18
Rizzuto's | **multi.**	20
Route 22 | **Armonk**	14
Rue/Crêpes | **Harrison**	19
Rye Roadhse. | **Rye**	18
Sakura | **Westport**	21
Sally's Apizza | **New Haven**	25
☑ Shady Glen | **Manchester**	21
Sono Seaport | **S Norwalk**	15
Southport Brew. | **multi.**	16
Steak Loft | **Mystic**	18
Super/Weenie | **Fairfield**	23
Sycamore Drive-In | **Bethel**	17
Tandoori Taste | **Port Chester**	21
Tequila Mock. | **New Canaan**	18
Tiger Bowl | **Westport**	15
Tratt. Lucia | **Bedford**	18
☑ Valencia Lunch. | **Norwalk**	27
Vazzy's | **Bridgeport**	20
Village Sq. Bagels | **Larch**	18

Restaurant	Location	Rating
Waters Edge at Giovanni's	**Darien**	19
Yorkside	**New Haven**	15

TRENDY

Restaurant	Location	Rating
Acqua	**Westport**	22
NEW Arrosto	**Port Chester**	23
Asian Tempt.	**White Pl**	20
Aspen	**Old Saybrook**	20
Aurora	**Rye**	21
Ay! Salsa	**New Haven**	-
Azu	**Mystic**	23
Baang Cafe	**Riverside**	23
Ballou's	**Guilford**	18
Bambou	**Greenwich**	21
Barça	**Hartford**	20
Z Barcelona	**multi.**	24
NEW Bartaco	**Port Chester**	-
Basta	**New Haven**	25
Bedford Post/Barn	**Bedford**	23
NEW Bellota/42	**White Pl**	-
Besito	**W Hartford**	22
Bespoke	**New Haven**	24
Bin 228	**Hartford**	22
BLT Steak	**White Pl**	23
Blue	**White Pl**	20
Bonda	**Fairfield**	27
Bond Grill	**Norwalk**	21
Z Bricco	**W Hartford**	27
Café Manolo	**Westport**	23
Carmen Anthony Fish.	**multi.**	22
Carmen Anthony Steak	**Waterbury**	22
Z Carole Peck's	**Woodbury**	26
NEW Cask Republic	**New Haven**	-
Chat	**Larch**	18
NEW Cienega	**New Roch**	-
Community Table	**Washington**	27
Z Coromandel	**S Norwalk**	25
Costa del Sol	**Hartford**	25
Craftsteak	**Ledyard**	24
Dish B&G	**Hartford**	20
Z Dressing Room	**Westport**	24
Elbow Room	**W Hartford**	18
Z Elm St. Oyster	**Greenwich**	24
Eos Greek	**Stamford**	24
Fat Cat Pie	**Norwalk**	23
Feng Asian	**Hartford**	22
NEW Fez	**Stamford**	20
Firebox	**Hartford**	24
Flipside Burgers	**Fairfield**	17
Forbidden City	**Middletown**	25
42	**White Pl**	22
Z Frank Pepe	**New Haven**	24
Full Moon	**White Pl**	24
Geronimo	**New Haven**	20
Ginban Asian	**Mamaro**	23
Ginger Man	**S Norwalk**	18
Haiku	**multi.**	22
Z Harvest Supper	**New Canaan**	27
Hot Tomato's	**Hartford**	20
Z Ibiza	**multi.**	27
Koo	**Rye**	23
Kotobuki	**Stamford**	24
Kudeta	**New Haven**	21
Z Le Farm	**Westport**	27
Lolita Cocina	**Greenwich**	22
Market	**Stamford**	20
Max-a-Mia	**Avon**	24
Max Amore	**Glastonbury**	23
Max Burger	**W Hartford**	25
Z Max Downtown	**Hartford**	27
Max Fish	**Glastonbury**	23
Max's Oyster	**W Hartford**	26
Mediterranean Grill	**Wilton**	18
Mediterraneo	**Greenwich**	21
Métro Bis	**Simsbury**	25
Z Mill/2T	**Tariffville**	28
Miya's Sushi	**New Haven**	25
NEW Moderne Barn	**Armonk**	22
Molto Wine	**Fairfield**	21
Morgans Fish	**Rye**	21
Z Napa & Co.	**Stamford**	24
NEW Oaxaca Kitchen	**New Haven**	-
Oliva Cafe	**New Preston**	24
116 Crown	**New Haven**	21
Osetra	**S Norwalk**	23

Vote at ZAGAT.com

Paci | **Southport**	26
Pastorale | **Lakeville**	23
Piccolo Arancio | **Farmington**	25
🆉 PolytechnicON20 | **Hartford**	28
Rebeccas | **Greenwich**	26
🆕 Red Lulu | **S Norwalk**	24
Red Plum | **Mamaro**	21
🆕 Rest. North | **Armonk**	26
Rizzuto's | **multi.**	20
Rouge Winebar | **S Norwalk**	21
RSVP | **W Cornwall**	28
Ruby's Oyster | **Rye**	23
Sally's Apizza | **New Haven**	25
Scoozzi Tratt. | **New Haven**	22
Solé Rist. | **New Canaan**	21
SolToro | **Uncasville**	20
Sonora | **Port Chester**	24
Splash | **Westport**	22
Still River | **Eastford**	28
Tapas/Ann | **W Hartford**	23
🆕 Tappo | **Stamford**	-
Tarry Lodge | **Port Chester**	24
🆉 Tengda | **multi.**	22
Thali | **New Haven**	24
🆉 Thomas Henkelmann | **Greenwich**	28
Tre Scalini | **New Haven**	24
Trumbull Kitchen | **Hartford**	22
🆉 Valencia Lunch. | **Norwalk**	27
V Rest. | **Westport**	18
Wasabi Chi | **S Norwalk**	23
Watermoon | **Rye**	23
West St. Grill | **Litchfield**	24
Zinc | **New Haven**	24
Zitoune | **Mamaro**	19

VALET PARKING

🆉 Arch | **Brewster**	27
Baang Cafe | **Riverside**	23
Bedford Post/Barn | **Bedford**	23
Bedford Post/Farm | **Bedford**	25
🆉 Bernard's | **Ridgefield**	27
BLT Steak | **White Pl**	23
Blue | **White Pl**	20
California Pizza | **Ledyard**	17

🆉 Capital Grille | **Stamford**	25
Carmen Anthony Steak | **New Haven**	22
Cedars | **Ledyard**	28
Christopher Martins | **New Haven**	20
Craftsteak | **Ledyard**	24
David Burke | **Ledyard**	26
Dish B&G | **Hartford**	20
Don Coqui | **New Roch**	23
🆕 Eclisse Med. | **White Pl**	21
Feng Asian | **multi.**	22
Firebox | **Hartford**	24
Fonda La Paloma | **Cos Cob**	19
42 | **White Pl**	22
🆕 Gabriele's | **Greenwich**	-
Gervasi's | **White Pl**	20
Hard Rock | **Ledyard**	15
Heirloom | **New Haven**	20
Il Castello | **Mamaro**	24
Il Sogno | **Port Chester**	24
Johnny Rockets | **Uncasville**	16
Kelly's Corner | **Brewster**	17
Kona Grill | **Stamford**	17
La Bocca | **White Pl**	23
🆉 La Crémaillère | **Bedford**	27
🆉 La Panetière | **Rye**	27
Le Château | **S Salem**	25
Legal Sea Foods | **White Pl**	19
L'Escale | **Greenwich**	23
🆉 Max Downtown | **Hartford**	27
🆉 Mayflower Inn | **Washington**	24
Milonga | **N White Plains**	22
Morton's | **multi.**	24
Mulino's | **White Pl**	24
Octagon | **Groton**	24
Pellicci's | **Stamford**	19
Peppercorn's Grill | **Hartford**	26
Polpo | **Greenwich**	24
Positano's | **Westport**	22
Posto 22 | **New Roch**	21
Primavera | **Crot Falls**	24
Reka's | **White Pl**	19
Rest./Rowayton Sea. | **Rowayton**	22

Rest./Water's Edge | **Westbrook** 23

Roger Sherman | **New Canaan** 24

Rye Grill | **Rye** 18

SolToro | **Uncasville** 20

Sonora | **Port Chester** 24

Stonehenge | **Ridgefield** 22

Tango Grill | **White Pl** 21

☑ Tengda | **Greenwich** 22

☑ Thomas Henkelmann | **Greenwich** 28

Todd English's | **Uncasville** 22

Tre Scalini | **New Haven** 24

Trumbull Kitchen | **Hartford** 22

☑ Valbella | **Riverside** 25

Vito's | **Hartford** 21

Waters Edge at Giovanni's | **Darien** 19

Winvian | **Morris** 27

Wood-n-Tap | **multi.** 17

VIEWS

Abbott's Lobster | **Noank** 23

Abruzzi Tratt. | **Patterson** 21

Apricots | **Farmington** 23

☑ Arch | **Brewster** 27

Back Porch | **Old Saybrook** 18

Beach House | **Milford** 22

Bill's Seafood | **Westbrook** 19

Bloodroot | **Bridgeport** 23

NEW Boathse./Saugatuck | **Westport** 25

Boom | **Westbrook** 22

Boulders Inn | **New Preston** 21

Brasserie Pip | **Ivoryton** -

Bull's Bridge | **Kent** 16

Café/Green | **Danbury** 22

Dock/Dine | **Old Saybrook** 14

Dolphins Cove | **Bridgeport** -

80 West | **White Pl** 19

Flood Tide | **Mystic** 21

42 | **White Pl** 22

Grist Mill | **Farmington** 23

G.W. Tavern | **Wash Depot** 20

Harbor Lights | **Norwalk** 20

Hopkins Inn | **New Preston** 19

Jasper White's | **Uncasville** 21

Jeffrey's | **Milford** 26

Le Château | **S Salem** 25

Lenny's Indian | **Branford** 21

Leon's | **New Haven** 18

L'Escale | **Greenwich** 23

Mamma Francesca | **New Roch** 19

☑ Mill/2T | **Tariffville** 28

Mill/River | **S Windsor** 20

Olive Tree | **Southbury** 21

Paradise B&G | **Stamford** 13

☑ PolytechnicON20 | **Hartford** 28

Positano's | **Westport** 22

Quattro Pazzi | **Norwalk** 23

Rani Mahal | **Mamaro** 23

Reka's | **White Pl** 19

Rest./Rowayton Sea. | **Rowayton** 22

☑ Rest./Water's Edge | **Westbrook** 23

River House | **Westport** 17

Sage | **New Haven** 19

Saltwater Grille | **Stamford** 17

Seaside Johnnie's | **Rye** 12

Sharpe Hill/Vineyard | **Pomfret** -

Sono Seaport | **S Norwalk** 15

Splash | **Westport** 22

Still River | **Eastford** 28

Stonehenge | **Ridgefield** 22

Stone House | **Guilford** 18

Terra Mar | **Old Saybrook** 23

☑ Thomas Henkelmann | **Greenwich** 28

Tratt. Vivolo | **Harrison** 25

Tre Scalini | **New Haven** 24

Trumbull Kitchen | **Hartford** 22

☑ Union League | **New Haven** 27

Vazzy's | **Fairfield** 20

Village | **Litchfield** 20

Vito's | **multi.** 21

Viva Zapata | **Westport** 17

Vox | **N Salem** 21

Wandering Moose | **W Cornwall** 16

White Horse | **New Preston** 19

Winvian	**Morris**	27
Woodland	**Lakeville**	22
Wood-n-Tap	**Farmington**	17
Zinc	**New Haven**	24

VISITORS ON EXPENSE ACCOUNT

Z Arch	**Brewster**	27
NEW Bar Bouchée	**Madison**	28
Basta	**New Haven**	25
Beach House	**Milford**	22
Bedford Post/Farm	**Bedford**	25
NEW Benjamin Steak	**White Pl**	24
Bentara	**New Haven**	24
Z Bernard's	**Ridgefield**	27
Bistro 22	**Bedford**	24
Blackstones	**Norwalk**	25
BLT Steak	**White Pl**	23
NEW Boathse./Saugatuck	**Westport**	25
Z Capital Grille	**Stamford**	25
Carmen Anthony Fish.	**multi.**	22
Carmen Anthony Steak	**Waterbury**	22
Craftsteak	**Ledyard**	24
David Burke	**Ledyard**	26
Z Dressing Room	**Westport**	24
Ferme	**Avon**	21
Ferrante	**Stamford**	20
42	**White Pl**	22
NEW Gabriele's	**Greenwich**	-
NEW Goose	**Darien**	-
Graziellas	**White Pl**	19
Z Ibiza	**Hamden**	27
Z Jean-Louis	**Greenwich**	28
Joseph's	**Bridgeport**	24
Z La Crémaillère	**Bedford**	27
Z La Panetière	**Rye**	27
La Tavola	**Waterbury**	26
Le Château	**S Salem**	25
Longwood	**Woodbury**	18
Luca Rist.	**Wilton**	26
Lusardi's	**Larch**	24
Market	**Stamford**	20
Max Burger	**W Hartford**	25

Z Max Downtown	**Hartford**	27
Max Fish	**Glastonbury**	23
Melting Pot	**Darien**	17
Michael Jordan's	**Uncasville**	23
NEW Moderne Barn	**Armonk**	22
Morton's	**multi.**	24
Mulino's	**White Pl**	24
Octagon	**Groton**	24
Pascal's	**Larch**	23
Z PolytechnicON20	**Hartford**	28
Rebeccas	**Greenwich**	26
Rest. L&E	**Chester**	24
Roger Sherman	**New Canaan**	24
Ruth's Chris	**Newington**	25
Still River	**Eastford**	28
Strada 18	**S Norwalk**	26
Tango Grill	**White Pl**	21
Z Tengda	**Darien**	22
Z Thomas Henkelmann	**Greenwich**	28
Z Valbella	**Riverside**	25
Willett House	**Port Chester**	24
Winvian	**Morris**	27
Z Woodward Hse.	**Bethlehem**	27

WINNING WINE LISTS

Alba's	**Port Chester**	23
Assaggio	**Branford**	24
Bacchus	**S Norwalk**	-
Ballou's	**Guilford**	18
NEW Bar Bouchée	**Madison**	28
Z Barcelona	**multi.**	24
Beach House	**Milford**	22
NEW Benjamin Steak	**White Pl**	24
Bentara	**New Haven**	24
Z Bernard's	**Ridgefield**	27
Bin 100	**Milford**	26
Bin 228	**Hartford**	22
Bistro 22	**Bedford**	24
BLT Steak	**White Pl**	23
Boulders Inn	**New Preston**	21
Cafe Lola	**Fairfield**	24
Café Manolo	**Westport**	23
Z Café Routier	**Westbrook**	27

☑ Capital Grille	**Stamford**	25
Carbone's	**Hartford**	24
Carmen Anthony Fish.	**multi.**	22
Carmen Anthony Steak	**multi.**	22
Cava Wine	**New Canaan**	22
Cavey's	**Manchester**	26
Central Steak	**New Haven**	24
Chez Jean-Pierre	**Stamford**	24
Craftsteak	**Ledyard**	24
DaPietro's	**Westport**	27
☑ Elm St. Oyster	**Greenwich**	24
Emilio Rist.	**Harrison**	25
Enzo's	**Mamaro**	20
Esca	**Middletown**	19
Fat Cat Pie	**Norwalk**	23
42	**White Pl**	22
Frankie/Johnnie's	**Rye**	24
NEW Gabriele's	**Greenwich**	–
Geronimo	**New Haven**	20
Gnarly Vine	**New Roch**	17
☑ Ibiza	**multi.**	27
☑ Jean-Louis	**Greenwich**	28
John's Café	**Woodbury**	23
La Bretagne	**Stamford**	24
☑ La Crémaillère	**Bedford**	27
☑ La Panetière	**Rye**	27
☑ Le Farm	**Westport**	27
Le Fontane	**Katonah**	22
☑ Le Petit Cafe	**Branford**	29
Litchfield/Grille	**Litchfield**	20
L'Orcio	**New Haven**	23
Luca Rist.	**Wilton**	26
Lusardi's	**Larch**	24
Max Burger	**W Hartford**	25
Max Fish	**Glastonbury**	23
Melting Pot	**Darien**	17
Michael Jordan's	**Uncasville**	23
Michael's	**Wallingford**	24
☑ Mill/2T	**Tariffville**	28
NEW Moderne Barn	**Armonk**	22
Morton's	**multi.**	24
☑ Napa & Co.	**Stamford**	24
Nessa	**Port Chester**	21
Octagon	**Groton**	24
Ondine	**Danbury**	26
O'Porto	**Hartford**	23
Peppercorn's Grill	**Hartford**	26
Piccolo Arancio	**Farmington**	25
Pizzeria Lauretano	**Bethel**	22
Plates	**Larch**	25
☑ PolytechnicON20	**Hartford**	28
Rebeccas	**Greenwich**	26
Rest. L&E	**Chester**	24
NEW Rest. North	**Armonk**	26
Rist. Luce	**Hamden**	22
River Tavern	**Chester**	26
Rouge Winebar	**S Norwalk**	21
Sal/Pepe	**Newtown**	24
Strada 18	**S Norwalk**	26
NEW Suburban	**Branford**	24
Taberna	**Bridgeport**	28
Tango Grill	**White Pl**	21
NEW Tappo	**Stamford**	–
Tarry Lodge	**Port Chester**	24
Telluride	**Stamford**	21
☑ Thomas Henkelmann	**Greenwich**	28
Tre Scalini	**New Haven**	24
☑ Valbella	**Riverside**	25
West St. Grill	**Litchfield**	24
Willett House	**Port Chester**	24
Winvian	**Morris**	27

THE BERKSHIRES RESTAURANT DIRECTORY

	FOOD	DECOR	SERVICE	COST

TOP FOOD

<u>27</u> Old Inn/Green | *American*
Blantyre | *American/French*

<u>25</u> Wheatleigh | *Amer./French*
Nudel | *American*
Tratt. Rustica* | *Italian*

TOP DECOR

<u>29</u> Blantyre | *American/French*
Wheatleigh | *American/French*

<u>26</u> Old Inn/Green | *American*

<u>25</u> Cranwell Resort | *American*

<u>24</u> Old Mill | *American*

Aegean Breeze *Greek*

| 19 | 16 | 19 | $39 |

Great Barrington | 327 Stockbridge Rd. (bet. Cooper & Crissey Rds.) |
413-528-4001 | www.aegean-breeze.com

It's "not quite Santorini", but this "comfortable" Great Barrington
Greek is "a reliable choice" for "tasty taverna food"; white stucco
decor with blue accents creates a "relaxing" backdrop for "friendly,
informal service", and while a few find the menu "pricey", "terrific"
daily specials offer "reasonable" value.

Allium *American*

| 18 | 19 | 17 | $46 |

Great Barrington | 42-44 Railroad St. (off Main St.) | 413-528-2118 |
www.alliumberkshires.com

Fans of this "upscale" Great Barrington sibling of Williamstown's
Mezze praise the "smashing", "ambitious" New American "comfort
food for locavores" and "hip" digs; the less enthused complain that
lately the "limited menu" "misses the mark", tabs are "a bit expensive" and service "varies from ok to clueless"; even so, it remains
a "happening place."

Alta *Mediterranean*

| 21 | 18 | 22 | $44 |

Lenox | 34 Church St. (bet. Housatonic & Walker Sts.) | 413-637-0003 |
www.altawinebar.com

"Locals and visitors alike" head to this "congenial" Lenox eatery and
wine bar for "delicious" Mediterranean fare and "top-notch" *vini* at
"upper-moderate" prices; service is "lovely", while the "porch on a
breezy summer night" suits "those of a certain age" who find the
"pretty" but "generally crowded" interior on the "noisy" side.

Aroma Bar & Grill *Indian*

| 22 | 13 | 19 | $27 |

Great Barrington | 485 Main St. (South St.) | 413-528-3116 |
www.aromabarandgrill.com

"What a surprise!" declare Great Barrington denizens of this "rare
find" "run by a lovely family", which prepares its "authentic" Indian
fare "as spicy as you like"; "well-chosen wines" and "affordable"
rates are pluses, and there's always takeout for those who don't care
for the "informal" setting.

Baba Louie's Sourdough Pizza *Pizza*

| 24 | 13 | 18 | $23 |

Great Barrington | 286 Main St. (bet. Elm & Railroad Sts.) | 413-528-8100
NEW **Pittsfield** | 34 Depot St. (McKay St.) | 413-499-2400
www.babalouiespizza.com

"Superb" pizza with "paper-thin" sourdough crusts and "creative,
sophisticated" toppings lead to "lines out the door" at this Great
Barrington spot where "scrumptious" salads, soups and sandwiches

---

* Indicates a tie with restaurant above

round out the "bargain" menu; staffers "aim to please", and although it's "cramped", there's much more "elbow room" at the "attractive" Pittsfield newcomer.

Barrington Brewery & Restaurant *American*

14 | 14 | 17 | $24

Great Barrington | 420 Stockbridge Rd./Rte. 7 N. (Crissey Rd.) | 413-528-8282 | www.barringtonbrewery.net

"It's all about the beer" at this "bustling" Great Barrington microbrewery, but there's "something for everyone" in the way of food too, namely "plentiful" portions of "homey" American eats with "no pretense"; "quick service", "modest" tabs and a "casual" if "chaotic" vibe in a "rustic, barnlike" setting make it "fun" for "families."

Bistro Zinc *French*

21 | 22 | 19 | $48

Lenox | 56 Church St. (bet. Housatonic & Tucker Sts.) | 413-637-8800 | www.bistrozinc.com

"Sophisticated" Gallic fare pairs with "polished" decor at this Lenox bistro where patrons can sit in the "sleek" dining room or "be part of the buzz" at the bar; although a few are annoyed by "Manhattan prices" and the "attitude problem" of many of "the people you're supposed to be tipping" (others are "friendly and accommodating"), it's nevertheless a "go-to" "for a special night out", so "reserve early."

Bizen *Japanese*

24 | 18 | 19 | $40

Great Barrington | 17 Railroad St. (Rte. 7) | 413-528-4343

"Sparklingly fresh, creative" sushi and a "huge menu" of "memorable" grilled fare "worth" the price keep this "popular" Great Barrington Japanese "always packed"; the "can-be-spotty" service is made up for by "engaging" chef Michael Marcus (BTW, that's his "wonderful pottery on view"), while those who consider the "noisy", "close quarters" "less than Zen" find "the tatami rooms a boon", especially when splurging on the prix fixe kaiseki.

⚊ Blantyre *American/French*

27 | 29 | 28 | $107

Lenox | Blantyre | 16 Blantyre Rd. (Rte. 20) | 413-637-3556 | www.blantyre.com

With a "romantic, intimate" setting that conjures "Gilded Age" "luxury" and staffers who give patrons the "royal treatment", this "outstanding" prix fixe–only French–New American dining room in a Lenox inn earns The Berkshires' No. 1 scores for Decor and Service; the fare "makes you swoon" as much as the "megabucks" needed to pay for it, yet "it's worth every penny" for an experience that's "special in every sense"; P.S. it's "formal", so jacket and tie required at dinner, and no children under 12.

Bombay ⓜ *Indian*

22 | 14 | 18 | $30

Lee | Quality Inn | 435 Laurel St./Rte. 20 (Lake Rd.) | 413-243-6731 | www.fineindiandining.com

Indian fare that's "sizzling with flavor" and "prepared to your liking" draws Lee curryphiles in to this "comfortable" spot where a lunch buffet that "can't be beat for value" is upstaged only by the "extraordinary" Sunday brunch; "service is willing", and if you "sit where you can view" Lake Laurel, it takes your mind off the "drab" decor

Brix Wine Bar ⓜ *French* | 23 | 20 | 22 | $42 |

Pittsfield | 40 West St. (bet. McKay & North Sts.) | 413-236-9463 | www.brixwinebar.com

"What's not to like?" asks the "younger crowd" who hie to this "hip" Pittsfield bistro for its "excellent" French bistro fare, "well-chosen wines", "reasonable prices" and "chic", "brick-lined" setting; "personable" service and an "*intime*" vibe help to make it "perfect for a date", as long as you don't mind a little "noise" (and a no-rez policy).

🆕 Brulées ⓜ *American/European* | ▽ 21 | 23 | 22 | $33 |

Pittsfield | 41 North St. (bet. East & School Sts.) | 413-443-0500 | www.brulees.com

"Everyone's excited" about this "promising" midpriced Pittsfield newcomer offering a "good variety" of "great" American-European eats, ranging from its signature pan-seared scallops to steaks, seafood and pastas, plus vittles for vegetarians and young 'uns; the roomy, "comfortably elegant" digs include a lounge, which hosts live music on weekends.

Cafe Adam ⓜ *European* | 23 | 17 | 20 | $43 |

Great Barrington | 325 Stockbridge Rd. (bet. Cooper & Crissey Rds.) | 413-528-7786 | www.cafeadam.org

"Skillful" chef-owner Adam Zieminski turns out a "small" but "fabulous" menu of "inspired" "European bistro cuisine" at this "comfortable" Great Barrington outpost; a "soothing" environment with a "nice porch" for when it's warm, "welcoming" staffers, "fair prices" and a "wonderful" "wine list that has real value" all factor into the "satisfying" experience.

Café Lucia 🛇ⓜ *Italian* | 23 | 20 | 22 | $51 |

Lenox | 80 Church St. (bet. Franklin & Housatonic Sts.) | 413-637-2640 | www.cafelucialenox.com

"Sophisticated", "wonderful" Italian cooking ("you'll swoon for the osso buco") plus a staff that "aims to please" make this Lenox venue in an "elegant" 1839 farmhouse an "'in' spot", despite somewhat "elevated tariffs"; surveyors seeking "lots of energy" choose to sit inside, while those who find it too "cramped" and "noisy" (especially when they "pack them in during Tanglewood") ask for the "lovely deck"; P.S. closed in winter.

Castle Street Cafe *American/French* | 20 | 18 | 20 | $41 |

Great Barrington | 10 Castle St. (Main St.) | 413-528-5244 | www.castlestreetcafe.com

"An old standby and deservedly so", this "reliable" Great Barrington American-French "charmer" draws "repeat customers" for "bargain" "quick bites" in the bar or "solid" bistro "standards" at more expensive tabs in the dining room; the service is "warm", the wine list is "moderately priced" and "great" live jazz on weekends gives the "homey" digs a "festive" feel, so no wonder it's "still going strong."

Chez Nous *French*

24 | 20 | 24 | $48

Lee | 150 Main St. (Academy St.) | 413-243-6397 | www.cheznousbistro.com

"Wonderful all around" declare Lee locals of this "delightful" destination where chef Franck Tessier's "fantastic" French bistro fare is matched by spouse Rachel Portnoy's "scrumptious desserts", not to mention her "charming" greetings; an "impressive", "well-priced wine list" adds to the "good value", while "marvelous service" "without hauteur" and a setting in a "historic house" with "quiet, romantic corners" add to the "appeal."

Church Street Cafe *American*

20 | 18 | 20 | $41

Lenox | 65 Church St. (bet. Franklin & Housatonic Sts.) | 413-637-2745 | www.churchstreetcafe.biz

This "casual" 30-year-old gets "mobbed in summer" not only for its convenient Lenox location (e.g. for "before-concert dining"), but because the New American fare is "reliably good"; a "most pleasant" staff plus three "nice", "simple" dining rooms add up to a "relaxing" mood, and even critics who complain it's "nothing to rave about" with tabs that are "a little pricey" admit that the "porch is special."

Coyote Flaco Ⓜ *Mexican*

23 | 18 | 22 | $34

Williamstown | 505 Cold Spring Rd. (Bee Hill Rd.) | 413-458-4240 | www.mycoyoteflaco.com

"Come hungry" for "real Mexican" "served with flair" advise amigos of this "family-owned" chainlet; even those who declare it "generally mediocre" find places in their hearts for "not-to-be-missed" margaritas and the occasional "mariachi serenade."

Cranwell Resort,
Spa & Golf Club *American*

21 | 25 | 22 | $51

Lenox | 55 Lee Rd./Rte. 20 (Rte. 7) | 413-637-1364 | www.cranwell.com

"Swellegant" sums up this "beautiful" Tudor-esque mansion resort in Lenox, where "people come from all over" for "well-prepared" New American fare served in an "unrushed" fashion in the "grand" Wyndhurst or Music Room restaurants; those who don't want to "go broke" "eat smart" at the more "moderate" Sloane's Tavern, dispensing "publike" provisions, while calorie counters hit the Spa Cafe.

Dakota Steakhouse *Steak*

17 | 17 | 18 | $36

Pittsfield | 1035 South St. (Dan Fox Dr.) | 413-499-7900 | www.steakseafood.com

"You get a lot for your money" at this Pittsfield steakhouse famed for its "pig-out Sunday buffet" brunch, "well-stocked salad bar" and "generous" if "pedestrian" "proteins, be they seafood or land-based"; the "Western motif" complete with "stuffed animals" may be "tired" and service can be "lackluster", but it nevertheless "hits the spot", especially for "families", as it's quite "child-friendly."

	FOOD	DECOR	SERVICE	COST

Dream Away Lodge 🅜⌖ *American* — 17 | 21 | 19 | $34

Becket | 1342 County Rd. (bet. Lenox-Whitney Place Rd. & McNerney Rd.) | 413-623-8725 | www.thedreamawaylodge.com
"A true original", this "oddball" New American "in the middle of no-where" in Becket puts the "kitsch in kitchen" with an affordable, "un-usual menu" running from burgers to tagines served by a "pleasant" crew; even those who consider the eats "average" admit the "hoote-nanny atmosphere" (a 19th century farm–cum–"old cathouse"–cum-speakeasy) "makes up for it", as does the nightly live music.

Elizabeth's 🅈🅜⌖ *Eclectic* — 24 | 13 | 23 | $35

Pittsfield | 1264 East St. (Newell St.) | 413-448-8244
"Utterly delicious" pastas, "legendary salads" and one "tantalizing" fish and meat dish per night comprise the roster at this "off-the-beaten-track" Pittsfield Eclectic "institution" with a "devoted fan base"; a "dinerlike" setting prompts the question "what decor?", but tabs are "a true bargain" and chef-owner Tom Ellis is a "trip" who'll accept "an IOU" if you haven't got "good old cash or a check."

Fin *Japanese* — 23 | 19 | 19 | $44

Lenox | 27 Housatonic St. (Church St.) | 413-637-9171 | www.finsushi.com
Even though it's "far from the ocean", this "easygoing" Lenox Japanese stocks sushi "so fresh it wiggles", along with some "cre-ative specials" among the cooked fare; such "big quality" helps off-set the "small", "noisy" digs dominated by a red lacquered bar, while takeout's an option when it's "hard to get into."

Firefly *American* — 17 | 17 | 17 | $38

Lenox | 71 Church St. (Housatonic St.) | 413-637-2700 | www.fireflylenox.com
"Berkshires casual" is the style of this Lenox New American where "lo-cals meet" in the "cozy" dining rooms or on the "pleasant" porch when it's warm; some say the midpriced fare is "imaginative" and "well pre-pared" while others claim it's "mediocre" – but there's consensus on the "erratic service" and the appeal of the "late-night bar."

Flavours of Malaysia 🅜 *Asian* — 21 | 12 | 20 | $29

Pittsfield | 75 North St. (McKay St.) | 413-443-3188 | www.flavoursintheberkshires.com
An "elaborate" assortment of dishes from China, Malaysia, India and Thailand come "cooked to order" and as "spicy" as you like at this "wonderful" Pittsfield Asian; though "remodeling" wouldn't hurt and the live bands on weekends "change the atmosphere", the "accommodating" staff and "outstanding value" help make it "de-serving of the crowds it attracts."

Frankie's Ristorante Italiano *Italian* — 18 | 18 | 20 | $41

Lenox | 80 Main St. (Cliftwood St.) | 413-637-4455 | www.frankiesitaliano.com
"Enjoyable" "red-sauce preparations" "entice" "families" to this "welcoming" Lenox Italian where a "young", "on-the-ball" staff serves in dining rooms warmed up with "old photos on the walls";

true, it's "not high end", but it's "not stuffy" either, just a "good spot" for those "on a budget"; P.S. the "porch in summer is a plus."

Gramercy Bistro *American/Eclectic*   23 | 21 | 22 | $43

North Adams | MASS MoCA | 87 Marshall St. (bet. River St. & Rte. 2) | 413-663-5300 | www.gramercybistro.com

After a move across the street to Mass MoCa, this "standout" chef-owned North Adams bistro now feeds "famished" museumgoers its "diverse menu" of "stellar" seasonal American-Eclectic fare; "reasonable pricing", an "attentive" crew, "comfortable" modern surroundings and a summertime patio all add to the "pleasure."

Gypsy Joynt Ⓜ *American*   ∇ 16 | 13 | 16 | $17

Great Barrington | 389 Stockbridge Rd. (Crissey Rd.) | 413-644-8811 | www.yallsjoynt.com

Great Barrington "locals love" to "hang out and relax" at this "deli-style" American where the affordable salads, sandwiches, pizzas and pastas are made with organic produce; some say the eats are "just ok", but the "friendly service", "delightfully random decor" and "great music" on weekends add up to a "funky good time."

Haven *American/Bakery*   23 | 15 | 16 | $21

Lenox | 8 Franklin St. (Main St.) | 413-637-8948 | www.havencafebakery.com

The "elite meet to eat" "wonderful", "high-end" breakfasts" and "flavorful, hearty" lunches (plus "indulgent" "homestyle" dinners in season) at this "low-key" American cafe and bakery in "trendy" Downtown Lenox; "gourmet coffees, teas" and "cocktails based on Berkshire mountains spirits" are also available in the "spacious, unassuming" room – and "oh yeah, they have wireless" too.

Hub, The Ⓢ *American*   ∇ 23 | 21 | 22 | $36

North Adams | 55 Main St. (State St.) | 413-662-2500 | www.thehubrestaurant.com

Often "packed", this North Adams American "upscale diner" "lives up to its name" as a "hangout" that's "tough to beat" for "comfort food"; "professional" servers patrol the storefront setting where the eats are "priced right" and the house wines are a similarly "good value."

Isabella's Ⓜ *Italian*   – | – | – | M

North Adams | 896 State Rd. (bet. Georgia & Hawthorne Aves.) | 413-662-2239 | www.isabellasrest.com

"Good food and good service at a fair price" sums up this casual North Adams Italian turning out "reliable" regional standards that make it a "favorite place to bring the family"; soft colors create a "pleasant" mood in the 19th-century farmhouse where every table overlooks the garden, while the porch offers "nice" seating in summer.

Jae's Spice *American/Asian*   22 | 23 | 20 | $40

Pittsfield | 297 North St. (bet. Summer & Union Sts.) | 413-443-1234 | www.eatatjaes.com

Don't worry if the "adventurous menu" of midpriced "designer" Pan-Asian fare at Jae Chung's "beautiful" Pittsfield "gem" "seems daunting", because "you can't go wrong" – there are even "tasty" "American choices" "for the non-chopstick crowd"; although it's "warehouse-sized", the "richly renovated" space has a "warm atmosphere", with the "bonus" of being "close to the Barrington Stage" theater and a "nice staff" to ensure you "make the curtain."

John Andrews *American*   24 | 22 | 23 | $54
South Egremont | Rte. 23 (Blunt Rd.) | 413-528-3469 | www.jarestaurant.com

A "nicely dressed, soft-spoken clientele" gathers at this "fine-dining rendezvous" "in the woods" of South Egremont to "sit back and en-joy" "superior" New American cooking served by an "informed, friendly" staff in "delightful", "romantic" surroundings; naturally, such a "celebratory" experience commands an "expensive" tab, al-though the budget-conscious claim "even the bar menu is a class act", and "more reasonable" to boot.

John Harvard's Brew House *Pub Food*   16 | 17 | 17 | $25
Hancock | Country Inn at Jiminy Peak | 37 Corey Rd., 3rd fl. (Brodie Mountain Rd.) | 413-738-5500 | www.johnharvards.com

"Terrific beer" is all you need to know about this "casual" Manchester outpost of the national brewpub chain dispensing a "wide selection" of "craft-brewed" suds to wash down "ok" American "comfort food"; though it can "feel like a frat house" ("ex-pect a drinking crowd"), it's perfectly "adequate" as an "after-work hangout" with "reasonable prices."

Jonathan's Bistro *American*   20 | 17 | 19 | $37
Lenox | Lenox Commons | 55 Pittsfield Rd. (bet. Dugway Rd. & Main St.) | 413-637-8022

"A pleasant surprise hidden in a shopping center", this "casual" Lenox New American turns out "something for all appetites", rang-ing from "tasty sandwiches" to "original" entrees; although a few find the fare "uneven", most say it's "on the mark" and laud the "lovely wine list", "good prices", "comfortable" digs and patio for summer dining.

La Terrazza *American/Italian*   ▽ 23 | 24 | 20 | $55
Lenox | Gateways Inn | 51 Walker St. (bet. Church & Kemble Sts.) | 413-637-2532 | www.gatewaysinn.com

You "walk into what looks like someone's house" at this Italian-American eatery in Lenox's "lovely" Gateways Inn (it was the Procter mansion, back in the day); terra-cotta walls and soft music in the dining room create an "elegant" backdrop for somewhat pricey but "outstanding homemade pastas" and such, while the "excellent wine and spirits" include an extravagant selection of single-malt scotch.

Marketplace Kitchen *American/Sandwiches*   - | - | - | I
Sheffield | 18 Elm Ct. (Main St.) | 413-248-5040 | www.marketplacekitchen.com

"Breakfast wraps that will fortify you until dusk", plus "terrific soups", "amazing burgers" and flatbread pizzas are among the

	FOOD	DECOR	SERVICE	COST

American eats on offer at this Sheffield spin-off of Marketplace, the specialty foods shop nearby; the "diner"-style digs are cheery and the rates "inexpensive", especially on Tuesday nights when "home-cooked meals" that feed a family of four cost only $20.

Mezze Bistro + Bar *American*

| 22 | 22 | 22 | $51 |

Williamstown | 777 Cold Spring Rd./Rte. 7 (Taconic Trail) | 413-458-0123 | www.mezzebistro.com

Now ensconced in an "inviting", "airy" 19th-century farmhouse (reflecting its farm-to-table philosophy), this "exciting" Williamstown New American still dispenses "sophisticated" dishes via staffers who "know the right pace"; even those who say it "lost its amiability" after the move, and complain of "inflated" prices and quality that's "slipped a bit", agree it's "the place to impress your out-of-town friends."

Mill on the Floss Ⓜ *French*

| 23 | 23 | 24 | $51 |

New Ashford | 342 Rte. 7 (Rte. 43) | 413-458-9123 | www.millonthefloss.com

It's "a little old-fashioned" and "that's a good thing" declare the "discerning clientele" of this "long-established" New Ashford French "classic" where "everything is superb", from the "quality" "country fare" and "personal" service to the "glorious" 18th-century farmhouse setting; sure, it's "special" (read: pricey), but there's a nightly three-course prix fixe that's "the bargain of the century."

Mission Bar & Tapas ◑ *Spanish*

| 23 | 19 | 22 | $30 |

Pittsfield | 438 North St. (Maplewood Ave.) | www.missionbarandtapas.com

A "slice of SoHo in Downtown Pittsfield", this "trendy" Spanish "hangout" has "mastered" a menu of "tasty" tapas to match its "wonderful" Iberian wines – and for pretty "low prices" too; a staff that "aims to please" works the "funky", low-lit room where musicians and a "kitchen open until midnight" mean it stays "lively" until "late."

Morgan House *New England*

| 15 | 16 | 17 | $39 |

Lee | Morgan House | 33 Main St. (Mass. Tpke., exit 2) | 413-243-3661 | www.morganhouseinn.com

"Comforting in an old country inn kind of way", this "friendly" spot in Lee has "been around for years", dishing up moderately priced, "traditional" New England fare in an early-19th-century onetime stagecoach stop; some complain the eats are "ordinary" and the vibe "touristy", but the "good bar crowd" might disagree.

Napa *Eclectic*

| 18 | 19 | 17 | $41 |

Great Barrington | 293 Main St. (Church St.) | 413-528-4311 | www.napagb.com

Smack "in the middle of everything" in Great Barrington, this "cool" Eclectic cafe and vino bar delivers a "well-priced" menu of "good, basic" fare, plus "wines from every region" to go with; the "pretty" digs exude a "New York feeling", abetted by sometimes "surly service" but enhanced by "great jazz on Friday nights."

⚡ Nudel Ⓜ *American*
| 25 | 15 | 21 | $41 |

Lenox | 37 Church St. (bet. Housatonic & Walker Sts.) | 413-551-7183 | www.nudelrestaurant.com

"Wow", "this man can cook!" exclaim those taking a "culinary romp" at chef Bjorn Somlo's "vibrant" New American enlivening "sleepy" Lenox with an "excellent", "ever-changing", midpriced menu of "ingenious cuisine", which highlights pastas (aka nudels) and "whatever's fresh" that day; the "no-reservations scenario" makes it "tough to get into" the "cubbyhole" of a space, so "show up early" or expect "a big wait."

⚡ Old Inn on the Green *American*
| 27 | 26 | 26 | $63 |

New Marlborough | Old Inn on the Green | 134 Hartsville-New Marlborough Rd./Rte. 57 (Rte. 272) | 413-229-7924 | www.oldinn.com

"You need a compass to find" this "idyllic" New Marlborough "treasure" set in a "romantic" 1760s inn, but once there you'll be "blown away" by chef-owner Peter Platt's "prodigious menu" of "fabulous" New American cuisine, voted No. 1 for Food in The Berkshires; a "superb wine list", "professional staff" and "lovely" rooms "lit only by candles and fireplaces" are part of the package, and while it'll "empty your pocketbook", "it's worth it" for such a "magical experience"; P.S. the $30 prix fixe offered on some nights is a "fantastic" "steal."

Old Mill *American*
| 24 | 24 | 25 | $47 |

South Egremont | 53 Main St. (Rte. 41) | 413-528-1421 | www.oldmillberkshires.com

It's "pure country charm" at this "quaint" South Egremont veteran turning out "first-rate" American fare via the "best-trained staff" in a "pretty" 1797 old mill with "crooked floors" and "a gorgeous fireplace"; one "drawback" is no reservations for fewer than five, but there's a "cozy bar to warm your cockles while you wait", or you can eat there from a lighter menu – it's "easier on the budget" and you "get the best of both worlds."

Once Upon a Table *American/Continental*
| 21 | 15 | 19 | $38 |

Stockbridge | The Mews | 36 Main St. (bet. Elm St. & Rte. 7) | 413-298-3870 | www.onceuponatablebistro.com

"Blessed with a loyal following", this "delightful" Stockbridge American-Continental "hidden away" in a mews beside the Red Lion Inn dispenses "well-prepared" dishes deemed "worth the squeeze" in the "intimate" (make that "*very* small") setting; "quick service" means it's "good for lunch", while you "can take your time" at dinner, "if you can get in."

Perigee *Eclectic/New England*
| 19 | 18 | 20 | $46 |

Lee | 1575 Pleasant St. (bet. Church & Willow Sts.) | 413-394-4047 | www.perigee-restaurant.com

This "casual", "off-the-beaten-path" Lee sophomore offers Eclectic–New England fare (trademarked as Berkshire cuisine) that some say is "consistently good" and others find sometimes "too elaborate", with tabs a tad "high for the area"; still, given the "appealing" two-story setting and a "wonderful owner" heading up an "accommodating" staff, they probably just need time to "work out the kinks."

Pho Saigon *Vietnamese*

22 | 12 | 18 | $22

Lee | 5 Railroad St. (Main St.) | 413-243-6288

"Who'd have thought you'd find authentic Vietnamese in Lee?" ask astonished newcomers to this "tiny place" run by a "friendly, talkative owner" turning out "homestyle" pho and other dishes, plus "excellent pad Thai" to boot; yes, it's "low on decor, but high on taste and value", and it "hits the spot" after a "night of partying."

Prime Italian
Steakhouse & Bar ● *Italian/Steak*

▽ 21 | 22 | 22 | $48

Lenox | 15 Franklin St. (Rte. 7) | 413-637-2998 | www.primelenox.com

"A good bet" for "red meat and red wine" plus "old favorite dishes" like chef-owner Gennaro Gallo's homemade gnocchi, this Lenox Southern Italian steakhouse beloved of the "business" set makes everyone "feel welcome"; yes, it's "pricey", but unsurprisingly so given the upscale touches that abound in both the fare and the "hip decor" with a backlit bar.

Red Lion Inn *New England*

18 | 22 | 21 | $46

Stockbridge | Red Lion Inn | 30 Main St./Rte. 102 (bet. Main & Water Sts.) | 413-298-5545 | www.redlioninn.com

Stockbridge's "grande dame", this 1773 inn simply "screams Norman Rockwell" while dispensing "safe" New England "classics" in the "fine, old", "formal" dining room, "rustic" Widow Bingham's Tavern or "casual" Lion's Den pub, where tariffs are "lower"; "service is top-notch", and even though grumps grumble it's "only for tourists", it's practically "mandatory" to "go once."

Rouge Ⓜ *French*

22 | 18 | 17 | $49

West Stockbridge | 3 Center St. (Rte. 41) | 413-232-4111 | www.rougerestaurant.com

Chef William Merelle's "mouthwatering" French cuisine coupled with spouse Maggie's "warm hospitality" make this West Stockbridge bistro a "popular" "go-to" for the "elite and hoi polloi" alike; a recent expansion doubled the rouge-accented space, although it still gets "jammed" in the "lively" bar where the less "expensive", "interesting tapas menu" is "a treat", leaving only "loud" decibels and sometimes "lackadaisical service" as issues.

Route 7 Grill *BBQ*

18 | 13 | 19 | $36

Great Barrington | 999 S. Main St. (bet. Brookside & Lime Kiln Rds.) | 413-528-3235 | www.route7grill.com

"Awfully good babyback ribs" are among the "well-priced", "finger-licking" fare at this "unpretentious" Great Barrington BBQ specialist focusing on "locally raised meats and produce"; "Texans" and others less enthused declare it "just ok" and the "cost not merited", but

	FOOD	DECOR	SERVICE	COST

most enjoy the "nice buzz" in the "plain", "family-friendly" space, made cheery by its "raging fire" and "horseshoe bar."

Shiro Sushi & Hibachi *Japanese*   20 | 16 | 18 | $34

Great Barrington | 105 Stockbridge Rd. (bet. Blue Hill Rd. & Brooke Ln.) | 413-528-1898

Shiro Lounge *Japanese*

Pittsfield | 48 North St. (School St.) | 413-236-8111
www.berkshiro.com

Sushi is "difficult to find in the Berkshires", but "the art is alive" at this Japanese duo purveying "first-class", "artistic" fare; true, the digs have all "the ambiance of a tire shop", but the staff is "pleasant" and the prices moderate, plus the "hilarious" hibachi chefs grilling "bountiful" meals at the Great Barrington original "make it fun for the whole family."

Siam Square Thai Cuisine *Thai*   19 | 16 | 20 | $25

Great Barrington | 290 Main St. (Railroad St.) | 413-644-9119 | www.siamsquares.com

"The only game in town" for Thai, this "casual", somewhat "quiet" Great Barrington spot draws many "regulars" with its "wide array" of "terrific" fare featuring the occasional "kick"; it's "a good value" and the dishes come "served quickly and with a smile", making it "one of the best pre-movie" options around.

Stagecoach Tavern Ⓜ *American*   ▽ 17 | 23 | 20 | $40

Sheffield | Race Brook Lodge | S. Undermountain Rd./Rte. 41 (Berkshire School Rd.) | 413-229-8585 | www.stagecoachtavern.net

It's so "atmospheric", "you can imagine tying your horse outside" this "inviting" 1829 tavern in Sheffield, where a seasonal menu of "dependable" American fare comes served in "cozy", "candlelit" rooms with fireplaces, making it "perfect on a snowy night"; the "sweet" staff adds to the "convivial" vibe, while moderate tabs are another reason it's "worth going."

Sullivan Station Restaurant Ⓜ *New England*   15 | 18 | 20 | $30

Lee | 109 Railroad St. (Mass. Tpke., exit 2) | 413-243-2082 | www.sullivanstationrestaurant.com

"A Lee standby", this restored "historic" onetime train depot is all "old-fashioned charm", from its "large portions" of affordable, "plain" New England eats to its "homey" digs with "decor featuring locomotive pictures and railroad nostalgia"; "lunch is always good" and just the ticket if you're with kids, especially when the Berkshire Scenic Railway toots by.

Sushi Thai Garden *Japanese/Thai*   ▽ 20 | 15 | 21 | $30

Williamstown | 27 Spring St. (Rte. 2) | 413-458-0004 | www.sushithaigarden.com

The "Thai food is hearty and hot" and the sushi "surprisingly good" at this "dependable" Williamstown spot; although the "tables are close together", the decor in the "casual" brick storefront setting is "fine", while "bargain" rates, "attentive service" and overall menu "variety" make it a "good place to go with a group of friends."

Taylor's 🏷 *American*
— | — | — | M

North Adams | 34 Holden St. (Center St.) | 413-664-4500 | www.taylorsfinedining.net

White tablecloth restaurants are rare in North Adams, so this American near Mass MoCa serves as a "good place" for locals in search of reasonably priced steaks, seafood and pastas, as well as affordable comfort fare – and there's even sushi Thursdays–Saturdays; "inviting" brick-walled rooms and a staff that "works hard" are added attractions.

Trattoria Il Vesuvio *Italian*
19 | 17 | 20 | $41

Lenox | 242 Pittsfield Rd. (bet. Lime Kiln & New Lenox Rds.) | 413-637-4904 | www.trattoria-vesuvio.com

Fans of this "reliable" Lenox Italian claim the menu of "traditional" red sauce may "not change much", but it's as "comforting as a warm blanket on a cold day", plus the "homemade bread is great"; the converted hundred-year-old stable is "cavernous" but cozy, thanks to the wood-fired brick oven and "family-owned" feeling.

Trattoria Rustica *Italian*
25 | 21 | 21 | $48

Pittsfield | 27 McKay St. (West St.) | 413-499-1192 | www.trattoria-rustica.com

This "charming" Southern Italian is "worth a detour" to Pittsfield declare devotees of chef-owner Davide Manzo's "delicious", "sophisticated" cooking; the lantern-lit, brick-and-stone setting creates a "romantic" vibe in winter, while courtyard dining is "wonderful" when it's warm, so even though it's a little "expensive", it's a "special place."

Truc Orient Express *Vietnamese*
22 | 19 | 20 | $32

West Stockbridge | 3 Harris St. (Main St.) | 413-232-4204

"A Berkshires legend", this "amazing", over-30-year-old West Stockbridge Vietnamese offers its "splendid", "artfully presented" fare for "great prices"; the owners provide a "quiet", "welcoming" mood in "easygoing" digs, which are adorned with art from their homeland and augmented with an "extraordinary" attached gift shop.

Viva 🅜 *Spanish*
23 | 19 | 21 | $38

Glendale | 14 Glendale Rd. (Rte. 102) | 413-298-4433 | www.vivaberkshires.com

"Excellent paella" and "wonderful tapas" are representative of the "confident Spanish cooking" that draws Glendale denizens to this "out-of-the-way" spot near the Norman Rockwell museum; an "unobtrusive" staff serves in the "spacious", colorful room where a Picasso-like mural adds to the "fun" environment.

🏷 Wheatleigh *American/French*
25 | 29 | 27 | $93

Lenox | Wheatleigh | 11 Hawthorne Rd. (Hawthorne St.) | 413-637-0610 | www.wheatleigh.com

"Gatsby would have been proud" of Lenox's "magnificent" Italianate mansion, where it's "class all the way", from rooms exuding "elegance by the cartload" to the "fabulous" New American–French fare and "pampering" staff; a few fret about "prohibitive" tabs, but most suggest you "take out a second mortgage" and "splurge", because "life doesn't get much better than this"; P.S. jackets suggested.

Xicohtencatl *Mexican*   21 | 19 | 20 | $33

Great Barrington | 50 Stockbridge Rd. (Rte. 7) | 413-528-2002 |
www.xicohmexican.com

"No average Mexican", this Great Barrington spot dispenses "inspired", "flavorful" eats via a "crowd-pleasing staff" "who can discuss the subtleties"; "lively decor", a "huge margarita list" and "moderate prices" add to the "fun", while the patio is "mellow."

THE BERKSHIRES
INDEXES

Cuisines

Includes names, locations and Food ratings.

AMERICAN

Allium | **Great Barr**	18
Barrington Brew | **Great Barr**	14
Ⓩ Blantyre | **Lenox**	27
NEW Brulées | **Pittsfield**	21
Castle St. | **Great Barr**	20
Church St. Cafe | **Lenox**	20
Cranwell Resort | **Lenox**	21
Dream Away | **Becket**	17
Firefly | **Lenox**	17
Gramercy | **N Adams**	23
Gypsy Joynt | **Great Barr**	16
Haven | **Lenox**	23
Hub | **N Adams**	23
Jae's Spice | **Pittsfield**	22
John Andrews | **S Egremont**	24
Jonathan's | **Lenox**	20
La Terrazza | **Lenox**	23
Marketplace | **Sheffield**	-
Mezze Bistro | **Williamstown**	22
Ⓩ Nudel | **Lenox**	25
Ⓩ Old Inn/Green | **New Marl**	27
Old Mill | **S Egremont**	24
Once Upon | **Stockbridge**	21
Stagecoach Tav. | **Sheffield**	17
Taylor's | **N Adams**	-
Ⓩ Wheatleigh | **Lenox**	25

ASIAN

Flavours/Malaysia | **Pittsfield**	21
Jae's Spice | **Pittsfield**	22

BAKERIES

Haven | **Lenox**	23

BARBECUE

Rte. 7 Grill | **Great Barr**	18

CONTINENTAL

Once Upon | **Stockbridge**	21

ECLECTIC

Elizabeth's | **Pittsfield**	24
Gramercy | **N Adams**	23
Napa | **Great Barr**	18
Perigee | **Lee**	19

EUROPEAN

NEW Brulées | **Pittsfield**	21
Cafe Adam | **Great Barr**	23

FRENCH

Ⓩ Blantyre | **Lenox**	27
Mill/Floss | **New Ashford**	23
Ⓩ Wheatleigh | **Lenox**	25

FRENCH (BISTRO)

Bistro Zinc | **Lenox**	21
Brix Wine | **Pittsfield**	23
Castle St. | **Great Barr**	20
Chez Nous | **Lee**	24
Rouge | **W Stockbridge**	22

GREEK

Aegean Breeze | **Great Barr**	19

INDIAN

Aroma B&G | **Great Barr**	22
Bombay | **Lee**	22

ITALIAN

(N=Northern; S=Southern)

Café Lucia | **Lenox**	23
Frankie's Rist. | **Lenox**	18
Isabella's | **N Adams**	-
La Terrazza | **Lenox**	23
Prime Italian | S | **Lenox**	21
Tratt. Il Vesuvio | **Lenox**	19
Tratt. Rustica | S | **Pittsfield**	25

JAPANESE

(* sushi specialist)

Bizen* | **Great Barr**	24
Fin* | **Lenox**	23
Shiro* | **multi.**	20
Sushi Thai Gdn.* | **Williamstown**	20

MEDITERRANEAN

Alta | **Lenox**   21

MEXICAN

Coyote Flaco | **Williamstown**   23

Xicohtencatl | **Great Barr**   21

NEW ENGLAND

Morgan Hse. | **Lee**   15

Perigee | **Lee**   19

Red Lion Inn | **Stockbridge**   18

Sullivan Station | **Lee**   15

PIZZA

Baba Louie's | **multi.**   24

PUB FOOD

John Harvard's | **Hancock**   16

SANDWICHES

Marketplace | **Sheffield**   –

SPANISH

(* tapas specialist)

Mission Bar* | **Pittsfield**   23

Viva* | **Glendale**   23

STEAKHOUSES

Dakota Steak | **Pittsfield**   17

Prime Italian | **Lenox**   21

THAI

Siam Sq. Thai | **Great Barr**   19

Sushi Thai Gdn. | **Williamstown**   20

VIETNAMESE

Pho Saigon | **Lee**   22

Truc Orient | **W Stockbridge**   22

Locations

Includes names, cuisines and Food ratings.

BECKET

Dream Away | *Amer.*   17

GLENDALE

Viva | *Spanish*   23

GREAT BARRINGTON

Aegean Breeze | *Greek*   19
Allium | *Amer.*   18
Aroma B&G | *Indian*   22
Baba Louie's | *Pizza*   24
Barrington Brew | *Amer.*   14
Bizen | *Japanese*   24
Cafe Adam | *Euro.*   23
Castle St. | *Amer./French*   20
Gypsy Joynt | *Amer.*   16
Napa | *Eclectic*   18
Rte. 7 Grill | *BBQ*   18
Shiro | *Japanese*   20
Siam Sq. Thai | *Thai*   19
Xicohtencatl | *Mex.*   21

HANCOCK

John Harvard's | *Pub*   16

LEE

Bombay | *Indian*   22
Chez Nous | *French*   24
Morgan Hse. | *New Eng.*   15
Perigee | *Eclectic/New Eng.*   19
Pho Saigon | *Viet.*   22
Sullivan Station | *New Eng.*   15

LENOX

Alta | *Med.*   21
Bistro Zinc | *French*   21
� Blantyre | *Amer./French*   27
Café Lucia | *Italian*   23
Church St. Cafe | *Amer.*   20
Cranwell Resort | *Amer.*   21
Fin | *Japanese*   23

(column 2)

Firefly | *Amer.*   17
Frankie's Rist. | *Italian*   18
Haven | *Amer./Bakery*   23
Jonathan's | *Amer.*   20
La Terrazza | *Amer./Italian*   23
🅩 Nudel | *Amer.*   25
Prime Italian | *Italian/Steak*   21
Tratt. Il Vesuvio | *Italian*   19
🅩 Wheatleigh | *Amer./French*   25

NEW ASHFORD

Mill/Floss | *French*   23

NEW MARLBOROUGH

🅩 Old Inn/Green | *Amer.*   27

NORTH ADAMS

Gramercy | *Amer./Eclectic*   23
Hub | *Amer.*   23
Isabella's | *Italian*   -
Taylor's | *Amer.*   -

PITTSFIELD

Baba Louie's | *Pizza*   24
Brix Wine | *French*   23
🆕 Brulées | *Amer./Euro.*   21
Dakota Steak | *Steak*   17
Elizabeth's | *Eclectic*   24
Flavours/Malaysia | *Asian*   21
Jae's Spice | *Amer./Asian*   22
Mission Bar | *Spanish*   23
Shiro | *Japanese*   20
Tratt. Rustica | *Italian*   25

SHEFFIELD

Marketplace | *Amer./Sandwiches*   -
Stagecoach Tav. | *Amer.*   17

SOUTH EGREMONT

John Andrews | *Amer.*   24
Old Mill | *Amer.*   24

STOCKBRIDGE

Once Upon | *Amer./Continental*   21
Red Lion Inn | *New Eng.*   18

WEST STOCKBRIDGE

Rouge | *French*   22
Truc Orient | *Viet.*   22

WILLIAMSTOWN

Coyote Flaco | *Mex.*   23
Mezze Bistro | *Amer.*   22
Sushi Thai Gdn. | *Japanese/Thai*   20

Special Features

Listings cover the best in each category and include names, locations and Food ratings. Multi-location restaurants' features may vary by branch.

BRUNCH

Bombay	Lee	22
Cafe Adam	**Great Barr**	23
Dakota Steak	**Pittsfield**	17
☑ Wheatleigh	**Lenox**	25
Xicohtencatl	**Great Barr**	21

BUSINESS DINING

Allium	**Great Barr**	18
Cranwell Resort	**Lenox**	21
Jae's Spice	**Pittsfield**	22
La Terrazza	**Lenox**	23
Napa	**Great Barr**	18
Taylor's	**N Adams**	-

CATERING

Bizen	**Great Barr**	24
Bombay	Lee	22
Castle St.	**Great Barr**	20
John Andrews	**S Egremont**	24
Mezze Bistro	**Williamstown**	22

CHILD-FRIENDLY

(Alternatives to the usual fast-food places; * children's menu available)

Aegean Breeze	**Great Barr**	19
Baba Louie's	**Great Barr**	24
Barrington Brew*	**Great Barr**	14
Bistro Zinc*	**Lenox**	21
Café Lucia	**Lenox**	23
Castle St.	**Great Barr**	20
Church St. Cafe*	**Lenox**	20
Coyote Flaco*	**Williamstown**	23
Dakota Steak*	**Pittsfield**	17
Elizabeth's	**Pittsfield**	24
Marketplace	**Sheffield**	-
Morgan Hse.	**Lee**	15
Old Mill	**S Egremont**	24
Once Upon	**Stockbridge**	21
Red Lion Inn*	**Stockbridge**	18
Rouge	**W Stockbridge**	22

Rte. 7 Grill*	**Great Barr**	18
Shiro	**Great Barr**	20
Siam Sq. Thai	**Great Barr**	19
Sullivan Station*	**Lee**	15
Sushi Thai Gdn.	**Williamstown**	20
Tratt. Il Vesuvio*	**Lenox**	19
Xicohtencatl*	**Great Barr**	21

DINING ALONE

(Other than hotels and places with counter service)

Alta	**Lenox**	21
Baba Louie's	**multi.**	24
Cafe Adam	**Great Barr**	23
Castle St.	**Great Barr**	20
Coyote Flaco	**Williamstown**	23
Fin	**Lenox**	23
Gypsy Joynt	**Great Barr**	16
Marketplace	**Sheffield**	-
Mission Bar	**Pittsfield**	23
Napa	**Great Barr**	18
Once Upon	**Stockbridge**	21
Pho Saigon	**Lee**	22
Rte. 7 Grill	**Great Barr**	18
Sullivan Station	**Lee**	15

ENTERTAINMENT

(Call for days and times of performances)

☑ Blantyre	piano	**Lenox**	27
Castle St.	jazz/piano	**Great Barr**	20
Dream Away	live music	**Becket**	17
Mission Bar	folk/indie rock	**Pittsfield**	23
Napa	jazz	**Great Barr**	18
Red Lion Inn	varies	**Stockbridge**	18

FIREPLACES

Aegean Breeze	**Great Barr**	19
Barrington Brew	**Great Barr**	14

☑ Blantyre | **Lenox**	27
Cranwell Resort | **Lenox**	21
Dakota Steak | **Pittsfield**	17
Dream Away | **Becket**	17
John Andrews | **S Egremont**	24
La Terrazza | **Lenox**	23
Mezze Bistro | **Williamstown**	22
Mill/Floss | **New Ashford**	23
Morgan Hse. | **Lee**	15
☑ Old Inn/Green | **New Marl**	27
Old Mill | **S Egremont**	24
Red Lion Inn | **Stockbridge**	18
Rte. 7 Grill | **Great Barr**	18
Stagecoach Tav. | **Sheffield**	17
Truc Orient | **W Stockbridge**	22
☑ Wheatleigh | **Lenox**	25

HISTORIC PLACES

(Year opened; * building)

1760 | Old Inn/Green* | **New Marl**	27
1773 | Red Lion Inn* | **Stockbridge**	18
1797 | Old Mill* | **S Egremont**	24
1810 | Dream Away* | **Becket**	17
1817 | Morgan Hse.* | **Lee**	15
1829 | Stagecoach Tav.* | **Sheffield**	17
1839 | Café Lucia* | **Lenox**	23
1840 | Jae's Spice* | **Pittsfield**	22
1841 | Chez Nous* | **Lee**	24
1852 | Church St. Cafe* | **Lenox**	20
1893 | Sullivan Station* | **Lee**	15
1893 | Wheatleigh* | **Lenox**	25
1894 | Cranwell Resort* | **Lenox**	21
1900 | Tratt. Il Vesuvio* | **Lenox**	19
1924 | Brix Wine* | **Pittsfield**	23

HOTEL DINING

Blantyre

☑ Blantyre | **Lenox**	27

Gateways Inn

La Terrazza | **Lenox**	23

Morgan House

Morgan Hse. | **Lee**	15

Old Inn on the Green

☑ Old Inn/Green | **New Marl**	27

Quality Inn

Bombay | **Lee**	22

Race Brook Lodge

Stagecoach Tav. | **Sheffield**	17

Red Lion Inn

Red Lion Inn | **Stockbridge**	18

Wheatleigh

☑ Wheatleigh | **Lenox**	25

MEET FOR A DRINK

Alta | **Lenox**	21
Bistro Zinc | **Lenox**	21
Brix Wine | **Pittsfield**	23
NEW Brulées | **Pittsfield**	21
Castle St. | **Great Barr**	20
Chez Nous | **Lee**	24
Gramercy | **N Adams**	23
Jae's Spice | **Pittsfield**	22
Mission Bar | **Pittsfield**	23
Napa | **Great Barr**	18
Old Mill | **S Egremont**	24
Prime Italian | **Lenox**	21
Red Lion Inn | **Stockbridge**	18
Stagecoach Tav. | **Sheffield**	17

MICROBREWERIES

Barrington Brew | **Great Barr**	14

NEWCOMERS

Brulées | **Pittsfield**	21

OFFBEAT

Barrington Brew | **Great Barr**	14
Elizabeth's | **Pittsfield**	24
Gypsy Joynt | **Great Barr**	16

OUTDOOR DINING

(G=garden; P=patio; S=sidewalk; T=terrace; W=waterside)

Aegean Breeze | P | **Great Barr**	19
Alta | T | **Lenox**	21
Barrington Brew | G | **Great Barr**	14
Cafe Adam | P | **Great Barr**	23
Café Lucia | G, T | **Lenox**	23

Church St. Cafe	T	**Lenox**	20
Firefly	P	**Lenox**	17
Frankie's Rist.	T	**Lenox**	18
Gramercy	P	**N Adams**	23
Isabella's	T	**N Adams**	-
John Andrews	T	**S Egremont**	24
Jonathan's	P	**Lenox**	20
☑ Old Inn/Green	T	**New Marl**	27
Red Lion Inn	P	**Stockbridge**	18
Rouge	T	**W Stockbridge**	22
Shiro	P	**Great Barr**	20
Sullivan Station	T	**Lee**	15
Tratt. Il Vesuvio	T	**Lenox**	19
Tratt. Rustica	P	**Pittsfield**	25
Xicohtencatl	T	**Great Barr**	21

PEOPLE-WATCHING

Allium	**Great Barr**	18
Alta	**Lenox**	21
Bistro Zinc	**Lenox**	21
Mezze Bistro	**Williamstown**	22

POWER SCENES

| Bistro Zinc | **Lenox** | 21 |
| Mezze Bistro | **Williamstown** | 22 |

PRIVATE ROOMS

(Restaurants charge less at off
times; call for capacity)

Bizen	**Great Barr**	24
☑ Blantyre	**Lenox**	27
Castle St.	**Great Barr**	20
Church St. Cafe	**Lenox**	20
Cranwell Resort	**Lenox**	21
Dakota Steak	**Pittsfield**	17
Mill/Floss	**New Ashford**	23
Red Lion Inn	**Stockbridge**	18
Rouge	**W Stockbridge**	22
Stagecoach Tav.	**Sheffield**	17
☑ Wheatleigh	**Lenox**	25

PRIX FIXE MENUS

(Call for prices and times)

Bizen	**Great Barr**	24
☑ Blantyre	**Lenox**	27
☑ Old Inn/Green	**New Marl**	27
☑ Wheatleigh	**Lenox**	25

QUIET CONVERSATION

☑ Blantyre	**Lenox**	27
Cranwell Resort	**Lenox**	21
Gramercy	**N Adams**	23
John Andrews	**S Egremont**	24
La Terrazza	**Lenox**	23
Mill/Floss	**New Ashford**	23
Stagecoach Tav.	**Sheffield**	17
Taylor's	**N Adams**	-
☑ Wheatleigh	**Lenox**	25

ROMANTIC PLACES

☑ Blantyre	**Lenox**	27
Chez Nous	**Lee**	24
Cranwell Resort	**Lenox**	21
John Andrews	**S Egremont**	24
Mill/Floss	**New Ashford**	23
☑ Old Inn/Green	**New Marl**	27
Taylor's	**N Adams**	-
Tratt. Rustica	**Pittsfield**	25
☑ Wheatleigh	**Lenox**	25

SENIOR APPEAL

Aegean Breeze	**Great Barr**	19
Cranwell Resort	**Lenox**	21
La Terrazza	**Lenox**	23
Morgan Hse.	**Lee**	15
Red Lion Inn	**Stockbridge**	18
Taylor's	**N Adams**	-

SINGLES SCENES

Alta	**Lenox**	21
Brix Wine	**Pittsfield**	23
Castle St.	**Great Barr**	20
Jae's Spice	**Pittsfield**	22
Napa	**Great Barr**	18
Prime Italian	**Lenox**	21
Sushi Thai Gdn.	**Williamstown**	20

SLEEPERS

(Good food, but little known)

Aroma B&G	**Great Barr**	22
Fin	**Lenox**	23
Gramercy	**N Adams**	23
Haven	**Lenox**	23

Hub | **N Adams** 23

La Terrazza | **Lenox** 23

Mezze Bistro | **Williamstown** 22

Mill/Floss | **New Ashford** 23

Mission Bar | **Pittsfield** 23

☒ Nudel | **Lenox** 25

Pho Saigon | **Lee** 22

Tratt. Rustica | **Pittsfield** 25

Truc Orient | **W Stockbridge** 22

Viva | **Glendale** 23

TAKEOUT

Aegean Breeze | **Great Barr** 19

Baba Louie's | **Great Barr** 24

Barrington Brew | **Great Barr** 14

Bistro Zinc | **Lenox** 21

Bizen | **Great Barr** 24

Café Lucia | **Lenox** 23

Castle St. | **Great Barr** 20

Church St. Cafe | **Lenox** 20

Dakota Steak | **Pittsfield** 17

John Andrews | **S Egremont** 24

Marketplace | **Sheffield** –

Morgan Hse. | **Lee** 15

Once Upon | **Stockbridge** 21

Rouge | **W Stockbridge** 22

Shiro | **Great Barr** 20

Siam Sq. Thai | **Great Barr** 19

Stagecoach Tav. | **Sheffield** 17

Sushi Thai Gdn. | **Williamstown** 20

Truc Orient | **W Stockbridge** 22

TEEN APPEAL

Baba Louie's | **multi.** 24

Barrington Brew | **Great Barr** 14

Coyote Flaco | **Williamstown** 23

Dakota Steak | **Pittsfield** 17

TRENDY

Allium | **Great Barr** 18

Bistro Zinc | **Lenox** 21

Bizen | **Great Barr** 24

Brix Wine | **Pittsfield** 23

Cafe Adam | **Great Barr** 23

Castle St. | **Great Barr** 20

Fin | **Lenox** 23

Jae's Spice | **Pittsfield** 22

John Andrews | **S Egremont** 24

Mission Bar | **Pittsfield** 23

Napa | **Great Barr** 18

Prime Italian | **Lenox** 21

Rouge | **W Stockbridge** 22

Xicohtencatl | **Great Barr** 21

VIEWS

Bombay | **Lee** 22

Cranwell Resort | **Lenox** 21

☒ Wheatleigh | **Lenox** 25

WINNING WINE LISTS

Alta | **Lenox** 21

Brix Wine | **Pittsfield** 23

Cafe Adam | **Great Barr** 23

Castle St. | **Great Barr** 20

Chez Nous | **Lee** 24

Gramercy | **N Adams** 23

John Andrews | **S Egremont** 24

Jonathan's | **Lenox** 20

La Terrazza | **Lenox** 23

Mezze Bistro | **Williamstown** 22

Mission Bar | **Pittsfield** 23

☒ Old Inn/Green | **New Marl** 27

Wine Vintage Chart

This chart is based on our 0 to 30 scale. The ratings (by U. of South Carolina law professor **Howard Stravitz**) reflect vintage quality and the wine's readiness to drink. A dash means the wine is past its peak or too young to rate. Loire ratings are for dry whites.

Whites	95	96	97	98	99	00	01	02	03	04	05	06	07	08	09
France:															
Alsace	24	23	23	25	23	25	26	23	21	24	25	24	26	25	25
Burgundy	27	26	22	21	24	24	24	27	23	26	27	25	26	25	25
Loire Valley	-	-	-	-	-	-	26	21	23	27	23	24	24	26	
Champagne	26	27	24	23	25	24	21	26	21	-	-	-	-	-	-
Sauternes	21	23	25	23	24	24	29	24	26	21	26	24	27	25	27
California:															
Chardonnay	-	-	-	-	22	21	25	26	22	26	29	24	27	25	-
Sauvignon Blanc	-	-	-	-	-	-	-	-	-	26	25	27	25	24	25
Austria:															
Grüner V./Riesl.	22	-	25	22	25	21	22	25	26	25	24	26	25	23	27
Germany:	21	26	21	22	24	20	29	25	26	27	28	25	27	25	25

Reds	95	96	97	98	99	00	01	02	03	04	05	06	07	08	09
France:															
Bordeaux	26	25	23	25	24	29	26	24	26	25	28	24	23	25	27
Burgundy	26	27	25	24	27	22	24	27	25	23	28	25	25	24	26
Rhône	26	22	23	27	26	27	26	-	26	25	27	25	26	23	26
Beaujolais	-	-	-	-	-	-	-	-	-	27	24	25	23	27	
California:															
Cab./Merlot	27	25	28	23	25	-	27	26	25	24	26	23	26	23	25
Pinot Noir	-	-	-	-	-	-	25	26	25	26	24	23	27	25	24
Zinfandel	-	-	-	-	-	-	25	23	27	22	24	21	21	25	23
Oregon:															
Pinot Noir	-	-	-	-	-	-	-	26	24	26	25	24	23	27	25
Italy:															
Tuscany	25	24	29	24	27	24	27	-	25	27	26	26	25	24	-
Piedmont	21	27	26	25	26	28	27	-	24	27	26	25	26	26	-
Spain:															
Rioja	26	24	25	-	25	24	28	-	23	27	26	24	24	-	26
Ribera del Duero/ Priorat	26	27	25	24	25	24	27	-	24	27	26	24	26	-	-
Australia:															
Shiraz/Cab.	24	26	25	28	24	24	27	27	25	26	27	25	23	-	-
Chile:	-	-	-	-	25	23	26	24	25	24	27	25	24	26	-
Argentina:															
Malbec	-	-	-	-	-	-	-	-	-	25	26	27	25	24	-

Vote at ZAGAT.com